COMPOSITIONAL CROSSROADS

Compositional Crossroads

Music, McGill, Montreal

Edited by

ELEANOR STUBLEY

McGill-Queen's University Press
Montreal & Kingston • London • Ithaca

ISBN 978-0-7735-3277-9 (cloth)
ISBN 978-0-7735-3278-6 (paper)

Legal deposit first quarter 2008
Bibliothèque nationale du Québec

Printed in Canada on acid-free paper that is 100% ancient forest free (100% post-consumer recycled), processed chlorine free.

This book has been published with the help of a grant from the Schulich School of Music, McGill University.

McGill-Queen's University Press acknowledges the support of the Canada Council for the Arts for our publishing program. We also acknowledge the financial support of the Government of Canada through the Book Publishing Industry Development Program (BPIDP) for our publishing activities.

Library and Archives Canada Cataloguing in Publication

Compositional crossroads: music, McGill, Montreal / edited by Eleanor Stubley.

Includes bibliographical references and index.
ISBN 978-0-7735-3277-9 (bound)
ISBN 978-0-7735-3278-6 (pbk.)

1. McGill University. Faculty of Music – History and criticism.
2. Composers – Canada – 20th century. I. Stubley, Eleanor Victoria, 1960– II. Title.

MT5.M81M14 2007 780.71'171428 C2007-903788-7

This book was typeset by Interscript in 9.25/13 Stone serif.

Contents

From the Dean

McGill   Schulich School of Music
École de musique Schulich

Dear Friends

Welcome to *Compositional Crossroads*. As Dean of the Schulich School of Music of McGill University, it gives me great pleasure to introduce this volume of essays that are both reflections on, and a celebration of, "new music" at McGill: reflective because new music continues to require careful introspection to meet its challenging and challenged status in contemporary society; celebratory because *Compositional Crossroads* marks both an intersection and a turning point in the history of music at McGill. The idea for this volume evolved during the planning of our one-hundredth anniversary season in 2004–05. That same season witnessed an exceptional range of events, including – to cite but a few of the more than 650 concerts and special projects that took place – honorary degrees for Joni Mitchell and Jane Eaglen; the successful revival of Canada's national opera *Louis Riel*, by Harry Somers and Mavor Moore; the second edition of the international new music Montréal, Nouvelles musiques festival international; the official opening of our state-of-the-art New Music Building expansion; and the naming of the Faculty as the Schulich School of Music in recognition of an unprecedented philanthropic gift to arts and higher education in Canada from McGill alumnus and businessman Seymour Schulich. New music at McGill has been a driving force in the development of our unique profile, which today balances the finest professional training in musical creation and performance with demanding humanities-based study of music and groundbreaking scientific-technological and interdisciplinary research on music and sound. Without losing its championship of traditional compositional craft, new music at McGill has taken us from early specialization in electronic music, to sound recording, to music technology, to digital composition, to a university-leading interdisciplinary position in musical research and creation. We do not know what the future will bring, but if the past is any indication we can expect many exciting new directions to emerge. Now, I invite you to pause with us at this intersection, and then to continue the journey together as we forge new paths for new music in the times ahead.

Don McLean,
Dean, Schulich School of Music of McGill University

Acknowledgments

We gratefully acknowledge the following people without whom this volume would not have been possible: McGill University, Schulich School of Music, Dean Don McLean, Associate Dean Bruce Minorgan, Department of Theory Chair Brian Cherney, the Marvin Duchow Library, McGill University Archives, Steven Huebner, Marc Edery, Heather White, Matthew Testa, Jonathan Ayers, and Neil Middleton. Thanks are also owed to Ruth Pincoe and Joan McGilvray whose care and diligence facilitated the preparation of the volume for press.

McGill-Queen's University Press provided permission to reprint Pamela Jones' "The Soles of the Feet: alcides lanza Reconnects with Lis Roots," which was originally published as chapter 9 of *alcides lanza: portrait of a composer* (McGill-Queen's University Press, 2007). Belmont Music Publishers provided permission to reprint a passage from their edition of Arnold Schoenberg's *Pierrot Lunaire*.

COMPOSITIONAL CROSSROADS

INTRODUCTION

Crossroads

Crossroads ...
– a place where two or more roads intersect
– an oasis between destinations where travellers gather for refreshment and renewal before continuing their own individual journeys
– a critical turning point in a spiritual quest for self-hood.[1]

The idea that Canada has a musical history worthy of being told is relatively recent, having first been articulated by Helmut Kallmann in 1960.[2] Rather than harvesting the fruits of a thousand generations of civilization, however, that story has been one of an emerging "new music" culled from the struggle and toil of pioneers preoccupied not with matters of high culture but with the physical and economic realities of founding a nation. Initially the story focused on the musical pastimes of the people of Canada, the concern being not so much the music itself as the role it played in people's lives. Then, as the nation evolved, this musical history became a quest for the seeds of a national identity, a search to discover what aspects of this "new music" made it distinctly Canadian. It was an approach plagued with problems, the very variety of compositional techniques and sonorous languages used by Canadian composers reflecting a global musical landscape that, like "new music," was continually changing and evolving. We have subsequently entered what Linda Hutcheson describes as a post-national era.[3] While all that is Canadian remains its ground, the goal is to understand that which is "new" in music.

In this task, *Compositional Crossroads* charts untravelled terrain, taking as its object the emergence of the Faculty of Music, McGill University as "a centre of new music." In so doing, it conceptually aligns itself with recent studies of nineteenth-century musical life in the Royal Academy and the Paris Conservatoire, as well as Henry Kingsbury's ethnomusicological study of the twentieth-century American conservatory.[4] Only where these studies focus primarily on the internal life of the academy as a place apart, *Compositional Crossroads* recognizes the integral public role that the Canadian university music academy plays, both in the training of musicians and in the production and celebration of "new music" more generally. It is also written by the creative musical voices of insiders – the composers, students, and musicologists who, having invested the place with the richness of their own imaginations, are its life. The approach acknowledges the growing importance currently attached to memory and self-representation in archival documentation, while simultaneously recognizing the intricate inter-relatedness between place and identity, community and individual, faculty and students. The result is a series of snapshots that, flashed one after the other in quick succession, capture the vibrant life of a prestigious North American music academy at the turn of the twenty-first century standing on the threshold of a new beginning as the McGill University, Schulich School of Music.

The study is divided into two parts. Part one considers the various institutional pathways that, through a confluence of historical circumstances, have come to define the architectural infrastructure of the Faculty of Music as "a centre of new music" – the compositional programs, the Electronic Music Studio and its supporting research facilities, the visiting scholar programs, the catalytic inspiration of composer-performer collaborations, and the impact of McGill Records. Part two uses composer-work studies to explore the different musical languages sustaining this architectural infrastructure. The intent is not to provide a comprehensive listing of those languages but to document how the musical expression of composers, musicologists, and students, while part of this place, both feeds on and enriches the global "new music" landscape more generally. A closing epilogue uses the sound of the "new" at the beginning of the twenty-first century as a means of looking to the future. It, in turn, is followed by a chronology and an appendix that lists commercial recordings of the works cited in the body of the study.

As historical self-representation, the study focuses primarily on the explosion of "new music" activity that occurred during the last half of the twentieth century and through which the Faculty's sense of itself as a "centre of new music" evolved. Chapter topics were the outgrowth of an internal dialogue begun in 2004 during the Faculty's celebration of 100 years of music at McGill. Authors were selected for their expertise or relationship to a particular institutional pathway (for example, director of the Electronic Music Studio, founder of McGill Records, active role in a visiting artist program), musical genre, compositional language, or composer's work to allow for a mixing of individual personalities, as well as faculty, student, and research perspectives, that would reflect what McGill composer and Canadian music scholar Brian Cherney has described as the "eclecticism of the period."[5] Since this eclecticism defies a linear approach, the two parts are preceded by introductions designed to outline the broad strokes of the over-arching historical narrative. The brief biographical sketches placed at the beginning of each chapter serve to contextualize authors and their methodological approaches. As self-representation, moreover, individual chapters should be read not only for their scholarly content but also for the ways in which various themes, events, and people identified by the different authors recur, resonate, and otherwise interact with one another. Readers are, consequently, encouraged to explore the book's offerings in a variety of ways, allowing the authors' voices to be heard against the background of their own memories and experiences, the "snapshots" that, according to ethnographer Caroline Brettell, are the essence of self-representation "lying not only in the record, but also the ways in which readers find meaning in it."[6]

The story begins not in 2004, however, but in 1899. Montreal lies in the fork of the Ottawa and St Lawrence Rivers at the exact point where, according to Prime Minister Sir Wilfrid Laurier, the two founding directorates of Canada meet.[7] A traveller coming up the St Lawrence sees glittering steeples and copper domes against the pastoral grandeur of a distant mountain and finds in the scene an ancient spiritualism that seems to emanate from the land itself.[8] Another coming across from the mainland admires the beauty of a bridge, seeing in its contoured arcs and finely tuned suspension a city of the future.[9] Yet another, arriving by rail from New York, sees the city first from the inside and compares it to the fruits of the Dead Sea, "fair and tempting to look upon, but when tasted ... against the bite of the cold wind ... nothing but ashes and bitterness."[10] All three travellers are going to McGill University. Two are visitors curious to see what pen and pencil artist John Argyll described in 1885 as "a seat of wisdom, well worth taking in."[11] The third, Clara Lichtenstein, has been invited by Chancellor Lord Strathcona to develop a music program for young women at the Royal Victoria College. His is the vision of a colonial imagination that sees Montreal as a city in need of cultural reproduction, a makeover befitting its status as the largest and wealthiest city in Canada. He has chosen Clara Lichtenstein because of her reputation as both a talented performer and an inspired pedagogue. "Tall, willowy, with well-formed shoulders and thighs, and a pale face suggesting frailty," she is also the perfect image of the Victorian woman born of class and privilege.[12]

Music having always lent a certain dignity to the ambience of the University as a "seat of wisdom," it is not the first time that music has been heard at McGill. Nor is Lord Strathcona's vision shared by all. While many would agree that musical training is an essential attribute of the cultivated young woman about to be wed, most would argue that it is not an intellectual pursuit worthy of academic credit.[13] But Clara Lichtenstein, in addition to instilling in her students "a good and proper technique," will introduce classes in theory and music history, believing that the application of expressive performance techniques demands an understanding of the language of music itself.[14] Her vision more closely aligns the study of music with the formalist aesthetic feeding the University's other arts and literature courses.[15] Several of her more talented students receive rave reviews in Europe and New York, making it possible to re-envision Lord Strathcona's cultural makeover not simply as a matter of recapturing a way of life left behind but as an integral part of the commodity exchange that financially sustains Montreal itself.[16] Capitalizing on the change in the prevailing wind, Charles Harriss, "a veritable musical Napoleon, always engaged in a tonal campaign somewhere,"[17] forges an alliance with the Associated Board of the Royal Schools of Music in London and in 1904 music achieves what philosopher Edward Casey defines as the first two attributes of place: a name – The McGill Conservatorium of Music – and a physical space of its own – the Workman Mansion at 799 Sherbrooke Street West.[18]

With the change in status, there is much to applaud. New instructors are hired to extend course offerings to include selected orchestral instruments. Distinguished Montreal composer, conductor, and critic Guillaume Couture, later described by Léo-Pol Morin as "the first great musician in the history of Canadian music," improves instruction in voice and sight-singing.[19] Ties to the larger academic community are strengthened through the addition of two science courses, one in musical acoustics, the other in vocal physiology and hygiene. Degree requirements in turn demand that students demonstrate their mastery of the language of music by completing at the bachelor's level a "compositional exercise," a twenty-minute work for four-part chorus with string accompaniment, and at the doctoral level a fully orchestrated oratorio, opera, or cantata containing eight-part writing and a fugue.[20]

McGill Conservatorium of Music, the Workman Mansion. Reproduced by permission of the McGill University Archives, www.archives.mcgill.ca/resources/db/photosarchives.

For the first time, Director Charles Harriss notes in his end of year report, the musical offerings at McGill cater to the needs of both the "cultivated woman and the educated man of letters."[21] The language spoken, however, is largely that of the British Anglican cathedral tradition, a situation that ultimately serves to enflame the deep-seeded religious and linguistic tensions dividing the French and the English. Although many continue to assert that the Conservatorium has the potential to "propagat[e] a high musical standard across the Dominion," the Mountain that casts its shadow across the Workman Mansion and that has historically made McGill "a seat of wisdom, well worth taking in," appears an obstacle yet to be surmounted.[22]

The next chapter of the story begins in 1920. In 1909, in an effort to improve community relations, Charles Harriss's successor H.C. Perrin had used his newly acquired powers and privileges as a professor to develop a uniquely Canadian system of examinations supported by graded syllabi that included, in addition to standard repertoire, compositions by local musicians – himself, Charles Harriss, Graham Moore, Saul Brant, H. Barbieri, and two French composers who had once taught at the Conservatorium, Guillaume Couture and T. Dubois. This new system severed the Conservatorium's relationship with the Associated Board of Royal Schools of Music. Tied to the development of a Canadian music publishing industry, it also initiated a tradition of writing music that lay outside the ritual of the Church, which subsequently linked compositional identity to Canada as a distinct nation (albeit for educational purposes). The Conservatorium, however, remained largely isolated, geographically and metaphorically, on the peripheral edges of the University, the director's elevation to professor, the first such appointment in Music, having come at the expense of a reduction in teaching staff that left instruction a reflection of the tattered sitting rooms and parlours in which it unfolded. The First World War had also had an impact, music, as one examiner put it, "being essentially an art for times of peace."[23]

In 1920, though, hope springs eternal. Montreal, swollen by a giant wave of immigrants and a renewed measure of prosperity, has grown such that the Mountain now marks the place where country and city, old and new, meet. The once colonial imagination has been replaced by a sense of national pride, an awareness of the way in which battles won and lost overseas have come to define us not as French or English but as Canadian. And everywhere music seems to be bringing people together, using the cloak of darkness on long and blustery winter evenings to build bridges between communities that would otherwise be divided by language or social class. As one railway porter working the Chicago-Montreal run will recount thirty years later, it was not unusual to look in the window of a tavern and see a Negro at the piano, a French-Canadian with a cello, and a singer, "face hidden, bending over the piano ... held together in the strange rapture" of a moment that despite "its curious discords" knows "nothing but the lonely little theme being repeated over and over."[24]

In these times of change, H.C. Perrin, quoting William Blake, writes to the new principal, "Music need only follow its own example as an art in which the ordering of materials aligns itself with the soul."[25] This short letter, couched in a language that appeals to the principal's sense of moral responsibility as the general who led Canadians to victory at Vimy Ridge, is enough for Sir Arthur Currie. Music at McGill is reborn – this time as a Faculty, an autonomous space within the University that has equal stature as a particular domain of knowledge with the other arts and sciences. Its future, however, is anything but secure. The University lacks both the concert hall facilities and the critical body of musicians necessary to sustain the first-rate orchestra on which Perrin's vision hangs.[26] There is also a growing perception amongst the intellectual elite of the University that the curriculum is "falling behind the times."[27] Part of this stems from Perrin's public disdain for what he describes as "ultra-modern" music, music that in its "freedom from restraint ... hair-raising chords ... [and] unexpected endings" fills the listener's ears "with such a jumble of sounds as to stupefy him [sic]."[28] Equally important is an emerging new aesthetic that, fed by a growing historical consciousness and the literary criticism of the McGill Modern Movement, frames art as an emotional expression of or a response to a particular time and place.[29] Perrin's orchestral programming, while presenting Montreal premieres of works by Beethoven and Schubert, reflects a romantic idealism out of step with the harsh urban dissonances that, not unlike the effect of "a broken and wind-battered branch" in a Group of Seven landscape, make Montreal a "scarred" and "lonely land."[30]

The situation is not helped by the Depression and the economic devastation resulting from a city plan that, in failing to anticipate the winter closure of the harbour, leaves Montreal trapped four months of the year. The idea of Montreal as a "lonely land," however, fosters a new sense of identity, not merely as a crossroads but as a place to be mined for its own riches.[31] It is a sense of self as unique that, when combined with the emerging expressionistic aesthetic, manifests itself artistically in new poetic forms and in what has since become known as the Beaver Hall Group, an educational program in the visual arts that encourages the development of the artist's individual voice.[32] The new climate initiates a gradual change in the focus of instruction within the Faculty that transforms composition from an activity or "exercise" through which one demonstrates one's mastery of a language into an expressive act in and of itself.[33] Central to the process is the inspired teaching of Alfred Whitehead and Claude Champagne, both of whom emphasize a consummate technique put to the service of originality. Claude Champagne also leads by example, having developed through his *Suite Canadienne* (1927) a reputation with the French elite in Paris for investing the arts of modern Canada with a really homegrown flavour.

Perrin's successor, Douglas Clarke, uses his position as conductor of the newly formed, fully professional Montreal Orchestra to showcase the compositions of both staff and students, arguing that if students are to develop their own voices they must be able to hear their works.[34]

His programming is part of a larger vision that promotes music not as a form of social entertainment but as a human need, a spiritual essential with the power to "transmute ... the dullness of grubbing minds ... into something which shines with the stars."[35] His vision is intended to strengthen the position of the Faculty within the University by framing it as (what we today would call) a Foucaultian hub or centre that feeds and sustains the needs of the masses in a time otherwise seemingly bereft of hope.[36] Unfortunately Clarke's modern tastes rarely extend beyond Vaughan Williams, Grainger, Elgar, and Holst, while the French embrace Bartók, Debussy, Ravel, and Scriabin. By the 1940s the Montreal Orchestra has folded, Claude Champagne has left to assume a position at the Conservatoire de musique de Montréal, and the Faculty once again stands lost in the shadow of the Mountain, at odds with the French and curtailed by the tragedy and despair of another world war.

The next chapter of the story begins in the early 1950s. Canada's war efforts have capped our growing sense of nationhood through a seat at the United Nations. Montreal, however, despite its contributions to those efforts, seems once again trapped within itself, this time as a haphazard urban sprawl shackled by the conservative and Catholic policies of a Union National government intent on preserving a French way of life found only in the spiritual havens of the rural countryside. It is, in the words of the avant-garde painter Paul-Émile Borduas, a time for "refus global," a time for the people to reject the "prejudices of the past" and take "charge of their own destiny."[37] But union calls for the separation of church and state go unheard. Veterans have joined the ranks of the unemployed that "flow in two rivers along St Catherine Street," oblivious to the glitter of the unobtainable goods hidden behind the street's glass facades and the grittiness of its sidewalks.[38] The port, its impending facelift as part of the new St Lawrence Seaway not yet imagined, is "a jumble of ancient relics," filled with what poet/songwriter Leonard Cohen calls "public men" who speak what are now "Montreal's many different languages."[39]

The Mountain, with the city now sprawled haphazardly around it, has become, in the words of poet F.R. Scott, "a house of peace amidst the tumult," "an oasis away from unruly wilderness or the floodtide of faraway seas" where one can envision the possibilities of the future.[40] At its foot, the Faculty of Music seeks to resurrect itself from the rubble of the demolished Workman Mansion in the Shaughnessey House, another old mansion located at 40 Drummond St. Spearheading the effort are three men. Two – Alexander Brott and Marvin Duchow – are homebred, having completed compositional studies with Claude Champagne. The third, Helmut Blume, is a relatively new arrival whose long and circuitous journey to McGill from internment camps for "enemy aliens" includes a continuing career with the CBC as head of the International Service. While the University administration actually believes that the Faculty has become a corpse, their talk is only of expansion and growth, the goal a program of study that will distinguish the offerings of the Faculty from those of the government-supported Conservatoire de Montréal.[41]

Their proposal resembles the star-shaped urban map of Copenhagen that will come to serve as the template for the redevelopment of Montreal in the 1960s and 1970s – with the five prongs representing professional career options jutting out from a core of theoretical and historical studies. These career options, embracing performance, composition, radio, opera, and school music, are innovative for the time, and are, the three men believe, a Canadian-made solution designed to fit the needs of the community and carry the reputation of the University into the future as a leader.[42] Principal Cyril James is not easily persuaded. First, the Faculty has only three full-time staff and virtually no students. Second, the plan, by disassociating the curriculum of the Conservatorium from that of the Faculty, grants degree status to performance. It is not the first such degree in Canada, performance degrees having been introduced at Acadia University some years earlier, but for James, there remains, as in 1899, a question of academic integrity.

As discussions continue, a fourth man, István Anhalt, is using cold and blustery winter evenings to introduce Montreal audiences to the music of Bartók, Stravinsky, and Schoenberg. He has come to McGill through the philanthropy of Lady Isabelle Henriette Davis, a wealthy aristocratic woman dedicated to the betterment of humanity through scholarship and the arts. Anhalt finds Canada "a wonderfully, exotic, interesting, exciting country full of opportunities," a place where he can put down roots, "a country with which he can grow."[43] Intent on understanding Canada's "keys" and developing his own artistic voice as a response to them, he also frames composition as an experiment. In the eyes of Cyril James, his is an approach that aligns music with the progressive character of research in the sciences.[44] It is not much, but when combined with the persistence of the "three deans" as they had come to be known, it is enough to prevent the immediate closure of the Faculty. For Marvin Duchow, and later Helmut Blume, it is an opportunity to "make the impossible happen."[45] And although the five prongs of the original star have been reduced to three – composition, school music, and performance – the seeds that will ultimately define the potential of the Faculty of Music as a "centre of new music" (among other things) have been sown.

NOTES

1 This definition of a crossroads was metaphorically composed from a variety of sources, including *The Oxford Dictionary of Modern English* (Oxford: Clarendon Press, 1992); *Kopernickus*, an opera by Montreal composer Claude Vivier; and John Argyll's *Canadian Pictures: Drawn with Pen and Pencil* (London: Clay and Sons, 1885).

2 Helmut Kallmann, *A History of Music in Canada, 1534–1914* (Toronto: University of Toronto Press, 1960).

3 Benedict Anderson, *Imagined Communities: Reflections on the Origin and Spread of Nationalism* (New York: Verso, 1991).

4 See, for example, Rafael Cadoso Denis and Colin Trodd, *Art and the Academy in the Nineteenth Century* (Manchester: Manchester University Press, 2000); Henry Kingsbury, *Music, Talent, and Performance: A Conservatory Cultural System* (Philadelphia: Temple University Press, 1988).

5 Email correspondence with Eleanor Stubley, 14 September 2006.

6 Caroline Brettell, *Writing against the Wind: A Mother's Life History* (Wilmington, Delaware: S. R. Books, 1999), 12.

7 See, for example, Sir Wilfrid Laurier's speech on the occasion of his inauguration as prime minister of Canada, 11 July 1896. It is a theme that runs throughout his tenure.

8 Clara Lichtenstein, letter to Lord Sherbrooke, 12 July 1899, McGill University Archives, RG39, Administration Records, 1904–1966, Subject and Information Files, ca. 1908–1968, container 0028, file 00120, Clara Lichtenstein.

9 Geologist B.W. Sleigh, letter to Principal William Peterson, 14 September 1899, McGill University Archives, RG2, Office of the Principal and Vice Chancellor, Office of the Principal William Peterson, Administrative Records, Memorandum, container 0017, file 00016. One of McGill's famous landmarks at the time was a geology museum.

10 Sara James, letter to her husband, 13 February 1899, *Scenes of Montreal*, McCord Museum Archives, RG147, Miscellaneous Correspondence, container 49, file 13.

11 John Argyll, *Canadian Pictures: Drawn with Pen and Pencil* (London: Clay and Sons, 1885), 66.

12 Lord Sherbrooke, memo to Principal William Peterson, 12 October 1898, McGill University Archives, RG 2, Office of the Principal and Vice Chancellor, Office of the Principal William Peterson, Administrative Records, Royal Victoria College, container 0010, file 0003.

13 Associate Dean Bruce Minorgan notes, for example, that as early as 1894 G. (presumably Guillaume) Couture is reported as suggesting that a chair of music theory be created at McGill, as it "would be of much greater benefit to the country than the establishment of a conservatory," email correspondence with Eleanor Stubley, 12 October 2005.

14 Lord Sherbrooke quotes Graham Moore in a memo of 2 February 1904 to Principal Peterson. Moore makes the point himself in his 1905 end of the year Examiner's Report on the Conservatory, McGill University Archives, RG2, Office of the Principal and Vice Chancellor, Office of the Principal William Peterson, Administrative Records, Royal Victoria College, container 10, file 00229; RG39, Faculty of Music and Curriculum, Administrative Records, container 0010, file 00229.

15 At the time, the basic premise behind arts courses was that one taught literature as a means of acquiring the language of writing and that the best instructors were those who were writers themselves. This can be seen most directly by the list of instructors and the titles of the courses offered. The power of this formalist aesthetic within the academic setting has also been noted by Denis and Trodd in *Art and the Academy in the Nineteenth Century.*

16 In a memo to Lord Sherbrooke of 13 March 1905, Principal William Peterson writes, "we can no longer think of ourselves as a land to be tamed, but a homestead capable of spawning and sustaining its own expressive artistic voices." McGill University Archives, RG2, Office of the Principal and Vice Chancellor, Office of Principal William Peterson, Administrative Records, Royal Victoria College, container 0010, file 0003.

17 Percy Scholes, quoted in "Charles A.E. Harriss," in *Encyclopedia of Music in Canada*, ed. Helmut Kallmann and Gilles Potvin, 2nd ed. (Toronto: University of Toronto Press, 1992), 587c.

18 Edward Casey, "How to Get from Space to Place in a Fairly Short Stretch of Time: Phenomenological Prolegomena," in *Senses of Place*, ed. Steven Feld and Keith Basso (New York: School of American Research Press, 1996).

19 Léo-Pol Morin goes on to describe Couture as "the most intelligent, the most learned, and the most cultured (musician) of his time." See "Guillaume Couture," Papiers de musique, Archives Université de Montréal, 1930. Guillaume Couture was the grandfather of composer Jean Papineau-Couture, who taught at the Conservatoire de musique du Montréal (1946–63) and the Faculté de musique, Université de Montréal (1951–82).

20 McGill Conservatorium Syllabus, 1904–05.

21 Charles Harriss, 1904–05 End of Year Report to Principal William Peterson, McGill University Archives, RG39, Faculty of Music and Conservatorium, Administrative Records, container 0010, file 00229.

22 Graham Moore, "Examiner's Report," 1905. Moore, the representative of the Associated Board of the Royal Schools of Music, composed several examination pieces in the early years.

23 Saul Brant, "Conservatorium Sessional Report, 1915–16," in *Conservatorium Calendar, 1915–16*, McGill University Archives, RG39, Faculty of Music and Conservatorium, Administrative Records, container 0010, file 00231.

24 This scene was told to author Morley Callaghan in a café on St Antoine St. Callaghan later incorporated it in *The Loved and the Lost* (Toronto: MacMillan, 1951), a novel which explores the sensitive subject of race relations in Montreal.

25 Perrin, letter to Sir Arthur Currie, 13 March 1920, McGill University Archives, RG39, Faculty of Music and Conservatorium, Administrative Records, Records of the Dean and Director, container 0001, file 0015.

26 Charles Harriss had given performances in the large, open-air stadium used for sports events. Perrin's model of the ideal concert hall, similar to halls in London, is held in McGill University Archives; see, www.archives.mcgill.ca/resources/db/photosarchives, PR 027736.

27 Sir Arthur Currie, letter to the chancellor, 22 October 1929, McGill University Archives, RG2, Office of Principal and Vice-Chancellor, Office of the Principal Arthur Currie, Arthur Eustace and Lewis Williams Douglas, Administrative Records of Principal Currie, Records Relating to Academic Matters, container 0061, file 00132; Currie's letter is concerned primarily with a conversation with two Montreal poets, F.R. Scott and A.J.M. Smith, who eventually became part of the McGill Movement. See note 29 below.

28 H.C. Perrin, "Some Thoughts on Contemporaneous Music," lecture notes, McGill University Archives, RG39, Faculty of Music and Conservatorium, Administrative Records, Curriculum, container 0046, file 02494. Beginning in 1916, Perrin also gave regular public lectures on "Mannerisms of Music from Different Times."

29 In the first years of the Conservatorium, the compositional thread was understood as the "modern." The growing historical consciousness was part of a larger world phenomenon that led to history courses entitled "Historical and Modern Musics." Within the University it was fed by Perrin's centenary celebration performances of works by Beethoven and Schubert. The McGill Movement, later known as the Montreal Movement, was a group of anglophone Montreal poets who, rejecting the pastoral images of the countryside typical of Québec and Canadian poetry at the turn of the century, cultivated a more socially

critical orientation inspired by T.S. Eliot. It was to become a poetic genre that was to be embraced by English Canada at large. See Peter Stevens, *The McGill Movement: Critical Views on Canadian Writers* (Toronto: Ryerson Press, 1969).

30 A.J.M Smith, "The Lonely Land," in Stevens, *The McGill Movement,* 96; Smith was one of the founders of The McGill Movement.

31 For further discussion of the mythology of isolation as it pertains to Canadian identity and islands more generally, see Margaret Atwood, *Survival: A Thematic Guide to Canadian Literature* (Toronto: McClelland and Stewart, 1972); Carolyn Strange, *Isolation: Places and Practices of Exclusion* (New York: Routledge, 2003).

32 The Beaver Hall Group was a group of Montreal artists who developed an educational program for the community that made mastery of language and technique subservient to imagination or vision. One of the primary forces behind this movement was Anne Savage.

33 This shift is documented in the end of year sessional reports that make specific reference to the compositional teaching, rather than simply documenting the appearances of Faculty and Conservatorium staff as performers. See also Alexander Brott's *My Lives in Music* (Oakville, Ont.: Mosaic Press, 2005).

34 This viewpoint is most fully and clearly expressed in Graham Clarke's article, "Young Composer Needs Guidance in His Writing," in *McGill News,* 1954, commemorating the fiftieth anniversary of the Conservatorium; McGill University Archives, RG39, Faculty of Music and Conservatorium, Records of Director and Dean, container 0001, file 00090.

35 Douglas Clarke, undated lecture to students, McGill University Archives RG39, Faculty of Music and Conservatorium, Administrative Records, Curriculum, container 46, file 02496.

36 This position is articulated in particular in Douglas Clarke's 1937 end of session report, McGill University Archives, RG39, Faculty of Music and Curriculum, Administrative Records, Annual Reports, container 0046, file 02451.

37 See Paul-Émile Borduas, *Écrits/Writings, 1942–58* (New York: New York University Press, 1978).

38 Hugh McLennan reflecting on his memories of the years leading to the Quiet Revolution of the sixties, cited in Bryan Demchinksy and Elaine Kalman Naves, *Storied Streets: Montreal in the Literary Imagination* (Toronto: MacFarlane, Walter and Ross, 2000), 89.

39 Leonard Cohen, "Les Vieux," in *Let Us Compare Mythologies* (Toronto: McClelland and Stewart, 1956), 17.

40 The McGill Movement, F.R. Scott, "Reflections on Montréal," McCord Museum Archives RG 169, The McGill Movement, container 62, file 12.

41 Paul Helmer, "McGill University," unpublished manuscript, 2005, notes that this was a goal imposed by Principal Cyril James, who saw music at McGill best

defined not as a faculty but as a department that taught the language of music and trained teachers for the schools.

42 This plan is detailed in a twenty-five-page report completed in 1955, "On Plans for the Re-organization of the Faculty and the Conservatorium of Music of McGill University," McGill University Archives, RG 39, Faculty of Music and Conservatorium, Curriculum Records, container 36, file 00433. There were plans to include at a later date a ballet school and a national theatre school. This is the first document that defines the Faculty of Music as a "centre," though it was framed as a centre for music within the University. Emphasis is also placed on McGill as the university that would serve the English community.

43 Quoted in Helmer, "McGill University," 14–15.

44 See, for example, Cyril James' letter to Helmut Blume, 14 April 1958, McGill University Archives, RG 39, Faculty of Music and Conservatorium, Administrative Records, Records of the Dean, container 0044, file 02371. This phenomenon was experienced more generally in the academy in the United States and Europe at this time – the idea of the university as being a place for not only passing on knowledge but creating new knowledge, a place of experimentation.

45 Helmer, "McGill University," 15.

PART ONE

Mapping the Infrastructures of the Faculty of Music, McGill University, as a Centre of New Music

Introduction

Edward Casey writes that while place begins with a name and a physical space, its identity ultimately hangs on the way in which it "gathers" and "holds" people "to reflect the continuous contours or layout of the local landscape."[1] The Faculty of Music, as a school, is by definition a crossroads, a stopping off place or "oasis between destinations" where students gather to learn the craft of their art. And it is, given the nature of that craft, as much a spiritual quest for voice as a path to knowledge. At the beginning of the 1960s, however, the Faculty had few students. It was a crossroads primarily in terms of the cosmopolitan nature of its staff and the way in which the European experiences of István Anhalt and Helmut Blume mixed with the Canadian experiences of other staff to sustain a vision of the "new" that was shaped not by the tastes of the French or the English but by an understanding of a larger new music landscape that was continually evolving. As an "unwanted" Faculty, it also had a certain openness about its walls that made it easy to reach beyond the University to cultivate musical relationships with other composers and musicians who had similar interests and proclivities. Not all were associated with the leading edge of the "new" – Kelsey Jones's mark was contrapuntal ingenuity while Morley Calvert used dissonance only for dramatic purposes – but all were bound together by a pioneering spirit and a belief in themselves as visionary artists, "senses on full alert, wits sharpened, soul attuned, caught up in the mortal game of life."[2]

New appointments necessitated by departures and a growing student population did little to change the cosmopolitan atmosphere, even when a new public policy demanded that hiring priority be given to Canadian citizens: the first Canadian professors – Bruce Mather, Alan

Heard, John Rea, Paul Pedersen, and Brian Cherney – had been schooled in the diverse languages of the "new" and were themselves travellers, each having completed comprehensive studies at the University of Toronto with John Weinzweig and/or at one of the major "new music" centres in Europe and the United States – Paris, Darmstadt, Cologne, Princeton, and New York – with now legendary musicians such as Pierre Boulez, Karlheinz Stockhausen, Pierre Schaeffer, Olivier Messiaen, Vladimir Ussachevsky, Milton Babbitt, and György Ligeti. The Canadians were also young composers and were – just as their future students would be – in search of their own individual voices. The travellers from outside Canada – Bengt Hambræus from Sweden, alcides lanza from Argentina, Robert Jones from the United States, and Peter Paul Koprowski from Poland – brought other "global" connections, such that by the end of the 1970s, through a series of visiting professorships, the Faculty had become a crossroads where, as John Rea describes it, "East meets West," "North meets South." With exchanges between travellers inspiring and shaping compositions by both students and faculty, these meetings spawned a "world" awareness that, like the evolving multicultural character of Montreal at the time, was itself new.[3]

The draw or pull of the Faculty as a "centre of new music" first revolved around the Electronic Music Studio (EMS). It was not the first electronic music studio in Canada,[4] nor was it anything special in design or conception. But Montreal had a reputation as a centre for technological innovation and sound experimentation dating back to the 1950s that made it of immediate interest. At the National Film Board, for example, Norman McLaren was using a technique that had originated in Russia to create utterly captivating percussive soundtracks by "drawing" directly onto film. In Europe young Montreal musicians such as Andrée Desautels, Gilles Tremblay, Serge Garant, Pierre Mercure, and Micheline Coulombe Saint-Marcoux were distinguishing themselves as students of sound, an orientation inspired by the avant-garde ideas of the automatiste painters who had penned the 1948 *Refus global* manifesto. There was also the interest generated by the creative fervour leading up to Expo '67. Not only did the theme "Man and His World" provide an opportunity for Montreal to present itself to the international community as a city of the future, Expo '67 was supported by government funds that, linked with the celebration of Canada's centennial, placed a high value on the arts.[5]

The success of the EMS in those first years was due in large part to a sense of creative freedom that allowed composers to "harmonize a

Royal Victoria College (later, the Strathcona Music Building), 1904. Reproduced by permission of McGill University Archives, www.archives.mcgill.ca/resources/db/photosarchives, PR 002669.

personal path with the evolution of the world in which" they were living.[6] At the heart of this creative freedom was the capacity of the EMS to evolve with technological changes and developments in electroacoustic music. This capacity was cultivated by each EMS director (István Anhalt, Paul Pedersen, Bengt Hambræus, and alcides lanza), and was aided by their ability to garner financial support from within McGill University, and the studio's continuing collaboration with inventor Hugh Le Caine and with Eric Johnstone, one of its supporting technicians.[7] While neither Le Caine nor Johnstone regarded themselves as composers,[8] both were involved in continual experimentation in an effort to understand the composer's interest and, as was later the case with the Polyphone commissioned by Paul Pedersen, often worked closely with a composer as an instrument was being designed and built. Le Caine's pursuit of touch-sensitive instruments that would allow "nuance-filled expressive performances," moreover, balanced the "measure/control/check the UV meter" approach used in Cologne with the "sentire" approach (feel and/or listen) favoured in Milan.[9] It was a model, according to Bengt Hambræus, that even composers untrained in the mechanics of science felt capable of emulating.[10] It also nurtured composer-performer relationships like those formed between István Anhalt and violinist Otto Joachim, Micheline Coulombe Saint-Marcoux and percussionist Pierre Béluse, that were to have a profound effect on the development of the performance department in later years and on the performance and production of electroacoustic music in Montreal more generally.[11]

Initially, however, the EMS existed on the periphery of the Faculty where its creative mission outside the curriculum – as a space apart – was seen in much the same way as a scientist's laboratory. For the undergraduate student, the path to the "new" was the last step of a journey that traced the evolution of genres and the development of tonal languages through the history of western music. This approach was, in one sense, an extension of the Faculty's past and reflected the importance that the British Cathedral tradition had attached to the development of a consummate technique through mastery of tonal harmony and counterpoint. Not to be dismissed, though, was an internal debate that, having defined the curriculum around a core set of skills and knowledge to be shared by all musicians, pitted the needs of the performer, whose career trajectory revolved around the masterpieces of the Western canon, against the needs of the composer who, in developing a new Canadian voice not yet in existence, would be charting new frontiers. Over the years this debate has been fanned by the bias of the University administration toward an academic composer-musicologist model[12] as well as the pedagogical authority of ear training instructors such as Donald Mackey, who as McGill graduates often trained under the watchful ear of Kelsey Jones, treated the composer's hand as an extension of the ear best developed through that which has already been heard.[13]

In the early 1970s two developments allowed composition to disentangle its path from that of the core music theory and music history courses: the disciplinary evolution of musicology and theory as distinct career paths in and of themselves, and the recognition achieved by Canadian composers through the commissioning and programming policy of the Canadian Broadcasting Corporation (CBC). These developments changed not only the profile of the composers as teachers but also the sequence and range of courses offered. The composition area now supports an undergraduate program, a master's in music program, and two doctoral programs: a DMus and a more research-oriented PhD. While each has its own curricular integrity, the programs are bound together by an approach that views the "new" as the music of our time in all its historical depth, placing understanding at the service of the composer's individual voice. Andrew Culver, a McGill graduate and a former assistant to John Cage, describes this approach as an outgrowth of the new music landscape itself, Luciano Berio having said that the "easiest way for a musician to talk coherently about himself is to talk about other people, about things he has around him and behind him ... about those things richly impregnated with history" and about those things which, while not the language of music per se, inspire it, sustain it, and feed it.[14] Although expanded in scope, the approach remains rooted in the foundational practice of István Anhalt, maintaining the importance of listening, the inspiration to be gained from guest composers, and the use of analytical models drawn from a wide variety of disciplines.

While the compositional programs provide the core of the Faculty's infrastructure as a centre of new music, their internal synergy and dynamic is fed in part by a labyrinth of spaces shared with the department of performance.[15] In the early years of the Faculty's rebirth, the performance of new music was restricted largely to a Friday Composers Series driven solely by the industry and energy of the Faculty's composers as performer-producers. Today, it is a specialty sustained by a student composer-in-residence program, various ensembles associated with the Electronic Music Studio, the Contemporary Music Ensemble (CME), and the Percussion Ensemble. While the latter two ensembles struggled for resources in their first years, under the leadership of conductors Pierre Béluse, D'Arcy Gray, Bruce Mather, and Denys Bouliane they have become a regular forum for the performance of student compositions. The scope of new music heard at McGill has increased in both breadth and depth to include some of the most difficult and complex scores of our time. What is more, since the early 1980s the performer-composer dialogues nurtured in these shared spaces have also been constantly renewed and invigorated by initiatives such as the Contemporary Music Festival, the Electroacoustic Music Festival, and, more recently, MusMars and Montréal/Nouvelles musiques festival international. These festivals, which offer a series of concerts, lectures, and workshops with internationally recognized composers and performers, have made McGill and Montreal, if only for a few short days every year, the locus of the "new" as a "vibrating field hypnotically shared by people."[16]

Over the years, a variety of factors have shaped the cultivation of these shared spaces. In the beginning, it was Helmut Blume's persistent representation of performance to the University administration as a peer-reviewed activity equivalent to the research report.[17] His success in making the case led to the first full-time appointments in performance, a number of which were filled by musicians with well-developed interests in and established reputations for the performance of new music.[18] The long tenure of Paul Pedersen, first as chair of the theory department and then as dean, led to the development of a balanced large ensemble programming policy that required representation from all genres, styles, and historical periods and encouraged ensemble conductors to commission faculty composers.[19] Such collaborations, as noted by historian Gilles Potvin, played a particularly important role in the early 1970s when one of the major challenges facing the evolution of new music in Canada was the absence of an interested audience and opportunities to perform works that required larger choral, wind, and orchestral resources, the "new" as something other than the revitalization of Canadian folk songs having been associated primarily with dissonance and noise.[20] As an educational forum, the McGill large ensembles were a required component of the core program for all students, which would ensure, as Pedersen noted at the time, a ready-made audience by simultaneously nurturing understanding and interest in the students who would become the performers and audiences of the future.[21] The programming policy has since been facilitated by a flexible administrative structure that, allowing a performer – John Grew – to be appointed dean, and a composer – Donald Steven – to be appointed chair of the performance department, has ensured the continuing cross-fertilization of perspectives and interests. John Rea's tenure as dean, in turn, fuelled the growth of the opera program and nurtured joint initiatives with various francophone universities and new music ensembles in the larger Montreal community.[22] The ingenuity and initiative of students have also played an important role; lasting friendships grounded in the pursuit of both shared and divergent interests motivated GEMS (The Group of the Electronic Music Studio), various performer-composer collaborations sponsored by the Graduate Student Symposium, and an ever-increasing number of recitals, master classes, and workshop demonstrations.[23]

But the dynamic synergy of the shared spaces could not have been maintained for any length of time without the opening of Pollack Hall in 1975. By 1970, the Faculty had outgrown the mansion on Drummond Street; the pursuit of the "new" – or anything else musical for that matter – involved a journey that took students across the University campus from one mansion to another. There were no large ensemble rehearsal spaces, and concert venues were limited to Redpath Hall, a renovated reading room that had been McGill University's first library, and Moyse Hall, a theatre in the Arts Building. While Redpath Hall remains an important performance venue today, its live resonance and historical aura providing a beautiful ambience for many choral works, recitals, and small chamber ensembles, particularly in the field of early music, the acoustics, size, and performance resources of Moyse Hall in the Arts Building were "less than adequate for large orchestral, wind ensemble, and new music concerts requiring extensive technical support." As Associate Dean Bruce Minorgan recalls, "everything changed with the move in 1971 to the Strathcona Music Building,"[24] the refurbished east wing of the Royal Victoria College Residence at 555 Sherbrooke Street West. Where sense of place had initially been a function solely of curriculum, it now coalesced around the physical geography of the music building itself, with Pollack Hall as its gravitational centre. Not only did imagination have room to fly, but collaborative exchanges became a product of the way in which staff and students moved in, around, and through the building. Pollack Hall, the gravitational centre of that building, with its state-of-the-art acoustical design – at the time, the "envy of even Montreal's premiere venue for the performing arts, Place des Arts" – and its close proximity to the EMS and to what McGill graduate and frequent guest instructor Laurie Radford describes as the "new's changing instrumentarium," ensuring a steady stream of visitors from the outside, including the Société de musique contemporain à Québec (SMCQ), the professional Montreal ensemble most frequently associated with the leading edge of the "new."[25]

Beginning in 1977, the flow of the "new" through Pollack Hall has also been shaped by McGill Records, with commissions drawing in outstanding Canadian performers including Maureen Forrester, Lawrence Cherney, Tsuyoshi Tsutsumi, Arminda Canteros, and Rivka Golani, and celebrating the "exuberant performances and brilliant techniques" of the Gerald Danovitch Saxophone Quartet, the "precision and versatility" of the McGill Percussion Ensemble,[26] or the interpretative sensitivity of the piano teachers. A modern reworking of Helmut Blume's original vision of the Faculty as a "radio school," McGill Records was conceived by Paul Pedersen as part of a larger cultural initiative that, beginning with the CBC's Canadian composers series, sought to bring new music to a larger audience. According to Violet Archer, one of the Faculty's earliest composition graduates, the initiative represented a coming of age.[27] Not only did Canada now have its own musical culture, it was a tradition in which new music was meant to be listened to, appreciated, and valued over time. To this end, the top priorities of McGill Records were the development of a supporting infrastructure that would ensure the musical and technological distinction of its recordings on the open market, and a marketing plan that could distribute them across Canada. The latter was based on an alliance with Polygram forged in the early 1990s by Abe Kestenberg, the second director of McGill Records. For new music, however, sound recording has not had the democratizing impact seen with classical and popular music, the very fact that the "new" now embraces an entire century of diverse musical activity having endowed it, as cultural theorist Will Straw points out, with a longevity that renders it unmarketable as "new."[28] The financial viability of McGill Records has also been challenged by changing technology, the Internet, and its status as a small academic label, with the result, that sound recording as a shared space within the Faculty has become less about the production of new music per se and increasingly more about the ways in which sound recording research and techniques feed the timbral and spatial interests of composers.[29]

The change is part of an expanding internal network of pathways and corridors that has seen technology itself become a portal into the Faculty with a gravitational pull not unlike that of Pollack Hall. But where movement in, around, and through Pollack Hall is primarily a matter of musicians and their public audiences, technology, as a distinct career trajectory, also draws in computer scientists, engineers, sound technicians, and cognitive scientists. It is a portal that can be accessed from a variety of paths within the University as well as from outside.[30] Initially energized by the vision and efforts of composer Bruce Pennycook, first as chair of the music technology area, then as vice principal (information systems and technology), the change in many ways reflects the global landscape, technology having become so entangled and intertwined in our daily lives that it is difficult to remember a time, "just thirty or thirty-five years ago," when the fastest computers filled entire wings of buildings and the model used to send astronauts to the moon took twenty-eight minutes to generate an unperformable six-minute work in which all parameters were based on a single twelve-tone row.[31] Within the Faculty, the turn to technology has always been motivated by just such compositional challenges and – whether driven by notational problems, a need for more efficient computer code, or more sensitive performer-instrument interfaces, – was initially prompted by a musical vision, a sense of something that might be achieved if only one had the technological capacity.[32] As the computer has increasingly become a shared instrument through which sound is conceptualized by composers, performers, and scientists, music has literally become a space for the meeting of minds, with a notational problem inspiring research on the connection between sound and sight, research on gestures becoming the inspiration for composition. And, as with any instrument, the computer has left its own mark, ultimately engendering a self-reflexive dialogue that requires us to rethink the paradigms and models through which we understand the possibilities of music and what it means to compose in an era when, as Bruce Pennycook once put it, "sound has become a recyclable commodity, authorship the domain of the unschooled."[33]

This dialogue has spilled into and been nurtured by the Marvin Duchow Library. In the early years of the Faculty's rebirth, the library consisted of a small collection of recordings donated in 1939 by Deutsch Grammophon, and as such, was, as Marvin Duchow put it, the "Faculty's Achilles heel," the absence of books and scholarly material only serving to confirm the University's view that music was not a subject worthy of academic pursuit.[34] Today, the library is a microcosm of the Faculty itself, with book, score, journal, audio, and virtual collections providing a portal to seemingly limitless thinking in and about music. As a gathering place, it has been fed by open graduate seminars that draw together theorists, musicologists, performers, composers, opera singers, jazz performers, sound recording engineers, scientists, early music specialists, and music educators, each of which brings to the dialogue their own disciplinary ideologies, analytical approaches, and conceptions of what it means to be "new." With the passing of time, the library has come to have its own drawing power as the seat of the Faculty's memory, the repository where its ever-deepening history testifies to its longevity as place. As a crossroads, the Faculty is no longer defined only by what unfolds within its walls but also by the many roads taken by its visitors, faculty, and students as they continue their journeys out into and across the world.

NOTES

1 Edward Casey, "How to Get from Space to Place in a Fairly Short Stretch of Time: Phenomenological Prolegomena," in *Senses of Place*, ed. Steven Feld and Keith Basso (New York: School of American Research Press, 1996), 25.

2 Kelsey Jones, letter to Marvin Duchow, 10 July 1960, courtesy of estate of Kelsey Jones estate. Jones is quoting the *Refus global* manifesto written in 1948 by the group of avant-garde automatiste painters formed under the leadership of Paul-Émile Borduas. It is coincidental that this quotation also appears in the "Introductory Welcome" for the Montréal, Nouvelles musiques festival international 2005, as a characterization of the composer who creates new music today.

3 The major European centres drew students from all over the world and Messiaen spawned a world awareness, but the sense of "world" here in Montreal was about being multicultural, about living simultaneously together; the "other" was not the subject of the ethnomusicologist or anthropologist but part of our very character; in other words, the other was not simply a visitor.

4 The first electronic music studio in Canada was opened at the University of Toronto in 1959. The studio at the University of British Columbia was opened in 1965. All the early studios in Canada were equipped with instruments created by Hugh Le Caine. The largest studio today, located at l'Université de Montréal, was opened in 1985.

5 Six of the ten commissioned works for Expo '67 were associated with the McGill EMS. Such a level of funding for the arts has only been seen once since then – for the 2000 Millennium celebrations.

6 Micheline Coulombe Saint-Marcoux, in Canadian Music Centre, *Compositeurs au Québec: Micheline Coulombe Saint-Marcoux* (Montréal, 1985).

7 In "History of the Digital Orchestra Studio at McGill University, Schulich School of Music" Sean Ferguson describes Eric Johnstone as "the body, the glue, the binding" that made the studio work, "a valued private treasure"; document provided to Eleanor Stubley through email correspondence with Ferguson, 13 November 2005. Johnstone's inventions ranged from super-effective ring modulators and multi-mode filters to unique envelope and logic units to interfaces like the fiddler's foot-tapping jig-board, an automatic Irish jig writing program, and 3-D colour visualization software.

8 Hugh Le Caine did write compositions, believing that this was one of the few ways to understand a composer's interests: "the compositions arose in my attempting to understand what composers were after and particularly what use they could make of something I was working on"; quoted in Gayle Young, *The Sackbut Blues* (Ottawa: National Museum of Science and Technology, 1989), 114. Le Caine's compositions have been performed at McGill on several occasions.

9 See Chris Howard, "Completing the Circle," in *Crosscurrents and Counterpoints: Offerings in Honor of Bengt Hambræus at 70,* ed. Per Broman, Nora Engebretsen, and Bo Alphonce (Gothenburg: University of Gothenburg, 1998), 183.

10 Ibid., 183.

11 With Pierre Béluse, Saint-Marcoux formed the Ensemble Polycousmie to integrate electronic techniques with percussion and dance. During the 1970s she organized a number of electroacoustic concerts at various galleries in the historic district of Old Montréal.

12 Composers Marvin Duchow, Bengt Hambræus, and Brian Cherney are examples of this model, each having completed a doctorate in musicology. For further discussion of the importance that Cyril James placed on this model, see James's response to "On Plans for the Reorganization of the Faculty and the Conservatorium of Music of McGill University, April 1955," McGill University Archives RG39, Faculty of Music and Conservatorium, Curriculum Records, container 36, file 00433.

13 This theme runs through the minutes of meetings of the department of theory during the 1960s and 1970s on the topic of musicianship training, often as part of a larger pedagogical discussion on French and English approaches to sight-singing (the French use a fixed doh approach, the English a moveable doh approach). This viewpoint was first expressed by Donald Mackey but in later years it was also voiced by ear-training instructor Pierre Perron and composer Donald Patriquin.

14 Andrew Culver, who was John Cage's assistant from 1981 to 1992, made these remarks on a return visit as guest lecturer to the Faculty in September 2005 during his graduate seminar, "Chance Operations." For more details regarding Berio's perspective on history, see Paul Griffith, *The Substance of Things Heard: Writings about Music* (Rochester: University of Rochester Press, 2005).

15 Edward Casey, in "How to Get from Space to Place," uses the terms internal synergy and elasticism to describe the ways that these movements refresh and the newness and vitality of the place as being in synchronization with the changing times.

16 Arthur Kaptainis, "Review," *Montreal Gazette,* 9 March 2005. This phrase was originally used by alcides lanza to describe the music of his *acufenos V* (featured at the 1982 Contemporary Music Festival) and was requoted in 1985 by Canadian clarinetist James Campbell to capture the way in which the Contemporary Music Festival opened new music to an audience. In his introductory notes to the first Contemporary Music Festival John Rea notes the importance of this aspect in the evolution of the Faculty and new music generally: "During the last decade at the Faculty of Music in concerts of unusual variety and scope, the presence of twentieth century music has attracted appreciative audiences

from the Montreal public and student body … brings together these scattered efforts to reach an even broader spectrum of the public, as well as to involve students both as participants and as listeners."

17 Paul Helmer reports Blume as saying "every time a performer goes on stage he or she submits him/herself to peer review in a public forum and hence, for all intents and purposes, 'publishes'"; "McGill University," unpublished paper, 2005, p. 8.

18 Full-time appointments at the time included Otto Joachim, Pierre Béluse, Tom Plaunt, Louis-Philipe Pelletier, members of the Mount Royal Brass Quintet, and Gerald Danovitch.

19 It had been common practice in the early years of the Conservatorium and the Faculty for the choirs to perform music by staff composers. It was not until the 1970s that the instrumental ensembles began to commission works, including initially compositions by Donald Patriquin, alcides lanza, Bengt Hambræus, Brian Cherney, and John Rea. The most recent commissions include Sean Ferguson's *Les Bregmans* for the McGill Conservatory, the opera *Evangeline Revisited* by Julian Wachner for Opera McGill, and a group of fanfares by all the composers that were on staff for the reopening of the Faculty as the McGill University, Schulich School of Music, September 2005.

20 Gilles Potvin, "Music in Quebec," Radio-Canada interview, March 1989.

21 McGill University Archives, Minutes of meetings of the Department of Performance and Faculty Council, April 1977, provided to Eleanor Stubley in email correspondence with Paul Pedersen, 14 November 2005.

22 The opera program by its very nature as a musical genre constitutes a shared space. Since the late 1980s the program has a history performing and premiering "new" works, with a particular emphasis on Canadian compositions. The most recent was a re-staging of *Louis Riel*, the centenary opera by Harry Somers and Mavor Moore, in 2005.

23 For example, the experience of MUD described by John Rea in chapter 3 of this book has recently been repeated as graduate seminar, team-taught by D'Arcy Gray (percussionist), Marcelo Wanderley (engineer), and Sean Ferguson (composer), in which students design new instruments. Today performance master classes typically feature repertoire from all eras. All master's and doctoral performance recital programs typically include some "new" repertoire.

24 Bruce Minorgan, interview with Eleanor Stubley, 16 October 2005.

25 John Bland, internal memo, 13 February 1975. John Bland is the architect from the firm Bland, Loyne, Shine and Lacroix, which designed the Hall. During the late 1970s and early 1980s Pollack Hall was the primary performance venue for the SMCQ.

26 Quotation from a review for the recording "Celebration" on the McGill Records website, www.music.mcgill.ca/resources/mcgillrecords/classical_thumbnails.html; John Ditsky, "Review of Percussion," *Fanfare* 5 (1982), 292.

27 Violet Archer, "Making Music," *Our Own Agendas: Autobiographical Essays by Women Associated with McGill University* (Montreal: McGill-Queen's University Press, 1995). Violet Archer graduated from the Faculty of Music in 1936 and was one of the first to graduate with the sense of herself as "composer." Alexander Brott and Marvin Duchow were students at the same time.

28 Will Straw, "Sound Recording," *The Cultural Industries in Canada*, ed. Michael Dorland (Toronto: Lorimer, 1996).

29 Of central importance has been the ear-training program designed by René Quesnel which is based, not on harmonic function, but on acoustic spatial relationships. Prof. Martha de Francisco writes: "we work in various areas of production and research trying to find better ways to represent sound with the means of recording. Our faculty and students have a particular interest in understanding and describing the spatial characteristics of sound. The scope of our efforts within the group goes from capturing and recreating music using a variety of surround sound arrays, to learning to hear the most subtle spatial differences, to capturing motion associated with the production of music in an acoustic space, to understanding the emotional impact that certain recording techniques may produce in the audiences" (email correspondence with Eleanor Stubley, 13 November 2005). Note also that while McGill Records is no longer as active as it once was, current projects include a series of DVDs containing Brian Cherney's complete works with detailed analytical notes.

30 For example, one can enter the undergraduate technology programs through the Faculty of Arts and Science, Computer Applications, etc.

31 The work referred to here is Paul Pedersen's *Serial Composition for Violin, Horn, Bassoon and Harp*, the first fully computerized composition written in Canada, composed in 1965 (the year before Pedersen came to McGill) on the IBM 7094 computer at the University of the Toronto. It has since been renamed *Cybernetic Steps*, and a computer-realized version of it was used to accompany a performance of the ballet ensemble, Le Groupe de la Place Royale.

32 This type of thought process was the very essence of early work done in the EMS, each new instrument requiring sound and its notation to be conceived afresh. See, for example, the writings and reflections of Hugh Le Caine in Gayle Young, *Sackbut Blues*, and Lyse Richer-Lortie, "Otto Joachim: Composer, Performer, Inventor," *Variations* 2 (Feb. 1979). The first programs to splinter off were the MMA in computer applications, the BMus in technological applications in music, and the PhD in music, media, and technology.

33 Bruce Pennycook, "Composition: A Paradigm for the Future," draft of unpublished paper, 2004. The lecture series for the fall 2005 semester reflected well this self-reflexivity, as it included a variety of different presentations that consider the composer as scientist, the composer as analyst, the composer as mixer, the composer as experimenter, and the composer as elaborator, in addition to the composer as collaborator model discussed by James Harley in chapter 5 of this book.

34 Marvin Duchow, letter to Principal James, 14 March 1958, McGill University Archives, RG2, Office of Principal and Vice Chancellor, Office of Principal Frank Cyril James, Annual Reports to the Principal, container 603, file 0413. There are many other examples of Duchow's concern. The musicology program was delayed in the initial rebirth of the Faculty in 1960 because the library could not support study of "historic" music.

1

István Anhalt and New Music at McGill

Robin Elliott, University of Toronto

One of the many visitors drawn to the Faculty in 2004, musicologist ROBIN ELLIOTT is the Jean A. Chalmers Chair in Canadian Music and the director of the Institute for Canadian Music at the University of Toronto. When Elliott first met István Anhalt at a summer gathering in his parents' Kingston garden, he was about to graduate from high school, and was himself at something of a "crossroads," unsure as to whether mathematics or music would be the path to his future. He recalls that Anhalt was "a large part of his decision to opt for music," and that although he took only one course with him at Queen's University (1974–78) – fourth-year analysis in twentieth-century music – it had a profound impact, fundamentally changing his sense of the possibilities of music and its potential in contemporary culture. Remembering Anhalt at McGill as an essential part of the institutional building that marked the early years of the Faculty's rebirth, he tells his story in a way that infuses the archival record with the voices of Anhalt's former students, fellow composers, friends, and Anhalt himself. The resulting snapshot, consequently, is more like one of Anhalt's own "pluri-dramas" or multi-vocal compositions than the faded, sepia images of time and place that we typically associate with historical black and white frontier photographs.

In 1949 two Central European intellectuals of Jewish origin with a passionate interest in new music crossed the Atlantic Ocean, each travelling to a new country to take up a university position; one travelling from east to west, and the other from west to east. At age twenty-nine István Anhalt, originally from Budapest, moved from Paris to Montreal to start work at McGill University; at age forty-six

Theodor W. Adorno returned from exile in Los Angeles to the University of Frankfurt.[1] Although the two men did not know each other, their views on new music were remarkably similar.

Adorno's book *Philosophie der neuen Musik* was first published in 1949, the same year as these two trans-Atlantic migrations. In it Adorno argues that Schoenberg was the most important creator of the "new music" of the twentieth century.[2] For Adorno, only music that embodied a progressive dialectical relationship with society could rightly be considered "*avancierte Kunst*" and thus worthy of the term "new music."[3] His arguments for this rested on an interpretation of the history of music as a steady progression to more evolved types of musical language, an idea of progress embodied in his term *Fortschrittsmoderne,* which Günter Seubold translates as "advancement modernity."[4]

Anhalt shared Adorno's view of music history and new music: according to his former pupil William Benjamin, Anhalt "was very committed to the idea of musical progress, or at least to the notion that music was an ever expanding domain of knowledge and possibility, rather like science. It was obvious that he was interested in the avant-garde of the time, and was, as he later put it himself, composing for Darmstadt."[5] Anhalt made it his mission to introduce new music, in Adorno's sense of the term, to Montreal during the course of his activities as a composer, theorist, teacher, and administrator at McGill University from 1949 to 1971.

Although the rhetoric of twentieth-century European new music has been resolutely internationalist (some might even say imperialist) in tone, like all other music it is deeply embedded in, and marked by, its particular time and place of origin. Upon his arrival at McGill in January 1949, Anhalt brought with him as part of his mental baggage first-hand familiarity with two particular European new music scenes: that of Budapest in the 1930s, and that of Paris in the immediate post-war years.[6] In Budapest, through studies with Zoltán Kodály and more restricted but still firsthand associations with Béla Bartók,[7] Anhalt had been exposed to the quest for an authentically Hungarian "new music" that was to be accomplished via the incorporation and transformation of what was perceived to be authentic folk music traditions. In Paris, through composition studies with Nadia Boulanger and piano lessons with Soulima Stravinsky, Anhalt became intimately familiar with neo-classical music (which Adorno dismissively terms "music about music")[8] and the works of its leading proponent, Igor Stravinsky (Soulima's father).

Also in Paris Anhalt made the first tentative discoveries (on his own) of the work of Arnold Schoenberg and his school. He also heard the music of younger composers there, including Pierre Boulez.[9] His early compositions in Montreal were influenced in part by both the Bartók/Kodály idiom and by Stravinskian neoclassicism, but he would soon be most closely identified with the techniques of the Schoenberg school (using both atonal and twelve-tone idioms), creating a musical language that did not reflect the precepts of either of his principal composition teachers in Europe.

Shortly after his arrival in Canada in 1949, Anhalt must have quickly realized that little new music of any variety had made its way to Montreal. There had been sporadic visits from a few leading European composers: Prokofiev was heard in recital in 1920,[10] Ravel presented his music in 1928,[11] and Stravinsky gave a recital of his violin and piano works in 1937.[12] Henry Cowell gave a lecture-recital at McGill in 1925, Léo-Pol Morin played Schoenberg's op. 11 and op. 19 piano pieces in 1927, Rodolphe Mathieu wrote atonal works in the 1920s, and Alfred Laliberté had promoted the music of his friends Scriabin and Medtner.[13] Jean Papineau-Couture, Clermont Pépin, François Morel, Pierre Mercure, and Serge Garant (all born within ten years of Anhalt) were either still students or at the beginning of their professional careers and had yet to create a substantial body of new music.

Anhalt was not at all frustrated by the lack of a new music scene in Montreal when he arrived; on the contrary, he found it made for a good situation in which to get work done.

> The fact that the terrain was not overcrowded, like it was in Paris, Budapest and every other largish European city, meant that I felt that there might be room for myself, if I worked hard enough ... So instead of being intimidated or disappointed, I thought 'There is room in Canada to do things, and there are a number of people around my age who are doing that [i.e. composing], and they are surviving, and so I found the environment very conducive to work ... The environment in Montreal was just rich enough and not too rich.[14]

Benjamin adds:

> This, I think, is the key to the man: his ability to look at the present, the here and now, and to see nobility and worth in it... It's hard to think of many other North American European-born artists who showed this talent to so remarkable a degree. Of course there were some – Ernst Krenek and Stefan Wolpe come to

> mind, as does Kurt Weill of course, and Herbert Brün – but they stand out. In Canada, which was a good deal harder to swallow than the U.S., Anhalt was certainly more the exception than the rule among émigré intellectuals in being willing to take a serious, non-condescending look at his new surroundings.[15]

Anhalt's sanguine outlook must have been sorely tested by the situation that greeted him in 1949. Music instruction had been offered at McGill for sixty-five years when Anhalt arrived, but it remained a decidedly peripheral part of the University's mandate and activities. For the first twenty years, as current Dean Don McLean recalls: "The Victorian and Edwardian rationale for music instruction was to train ladies in the appropriate parlour skills."[16] During the next twenty years, as Stanley Brice Frost has noted, there was "barely enough money to keep the Conservatorium and the faculty alive, and both operations suffered from a lack of appropriate premises and a dearth of adequate equipment."[17] When Anhalt arrived, Douglas Clarke was still the only full-time member of the faculty, and the instruction was as outdated as the buildings in which it was offered. The British model of music education, which emphasized the mastery of a historical repertoire, hardly seemed relevant to the development of an original compositional voice, and the resultant student exercises were about as far as can be imagined from Adorno's – or Anhalt's – conception of new music.

Nevertheless, Anhalt fulfilled his duties at McGill conscientiously and looked for other outlets to nurture his interest in new music. In the absence of a decent music library at McGill ("It was a joke – the McGill Music Library was a shelf in the office," Anhalt recalls),[18] and without much income to build up his own collection of scores, Anhalt relied on listening to new music whenever possible. One memorable event was hearing Alban Berg's opera *Wozzeck* for the first time, in a radio broadcast of the New York premiere (in April 1951) conducted by Dmitri Mitropoulos.[19] Anhalt was living over a dentist's office on Park Avenue at the time: "The only radio in the house was in his [the dentist's] office ... It was Saturday afternoon, no patients, and so I was sitting in the dentist's chair, amidst those instruments and those smells, and having one of the greatest experiences of my life."[20] Anhalt recalls also the influence of listening to LP recordings: "François Morel told me that he had a recording of Schoenberg's *Orchestral Variations*, op. 31. He invited me to his home – he had a record player in the dining room of his parents – and we listened several times to this marvellous work.[21]

When I wrote my Symphony, I still heard the power and the language of Schoenberg's *Orchestral Variations*, a wonderful work."[22] Helmut Blume also shared recordings of new European music with Anhalt. Blume acquired these recordings through his work for the CBC, as the host of shows such as *International Concert* and *The Composer Speaks* in the 1950s and 1960s.[23] It was on one of Blume's shows that Anhalt first heard electronic music: "It was Blume who played electronic music on the CBC for the first time – it was in the mid-1950s, and it was *Gesang der Jünglinge* – a great experience. The next day I went to the CBC and I said 'Can I listen to this piece again?' And it was possible. They put me in a listening booth and I listened to *Gesang der Jünglinge* several times."[24]

Anhalt soon became active in giving concerts of new music at McGill – including both works by other composers and his own compositions. On 20 January 1950 he organized a concert at Moyse Hall in McGill's old Arts Building[25] that featured the local premiere of two works: Stravinsky's *Sonata for Two Pianos* and Bartók's *Sonata for Two Pianos and Percussion* (Anhalt played piano in the former work and conducted the latter work).[26] Moyse Hall was also the venue for two concerts that Anhalt mounted of his own recent compositions, the first on 20 March 1952, the second (as part of the celebrations of the fiftieth anniversary of the founding of the McGill Conservatorium) on 6 December 1954. These two concerts presented a total of ten works by Anhalt, most of them in first performances, ranging in style from the neoclassicism of his ballet *L'Arc-en-ciel* (1951) to the serialism of his *Fantasia* (1954) for piano. Other important twelve-tone compositions by Anhalt followed later in the 1950s, including the *Violin Sonata* (1954, premiered in 1957), *Chansons d'aurore* (a song cycle completed and premiered in 1955), and *Symphony* (1954–58, premiered in 1959). Anhalt was soon regarded as "the heavyweight among Canadian composers."[27]

Despite his growing reputation as a composer, Anhalt's position at McGill remained tenuous at best. His initial status, as an assistant professor with a fellowship from the Lady Davis Foundation, came to an end in August 1952. For the next four years, Anhalt remained on staff as a part-time instructor of piano and composition and took on private piano pupils to make ends meet.

A new phase in the life of the Faculty of Music at McGill began in 1955 with the resignation of Douglas Clarke. Clarke's vision of a small faculty, with twelve hand-picked students ("Cambridge on the St Lawrence," as

Anhalt has termed it)[28] came to an end. Under the new dean, musicologist Marvin Duchow, the BMus program was soon North Americanized: a specialist option in composition was introduced in 1956, together with options in performance and school music. New administrative structures also divided the Faculty into three sections: theory, headed by Duchow; keyboard and vocal music, headed by Helmut Blume; and orchestral instruments, headed by the violinist and conductor Alexander Brott.

While these structural changes were taking place there was considerable tension behind the scenes. Duchow, a scholar of modesty and integrity, found it a demanding job to deal with his two ambitious colleagues. At the same time, Ellen Ballon, a former child prodigy pianist who had been a pupil at the McGill Conservatorium when it first opened in 1904, had returned to Montreal and was becoming an éminence grise at McGill. A wealthy woman, she endowed a lecture series and became generally involved in the workings of the Faculty, not always with Duchow's best interests in mind. To top it all off, Frost reports that when Duchow was appointed as dean, "it was widely understood that he would be the last person to hold that office and that the venture (that is, the Faculty of Music) would be allowed to run down and quietly expire."[29]

Although Duchow, Blume, and Brott all had some professional experience as composers, it was clear that none of them would be willing or able to offer the advanced instruction required for the reorganized curriculum. As a result, Anhalt was rehired on a permanent basis as an assistant professor in 1956 to teach composition and theory.[30] For the next ten years he was the only faculty member giving advanced training in composition; harmony and keyboard harmony instruction filled out his timetable.

It is common, in speaking of compositional pedagogy, to separate technique and craft from art and inspiration. Some teachers concentrate exclusively on craft and feel that inspiration cannot be taught or learned. Jean Boivin notes that Gilles Tremblay might begin a composition class by reading poetry for twenty minutes, presumably hoping to convey inspiration; Serge Garant, on the other hand, stressed technique and did not permit any discussion of aesthetic issues in his analysis and composition classes.[31] Anhalt's approach tended to be closer to that of Garant than Tremblay, although as we shall see, his concept of craft extended beyond purely technical details.

Speaking of his instructional duties at McGill, Anhalt has noted that "The first few years of teaching were a real struggle because there were few students. But when the three H's appeared, and Bill Benjamin, the situation changed; I was really stimulated by those students."[32] Anhalt's three H's (by analogy with the three B's of classical music) are Alan Heard, Hugh Hartwell, and John Hawkins.[33] Alan Heard, the first to be taught by Anhalt, arrived at McGill in 1958 to begin his BMus degree at age sixteen. Heard took numerous courses with Anhalt, including three years of harmony, two years of keyboard harmony, and four years of composition. Having received advanced standing upon admittance, he took second-year harmony and composition in his first year, and as a result, he completed the required courses by the end of third year, and was given a year of private lessons by Anhalt in his fourth year. Heard recalls the instruction offered by Anhalt in detail:

> The early composition courses – up to second year – dealt with traditional (i.e. tonal) styles. István believed that students should also be exposed to contemporary techniques, and gave classes for small groups of (mostly second-year) students in this area. This was totally beyond the call of duty and, like the private instruction, added to what I only later came to understand must have been a crushing workload, but it was a vital part of my education and that of many of my peers. It is hard to remember precisely what new music content was involved, but there was a lot of it – and most things were new to me then. I do remember being introduced to Varèse, Bartók, Kodály, Messiaen, Hindemith, Stravinsky, and Ives. Oddly enough, I don't remember looking at works by the Neo-Viennese School, although we did study serial procedures. In fact, as often as not, István would rely on the works of the tonal masters for examples. This is not as odd as it sounds, as in matters other than pitch organization they are often as instructive as contemporary masters. We studied pretty much all techniques – diatonic modes, modes of limited transposition, even a limited and nascent form of set theory.[34]

Beyond the techniques and craft of composition that Anhalt imparted, Heard recalls that he was an inspired pedagogue: "It would be difficult to exaggerate the influence István has had on my professional life, especially in the area of teaching. Even after more than forty years, when confronted with a tricky technical problem in dealing with a student, I ask myself 'What would István have done?'"[35] Benjamin adds, "He has been our special exemplar (if at times our rebuke), but his achievement is a touchstone for all artists."[36]

A Composition Class at McGill University's Faculty of Music, in Shaughnessy House on Drummond Street, ca. 1959. Left to right: Charles Palmer, Alan Heard, Gian Lyman, Gerrit Tetenburg, István Anhalt, Pierre Perron, Alice Postner. Jean Talon Photo. Source: http://www.collectionscanada.ca/4/7/m15-244-e.html.

One mark of the success of the reorganized music degree at McGill is that all students in Anhalt's class pictured in the above photograph [37] had professional careers in music. Alice Postner was already on staff at McGill, teaching dictation. Charles Palmer and Heard both went on to teach composition (Palmer at McGill for about six years[38] and Heard at the University of Western Ontario, where he has been on staff for the past thirty years). Gian Lyman was a professional viola da gambist and taught at McGill and the Longy School of Music before her untimely death in 1974 (there is a McGill scholarship for early music performance in her memory). Gerrit Tetenburg was also an early music specialist and taught at the Université de Montréal and Queen's University (and he was later involved in palliative care in Montreal). Pierre Perron was head of music education at Dalhousie University for nineteen years, and though now retired remains active as a choral conductor. One measure of Anhalt's success as a teacher of composition is that many of his students went on to advanced graduate studies. Of those mentioned, Heard and Benjamin went to Princeton, Hartwell studied with George Rochberg and George Crumb at the University of Pennsylvania, and Hawkins went on to graduate studies in composition at McGill with Anhalt.

Heard's last year at McGill was Benjamin's first. Benjamin's recollection of Anhalt's classes accords in general outline with Heard's, but it differs in some details. Benjamin recalls that all of the harmony classes covered conventional materials up to the second term of fourth year, when Anhalt introduced "what he called modal chromaticism – basically a conservative (diatonic) modern idiom in which the models included Britten, some music by Anhalt himself, some neoclassical music, etc."[39] Composition was taught in small classes of two or three students; it began with creating historical pastiches in second year, worked through various modern compositional techniques in third year, and finally arrived at contemporary new music:

> In fourth year, he had us listen to a range of then recent music: Carter, Stockhausen, Schafer, *Atmosphères* and *Aventures* by Ligeti, and some music by Rochberg, Beckwith, as well as other composers whom he knew or who interested him. He didn't take a systematic approach to very recent music – there was no detailed analysis of the new works, we just listened and looked at small sections (sometimes at the keyboard if it seemed appropriate) and he would comment on general features of the compositional language or on presumptions underlying the style.[40]

Both Heard and Benjamin stressed that Anhalt was gifted at conveying the craft of composition. As Heard explains, "I am using the word 'craft' in an extended sense to include not only local manipulation of pitches and rhythms, but also in the more profound sense of knowing where one is in a composition, and how to pace it."[41] Benjamin adds "He did make useful suggestions for how to get a piece started. In particular, he showed us his own method of composing short bits of music ('snippets' he called them) without any view as to how they might fit together, and then experimenting with various assemblages that might, of course, require much additional linking material and many changes to the original bits."[42]

Students not as gifted in traditional compositional techniques as the three H's and Benjamin could still benefit from Anhalt's teaching. Kevin Austin recalls "With me he was amazingly patient. I remember once, in my third year [the late 1960s], spending six weeks with one bar (the first bar) of a simple violin piece in G minor! I couldn't 'get' the next note. We spent an hour per week looking at this one bar. He showed me stuff that was interesting, but never 'expected' that I would really amount to much in (traditional) composition."[43]

In addition to his classroom duties, Anhalt looked after his students' interests in other respects. Hartwell remembers working for Anhalt at various paid summer jobs, such as cataloguing and identifying tape loops in the Electronic Music Studio and helping to prepare the score and parts of Anhalt's *Symphony of Modules*.[44] Heard was similarly employed in proof-reading the parts for Anhalt's *Symphony*,[45] and Donald Steven remembers providing technical assistance for a production of Anhalt's *Foci* in Toronto.[46] More importantly, Steven recalls that it was through Anhalt's intercession that he was allowed to study music at McGill in the first place: "I had worked as a professional folk singer (in The Raftsmen and other groups) and become an arranger in the process. Gradually, my interest turned to contemporary music and I wrote a couple of pieces which a friend showed to Professor Anhalt, who, overlooking my previous poor efforts, allowed me to return and study composition. His openness changed my life, for which I will ever be grateful."[47] Anhalt also arranged for his composition students to hear their music in performance, a necessary but often overlooked part of compositional pedagogy. He even hired professional performers or conducted student compositions himself.[48] In addition, Anhalt would invite students to spend time with distinguished visiting composers in informal surroundings; Hartwell remembers such events as the highlight of his undergraduate career.[49]

McGill composition students had the opportunity to participate in various student composers' symposia. Benjamin recalls one such event at the University of Toronto in the early 1960s to which McGill students were invited; on that occasion Morton Feldman was the principal guest speaker.[50] Student symposia in 1968 and 1969 involved students from McGill, Bennington College, and the New England Conservatory of Music. At the first of these two events, which took place in Bennington, Vermont, John Hawkins (piano), Alex Tilley (double bass), and Kevin Austin (tuba) performed virtuoso toccatas that they had improvised under Anhalt's direction; Anhalt recalls engaging in a long conversation with composers Pozzi Escot and Robert Cogan afterwards about the performance.[51] The second symposium, held on 14–16 March 1969 at McGill involved students from the Conservatoire de musique du Québec à Montréal as well as from the two US schools. This symposium featured lectures by Serge Garant, Anhalt (on his *Cento*), and Harry Somers. Instead of speaking, Somers performed an early version of his *Voiceplay*, a wordless demonstration of new vocal techniques. After the performance by Somers one of Gilles Tremblay's students jumped up from his seat and improvised his own demonstration of extended vocal techniques, complete with choreography: it was Claude Vivier.[52]

Important changes that guided Anhalt's pedagogical activities in the late 1960s included his own new-found interest in writing for and studying all aspects of the human voice, his work in the field of electronic music, and the introduction of McGill's master's program in composition in 1968.[53] Anhalt often had his graduate students in composition read articles in other fields (such as psychology or linguistics) about the use and characteristics of the human voice and then apply these ideas to the study of works by George Crumb, Luciano Berio (*Sequenza III*), and other composers. Anhalt himself was in the process of applying ideas from many different disciplines to the analytical study of compositions for voice, which resulted in a number of published essays and eventually, thirteen years after he left McGill, a book, *Alternative Voices*.[54] Not all students took kindly to being asked to read complex articles outside their own field, but some became interested in writing for the voice as a result of Anhalt's example.[55]

Anhalt's activities in electronic music, with which he was intensively engaged from the late 1950s onwards, tended to remain somewhat apart from his pedagogical work at the undergraduate level but were an important part of his own contribution to new music at McGill. Benjamin notes that with the exception of *Gesang der Jünglinge*, Anhalt did not even mention electronic music in his classes, and adds, "I'm sure he thought it was too difficult for undergrads as a creative medium. Thus, while the electronic studio was developed in 1964–66, when I was still around, I was not encouraged to spend time there. Istvan knew that it was an all or nothing proposition if one wanted to use it creatively and believed, I think, that young composers needed to learn first to compose in traditional media."[56] By the time the graduate degree in composition was implemented, Anhalt had hired Paul Pedersen to direct the EMS and teach the graduate courses in electronic music.

As mentioned above, Anhalt's first experience of electronic music was hearing a CBC radio broadcast of Stockhausen's *Gesang der Jünglinge*. He quickly found the new medium to be an absorbing area of research and creativity. Working in an electronic music studio fitted in well with the "research lab" environment and science-dominated curriculum of a contemporary North American university. Even descriptions of Anhalt's concert music from this time reflect this link to scientific research: "Serially oriented, contrapuntally conceived, his works are like complicated chemical reactions where multiple elements continuously interact with each other, creating new essences which in turn set into motion new reactions."[57] Anhalt visited the studios in Ottawa, Paris, and Cologne in 1958,[58] returned to Ottawa in the summer of 1959, and visited the Columbia-Princeton Electronic Music Studio at Columbia University and the Bell Telephone Laboratories at Murray Hill, New Jersey, in the summer of 1961. He was also responsible for the first public concert of tape music in Canada, given at Moyse Hall on 1 November 1959: the program included works by Anhalt, Hugh Le Caine, and John Bowsher, as well as Stockhausen's *Gesang der Jünglinge*.[59]

In the spring of 1964 Anhalt was finally able to create the McGill Electronic Music Studio (EMS) in the coach house behind the Victorian mansion that housed the Faculty of Music. Most of the equipment was obtained on permanent loan from the National Research Council in Ottawa, thanks to Anhalt's friendly associations with Hugh Le Caine, who had designed much of this equipment himself. Anhalt served as the director of the EMS from 1964 until he left McGill in 1971.

For the first few years, the McGill studio was not open to students, but by September 1968 regular classes were being offered. Kevin Austin, the most prominent of Anhalt's students at McGill to specialise in electronic music, recalls this period:

> I started to work in the [McGill] Electronic Music Studio in 1969 and was [like] a fish to water. I started with three hours of studio time, and within a month was spending 20-plus hours per week in the studio. Over the Christmas holidays, I spent 12–14 hours per day. Anhalt was of the "old school" and quite competent in the studio. His work is quite good within the styles and idioms of the day, and with the equipment available to him. By the end of my first year I had better technique than Anhalt, but he had more fluency and better ideas. In time, the technology became an impediment to him and ceased to grow rapidly enough to meet his needs. Other things took precedence in his life.[60]

Austin also notes one way that electronic music composition at this time differed from more traditional forms of musical creation: "Paper composition is easier to do than working in the studio, as paper composition can be done at the lake or in a hotel room, or on a slow Sunday afternoon, or in your basement or the office. Working in electronic music required the studio availability (booking it!), and living with constant problems that a technician would have to resolve."[61]

The McGill EMS was part of a wider postwar phenomenon that has been termed the "institutionalization of the musical avant-garde."[62] In Europe public funding for electronic music studios was primarily filtered through radio stations (for example, Radio-Télédiffusion française, Westdeutscher Rundfunk, RAI Milan, and Warsaw Radio);[63] in North America the universities provided the institutional home for such activity. In Canada the first two universities to set up electronic music studios were the University of Toronto (in 1959) and McGill. By the end of the 1970s there were more than a dozen such facilities in Canadian universities from coast to coast, and it soon became a matter of prestige to have extensive facilities with the most up-to-date equipment. Thanks to Anhalt's efforts, McGill was one of the pioneers in this field.

"Whoever speaks of culture speaks of administration as well," wrote Adorno in the opening lines of his 1960 essay "Culture and Administration."[64] Thus we turn to Anhalt's administrative duties at McGill. On Blume's recommendation, he succeeded Duchow as the chair of the theory department in 1963, and he remained in that position until 1969. Under Anhalt's leadership, BMus specializations in music theory and musicology were created in 1966 and as noted above, graduate degrees in composition and musicology were added in 1968. (Paul Pedersen, who succeeded Anhalt as chair of the theory department, added a graduate specialization in theory in 1970.) In the 1960s the position of departmental chair was more powerful than it has been either before or since. This was an era of great expansion in the Faculty of Music – especially in the late 1960s when student numbers grew from about fifty to 250[65] – and Anhalt had free rein to hire faculty members without a hiring committee or a protracted interviewing process. During this period the theory department grew from three to thirteen faculty members including Paul Pedersen and Bruce Mather, both of whom were hired by Anhalt in 1966 and went on to make their own important contributions to new music at McGill.

In addition to curriculum developments and faculty enrichment, both before and during his term as chairman of the theory department, Anhalt was able to attract many eminent avant-garde composers as visitors to McGill. Stockhausen, whom Anhalt had met in the summer of 1958 during a visit to Cologne, gave a talk at McGill on "New Electronic and Instrumental Music" on 9 December 1958, and made a return visit to Montreal in January 1964, sponsored jointly by McGill, the Université de Montréal, the Conservatoire de musique du Québec, Jeunesses musicales du Canada, and the CBC. During his second visit he lectured at Redpath Hall on 23 January on the subject of "Invention and Discovery: Development of Musical Forms since 1951," and the next day gave a seminar for music students at McGill, during which he played a recording of and discussed his recent work, *Carré*. Not everyone greeted the Stockhausen events favourably: Kelsey Jones circulated an internal memo that took Anhalt to task for his enthusiastic endorsement of Stockhausen's work at both the public lecture and at the seminar. Anhalt's response, in kind, led to a second memo and a second response before the issue was laid to rest.[66]

Other visitors to McGill included Milton Babbitt,[67] John Beckwith, Luciano Berio, Lejaren Hiller, George Rochberg, Jean Papineau-Couture, R. Murray Schafer, and Toru Takemitsu. In August 1961 Anhalt also hosted John Cage and David Tudor; the two were visiting Montreal to participate in the Semaine internationale de la musique actuelle, but they did not interact with McGill students as it was the summer holiday period.[68] Cage gave two public lectures in Redpath Hall at McGill University as part of the festival, on 4 and 8 August 1961; Anhalt moderated a bilingual public discussion after Cage's second lecture. Shortly thereafter David Tudor returned to perform at McGill, an occasion that Benjamin recalls: "The pianist Lili Krauss was giving master classes at the same time, and she sat in, fuming, at Tudor's demonstration. She regarded all music since Wagner as being on a one-way escalator to hell, and he had no interest at all in anything from the standard repertoire."[69]

EPILOGUE

In his writings Adorno developed at length the thesis that "mass culture" is imposed by the culture industry rather than chosen by the masses. More recently some musicologists have advanced the idea that "high culture," or at least the high modernist style of avant-garde composition that flourished in the post-Second World War era, was imposed (or at the very least artificially nourished) by the academy. Susan McClary, one of the first people to advance this position, states: "Perhaps only with the twentieth-century avant-garde ... has there been a music that has sought to secure prestige precisely by claiming to renounce all possible social functions and values."[70] Canadian writers were quick to take up this position, among them two of Anhalt's former pupils: John Hawkins and William Benjamin. Speaking at the *Fifth Stream* conference held at Wilfrid Laurier University in May 1989, Hawkins stated:

> In many areas of endeavour in the twentieth century, groups of highly specialized people have split off from the society which surrounds them. Their work and ideas become so esoteric and far-fetched that few can understand. These groups always tend to become self-serving, self-aggrandizing and self-fulfilling. They seek dominance through power, whether in politics, religion, the professions, or in human relations in general. The "Us" and "Them" mentality has been one of the most divisive and destructive forces in this century.[71]

Hawkins adds that while studying under Anhalt his compositional models were Berg, Webern, and the late (serial) works of Stravinsky, but he later rebelled against this music: it was "written in a kind of code. But once you had cracked the code, the message was just as unintelligible. I just couldn't find any music in it at all." [72] Benjamin, speaking at the same conference, notes "The brief and tragic life and times of radical modern music is a chapter in human cultural history of unparalleled interest ... to understand the provenance of this new, advanced music and the reasons for its failure would be to grasp some deep truths about our times and the meaning of music and the other arts in our lives." [73] "Where else in human history is there anything like it?" he asks rhetorically. "In a degenerate phase of the Chinese aristocratic literary tradition, perhaps?" Benjamin notes that a turning point came in 1970 when composers "began to turn from the imposing and imposed constraints of the musical avant-garde."[74]

It is perhaps not a coincidence that the story I have been telling comes to an end at this same time – when Anhalt left McGill in 1971. Anhalt himself gradually left the avant-garde stream of composition during the 1970s, at about the same time as that entire scene was imploding internationally on all fronts and losing whatever tenuous prestige it had once enjoyed in the North American academy. Other kinds of new music rushed in to fill the void, so many, in fact, that no one kind could ever again wield the influence that the postwar avant-garde had exercised on fertile imaginations on both sides of the Atlantic for a period of about twenty-five years. In Anhalt's case a number of reasons may have contributed to his own shift in compositional outlook, including the relative isolation of his new position in Kingston, his disaffection with electronic music and its expressive potential (combined with his ongoing interest in the expressive qualities and potential of the human voice), and his friendship with the late George Rochberg, one of the most eloquent and erudite philosophers of the new postmodern aesthetic. To this list, Benjamin adds what may well have been the most important factor: "Istvan began to realize, in the early 1980s, that his Jewish heritage was more important to him than he had been willing to admit, and this made him want to communicate more concretely, with music functioning as a symbolic language, a language of cultural (historically grounded) musical topics. There is no way the high modernist style could be adapted to this purpose."[75]

None of this is meant to downplay the significance and importance of what Anhalt achieved for the Faculty of Music at McGill University. As Paul Pedersen stated when McGill University conferred an honorary D.Mus. degree on Anhalt in 1982, Anhalt's works "mirror his unique synthesis of artist, scientist, and scholar."[76] It would not be overstating the case to maintain that Anhalt institutionalized and validated the links between music and scientific inquiry at McGill, and thus in a sense laid the groundwork for further developments in that field, up to and including the creation in 2001 of the Centre for Interdisciplinary Research in Music, Media and Technology. The seeds Anhalt planted years ago at McGill have certainly yielded a rich harvest.

NOTES

1 Some years ago Anhalt stopped using the accent in his given name, but it has been retained for this publication because his name appears this way on official McGill documents such as contracts of employment. I would like to thank István Anhalt for the time he spent with me on numerous occasions discussing his experiences at McGill University. I would also like to thank his many pupils from McGill who shared their reminiscences and ideas with me, in particular Kevin Austin, William E. Benjamin, John Fodi, Clifford Ford, Hugh Hartwell, John Hawkins, Alan Heard, and Donald Steven.

2 Theodor W. Adorno, *Philosophie der neuen Musik* (Tübingen: J.C.B. Mohr / Paul Siebeck, 1949); English transl. by Anne G. Mitchell and Wesley V. Blomster as *Philosophy of Modern Music* (New York: Seabury Press, 1973). For a history of the use of the term "new music," from *ars nova* to Adorno, see Carl Dahlhaus, "'New Music' as Historical Category," in *Schoenberg and the New Music*, trans. Derrick Puffett and Alfred Clayton (Cambridge: Cambridge University Press, 1987), 1–13.

3 In a 1934 essay on Schoenberg, Adorno specifically examines "the dialectical relationship between artist and material," i.e. the dialectics of creativity. The beginning of Adorno's essay, though, touches upon the dialectics of reception. Theodor W. Adorno, "The Dialectical Composer," *Essays on Music*, ed. Richard Leppert, transl. Susan H. Gillespie (Berkeley: University of California Press, 2002), 203–7.

4 See Günter Seubold, "Some Reflections on Th. W. Adorno's Music Aesthetics," *Canadian Aesthetics Journal* 6 (Fall 2001), online at http://www.uqtr.uquebec.ca/AE/Vol_6/articles/seubol.html (accessed 7 December 2006).

5 William E. Benjamin, email communication with the author, 15 August 2005. The period to which Benjamin is referring is 1962–66. Darmstadt refers to the Internationale Ferienkurse für Neue Musik, an annual summer course for the European musical avant-garde that has been held in that city since 1946; Adorno was a regular lecturer at the Darmstadt courses during the 1950s and 1960s.

6 See Robin Elliott, "Life in Europe" and "Life in Montréal," in *Istvan Anhalt: Pathways and Memory*, ed. Robin Elliott and Gordon E. Smith (Montréal and Kingston: McGill-Queen's University Press, 2001), 3–32 and 33–64 for biographical information on Anhalt's life in Budapest, Paris, and Montréal, from his birth in 1919 until he left McGill in 1971 to become the head of the Department of Music at Queen's University.

7 Anhalt turned pages at one of Bartók's last recitals in Budapest in 1940; the program included two-piano works performed with Ditta Pásztory, Bartók's second wife; Anhalt has called this one of his most profound musical experiences; "István Anhalt: A Portrait," *Musicanada* 15 (November 1968): 9. Bartók also gave the first performance of some of the Bulgarian dances from *Mikrokosmos*, and Anhalt turned pages from Bartók's manuscript (István Anhalt, interview with the author, Kingston, 26 October 2005).

8 Adorno, *Philosophy of Modern Music*, 181–4.

9 In his activities as a teacher, concert promoter, and author, René Leibowitz disseminated information about the Schoenberg School in Paris during the years that Anhalt was living there. Leibowitz's *Schoenberg et son école*, the first book in French on Schoenberg, Berg and Webern, was published in Paris in 1947 (by J.B. Janin). Anhalt heard Boulez's *Piano Sonata No. 1* when it was performed in the same concert as Anhalt's *Six Songs from Na Conxy Pan* in May 1948; see Elliott, "Life in Europe," 21–2.

10 *Montreal Star*, 24 Jan. 1920, 38.

11 See Gilles Potvin, "Maurice Ravel au Canada," *Musical Canada: Words and Music Honouring Helmut Kallmann*, ed. John Beckwith and Frederick A. Hall (Toronto: University of Toronto Press, 1988), 149–63.

12 See "Regards en arrière / Looking Back," *Dossier Stravinsky-Canada, 1937–1967*, published in *Les Cahiers canadiens de musique / The Canada Music Book* 4 (Spring/ Summer 1972): 21–2.

13 For further details see Marie-Thérèse Lefebvre, "Les Débuts du modernisme musical à Montréal," in *Célébration*, ed. Godfrey Ridout and Talivaldis Kenins (Toronto: Canadian Music Centre, 1984), 73–9, and Lefebvre, *Rodolphe Mathieu: L'émergence du statut professional de compositeur au Québec 1890–1962*, Cahiers des Amériques 10 (Sillery, QC: Septentrion, 2004); the latter source includes a list of contemporary music concerts in Quebec between 1903 and 1953, on pp. 251–9.

14 István Anhalt, interview with the author, Kingston, 26 October 2005.

15 William E. Benjamin, "On becoming a Canadian composer: István Anhalt (1919 ... 1949 ... 1999)," unpublished paper (1999), 1.

16 Patrick McDonagh, Helen Dyer, and Andrew Mullins, "The Century Club: Marking Some McGill Milestones. 100 Years of Music," *McGill News* (Fall 2004): available online at http://www.mcgill.ca/news/2004/fall/century/two/ (accessed 7 December 2006).

17 Stanley Brice Frost, *McGill University: For the Advancement of Learning* (Montréal and Kingston: McGill-Queen's University Press, 1980), 290, 293.

18 István Anhalt, interview with the author, Kingston, 26 October 2005. Anhalt notes that it was Marvin Duchow who built up the music library after Clarke's retirement.

19 This production – a concert performance in Carnegie Hall – was released by Columbia records and is still available as a CD reissue (Sony MH2K 62759). Despite some pitch inaccuracies, the performance is widely regarded as one of the most riveting interpretations of *Wozzeck* on record.

20 "István Anhalt: A Portrait," *Musicanada* 15 (November 1968): 9.

21 On the importance of recordings to Morel's knowledge of new music, see S. Timothy Maloney, "Les années 60 et la montée de la musique d'avant-garde au Québec," *Les arts et les années 60*, ed. Francine Couture (Montréal: Triptyque, 1991), 159. Morel's familiarity with the Second Viennese School and Edgar Varèse was initially attained through commercial recordings of these works released in the 1950s.

22 István Anhalt, interview with the author, Kingston, 26 October 2005. The first commercially available recording of Schoenberg's op. 31 was by the Columbia Symphony Orchestra under Robert Craft (Columbia ML5244), recorded 4 June 1957 and released early in 1958. Anhalt worked on his *Symphony* from 1954 to 1958 and conducted the first performance of it in Montreal on 9 November 1959; his original title for the work, *Variations*, may have been inspired by the Schoenberg work.

23 Blume, who was five years older than Anhalt to the day, had studied with Hindemith in Berlin. He came to Canada in 1940 and joined the staff at McGill University's Faculty of Music in 1946, later serving as acting dean, 1963–64, and as dean, 1964–76. A radio clip of Blume interviewing Jean Papineau-Couture for a 30 December 1961 broadcast of "The Composer Speaks" can be heard on the CBC Archives web site at http://archives.cbc.ca/IDC-1-112-1498-10080/1960s/1961/clip4 (accessed 7 December 2006).

24 István Anhalt, interview with the author, Kingston, 26 October 2005. Stockhausen's *Gesang der Jünglinge* was premiered in live performance in Cologne on 30 May 1956.

25 There is a photograph of a lecture taking place in Moyse Hall in 1956 on the Virtual McGill University Archives web site at http://www.archives.mcgill.ca/pictures/pr017149.gif (accessed 7 December 2006). The hall is named after Charles Moyse, a long-serving professor of English and former dean of arts at McGill.

26 The concert also included performances of Mozart's Sonata for two pianos in D major, K448, and Debussy's suite *En blanc et noir* (the last movement of which is dedicated to Stravinsky).

27 Udo Kasemets, "István Anhalt," *Contemporary Canadian Composers*, ed. Keith MacMillan and John Beckwith (Toronto: Oxford University Press, 1975), 8.

28 Istvan Anhalt, interview with the author, Kingston, 3 September 1997.

29 Frost, *McGill University*, 292.

30 Anhalt was promoted to associate professor in 1962 and full professor in 1967. Other composers hired at Quebec institutions at about the same time include Jean Papineau-Couture (Université de Montréal, 1951), Clermont Pépin (Conservatoire de musique du Québec à Montréal, 1955), and Roger Matton (Université Laval, 1956).

31 Jean Boivin, "La classe de composition de Serge Garant, ou le sentier de la création lucide," *Circuit* 7.2 (1996): 37–55; especially 45 and 47. If the discussion in Garant's class happened to turn to aesthetic or personal issues, Walter Boudreau states that Garant would say "Listen, children, this is a composition class, not a psychiatrist's office" (45, author's translation).

32 István Anhalt, interview with the author, Kingston, 26 October 2005.

33 Most of Anhalt's composition pupils at McGill, and all of those who pursued advanced studies, were males. This was characteristic of what some writers have referred to as the "homo-social" atmosphere of avant-garde music composition at the time. While the situation for women composition students has improved somewhat in the intervening years, composition remains the most male-dominated area of instruction in university music departments across North America.

34 Alan Heard, email communication with the author, 25 October 2005.

35 Ibid.

36 William E. Benjamin, "István Anhalt: a tribute and an appreciation," *The Music Scene* 340 (November–December 1984): 10–11.

37 This photograph is also reproduced on p. 54 of Stéphane Jean, *István Anhalt Fonds (MUS 164): Numerical List* (Ottawa: Minister of Public Works and Government Services Canada, 2004), which in turn is available on the Library and Archives Canada website at http://www.collectionscanada.ca/obj/028021/f2/01-e.pdf (accessed 7 December 2006). The date given there is 1952, but 1959, the date supplied by Alan Heard, is likely more accurate.

38 Palmer quit his job as an assistant professor of composition at McGill in the early 1970s, moved to a farm in Nova Scotia, and later left music. Alan Heard notes that "he was a decent composer and a truly fine teacher, so in balance this was a loss" (email correspondence with the author, 1 November 2005).

39 Benjamin, email correspondence with the author, 15 August 2005.

40 Ibid.

41 Heard, email correspondence with the author, 25 October 2005.

42 Benjamin, email correspondence with the author, 15 August 2005.

43 Kevin Austin, email correspondence with the author, 22 September 2005. As will become evident, Austin subsequently found his calling in McGill's Electronic Music Studio.

44 Hugh Hartwell, telephone conversation with the author, 17 August 2005.

45 Heard, email correspondence with the author, 25 October 2005.

46 Donald Steven, email correspondence with the author, 15 August 2005.

47 Ibid.

48 For instance, in 1964 or 1965 Anhalt hired players from the Montreal Symphony to perform Hugh Hartwell's *Rondo* for oboe, clarinet, and bassoon and conducted the performance himself (Hartwell, telephone conversation with the author, 17 August 2005). Anhalt himself compared the role of concerts of student compositions to the role of lab work in the training of chemistry or physics students; see Yolande Rivard, "L'enseignement de la composition à l'Université McGill," *Vie musicale* 8 (May 1968): 11.

49 Hartwell, telephone conversation with the author, 17 August 2005.

50 Benjamin, email communication with the author, 15 August 2005; he dates the event as some time around 1963 or 1964.

51 Anhalt, telephone conversation with the author, 27 November 2005; Escot and Cogan were on staff at the New England Conservatory of Music. Kevin Austin recalls this event as an "open form / open score / gentle improvisation in the modern avant-garde style ... John [Hawkins] 'hated!' the idea and did so only under extreme pressure. I was a 'kid;' John was a somewhat unbalanced

genius; Alex was balanced and bright beyond my comprehension" (email communication with the author, 22 September 2005).

52 Anhalt, telephone conversation with the author, 27 November 2005.

53 The new two-year graduate programs in composition and musicology are described as the "brainchild of Prof. István Anhalt and Dean Helmut Blume" in the article "Graduate Degree in Music," *McGill News* 49 (January 1968): 6 (copy in István Anhalt Fonds, Library and Archives Canada, MUS164, file C1, folder 1,4).

54 István Anhalt, *Alternative Voices: Essays on Contemporary Vocal and Choral Composition* (Toronto: University of Toronto Press, 1984).

55 Clifford Ford has said that he became interested in playing with words and vocal sounds (for example by playing the voice backwards on a tape) during his studies with Anhalt (telephone conversation with the author, 26 October 2005). Kevin Austin notes that many students (though not he himself) found the requirement to read articles from psychology journals "repulsive" (email communication to the author, 22 September 2005). John Fodi states that in his graduate composition class with Anhalt, students were required to read psychology papers more than they were asked to look at music (interview with the author, University of Toronto, Faculty of Music, 25 October 2005).

56 Benjamin, email correspondence with the author, 15 August 2005.

57 "István Anhalt," BMI pamphlet, as cited in Raoul Duguay, "Istvan Anhalt," *Musiques du Kébèk* (Montréal: Éditions du jour, 1971), 17. Duguay is one of the few francophone writers on music in Quebec to have included an extensive discussion of Anhalt's career. Although Anhalt was fluently bilingual and enjoyed a close professional association with many leading francophone composers (particularly Jean Papineau-Couture), his role in the history of music in Quebec is often downplayed or overlooked entirely by francophone writers. This is a reflection of the general lack of interaction between anglophone and francophone Canadian music historians, which Gordon E. Smith was the first to point out in his article "Dualité dans l'historiographie musicale canadienne," *Les Cahiers de l'ARMuQ* 13 (May 1991): 29–37.

58 Montreal composer Pierre Mercure was also studying electronic music in Paris with Pierre Schaeffer during this period (1957–58), with financial support from the Royal Society of Canada; see Johanne Rivest, "La représentation des avant-gardes à la Semaine internationale de musique actuelle (Montréal, 1961)," *Canadian University Music Review* 19 (1998): 50.

59 For further details on this concert, and on all other aspects of Anhalt's work in this area, see David Keane, "Electroacoustic Music," *István Anhalt: Pathways and Memory*, ed. Robin Elliott and Gordon E. Smith (Montréal and Kingston: McGill-Queen's University Press, 2001), 132–63.

60 Austin, email communication with the author, 22 September 2005.

61 Ibid.

62 Georgina Born, *IRCAM, Boulez and the Institutionalization of the Musical Avant-Garde* (Berkeley: University of California Press, 1995). Jean Boivin uses the same phrase: "Les années soixante ont vu, au Québec comme ailleurs au Canada, l'institutionalisation progressive de la création musicale dite d'avant-garde," and specifically mentions the McGill EMS in this regard, in his article "La recherche consacrée aux compositeurs Québécois depuis un quart de siècle," in *Traité de la culture*, ed. Denise Lemieux (Sainte-Foy, QC: Les éditions de l'IQRC, 2002), 684.

63 All of these radio stations sent representative electroacoustic works to be aired during the Semaine internationale de la musique actuelle held in Montréal in August 1961; see Rivest. "La représentation des avant-gardes," 52–3. Anhalt's *Electronic Composition No. 3* was heard as part of this new music festival on 6 August 1961; works by Penderecki, Mercure, and Yoko Ono, among others, were heard on the same program.

64 The essay was first delivered as a radio lecture; see Adorno, *Essays on Music*, 57.

65 Charles Lazarus, "Sentimental Visit to McGill's Music Faculty Where Cheerfulness Breaks In," *Montreal Star* (21 Sep 1968; clipping in the István Anhalt Fonds, Library and Archives Canada, MUS164, file C1, folder 1,1) notes that there are "well over 600" full-time and part-time students at the Faculty of Music, of whom 250 are full-time students.

66 The memos are in the István Anhalt Fonds at the Library and Archives Canada, MUS164, file C1, folder 1,1.

67 "He [Babbitt] once told me that McGill (the faculty club) was where he discovered how awful English cooking could be," Benjamin, email communication, 15 August 2005. Babbitt visited McGill in 1963; Bethany Beardslee performed Babbitt's *Vision and Prayer* and *Philomel* at McGill on 10 March 1967 (István Anhalt Fonds, Library and Archives Canada, MUS164, file B2,6).

68 See Rivest, "La représentation des avant-gardes," 66.

69 Benjamin, email communication to the author, 15 August 2005; Benjamin remembers this event as having taken place during the 1962–63 academic year.

70 See her article "Terminal Prestige: The Case of Avant-garde Music Composition," *Cultural Critique* 12 (Spring 1989): 57–81; the quoted passage is on p. 60. Susan McClary was herself a member of the McGill musicology faculty in the early 1990s.

71 John Hawkins, "Us Versus Them: The Twentieth-century Dilemma," *The Fifth Stream*, ed. Peter Hatch and John Beckwith (Toronto: Institute for Canadian Music, 1991), 43.

72 Ibid., 41

73 William E. Benjamin, "Perspectives on Concert Music, the 'Sick Man' of Contemporary Culture," *The Fifth Stream*, ed. Peter Hatch and John Beckwith (Toronto: Institute for Canadian Music, 1991), 79.

74 Ibid., 80.

75 Benjamin, email communication with the author, 16 August 2005.

76 Paul Pedersen, "István Anhalt, Doctor of Music *Honoris Causa*," *Music McGill* 11 (Fall 1982): 3.

2

A Brief History of McGill University's Electronic Music Studio, 1964–2004: alcides lanza in Conversation with Meg Sheppard

alcides lanza, McGill University
Meg Sheppard, Montreal

ALCIDES LANZA's journey to McGill began in his hometown Rosario, Argentina, and included studies at the Di Tella Institute in Buenos Aires with Alberto Ginastera, Luigi Dallapiccola, Olivier Messiaen, and Bruno Maderna (1963–64), as well as an extended stay in New York where he worked at the Columbia-Princeton Electronic Music Center (1965–71). Arriving shortly after István Anhalt's departure, he subsequently shepherded the growth of the McGill Electronic Music Studio (EMS) through three dramatic transformations spanning more than thirty years. The EMS quickly became for him a home, a place where he could nurture the developing voices of young composers as family and friends while simultaneously launching an international career as composer, conductor, and pianist. Having recently become the Studio's Director Emeritus, he speaks of its past with the pride of a paternal father who, having left his mark, entrusts its future to a new generation. His memories, often rhapsodic and reminiscent, unfold as a collaborative exchange that is itself revealing of the place, in that Meg Sheppard is a renowned musician whose own ongoing search for eloquence and expressiveness through the use of diverse media has inspired many electroacoustic composers, including lanza himself.

Meg Sheppard: What were some of the earliest explorations of sound that precipitated and shaped electronic music composition in the twentieth century?

alcides lanza: My lecture notes for the course I teach on the history of electronic music document a long fascination with the relationship between art and machine – a relationship that has actually characterized much of music history. Indeed, music has often been on the cutting edge of technology: the violins of Stradivarius and others, Bach's organs, and Adolphe Saxe's saxophone are familiar successful developments. The twentieth century, however, introduced the added element of electricity and its potential to contribute to music production. One of the first fully electronic instruments, the Singing Arc, was built in 1899 by English physicist William Duddell. In 1906 Thaddeus Cahill created the dynamophone (telharmonium) – a machine that produced music made by a group of dynamos run by alternating electrical current. As the loudspeaker was yet to be invented, the dynamophone proved somewhat impractical, since the only way people could hear the music was over the telephone. Early in the twentieth century Italian futurists explored "the art of noises." As the century progressed, electronic manipulation of sound became increasingly sophisticated – ranging from the balletic movement of hands between two high frequency oscillators in the theremin to the multiple timbral possibilities of the trautonium (featured on the soundtrack of Hitchcock's *The Birds*), to computer-generated and manipulated sounds.

MS: Who was instrumental in sparking electronic composition in Canada?

al: Canada had its own genius working in the field of creating electronic devices, Hugh Le Caine (1914–77). Having spent his youth playing the piano and tinkering with all kinds of practical projects, he was something of a musical and mechanical prodigy. After completing studies in atomic physics, Le Caine, like other amateur-musician–scientists before him, such as Galileo and Einstein, began to travel between the world of music and the world of science. Le Caine applied his considerable expertise as a scientist to the exploration of music technology, and his laboratory at the National Research Council in Ottawa was the birthplace of the many instruments created by his vision and genius. One of his inventions, the Oscillator Bank, produced sine tone electrical waves in three frequency ranges, controlled by a touch-sensitive polyphonic keyboard. This was the first time that multiple oscillators were combined in one machine and controlled with such a mechanism.

The Spectogram, another important invention, permitted composers to "draw" music in ink on a graph-paper grid, defining rhythm, intensity, and duration graphically. The Spectogram could read these drawings as "on-off" control signals activating the Oscillator Bank. The Spectrogram also had the ability to work with twenty tracks simultaneously, and did not require splicing. At a time when tape splicing was a requisite skill – and a very tedious task – this was really something! The research leading to these two inventions was done in Le Caine's laboratory at the National Research Council (NRC) in Ottawa in the late 1950s. Prototypes were provided to both the University of Toronto and McGill University in the early 1960s.

MS: So what were the beginnings of the Electronic Music Studio at McGill?

al: István Anhalt was the first to explore the idea of starting an Electronic Music Studio at the Faculty of Music of McGill University. He had for some years been collaborating with Hugh Le Caine in developing machinery suitable for the production of electronic music. It became a reality on 16 June 1964 when a truck carrying an Oscillator Bank and a Spectrogram arrived at McGill's Faculty of Music. These two instruments were added to the Special Purpose Tape Recorder (also known as the Multi-Track) that Le Caine had previously loaned to McGill in September 1963. The Special Purpose Tape Recorder was capable of modifying the playback speed of ten stereo tapes, and recombining these sounds into a single stereo output. During the summer, the Electronic Music Studio was established in a small cramped space in the coach house behind the mansion on Redpath Street that housed the piano area. The EMS opened officially at McGill's Faculty of Music in September 1964 under the direction of István Anhalt, with Paul Pedersen as his assistant and Hugh Le Caine as special advisor.

The EMS quickly acquired tape recorders and additional equipment including White-noise and wave-form generators, plus ring modulators, a variable-band filter, mixers, microphones and a Novachord (a specialized type of electronic organ). Recording equipment included two Ampex stereo tape recorders (models AG-350 and 351). Except for commercially produced gear, most of the equipment in that earliest version of the EMS had been designed, developed, and built by Hugh Le Caine. Since these machines were hand-built by Le Caine, components needing replacement had to be built by him or by a technician following his instructions, and equipment needing repair had to be sent to Ottawa. This did interfere with the practical usage of these unique

Hugh Le Caine (centre) demonstrates the internal mechanism of the Multi-Track Tape Recorder to István Anhalt (LEFT) and Helmut Blume at the EMS in the coach-house on Redpath Street, Summer 1964. Reproduced by permission of the Music Division, National Library of Canada.

instruments. At the same time, Le Caine's focus on responding to composers' growing demands for greater flexibility, variety, and user-friendliness remained an important influence on his ongoing research and development of new machines.

MS: Who were the Directors of the EMS over the years?

al: István Anhalt became the first EMS director in 1964 and stayed until 1971; Paul Pedersen was director from 1971 to 1973. During the academic year 1973–74, Bengt Hambræus and I were co-directors. I took over as Director in 1974 and continued for the next thirty years, until 2004.

MS: Who used the EMS in the early years?

al: The EMS was initially used only for the creation of new works by composers on staff and invited visiting composers. During Canada's Centennial Celebration (1967), for example, guest composer R. Murray Schafer created new works at the studio (*Kaleidoscope* and *Visual Illusions*), and a new piece by Anhalt was commissioned (*Cento*). The mandate of the studio at that time was to create music, rather than to focus on research or teaching.

MS: The EMS got its own space when the Faculty of Music moved to the Strathcona Music Building in January 1972. How did this change affect the EMS?

al: At the Strathcona Music Building the EMS quickly burgeoned into four separate but interconnected studios:

1 the Moog Studio, housing the Moog Mark II Synthesizer, plus the Le Caine Serial Sound Structure Generators acting as sequencers to the Moog
2 the Main Studio, housing the Le Caine equipment described above, plus a new addition, Le Caine's polyphonic synthesizer (usually referred to as "the Poly"), which was without question the first polyphonic voltage-controlled synthesizer in the world
3 the Back Studio, where an Arp 2600 Synthesizer was installed
4 a small Editing Studio with basic gear for editing tapes and a Moog Model 15 Synthesizer, later combined with Aries modules

EMS technician Eric Johnstone created a brilliantly designed system interconnecting these four separate electroacoustic music studios that included a system of trunk lines allowing sound signals (later, also voltage-control signals) to travel from studio to studio. The high quality EMT Echo Chamber could also be accessed from any studio, and tape recorders – two to four units in each room – could be activated by "remote control" with an ingenious device also developed by Johnstone. If a composer wanted to playback eight or ten tape recorders simultaneously, at the McGill EMS this was possible.

MS: The EMS soon developed a teaching mandate as well. Can you describe that for us?

al: It was only in September 1968 – once the Faculty of Music launched MMA programs in composition and musicology[1] – that the EMS began to function as a teaching centre. The teaching of electroacoustic music at the EMS quickly grew into two undergraduate courses, one for student composers (enrolment about nine students), the other open to non-composers and students from other faculties (enrolment about twenty students). This second course has always been very popular, and we felt it was important not to restrict exposure to electronic music to the experts, but to find room for the aficionados as well. Both courses usually had extensive waiting lists as our ability to accept students was limited by constraints of both space and time. Each student was allotted a minimum of six hours a week in the studios for hands-on work, and there was always a need for more time. For a number of years we also offered an intensive summer course that was open to all. This course was always full to overflowing as well. There was just a tremendous amount of interest.

At the graduate level the electronic music seminar (eight to nine students) included the nascent area of computer music; early classes occasionally used the big mainframe computers in the administration building, and sometimes even travelled to Ottawa to work with Le Caine at the NRC computer centre.

MS: What was the teaching philosophy at the EMS?

al: Electroacoustic music composition has different approaches. In most European studios the style has been that composers work closely with a technician in creating new works. The composers explain their needs and desires to the technician who then produces the sounds and mixes required. Composers are not permitted to touch the machinery. At the McGill EMS, the preferred aesthetic has always been that of teaching students how to build the sounds they need from scratch – making each work unique, and not subject to the influence of factory presets and other ready-made devices. The Le Caine machinery lent itself particularly well to this mode of teaching, the varied inventory, ranging from oscillator banks to synthesizers to tape recorders and microphones giving composers a rich field to explore musically. Even the digital revolution in later years did little to change this orientation. More recent software permits composers to tap into a library of available sounds more easily than traditional electronic instruments permitted, but students were still encouraged to ignore presets in favour of creating a unique and personal voice.

MS: How has the EMS accommodated what has now become a daunting number of users?

al: In order to permit the necessary hands-on experience, the studios are available for booking twenty-four hours a day, seven days a week, and often hum at capacity.

MS: What is the role of the EMS technicians working with composers and students?

al: The EMS technicians are responsible for maintaining the machines, and they also give a helping hand to students or composers who may be a little baffled by the technology. They have been absolutely essential in providing technical support for live-electronic and mixed-media works. The technicians also research new developments in the field and are responsible for purchasing and installing these novelties in collaboration with the EMS Director.

MS: Tell us about the performance of pieces created in the EMS.

al: As part of its teaching philosophy, the EMS has always been a leader in promoting the integration of electronics and live performance. While some composers prefer to work with the world of recorded sound exclusively, many others have taken advantage of the encouraging atmosphere to produce mixed-media works. In addition to the production of works, a need was felt to provide a platform for the performance of these works. GEMS – the Group of the Electronic Music Studio – was founded in 1983 after two graduate students, John Oliver and Claude Schryer, approached me on the steps in front of the Faculty of Music and expressed an interest in forming a group for the performance and promotion of electronic and instrumental/electronic works. The group was to be student-run, with students actively involved in programming, planning, publicizing, and concert production. The EMS director was to serve as faculty co-ordinator. The only criterion for admission to the group was a willingness to work to make concerts happen. During the next twenty years – with an ever-changing student membership – GEMS was responsible for premieres and recordings of more than 100 electroacoustic and interactive compositions created at the EMS (see Appendix 1).

James Tenney (left), Bengt Hambræus (centre), and alcides lanza (right) during Tenney's residence with GEMS, Clara Lichtenstein Recital Hall, 16 March 1998. Photograph by Meg Sheppard. Reproduced by permission of alcides lanza.

MS: What role did visiting professors and composers play in the life and teaching philosophy of the EMS?

al: The life of an electronic studio involves so much more than machinery. Machines don't make music – people do! Throughout the 1970s students had a unique opportunity to work with composers/teachers as a result of a program of visiting professorships that included Mario Bertoncini (Italy), Sergio Cervetti (Uruguay), Makoto Shinohara (Japan), Mariano Etkin (Argentina), and Edgar Valcárcel (Perú). The program, which I coordinated, was sponsored initially by the Cultural Exchange Program of the federal government of Canada, and then by the Visiting Professors Program of the Canada Council for the Arts in association with McGill University. In addition, every opportunity was taken to invite composers for short residencies and for lectures and demonstrations. The goals were to offer students as broad a view as possible of the world's electroacoustic community, and also to give them an opportunity to make connections with composers from diverse cultural backgrounds and perhaps to move away somewhat from the Eurocentric bias often found in traditional studies. Visiting composers working at the EMS were encouraged to follow their own interests in research and creation. Guest composer Mario Bertoncini, for instance, focussed his teaching and research on the recording and amplification of very small sounds, on the development of new performance instruments, and on live concert improvisation. His inspiring example led to the creation of MUD (a group that was later renamed SONDE; see also chapter 3, pp. 101–3).[2]

MS: You made a reference earlier to the digital revolution. How did this change affect the EMS?

al: The need to stay abreast of technological change is a constant challenge in any electroacoustic studio, particularly given budgetary restrictions and the need to continually upgrade personal expertise. During the early 1980s, in response to technological changes, the EMS decided to acquire the Synclavier II Digital Synthesizer, a large integrated system developed by New England Digital. This powerful system – with more than 100 sine tone oscillators, a high capacity polyphonic 16-track sequencer, and a sophisticated (but only monophonic) digital sampler (called sample-to-disk) – became the first all digital studio in Canada.

Another significant development took place in 1987 when McGill University hired Bruce Pennycook to design and develop a new music technology area in the department of theory. From the start, this area was heavily involved with the Electronic Music Studio, sharing some facilities and having overlapping areas of interest. Bruce Pennycook did brilliant and exceptional work in the exploration and promotion of the role of computers as tools for music creativity. Research centred on the creation of new technological tools for the understanding and manipulation of sound, and on music composition using digital media. About this time a decision was made to retire the Synclavier and adopt the faster and more powerful Macintosh computers, which later became the norm in both the EMS and the music technology area. The music technology area expanded rapidly as interest grew in the important application of computer technology to the exploration of sound.

MS: Did the relationship between composition and technical invention that characterized the early years of the EMS continue into the new digital era?

al: Yes. Although the primary mandate of the EMS has always been music composition, invention did not stop with the early work of Le Caine. I can give a couple of examples. Eric Johnstone invented an interface called the PodoBoard, which consists of roughly a square metre of thick flat board covered with small aluminium tiles. The user – perhaps a tap dancer? – wears shoes with metal plates on toes and heels. A dedicated computer extracts coordinates of the positions of the toes and heels on the tile board. Two piezoelectronic film microphones are embedded on each shoe allowing for the registration of velocity changes and rhythm and this data is sent as MIDI signals that can drive sound modules or external synthesizers. The PodoBoard was demonstrated during the celebrations for the twenty-fifth anniversary of the EMS, and it was really dazzling!

Bruce Pennycook is a leading figure in the area of interactivity between the computer and performance in real time. In 1992, again with the assistance of EMS technician Eric Johnstone, he developed the MIDI Time Clip (MTC). The idea was to provide "an economical means of communicating to a performer the state of computer-controlled accompaniment."[3] Physically, the MTC was a small unit that communicated with a computer via MIDI. It included six LCDs for alphanumerical display and one large red LED for flashing tempo cues. There was also a pedal input attachment in charge of registering volume, sustain, and trigger pedals. Pennycook also wrote a series of compositions utilizing the MTC, one of which, *Praescio VII, piano (and then some)* (1994) was written for me to perform. With the interaction between the computer and the MTC, the composer was able to achieve a successful blend of the computer generated sounds – digitally produced but also including analog sounds stored via sampling – at a pace largely dictated by the pianist's performance. The nuances of performance were precisely sensed by the computer, and at the same time – via the alphanumerical display of the MTC – flashed as visual information to the soloist. Unfortunately, due to changing technology, the MTC is no longer viable. This is a serious concern for composers as changes in technology can result in an inability to transfer information to new platforms that make it impossible to perform a work as originally conceived. If this is to be avoided, composers need to constantly revisit pieces to upgrade the technical data. Fortunately, *Praescio VII, piano (and then some)* can still be performed with compact disc playback for the electronic part, and continues to be enjoyed by audiences.

MS: Can you describe some of the major performance milestones for the EMS?

al: During the last quarter of the twentieth century, the EMS put special emphasis not only on the creation of new electroacoustic compositions, but also on the presentation of these works in public. The EMS tenth anniversary concert, held at Redpath Hall on 31 January 1975, was organized by myself in collaboration with Metamusic Québec (a group specializing in electroacoustic/instrumental improvisation) and the McGill Symphony Orchestra. The ambitious program included the original quadraphonic presentation of Bengt Hambræus's *Tides* (1974); István Anhalt's *Cento* (1966–67), a "cantata urbana for twelve speakers and tape" and one of the first works to be composed on Le Caine's early instruments employing the techniques of *musique concrète*; Paul Pedersen's *Fantasie* (1967), electronic music with projected images (done at the EMS for the Expo '67 exhibit), one of the few works composed entirely using the Spectrogram; and my *eidesis III* (1971-II), for two orchestral groups with electronic sounds, performed by the McGill Symphony Orchestra conducted by Eugene Plawutsky and myself (the tape part for *eidesis III* also includes sounds generated from Le Caine's Tone Mixture Generator.) This multi-media concert inspired Helmut Blume, then dean of the Faculty of Music, to write this interesting note: "your work *Eidesis III* ... I can't 'analyze' or 'understand' it, but there is a power which is as overwhelming and unknown as that in the bowels of the earth – a thousand miles below the cooled crust of the intellect ... The other work which, to my understanding, was outstanding was Bengt's *Tides*, a marvellously evocative imagery in sound."[4] It was particularly gratifying to receive such a letter from a devotee of the classical tradition, as avant-garde and electronic music were still (believe it or not) somewhat suspect in certain quarters.

Fifteen years later, the twenty-fifth anniversary of the EMS provided the occasion to mount a festival of electroacoustic music that included five concerts, guided tours of the EMS, and lecture-demonstrations highlighting the important role of electronics in the creation of new music. The concerts featured a wide variety of approaches used in electroacoustic music, and included works by professors, students and invited guest composers who had worked at the EMS over the previous twenty-five years, including, Anhalt, Le Caine, Hambræus, and myself. The festival also invited composers from studios at Concordia

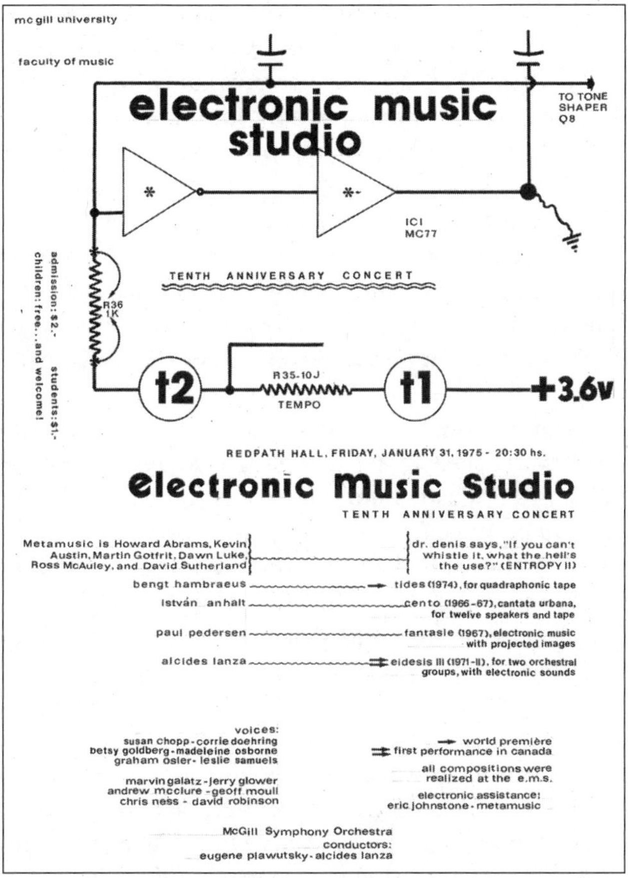

Program of the EMS tenth anniversary concert presented at Redpath Hall, 3 February 1975.

University, the Conservatoire de musique de Montréal and the Université de Montréal, including Robert Normandeau, Gilles Gobeil, Alain Thibault, Ned Bouhalassa, Francis Dhomont, Yves Daoust, and Christian Calon. In all, the festival featured performances by twenty-six different composers of electroacoustic music.

MS: I understand that the EMS and GEMS were instrumental in establishing the presence of contemporary music at McGill over the years at various international festivals and in providing a forum for the commissioning of many new works. Can you tell us about those efforts?

al: In partnership with the composition area, the EMS and GEMS contributed to the realization of the McGill Contemporary Music Festivals from 1982 to 1989. These festivals commissioned works from Alexina Louie, Steven Gellman, Denis Gougeon, John Burke, José Evangelista, and Michel-Georges Brégent, among others. The festivals were coordinated with a visiting professorship program, making it possible to have internationally-recognized artists lecturing at McGill and performing in concert. Among those artists was Carles Santos, the Catalan composer, film maker, pianist, and creator of provocative events. One of my best memories of his visit was when he put on a sandwich board advertising his concert and wandered the halls bellowing out an invitation to attend in the manner of a Catalan town crier. He opened his concert by tying a rope to the grand piano, which was offstage, and pulling it to centre stage by brute force, after which he sat down and played brilliantly for two hours. It was quite a night! Other artists included Bertram Turetzky, an avant-garde double bass virtuoso and composer from the United States; Manuel Enríquez, a violinist, organizer of international festivals, and composer from Mexico; and Werner Jacob, a composer and master of the contemporary organ repertoire from Germany.

On the international scene, many works created at the EMS have been selected for festivals and concert series devoted to electroacoustic and digital music worldwide. In 1991 the International Computer Music Society, coordinated by Bruce Pennycook and myself with technical assistance provided by the EMS technical staff, held its annual conference in Montreal. A studio exchange program also provided an opportunity to exchange music with similar organizations in Holland, Sweden, France, Argentina, and Brazil.

GEMS also took the initiative of commissioning Canadian composers. Among these works were new compositions by Michel-Georges Brégent and Kristi Allik. Brégent's massive chamber ensemble work *Mélorythmharmundi* (1983) was premiered by GEMS during the third Contemporary Music Festival in 1984, and subsequently recorded in studio for Radio-Canada. This incredibly complex work stretched the resources of GEMS to the limit. Kristi Allik's *Silicon Sidewinder* (1985), for two percussionists and tape, was premiered in 1986. GEMS – with the sponsorship of SOCAN – also produced a composer-in-residence series, resulting in important residences and mini-festivals built around compositions by James Tenney (1998), David Rokeby (2000), and Keith Hamel (2003). To mark its twentieth anniversary, GEMS staged a celebratory festival at

Pollack Hall on 25 October 2003. "GEMS in Concert" offered a program featuring Laurie Radford's *I was struggled ...* (2003), a theatre piece in which a pianist and a singer struggle to confront and inhabit a shared physical, acoustic and personal performance space – a metaphor for the composer's own struggles in composition; John Oliver's *Dust* (2002), which explores the sense of dilated time that occurs during a disaster; and Claude Schryer's intimate and introspective *Dans un coin...* (1982–83), a work that had been played at the first GEMS concert on 4 October 1983. The concert also included works by graduate student composers Henry Ng (*I Closed My Eyes ... and Saw Myself Running*) and Geof Holbrook (*Mightier than the Sword*). 2004 was the last season of GEMS.

MS: An observation that suggests the notion of change as well as history. What role does the EMS play in preserving its own history and that of electronic composition in general?

al: Music performance can be the stuff of ephemera, and it would seem that the recording of music – both in traditional performance and for electroacoustic works – would ensure the preservation of this music for all time. Unfortunately this is not the case when it comes to recordings made with pre-digital technology. Recordings made on acetate, polyester, or mylar tape are subject to inevitable deterioration and eventual destruction due to chemical corrosion of the magnetised iron particles in the coating of the tape. In 1997, in order to rescue tapes of compositions made at the EMS during these early years, with the collaboration of Bruce Pennycook, then vice-principal of information systems and technology, and Head Music Librarian Cynthia Leive, I initiated the EMS Tape Restoration Project. The transfers were realized by technicians Oles Protsidym, Ian Knopke, and Neil Middleton. All the rich history of composition and performance at the EMS is currently preserved at the Marvin Duchow Music Library in an archive of fifty-five compact discs of music created at the EMS, and twenty-two compact discs of GEMS in concert. Some recordings were plucked from this archive and commercially-released on a double compact disc entitled *Tornado*.

MS: What happened to the Le Caine instruments?

al: We ensured the preservation of the Le Caine instruments in 1987 by donating this historic instrumentarium to the National Museum of Science and Technology in Ottawa where it can be viewed by special request. Several groups of students from the EMS have taken advantage of the opportunity to visit the museum. The visit in 2004 included a videotaping of the tour of the instrumentarium with commentary by myself.[5]

MS: In your opinion, what is the legacy of the EMS?

al: From its start as the first electronic studio in the province of Quebec, the legacy of the McGill EMS has been its role in the training of generations of electroacousticians and in the production, promotion, and dissemination of electroacoustic music in all its forms. In reflecting on this past, we can understand both the historical importance of the McGill EMS and its impact on the cultural life of Montreal, Quebec, and Canada. Most telling, perhaps, is the fact that alumni from the studio are now working in the field across Canada and internationally. Those with university appointments include Kevin Austin (Concordia University), David Eagle (University of Calgary), Brent Lee (University of Windsor), Martin Gotfrit (Simon Fraser University), Laurie Radford (University of Alberta, and later City University, London, England) and Osvaldo Budón (University of Montevideo, Uruguay). Other composers who worked at McGill and have gone on to thriving international careers include among others Christian Calon, Gilles Gobeil, John Oliver, and Alain Thibault.

MS: What was the influence of the EMS on the development of music at McGill? And, finally, what is happening with the EMS today?

al: From its modest beginnings in the Redpath coach house, the EMS has played a major role in the development of sound recording, music technology, digital composition, and a myriad of recent interdisciplinary research and initiatives. These personal reflections end in 2004, but the legacy of the EMS continues. In response to changes in technology, the EMS has been renamed the Digital Composition Studio (DCS) and is under the direction of McGill EMS alumnus Sean Ferguson. In 2004 I was honoured with the title of Director Emeritus, but of course I have had no part in the most recent decisions concerning the studios: this has passed to a new generation. The music technology area and the newly formed Centre for the Interdisciplinary Research in Music Media and Technology (CIRMMT) are at the forefront of new research in music and sound. But all that is another story.[6]

NOTES

1 Editor's note: the Master of Musical Arts (MMA) in composition was replaced by the MMus in 1976.

2 MUD went on to create several recordings such as, SONDE, "Works by Culver, De Mestral, Pavelka, Dostie" (Toronto: Music Gallery Editions MGE 14 (Stereo LP), 1978). For a full listing of recordings of works created in the EMS, see Appendix I.

3 Bruce Pennycook and Eric Johnstone, "The MIDI Time Clip: A Performer/Machine Synchronization System for Live Performance," *ICMC Proceedings* (1994): 181–2.

4 Helmut Blume, personal correspondence to alcides lanza, 3 February 1975.

5 A copy of this DVD is available for viewing at both the Marvin Duchow Music Library and the archives of the National Museum of Science and Technology.

6 More information about the history of the EMS and electroacoustic music may be found at the following websites: www.music.mcgill.ca/~alcides; www.sonus.ca; www.cdemusic.org/artists/lanza.html; www.musiccentre.ca/home.cfm. See also "Souvenir Programme: The 25th Anniversary Festival of the Electronic Music Studio," Faculty of Music, McGill University, 7 and 9 December 1990; "GEMS: 20th Anniversary Programme," Faculty of Music, McGill University; alcides lanza, "McGill University: Its Electronic Music Studio Complex," *Interface* 9 (1980): 59–69; Gayle Young, *The Sackbut Blues: Hugh Le Caine, Pioneer in Electronic Music* (Ottawa: National Museum of Science and Technology, 1989); and Joel Chadabe, *Electric Sound: The Past and Promise of Electronic Music* (Upper Saddle River, NJ: Prentice Hall, 1997).

3

Better Than a Thousand Days of Diligent Study Is One Day with a Great Teacher:[1] Visiting Foreign Artist Residencies at McGill's Faculty of Music, 1975–1981

John Rea, McGill University

His own studies not yet completed when he arrived at McGill in 1973, JOHN REA's quest for voice has evolved with the institution, his travels expanding with the Faculty's reputation and his capacity as composer, pedagogue, producer, and administrator developing to creatively meet the exigencies of the moment. During his tenure as dean (1986–91), the Faculty, despite a climate of economic restraint, won a place on the international stage with the performances of the McGill Symphony Orchestra at Carnegie Hall, the revitalization of the opera program, and the successes of the Contemporary Music Festival, one of the first of its kind in Canada. His tenure also produced the first models for a new music building. In this chapter, however, Rea remembers the impact of four foreign visiting composer-pedagogues in the late 1970s and early 1980s. His memories unfold through a looking glass that frames the past, seemingly long forgotten in the successes of yesterday and today, as a future not quite realized. The sense of place that emerges is thus as revealing of the present as of the past, and the image, although a snapshot, is ultimately also a portrait of a man who will forever remain a student both of music and of life.

> The limits of my language mean the limits of my world.
>
> Wittgenstein, *Tractatus* (5.6)

It was another time. Not that long ago, thirty, thirty-five years or so, but unquestionably another time. It was a moment during which ideas in the world – and the often turbulent discourse arising from them, so difficult to understand or interpret even on the best of occasions – changed rapidly and, above all, convincingly, most notably in the wake of the inflamed social and political events that stirred both Europe and the Americas from about 1968. In Canada, one reckons from the symbolic date of 1967, whereas in Quebec, that date is 1970.[2]

As a span of time, thirty years is considerably longer than the period of the so-called "ceasefire" that delimited the end of one utterly catastrophic world war in 1918 and the beginning of another in 1939. Thirty years happens to be almost the exact time that elapsed between the first production of *Parsifal* (1882) and the paradigm-shaking premiere of *Le Sacre du printemps* (1913); between the emergence of the first twelve-tone music in Schoenberg's op. 23 (1923) and the establishment of the first electronic music studios in Cologne (1951) and Milan (1953).

Thirty years is a few years longer than the interval that separates the regrettable cancellation of the Visiting Foreign Artists Program by the Canada Council for the Arts from its surprising and much welcomed reincarnation in 2005, now qualified – rather disingenuously I would say – as a "pilot" program.[3] Initiated in the 1960s by Canada's Department of External Affairs, this forward-looking program (itself a part of a broader cultural exchange policy) was handed over to the Council to administer in the late 1970s, preserving the original objective of encouraging visits by individual professional artists from a wide variety of disciplines. In the area of composition, participation in the program meant stable financial support for visitors who devoted as much as an entire semester to guiding undergraduate and graduate composers by way of in-class teaching, workshops, master classes, talks, and so forth. Not only were new musical languages, new meanings explored and cultivated by our guests – through which our young student composers confronted and discovered other poetics and other catalysts for the creation of new music – but there was exploration of novel approaches to musical expression, and yes, to the limitless possibilities of thinking in music.

Another time it was, without a doubt. A moment so diverse and so distinct from our current one that, before proceeding with a recollection of some of the circumstances associated with the guest artist residencies of Mario Bertoncini (1975), Edgar Valcárcel (1976), Mariano Etkin (1977), and Makoto Shinohara (1978), I would like to describe, in a kind of thumbnail sketch, the spirit of those divergent times, albeit from my personal point of view. I do so in an effort to portray a social, educational, and artistic environment that, for all of its idiosyncrasies, and there were indeed many, seems almost impossible to imagine today.

My first observation is that in September 1973 when I began to teach at McGill, the Faculty of Music looked remarkably brand new, relocated since 1971 in its new home, the recently refurbished central block of the Royal Victoria College for Women, now rechristened the Strathcona Music Building. It appeared to me that Montrealers were also a bit more hopeful and a bit more optimistic about their futures, especially following the tumultuous events of 1969 and 1970. On 11 February 1969, for instance, Sir George Williams University (years before it merged with Loyola College to become Concordia University), saw the largest student riot in Canadian history as young people protested against a teacher accused of racism. A fire began and the resulting destruction of computer data produced more than $2 million worth of damage.[4] One month later, on 28 March 1969, as many as 10,000 militant Quebec nationalists, trade unionists, and students – including 200 McGill activists – joined forces in front of the Roddick Gates demanding *McGill français*! – the devolution of McGill University into a unilingual French, pro-worker institution.[5] In April, with much less tumult and much more optimism, a new francophone institution for higher learning, l'Université du Québec à Montréal, was founded, and that autumn the first courses were offered. By 1973 the terrible events known to us today as the October Crisis of 1970[6] (a socio-political event too complex for discussion here) seemed, to those around me, to be finished at last and to belong to an, albeit recent, past, providing some measure of comfort to citizens and institutions alike while at the same time affording them opportunities not only to reaffirm old commitments but also to start lives anew, to cultivate new associations with fresh ideas and innovative challenges.

So too, in 1973, the Faculty of Music's composition area seemed to be minted anew. With the departure to Queen's University in 1971 of István Anhalt (born 1919), former theory department chair and director of the electronic music studio (EMS), and the move of another

Charles Harriss, "a veritable musical napoleon" engaged in a "tonal campaign" at the Montreal Stadium, 1940s. Reproduced by permission of McGill University Archives, www.archives.mcgill.ca/resources/db/photosarchives, PR014042.

composition teacher, Alan Heard (born 1942), to the University of Western Ontario, the only remaining full-time teacher in our area was Bruce Mather (born 1939). And so, thanks to the concerted efforts of the dean, Helmut Blume, and of the new theory department chair (and future dean), Paul Pedersen, a goodly number of new composers joined the staff: alcides lanza (Argentina), who became next director of the EMS in 1971; Brian Cherney (Canada), Bengt Hambræus (Sweden), and Robert Jones (United States) in 1972; and Peter Paul Koprowski (Poland) and myself in 1973, each of us absolutely delighted with the new one-year visiting appointments. It must be remembered that in those days, in addition to their tutorial responsibilities, composers at the Faculty taught all of the music theory, analysis, and counterpoint courses as well as some of the history courses. Cherney and Hambræus, for example, had each received postgraduate training in musicology. Thus in the autumn of 1974, when it was confirmed that visiting foreign artist Mario Bertoncini from Italy would arrive at McGill to teach in the upcoming winter term, the words "foreign" and "visiting" obviously carried with them other connotations. Thanks to the great resourcefulness and expert administrative liaison of Professor lanza throughout the years we benefited from this cultural program, "newer" composer guests joined our ranks, even if only for a brief span of time: Edgar Valcárcel from Peru, Mariano Etkin from Argentina, and Makoto Shinohara from Japan.

A secondary group of observations from my vantage point is also telling. It was a time, broadly speaking, when the ideal future for a student composer (almost always a young man) consisted in imagining and thus directing his career – whatever that might mean in a country such as Canada – towards becoming a composer of concert music rather than, as it is very often the case today, becoming a composer for film or television, or perhaps even for computer games or portable telephones. During the last fifteen years or so, film, television, gaming, and ringtone industries have not only thrived in Canada but seem to be in expansion; concert music, however, is not necessarily on the decline.

It was a time prior to the extensive use of pocket calculators, photocopiers, videocassettes, and compact discs (introduced only in 1982), a time even before sushi and California maki. It was a time when, in a genuine effort to come to grips with new music, ensembles and symphony orchestras rehearsed new compositions in order to interpret them, rather than merely reading them through once, as they do nowadays, usually limiting the allotted rehearsal time to the performance duration of the new work. More importantly, it was a time before the personal computer, the ubiquitous personal computer that adorns every composer's private studio nowadays, spewing forth cascading streams of sonic glossolalia more or less efficiently filtered, channelled, and shored up, so to speak, by software bundles manufactured by multinational corporations. It may be difficult to appreciate now (or to remember, as the case may be), but thirty-five years ago the words "memory," "ram," "desktop," and "mouse" all conveyed other more convivial meanings and imagery. It was also some time before the foundation of the Institut de recherche et de coordination acoustique-musique (IRCAM) in France, before the arrival of the concept of inharmonicity, which would later serve as the psychoacoustic source of inspiration for creative composition,[7] before the crucial, and today almost doctrinaire, notion of "timbre as a metaphor for composition."

During this complex and transpicuous period, thirty, thirty-five years ago, during this interregnum delimiting a span of time between, on the one hand, the shared conceptualizations (paradigms) for new musical composition that had been attached to serialist and postserialist preoccupations (1950s–60s) and, on the other hand, the as yet to be imagined conceptualizations linked to acoustic and/or spectral modelling (1980s–90s) – where the "inside" of sound would be brought forward to the very forefront of audibility, that is, to the surface of the composition – thinking in music seemed to be truly limitless, free from dogmatic assertions and considerations, exempt from cliques and coteries – autonomous and independent. Perhaps this was an illusion. Perhaps there had been, and still were, competing dogmas to which, happily, no one was listening. Perhaps it was nothing but joyful chaos. Nevertheless, during the decade of the 1970s, the greatest exemplifications of this free thinking spirit in the creation of new music would be found in the rise of neoromanticism and of minimalism, to name but two types of postmodern music being composed in Europe and the United States then. The former belonged to an a-critical world of musical expression, the latter to a critical and systematic one. All the same, this social and culturally enriched environment both at home and abroad furnished the multi-coloured setting into which our composer guests arrived on stage, in Montreal, one after another.

MAKOTO SHINOHARA

> The bamboo that bends is stronger than the oak that resists.
>
> Japanese proverb

Although his was the last residency for which the Faculty of Music would be able to count on support from the visiting foreign artists program of the Canada Council, Makoto Shinohara (born 1931) was actually the first of our four guest composers to have his music presented in Montreal. His arrival in January 1978 was in some sense a reappearance because he was already quite well known to the group of composers associated with the Société de musique contemporaine du Québec (SMCQ), which had introduced his work to Montrealers on two previous occasions. Shinohara's youthful *Altérnance* (1961–62) for six percussionists, written for Les Percussions de Strasbourg, received its North American premiere at Théâtre Maisonneuve of the Place des Arts, on 22 October 1970 (in the midst of the unfolding October Crisis), in the opening concert of the society's first season. On 27 January 1977, this time in Pollack Concert Hall, the SMCQ presented his *Consonance* (1964–67), for flute, horn, harp, two percussionists, and cello.

In 1954, at the age of twenty-three, leaving behind the morose surroundings of postwar Japan now that he had completed his undergraduate studies in composition, piano, and conducting at the Fine Arts University of Tokyo, Shinohara traveled to Europe. Thanks to a grant offered to him by the government of France, he moved to Paris, where he studied with Tony Aubin (composition), Simone Plé-Caussade (piano), Pierre Revel (harmony), and Louis Fourestier (conducting). His encounter with Olivier Messiaen, an undeniably great teacher, some time later at the Conservatoire national supérieur in the well-known annual seminar on musical aesthetics, was to mark him in the most meaningful of ways. Messiaen is known for imparting unusual perspectives and singular interpretations of non-Western music and cultures to his seminar students – an east meets west for composers, so to speak – a "world music" approach to creative composition (*métissage avant la lettre,* one might say) that is still vibrant and meaningful for many composers today. It was also in these seminars that Shinohara chanced upon fellow student Gilles Tremblay, just as Serge Garant and Clermont Pépin had encountered Stockhausen there in 1951–52. This meeting with Olivier Messiaen helped Shinohara to see and hear himself in a new way.

Throughout the 1960s, an era that in Europe and the United States witnessed the propagation of a serialist and postserialist creative paradigm already in decline, Shinohara lived in Germany. Between 1960 and 1962, with a grant from the provincial government of Bavaria, he studied composition at the Hochschule für Musik in Munich; then he transferred to a school in Cologne where he studied with Bernd Alois Zimmermann and Gottfried-Michael Koenig. The year 1964 found him at the Summer Courses for New Music at Darmstadt.[8] Having completed an assistantship with Stockhausen in 1965, Shinohara moved on to Berlin, where he remained from December 1966 through July 1968, thanks to an artist-in-residence fellowship in the Berliner Künstlerprogramm offered to him by the Deutscher Akademischer Austauschdienst (DAAD).[9]

Over the next few years, not unlike other Japanese composers of the time working in the West – Joji Yuasa (born 1929), Toru Takemitsu (1930–96), and Maki Ishii (1936–2003), to name but a few – Shinohara came to refine a musical style informed by innovative techniques, particularly aleatoric notation, and above all, by a sense of the tone quality or mood of specific instrumental timbres emanating from traditional Japanese music, sounds that he borrowed, decontextualized, and later recontextualized into his own music. This creative attitude in its broadest understanding resembles an approach to composing that not only suggests an acquaintance with the fruits of ethnomusicological research but also points to a desire to transform a musical anthropology from a pure science into, as it were, an applied one. The seminar teachings of Olivier Messaien in this respect cannot be overestimated.

Two general artistic strategies can be heard in Shinohara's compositions: one is characterized by the mood and colours of Japanese instruments, although the instruments themselves are absent; the other includes Japanese instruments played either as solo instruments or in combination with Western or additional Japanese instruments. At the end of his studies with Messiaen, for example, Shinohara wrote *Obsession* (1960), a work for oboe and piano originally intended for an oboe class competition at the Conservatoire. Here one senses the desire to create an "east meets west." Although no specific quotations are employed, there is a mysterious quality, even a repressed-like mood, between the two instruments that, after breaking through into the highest registers of the oboe with a sound almost like screaming – the work is quite virtuoso – resumes its mystery and brusquely confirms its repression at the end of the composition. To the ears of an occidental listener, this work sounds Japanese, or at least oriental or Asiatic. Today, forty-five years after its creation, *Obsession* sounds like an example of new contemporary concert music inspired by "world music," and here I imagine a listener being reminded of *gagaku*. *Mémoires* (1966), a four-channel electronic music work produced at the Institute for Sonology in Utrecht (where Shinohara would eventually reside), seems to replicate this mysterious atmosphere, suggesting the fragility of memory, a remembrance as return. The most successful of Shinohara's works with no Japanese instrument is *Fragmente* (1968–69), a work for solo tenor recorder. Commissioned by the Prince Bernhard Foundation (Netherlands) on behalf of early music specialist Frans Brüggen, this virtuoso recorder piece is often found on concert programs next to fourteenth- and fifteenth-century European works, for its world evokes the *shakuhachi* (a notched bamboo flute), singing of a music at least as ancient as its occidental counterparts.

During the 1970s Shinohara traveled from Germany to Italy, where he was a recipient of an important grant, and then to New York, where he worked at the Columbia-Princeton Electronic Music Center, and eventually settled in Utrecht after his 1978 sojourn in Montreal. In New York in 1971 he encountered Milton Babbitt again and met alcides lanza for the first time. His audiovisual work *City Visit* (1976), a work coming from his experiences living in New York, was heard at the beginning of his McGill residency during an EMS concert at Pollack Hall on 12 January 1978.

As he began to (re)examine his own musical heritage Shinohara quite naturally and perhaps inevitably moved to composing works that made direct use of Japanese instruments, especially in the years just before and just after coming to McGill. This approach involved learning to play these instruments, particularly the *koto* (a long zither). In 1972, once again in Berlin, he composed *Tayutai* (fluctuation) for a koto soloist who also plays percussion, speaks, and sings (with the option that the vocal parts be performed by a singer). On 6 April 1978, during a memorable new music concert at Pollack Hall organized by alcides lanza, Shinohara gave the Canadian premiere of this piece. In the program note he comments:

> This work is composed for a traditional Japanese instrument, the *koto*, but in an avant-garde language. The 13 strings of the instrument are to be tuned in a new scale and the performer not only plucks the strings with picks [plectra] in the traditional manner, but also strikes the instrument with different sticks. Moreover, he has to play additional percussion instruments, and to speak or to sing at the same time isolated Japanese words. The piece represents the psychological fluctuation between hope and despair, and has an introspective character.[10]

The twenty-seven spoken and sung Japanese words employed throughout the piece, often as fleeting interjections or motivic-like sighs or groans, are of significant interest and reveal much about the work's overall mood and dualistic projection of hope and despair, although the word "despair" is never heard: *tayutai* (fluctuation), *hitori* (alone), *iru* (being), *yübe* (evening), *urei* (anxiety), *utsuro* (emptiness), *tanomi* (hope), *osore* (fear), *kanashi* (sad), *omoi* (thought), *kirameki* (sparkle), *nozomi* (wish), *munashi* (vain), *naze* (why), *mayoi* (hesitation), *kurushimi* (suffer), *midare* (disorder), *ikari* (anger), *kokoro* (heart), *nayami* (trouble), *akogare* (yearning), *yorokobi* (joy), *kagayaki* (radiance), *tomoshibi* (light), *furusato* (home), *negai* (desire), *ai* (love). My recollection of this performance focuses on Shinohara's solid and paradoxically timeless presence on stage, not unlike that of a ritual or a temple ceremony. Within the setting of our then new concert hall, appropriately illuminated, his presence – his charisma – was for me something radiant and absolutely sensational.[11]

Although I am unaware whether, in addition to his concerns with timbre, Shinohara constructs large-scale time structures in the manner of, say, Toshiro Mayuzumi (1929–97),[12] there is no doubt that a distinctive pacing, a particular type of momentum, lies beneath the flow of Shinohara's music; it inevitably brings to mind, and thus suggests an affinity with, the music connected to traditional Japanese theatrical forms. Mayuzumi had tried in several works to make direct reference to the *jo-ha-kyu* time structure characteristic of *Noh* drama – slow introduction (*jo*), increasing complexity in an exposition (*ha*), which nevertheless develops, tending towards a rapid finale and climax (*kyu*), then slowing down briefly at the end – and some aspects of this overall shaping technique, as I hear them, typify Shinohara's music as well.

In 1983 Shinohara was honoured with the designation of principal composer at the Holland Festival, and in 1985 he returned to Montreal for a SMCQ concert featuring the music of Mayuzumi, Yuasa, Ishii, Takemitsu, and Takahashi. The program included the premiere of Shinohara's *Tabiyuki* (1984), scored for mezzo-soprano, flute (with piccolo, alto flute, slide whistle), oboe (english horn), clarinet (bass clarinet), bassoon, horn, trumpet, trombone, percussion, violin, viola, cello and double bass. *Obsession* – many years after its creation, and now a "classical" work performed around the world –was once again presented in Montreal on 15 May 2005 during the fifth season of the distinguished chamber music festival held at the Centre for Canadian Architecture (CCA). It is fitting that this duet for oboe and piano shared a concert with other works linked to "world music" sensibilities by composers such as Olivier Messiaen, Toru Takemitsu, and Ravi Shankar, as well as Lou Harrison, Henry Cowell, and Claude Vivier.

In my mind, "east meets west" is a notion forever associated with Shinohara's presence in Montreal during the winter of 1978. At that time Ramón Pelinsky, professor of ethnomusicology at l'Université de Montréal and another former classmate from the Messiaen seminars, together with José Evangelista, Matilde Asencio, and myself co-founded Traditions musicales du monde. In operation for only five seasons, this concert society was dedicated to the dissemination of world music traditions by way of concerts, lectures, and films.[13] At memorable events held around the city one heard authentic music from India, Japan, China, Spain, Indonesia, Iran, and Iraq. In 1981, during "Travel Journals," a concert-happening on behalf of Les Événements du neuf, another society that Evangelista, Vivier, and I had co-founded in 1977 together with conductor Lorraine Vaillancourt, I performed as a "samisen" soloist in my ensemble piece *Médiator (... pincer la musique aujourd'hui ...)*, a work that owes some of its inspiration to a transformative moment in 1978 when Shinohara sat before us to perform his *Tayutai*. For the concert booklet I would write:

> As in art, so too in travels: in the past as in the present, artists have tried to be travellers in other ethnic realities, to grasp distant worlds and their exoticism, and to make them serve as sources of inspiration.
> *Médiator (... pincer la musique aujourd'hui ...)* [plectrum, plucking music today] is, among other things, a musical "travel book," the testimony of an admiration for the musics of the Far East, which can be found in other works of mine. Just as the plectrum mediates between the hand and the string, *Médiator* is a friendly attempt at communication between musical instruments of our tradition and certain sounds and gestures of East Asian musics.

EDGAR VALCÁRCEL

> The teacher is like a candle which lights others in consuming itself.
>
> Giovanni Ruffini[14]

Looking back to the winter semester of 1976, when we welcomed our second visiting foreign artist, Peruvian composer, conductor, and pianist Edgar Valcárcel (born 1932), I am once again utterly astonished to recall the intensity with which he embarked upon all his activities, the ardour with which he participated in our pedagogical mission, and the sheer quantity of his public appearances. Perhaps more than any other guest composer-teacher during those years, Valcárcel gave himself entirely to the tasks at hand, without conditions, accomplishing his various duties with the greatest élan. He not only taught our undergraduate electronic music course and somehow secured a bit of free time in the EMS in order to work on his own projects, but he also appeared as soloist, chamber musician, co-coordinator, et cetera, in no less than seven out of the unprecedented nine Pollack Hall contemporary music programs between 2 March and 13 May 1976 that also witnessed the successful conclusion to the first complete season in the new hall.

Born at Puno, in the southeast corner of Peru near Lake Titicaca, Edgar Valcárcel completed his undergraduate studies in Lima at the Conservatorio Nacional del Música (1949–58) as a scholarship student in both piano and composition, working with Paris-born André Sás

(1900–67), one of Peru's most important composers. Valcárcel himself began teaching at the Conservatorio Nacional almost immediately after his own studies and he continued his association with that institution, with a few brief interruptions, for almost five decades. However, when the opportunity arose to pursue studies at the graduate level (he was already twenty-nine years old), he chose to leave Peru and travel to New York where his former classmate from the Conservatorio Nacional, César Bolaños (born 1931), had been working since 1958. Valcárcel received his Master's degree as a scholarship student at Hunter College (1961–62), studying with American composer Donald Lybbert (1923–81), who was also known as a counterpoint specialist. The following year (1963–64) Valcárcel returned to South America, where he completed his postgraduate work in Buenos Aires at the newly founded Centro Latinoamericano de Altos Estudios Musicales (CLAEM) del Instituto Torcuato Di Tella,[15] studying primarily with Alberto Ginastera but also with visiting artists including Olivier Messiaen, Yvonne Loriod, and Bruno Maderna. During these courses he saw his old friend César Bolaños again and met for the first time fellow classmate alcides lanza. During the later 1960s Valcárcel attended further lectures given by Messiaen in Paris and by Riccardo Malipiero, Maderna, and Luigi Dallapiccola in Italy.

Throughout this entire period and for many years subsequently, Valcárcel also concertized in performances with symphony orchestras in Lima, Havana, and Rio de Janiero, and in solo piano recitals and chamber music concerts in both the United States and South America. During those years, however, his desire to work in the field of electronic music – undoubtedly prompted by encounters with classmates Bolaños and lanza, and with other teachers of the CLAEM – had always been frustrated. It was a dream impossible to realize in Peru, due to the often dramatic if not depressed socioeconomic and cultural situation there. And so, with a new and substantial fellowship from the Guggenheim Foundation, Valcárcel spent a further two years in New York (1966–68), working and composing at the Columbia-Princeton Electronic Music Center. Here he studied with Vladimir Ussachevsky and alcides lanza and began his first compositions employing electronic sounds. Given his already considerable teaching experience, he also took up a position at Hunter College, his alma mater, teaching courses in advanced counterpoint.

When he arrived at McGill at the age of forty-four, Valcárcel's creative output was already quite remarkable, including almost fifty compositions. Even in 1976, I had to mull over a paradox: how was it that, in a small country like Peru, which had a chronic and "dramatic, if not depressed, socioeconomic and cultural situation" (to quote myself), composers somehow still managed to create music and have it performed in their own country? In Canada, a large and privileged nation, it seemed there was to be only one composer, R. Murray Schafer (born 1933), whose output even approached the scope and quantity of someone who, living in a profoundly disadvantaged environment, not only composed music but heard it performed as well. Were our cultural institutions doing as much as they could to encourage and to disseminate new Canadian music? Sadly, I did not seem to have a very optimistic answer to that question.

Valcárcel's electronic compositions at that time included *Invención* (1967), composed in New York and assembled with the technology of the day (sound wave generators, filtered white noise, editing and looping techniques), *Cantata* (1967) for choir and tape, and *Canto Coral a Túpac Amaru* (1968) for choir, percussion, and tape, also composed at the Columbia-Princeton studio. One further electronic work, *Zampoña Sónica* [Sonic Panpipes] was begun in New York (1968) but completed at the McGill EMS (1976). Scored for flute and electronic sounds, this work reminds me of the relationship Shinohara experienced in 1960 with *Obsession*, not so much because the two works are stylistically similar – they are not, although both employ woodwinds – but because, like Shinohara's "east meets west," Valcárcel was attempting for the first time to communicate in a way that we readily recognize today as a world music approach, a "south meets north."

Over the years, the compositional practice of creating sets of pieces, bringing works together in a way that reveals shared constructive principles, attracted Valcárcel a number of times: examples include a set of four trios entitled *Espectros* [Spectra, Spectres, Ghosts, Phantoms] and the *Homenaje* [Homage] series, which flirts in a perhaps postmodern way with quotation, paraphrase, and pastiche. Other compositions, though not designated with the word *Homenaje*, nonetheless point to Valcárcel's reverential approach and inspiration, and deserve special mention: *Responso para Ives* [Answer to Ives] (1978), for clarinet, violin, and percussion, and *Zorro, Zorrito* [Fox, Little Fox] (2003), a recent and elaborate work that brings to mind Prokofiev's *Peter and the Wolf*. Drawing upon an Aymaran Indian legend (Aymara is the aboriginal linguistic tradition to which Valcárcel belongs), he employs a specific set of instruments in order to delineate individual theatrical characters.

Replete with vibrant music, rowdy gestures, and the evocative colours of Andean folk music – performed out-of-doors in a public square – this cantata is scored for large orchestra, a forty-voice children's chorus, and a *tropa de zampoñas* [ensemble of panpipes] consisting of sixty Andean musicians from the two main Amerindian linguistic groups, Aymara and Quechua, who play various types of the *sico* (small Aymara panpipes) and the *antara* (large Quechua panpipes), as well as conch shells, *bombas* (drums), and other indigenous instruments.

Valcárcel's first performance in Pollack Hall took place on 2 March 1976 in a program entitled "Music from Latin America" that also featured alcides lanza in virtuoso works for two pianos, some of which incorporated percussion, tape, and sound diffusion. In addition to compositions by Claudio Santoro (1919–89) of Brazil, Enrique Iturriaga (born 1918) and Pedro Seiji Asato (born 1940) from Peru, and Oscar Bazán (born 1936) and Dante Grela (born 1941) from Argentina, two memorable works deserve particular mention: one just before intermission and the other at the end of the concert. César Bolaños's *ESEPCO II* (1970) for one piano (two performers), tape, and microphone amplification, was probably the earliest computer-assisted composition written in South America, having been constructed, like its sister piece *ESEPCO I*, at the electronic music studio of the Torcuato di Tella Institute: "the structure, order of sections, voice entrances, instrumental possibilities, sound event densities, 'harmonic' and 'melodic' density, length and timing have all been programmed through the computer. The piece is subtitled 'Song without Words' (Homage to Unpronounced Words)."[16] The title is an acronym for the Spanish phrase "estructura sonora expresiva por computación" [expressive sound structure by computerization].

The last piece on the program, *Concierto* for two pianos, percussion, tape, and audience participation, was written by Sergio Barroso (born 1946), a Cuban-born composer who eventually moved to Canada in 1980. Written in the crucible year of 1968 while Barroso was a student in Prague, this concerto requires the audience to undertake any of the following actions at specific moments indicated in the score and by numerals set up along the stage: (1) tap the floor with one's feet, (2) clap hands, (3) whistle, (4) whisper the consonants TRKBD, (5) whisper the vowels AEIOU, (6) sing in a soft as well as a loud voice while opening and closing one's mouth, (7) shout as well as remain silent (invent words), and (8) repeat a text many times in a loud voice, freely. The text in question, a quilt-like assemblage of utterances fashioned, I suppose, to sound like an agitprop of the times – albeit focused upon musical rather than sociopolitical revolutions – consists of eight quotations from six Latin American composers, an American composer, and an American musicologist, including these three:

It took us fifteen years of work in Mexico to liberate ourselves from a suffocating conservative tradition, an academic stagnation of the worse kind. We rediscovered ourselves by returning to the traditional cultures of the Indians who, still today, make up four fifths of the Mexican population. (Carlos Chavez)

The fundamental problem with Latin American music resides not in the assimilation of new techniques but rather in the discovery of the means to express the sociopolitical reality troubling this continent. (César Bolaños)

The territory of Latin American music history is so foreign to us that it practically constitutes a "terra ignota" (Gilbert Chase).[17]

For the concert of 15 March 1976 the McGill Percussion Ensemble under the direction of Pierre Béluse performed an end-of-year program that featured Valcárcel as soloist in *Variaciones* (1964) for piano and percussion by Bolivian composer Alberto Villalpando (born 1942). This concert was also notable for the student ensemble performance of Mario Bertoncini's *Tune* (1965), a work for multiple groups of suspended cymbals. Bertoncini was in residence for the second time at McGill, teaching a course called "Musical Design" (see pp. 97, 101–3). On 19 March 1976, in a concert featuring junior staff composers Brian Cherney, Donald Steven, and me, Valcárcel performed my piano piece *Anaphora II* (1971); during a rehearsal he told me that he had completely analyzed this serial composition, and ever so respectfully and with the greatest of tact, pointed out that I had made a number of copying errors! Obviously I was more than happy to correct them all, thanks to his perspicacity, and his subsequent performance sparkled with dazzling passion.

Valcárcel played *Anaphora II* again on 1 April 1976, in a concert that also featured four undergraduate student works, and he also gave the Canadian premieres of two pieces by Latin American composers. In the first, his own *Espectros I* for flute, viola, and piano, appropriately ghostly "micro-structures in each part can be played in any order," a performance practice dealing with polymetric and polytempo issues. In the second, Bolaños's *ESEPCO I* (1970) for piano and actress-singer –

a music-theatre piece requiring two flashlights and a wooden cage placed on stage near the piano – both pianist and singer (student Madeleine Osborne) are directed to imitate, in the style of a sarcastic dialogue, the tirade of a military dictator commanding a malevolent politician. The text for the vocal parts was drawn from a variety of sources: three unidentified political speeches, stock market reports, an invented newspaper story, the initials of various well-known political institutions, and a group of unrelated phonemes. It was another time, to be sure. It was another time.

On 14 April 1976 Valcárcel, Bertoncini, Cherney, Eugene Plawutsky (then conductor of the McGill Symphony Orchestra), and I functioned as coaches and/or conductors for a concert of student works. Among the young composers heard that evening were John Winiarz and Andrew Culver.[18] Two more concerts, on 29 April and 13 May 1976, brought Valcárcel's teaching duties at McGill to a magnificent conclusion. The first evening involved twenty-seven student performers in a variety of chamber music configurations, all under the guidance of either lanza or Valcárcel; two of the eight student compositions particularly stood out and deserve mention here. Harold Kilianski's *Crab-Seal-Tin* (1976), scored for bass clarinet and tape, was concerned with "further explorations in the seafood canning industry, presenting the serious bass clarinettist with a golden opportunity to be silly; concrete tape [was] poured from February to April; 76 wind chimes by Japan."[19] The bass clarinet soloist was Stephen McAdams, future director of the Centre for Interdisciplinary Research in Music, Media and Technology (CIRMMT), a multidisciplinary research group centred at McGill.[20] At that time the versatile McAdams was a student in the department of psychology, working in acoustics and perception, an area of research that, thanks to his supplementary knowledge of music, steered him a few years later to IRCAM in Paris. Elizabeth Szeremeta's *The Enchanted Star* (1976), based on the poem *Star and Dead Leaves* by Japanese poet Tsuboi Shigeji (1898–1975), was scored for sine tone generator, three whisperers, singer, two pianos, harp, and percussion. The work "is an experiment in cross-parallel symbolism," wrote Szeremeta. "It is written for interpretative artists who need not have the technical knowledge, otherwise necessary, to play an instrument. This is the composer's first attempt at [creating] a type of 'non-music, non-drama.'"[21]

The final concert was devoted to the assignment compositions written during the second semester of the EMS course. Two of the seven student works presented especially caught my attention. Raymond Boileau's *"want we Chopin??" – (prelude to time)*, scored for two pianos and tape, was more than twenty minutes long and sported the following brief program note: "(tic) Professor Valcárcel woke me up this morning in order to ask me to write something (tock) concerning my piece (tic). I would like to begin by saying tock." That's it – no further explanation for a piece that amused itself with quotations, paraphrase, and pastiche. *Whispers of Sunflower and Splendor (Earth, Fire, Water, Air)*, an elaborate work rich in poetic power, was composed by the multi-talented student of psychology Stephen McAdams who, thanks to the University's system of free electives, had made good use of six credits and enrolled in the EMS course. Scored for African xylophone, conga drums, erh-hu, water tam-tam, aquamarimba, paper wind, shakuhachi, and tape – with the players wearing exclusively designed masks[22] – McAdams' work drew inspiration from a lengthy poem (434 lines) entitled *A Letter from Li Po* (1956) by the American poet Conrad Aiken (1889–1973).[23] This poem, in part an examination of change and loss, a kind of Taoist poem in honour of a Taoist poet,[24] attracted the young psychologist-composer with its message of eternal transformation. As I see it, McAdams revealed in sound not only his sensitivity to the imagery of the poem but also his bewilderment with regard to the temper of his disquieting times. The following text, excerpted from the poem's fourth stanza, appears as the program note to this evocative composition: "Exiled are we. We're exiles born. The 'far away' language of desert, language of ocean, language of sky, as of the unfathomable worlds that lie between the apple and the eye, these are the only words we learn to say. Each morning we devour the unknown. Each day we find, and take, and spill, or lose, a sunflower splendour of which none know the source." Bringing together a myriad of cross-cultural influences and exotic sounds, many seemingly brought into existence from images of sky, desert, and ocean, McAdams created an environment on stage that encompassed not only an apparatus to undulate strips of paper (paper wind) and a performer manipulating an *erh-hu* (a two-stringed Chinese spike fiddle with the horsehair of the bow passing between the strings, causing them to sound simultaneously), but also an aquamarimba (a wooden idiophone struck while partially immersed in water).[25] Stephen McAdams himself performed on the shakuhachi.

Valcárcel's teaching at McGill was characterized by naturalness, direct generosity, accessibility, and open-mindedness. These precious human qualities (about which McAdams and I reminisced during the summer of 2005) seemed all the more telling and poignant in their intensity when he was confronted with a less than inspired student project or a reluctance on the part of a student to work assiduously on a creative task. Valcárcel would try to conceal his surprise and disappointment in young people who did not appear to be as impassioned as himself, students who did not recognize their good fortune in being able to work in a well-equipped laboratory for musical creation, students who could not detect the genuine opportunities offered them by a country neither subject to miserable economic conditions nor submerged by the chaos of social and cultural disorder so typical then of his native Peru. Like the dedicated and the enlightened teacher that he truly was for us, Edgar Valcárcel continuously encouraged young people, keen to light their way. He made things much brighter for our young composers.

MARIANO ETKIN

> He who speaks two languages is worth two people.
>
> Spanish proverb

The winter of 1977 arrived much like other winters in Montreal before and since. It would be cold, then very cold. Later the air would be humid, then very humid. On occasion the days would be bright, often very bright, due to those brilliant (but not always warm) rays of the northern sun illuminating freshly fallen white snow, often very white, in fact so undeniably white that, to the uninitiated, such white brilliance could easily be mistaken for a type of blindness, snow blindness, or the less severe condition known as snowblink, the eerie white glow in the sky (especially in polar regions) caused by the reflection of sunlight from distant snow-covered fields. To our third guest, composer and conductor Mariano Etkin (born 1943), who had left his native city of Buenos Aires (healthy air) at the beginning of January in order to teach at McGill University, the snow must have seemed fairly eccentric if not utterly exotic: his first encounter with a "real" winter – only hours after saying farewell to a "real" summer – was an occurrence that I would affectionately describe as a "snow job," experienced as a chilling event, literally. Stepping into the open air at Dorval airport on a nippy minus-eight-degree day, with hands, feet, face, ears, nose, and throat beginning to freeze, and walking for some distance, as if through a septentrional void, to a parked car (long before parking

Left to right: Mariano Etkin, Brian Cherney, alcides lanza, and Morton Feldman at a gathering at the lanza-Sheppard residence. Photograph by Meg Sheppard. Reproduced by permission of alcides lanza.

structures were built), trekking through snow the colour of funereal ash, he murmured: "me muero de frio, alcides ... hace frio, no?" [I'm dying of cold, alcides ... it's cold, isn't it?].

To know another language, as the adage goes, is to have a second soul. And this bit of wisdom held true with regard to our visiting foreign artists who, during those halcyon years, assisted us in our pedagogical mission. Each composer, in his individual way, understood the nature of music and was able to communicate with it to our students. But each artist also spoke a unique and creative musical idiom of his own, an idiom springing from distinctive cultural and social realities. Each artist explored novel approaches to musical expression and to the limitless possibilities of thinking in music. Each of them were also, in a real sense, newcomers to Canada, where they, like immigrants and other visitors, find that the "language of winter" is perhaps more unmanageable than the grammatical refinements of French or the colloquialisms of day-to-day English. Such a language is something else to manage and quite hard to learn, let alone master, with its unsettling syntax and meteorological morphologies. This was particularly the case for the insightful and resolute Etkin.

In 1965, at the tender age of twenty-two, Etkin received a two-year fellowship permitting him to enrol at the now legendary Di Tella Institute's Latin American Centre for Advanced Musical Studies (CLAEM). During this academic cycle the visiting artist-teachers were Earle Brown, conductor Maurice Le Roux, and Iannis Xenakis, together with Argentinean composers Gerardo Gandini and Alberto Ginastera. Upon completion of his courses, Etkin was awarded the 1967 Composition Prize of the Municipality of Buenos Aires. Precocious is a word I would use to describe the young Etkin; he had been more than well prepared for these singular moments with great teachers by his earlier private studies with musicologist Ernesto Epstein and composition and theoretical studies with the Viennese-born Guillermo Graetzer.[26] In 1968–69, thanks to an important fellowship from the Netherlands, Etkin went to Europe to study electronic music at the Institute for Sonology (Utrecht), as both Shinohara and Bertoncini had done some time earlier. The following year (1969–70), now in New York with a fellowship from the Organization of American States, Etkin completed his composition studies at the Juilliard School working with Luciano Berio. Returning home, and in demand himself as a teacher, he began to work at various regional universities (Littoral, Río Cuarto, Tucumán), and then at Buenos Aires. Today he is senior professor of composition and musical analysis and director of a research project on the analysis of new music at the National University of La Plata, where Graetzer, his former teacher, had taught for many years.

Etkin's creative output when he came to McGill in 1977, that is, up to the age of thirty-four, already displayed all the artistic traits that characterize the evolution of a unique and almost ascetic style nonetheless rich in uncommon timbres and delicate moods. *Muriendo Entonces* [Dying Then] (1969–70), scored for horn, trombone, tuba, two percussion, viola, and contrabass, had even caused a mini-sensation. It was inspired by *El Olvido* [Oblivion], an erotic poem by Idea Vilariño (born 1920), Uruguay's most famous and recondite poet; the first two lines read: "Cuando una boca suave boca dormida besa / como muriendo entonces" [When a soft mouth kisses a mouth sleeping / as if dying then]. I heard an early recording of this work during a talk given by Etkin at McGill, and I also remember well the performance at an SMCQ concert in Pollack Hall on 27 October 1977, a few months later after Etkin left Montreal, when conductor Serge Garant and his ensemble elegantly recreated the smoky atmosphere and the dreamy mystery of this exquisite world of sound: low sounds, muted sounds, velvet sounds, all operating as one in the fashioning of this special sensibility.

By the early 1970s Etkin's name had begun to circulate, starting with a brief mention in *Introducción a la música de nuestro tiempo* (1970) by Juan Carlos Paz,[27] an encyclopedia entry here, another book entry there, and also an article in an important daily Buenos Aires newspaper authored by the young composer himself, "reflecting upon the current state of the musical avant-garde in Latin America."[28] Even John Vinton's brand new American dictionary of contemporary music, published in 1974, seemed to have more to say about young composers working in Central and South America – including the young Etkin – than it did about the composers, all of whom were old (or so it seemed to me at the time), struggling away in Canada. I certainly was impressed, all the more so given the fact that I was essentially Etkin's age. And no one in Canada was talking about me, talking to me, or asking me – or anyone else for that matter of my generation – about my opinions on the avant-garde in North America!

Etkin's first McGill appearance took place in Pollack Hall on 19 February 1977. The constellations in the musical heavens on that luminous wintery Montreal night could not have been more evocative nor redolent of some other world, of some exotic but, in truth, lost world. The program booklet announced: "Quarter-tone Music of Ivan Wyschnegradsky" – one of Bruce Mather's first public presentations in his rediscovery of the microtonal music of this idiosyncratic Russian composer. However, for Etkin, who was to conduct two complex works, the air that evening could not have been more dense, more resonant, more theosophical, and, strangely enough, more gaunt than the eerie white glow onstage in our northern environment replicating a replication (reflection) of the vanished northern environment from pre-1917 Russia, a cultural and social reality that Wyschnegradsky had attempted while in exile to reconstitute if only in music. (Baudrillard might have called this exhibit "a simulacrum of a simulacrum.")[29] As I imagine it – I realize I am speculating here – this concert enactment appeared to Etkin, himself of Russian descent, as an incongruously atavistic event or perhaps even an artistic avowal, the essence of which was the very opposite of his own avant-garde sensibility.

His next appearance, a few days later on 23 February 1977, again in Pollack Hall, was in a concert devoted to instrumental and electroacoustic music. Of the variety of works on the program, the most compelling was Etkin's taut yet paradoxically reserved *Distancias* (1968) for piano solo, "a study in resonances, decays and durations as applied to the piano. The classical harmonic and melodic changes with their relevant periodicity have been avoided completely."[30] This work was conceived as if it were an electroacoustic composition, which is not surprising since it had been written while Etkin was studying at the Institute for Sonology in Utrecht. True, the composition inhabits a magical sound world, soft and slow moving, but the perception of time, the passage of time – the distances – delimited something quite diverse, as if a continuum of sound had been condensed in some unknown, disturbing way.

Etkin's main teaching responsibility during his residency semester at the Faculty required him to direct and coach chamber music groups for our Contemporary Music Ensemble, always a labour-intensive and challenging assignment even to this day. For the concert of 22 March 1977 Etkin had helped our students rehearse and refine pieces ranging from *Six epigrammes antiques* (Debussy), *Drei Lieder,* op. 25 (Webern), and *Vier Stücke,* op. 5 (Berg) all the way to *Couple – from 'Sette fogli'* (Bussotti) and *The Viola in My Life – 3* (Feldman) as well as *Hip'nôs I* (lanza), and *Vortices II,* a work by student composer John Winiarz scored for piano, cello, percussion, tape, and lights.

Although the EMS produced three more Pollack Hall concerts that semester (the 1987 renovations, including facilities for recording and tape playback, of the former dormitory parlour that eventually became Clara Lichtenstein Hall were still far off in the future), Etkin participated in only two, acting again as artistic co-director. A program presented on 5 April 1977 entitled "live electronics, instruments, tapes," included his *Umbrales* [Thresholds] (1976), scored for flute and alto flute (two players). The world of sound in this piece behaved much like that in *Muriendo,* with a dreamy atmosphere made up of low sounds, but it also evoked the world of *Distancias,* sparse, quiet, and mysterious with intent. The word "umbrales" refers to the thresholds of perception; in composing the duo, Etkin had considered the "relationships situated near the limits of perceptual mechanisms. Those relationships act then [fundamentally] with the thresholds of intensity, duration and timbrical perception."[31]

For the concert on 27 April 1977, just before he returned home to Argentina, Etkin guided the preparation of numerous student tape compositions, one of which must have given him (at least as I like to imagine it) the shivers all over again. *Memories of Winter,* a *musique concrète* work written by Wendy Prezament, one of my students in the regular composition tutorials, revealed its source materials quite poetically with recordings of natural outdoor sounds drawn from the winter just recently ended, the very winter through which Etkin had suffered. Constructed much like a rondo in which an assortment of sounds represent aspects of the season, dominating a section of the rondo form (the frosty sounds include walking on crunchy snow, wind, cars in traffic, slush, snow blowers, breaking twigs, birds in winter), this delightful work may have seemed to Etkin the most meaningful work on the program. As our winter was moving to an early spring in Montreal, summer was inexorably moving toward a sombre autumn in Buenos Aires, advancing along a road leading to a difficult and tragic period for Argentina. Several years would pass before Etkin managed to extricate himself from these arduous living conditions.

Etkin's second residency at the Faculty in 1980–81 involved full-time teaching responsibilities in composition, theory, and analysis. Soon after, for a further three years (1982–85), he was appointed professor at Wilfrid Laurier University where, besides teaching composition and analysis, he also directed the Contemporary Music Ensemble. During this sojourn in Canada a number of his compositions were performed, two of which particularly stand out. Etkin's *Otros Soles* [Other Suns] (1976) was heard in Pollack Hall on 7 April 1981, during program of works by staff composers. Partaking of that same fabric first employed in *Muriendo,* this elusive work scored for bass clarinet, trombone, and viola created a dark and sometimes menacing tone. The "other suns" were created with the "idea of putting into play the following concept: the relativity of perception within the distinguishable [i.e., the discernible elements] among all musical parameters," and with "the thresholds of the perception of differences, particularly and fundamentally the no-man's land which separates the binomial, equal/different."[32] In this respect, Etkin was working as he had with *Umbrales,* which was composed at the same time.

An SMCQ concert on 18 February 1982 entitled "Musiques nouvelles d'Amérique latine" and directed by guest conductor alcides lanza, introduced Montrealers to works of Mario Lavista (Mexico), Alfredo Del Monaco (Venezuela), Gerardo Gandini (Argentina), and Marlos Nobre (Brazil), as well as lanza and Etkin. Etkin's *Otros Tiempos* [At Other Times, Other Tempos] (1978; 1981) was originally written as a string quintet in 1977, just after his first return to South America from Canada, then adapted for string orchestra and performed by the National Symphony Orchestra of Argentina. Three years later, Etkin transformed his score once again, now for eleven strings, the version given at the SMCQ.

Looking back, I cannot help but think that, deep within Etkin's "other times," "other tempos," "other suns," "distances," and "thresholds," indeed within all of his music touched then by the dualities (binomials) of different/equal, variation/repetition, etc., there loomed ubiquitously the notion of alterity. At that point, thirty years ago, I was utterly unable to appreciate the significance of this concept or to comprehend how it might be operating (unconsciously?) within his music, even though I could – and did – recognize the enthralling worlds of sound he had so magically created. Today I believe that at such a crucial moment Etkin's disquieting music foreshadowed the changing times so prevalent in the social and political spheres of Latin America. The *Oxford English Dictionary* defines "alterity" as "the state of being other or different; diversity, 'otherness,'" but nowadays the term connotes a perilous lack of identification with some component of one's personality or one's community. Moreover, in the view of a philosopher such as Michel Foucault, the term alterity (the "other") is directly connected to "those who are excluded from positions of power, and are often victimized within a predominantly liberal humanist view of the subject."[33] In its extreme manifestation, alterity symbolizes dispossession, a state of existence that millions of Argentineans over the last thirty or thrity-five years have come to know more about than they ever had wanted.

Although he has been little affected by world music poetics – so much a part of the diverse creative approaches to composition and to sound today – Etkin has nevertheless shown more than a passing interest in this artistic attitude. There are a number of thought-provoking works in his catalogue, some of which focus upon the urban music of Buenos Aires: *Perpetual tango* (1989) for piano solo, and the somewhat ironic *Abgesang Mambo* (1992) scored for flute, oboe, clarinet, bassoon, horn, trumpet, trombone, and contrabass. "Abgesang" is a technical term in the medieval poetics of the Minnesingers and Meistersingers denoting the latter portion of a stanza (the former half being "Aufgesang"), but the word is also used in contemporary German to mean "swan song," a final accomplishment. In *Lo que nos va dejando* [That Which Leaves Us] (1998), a work for solo percussion, Etkin draws his inspiration from the Uto-Aztecan (Meso-American) concept of time: "cáhuitl" in the Náhuatl language, an exalted idea customarily translated as "that which leaves us."[34]

The final work I wish to mention is entitled *Taltal* (1993), scored for four percussionists. The very name seems to be percussive, like the "tintal" syllabifications used to denote rhythmic cycles in musical cultures of the Indian subcontinent. But, in reality, Taltal is the name of a village on the northern Pacific coast of Chile, south of the city of Antafogasta, near the Atacama Desert, one of the world's driest regions. Etkin writes:

"The precise meaning of the word Taltal is not known. One hypothesis associates this pre-Hispanic vocable with a predatory bird descending to earth, maybe a kind of raven. I was fascinated by the strange combination of this uncertain etymology, the percussive quality of the word, and the quietness of the area in which I was composing the piece. Extinctions, resonances, velocities and timbres were the main compositional concerns. Each musician plays a bass drum and a large tam-tam. It is worthwhile saying that *Taltal* has nothing to do with program music. In reference to other hypothetical remarks to be made in order to get [further] knowledge about [my composition], let me quote Elias Canetti: 'A demolishing thought: that perhaps there is nothing to know; that all falseness arises only because we want to know it.'"[35]

Extinctions ("that which leave us"), resonances, velocities, and timbres: all are residue elements of a paradoxically arid albeit sonorous terrain owned and cultivated by Etkin. But rather than demolish, it has given birth to many extremely beautiful desert flowers.

MARIO BERTONCINI

He gave me a bag made out of ox hide, flayed from a creature nine years old, and tied up in it all the winds that blow from every quarter, for Cronos' son has made Aeolus keeper of the winds, and he could calm or rouse them, as he wished.

Homer, *Odyssey*, book X

From almost any point of view, the events that came to pass on 7 October 1976 in our very own and brand new Pollack Concert Hall – where Mario Bertoncini (born 1932) appeared as composer and performer during the SMCQ's eleventh season – were, to say the least, unusual. Strange as it may seem, the incidents of that evening bore a strong resemblance to actions, let's call them supernatural happenings, described once upon a time in the epic poetry of antiquity. Only three compositions were scheduled for performance: *Scratch-a-Matic* (1970–71) for amplified grand piano excited by means of nine direct-current motors and tape playback, and *Chanson pour instruments à vent* (1974) for two aeolian harps and multiple aeolian gongs, both by Bertoncini, together with ... *chant d'amours* (1975), a large chamber piece composed and conducted by SMCQ artistic director Serge Garant. Whether due to the influence of predestination or not, the concert seemed to be risking fate, emerging as if under the power of magical or divine forces, proceeding in such a way that only Homer could have interpreted it with assurance and recounted it with grandiloquence.

Having successfully completed his tenure as the Faculty of Music's first visiting foreign artist in the spring of 1975 and subsequently provided us with a full year (1975–76) of creative and experimental teaching in a special project course in composition called Musical Design, the odyssean Bertoncini returned to Canada from Germany in the fatidic autumn of 1976 to prepare two performances, one (referred to above) for the SMCQ and the other for New Music Concerts (NMC) of Toronto on 8 November 1976. Bertoncini had concluded a DAAD residency in West Berlin in 1973. (Both Makoto Shinohara and alcides lanza had previously been invited to the same *Künstlerprogramm*, and, it was the outgoing lanza in 1972 who had suggested to the incoming Bertoncini the possibility of spending some future time at McGill.)

In October 1976, however, Bertoncini was concentrated on his efforts to make a success of the North American première of *Scratch-a-matic*. This remarkable *sui generis* artwork requires a bit of explanation. Springing forth as one of the earliest products of his poetics linked to a re-contextualized notion of the *bottega d'arte* – the Italian name for guilds or workshops in the Middle Ages and Renaissance where apprentices and journeymen converged to work with a master artist and teacher – Bertoncini's conception of and design for a "singing" grand piano makes one pause – and then utterly convinces. For one has only to think of a very elaborate if not fanciful *vielle à roue* (hurdy-gurdy) that is both mechanized and electrified, with a keyboard that is never touched. With its top cover removed, the grand piano reveals its hitch pins, wrest pins, soundboard, metal frame, and strings, dampers up (thus, pedal down), together with an apparatus delicately anchored upon its lacquered black wooden casing so that nine direct-current motors, under the control of the performer, drive nine small rubber wheels at variable speeds. The wheel units, positioned along selected strings in order to touch specific harmonic nodes, prompt or excite the individual strings into producing a full-bodied, resonating stream of tone, coloured as much by its inharmonics as by its natural partials. The combined acoustical effect is not easy to convey in words, since I wish to limit myself to the limits of the language of that time, to the then limits of my world. Suffice it to say, the resultant sound – continuous, modulated, and truly ethereal – resembled nothing less than the beautiful singing of invisible choruses of women, each intoning her own celestial and slow-moving vocalise, each engaged in creating a music so enchanting and so intoxicating that "he who listens will go on his way not only charmed, but wiser, for we [the Sirens] know all the ills that the gods laid upon the Argives and Trojans before Troy, and can tell you everything that is going to happen over the whole world."[36]

Nonetheless, in Pollack Hall that evening it was not entirely clear what variety of ills the gods had decided to lay upon the audience, for about half way through the performance of *Scratch-a-matic*, Bertoncini – like an Odysseus after the shock of not believing his ears – became aware of the spectre of a rogue Siren uniting her uninvited voice ever so insidiously into the heavenly mix. The high-pitched squeal of a new electronic fire alarm (the steady pitch of which was so fashionable in the 1970s) slowly began to pollute the sounds emanating from the stage. It took quite some time before audience members, many of whom were new to the new Pollack Hall,[37] understoood what was going on, since during those few moments both the music and the alarm hovered together, commingling within a narrow bandwidth of frequencies, a slender range of sound that, alas, exhibited the most inglorious of micro-polyphonies. No one was charmed nor any the wiser to learn later that, at some point during the previous year, in their rush to finish the construction of the Hall, workers had conjoined two fire security systems that should have been separated (one for the Strathcona Music Building, and one for the other buildings and residences of Royal Victoria College).

Following this awkward interruption of such a remarkable composition, and the obvious necessity for a long intermission during which our wayward siren still echoed along the walls until being obliged to go voiceless, Bertoncini chose to continue his performance with *Chanson pour instruments à vent* (1974), another *sui generis* work conceived for aeolian harps and aeolian gongs. Here he metamorphosed into yet another Homeric persona, Aeolus, "keeper of the winds" in order that "he could calm or rouse them, as he wished." Located discreetly on stage in the vicinity of two metal harp structures – the first, quadrilateral, about one metre square and, the second, circular, about one metre in diameter, and both draped with hundreds of tightly wrought, thread-like wires, the former vertically and the latter both vertically and horizontally – there was a large free-standing tank of compressed air. Next to these two harps was an assortment of aeolian gongs, mounted vertically on thin metal rods, some in the shape of spirals (the bronze chimes of former mantel and grandfather clocks), so that they too might be excited by silent jets of air traveling from the tank along small, transparent, plastics tubes each controlled by Bertoncini like a sculptor guiding a chisel. Here, as in *Scratch-a-matic,* he fashioned continuous and modulated inharmonic sounds, now with artful gestures near the harps, now with sudden thrusts near the gongs, thanks to the presence of numerous contact microphones sending signals to filters, amplifiers, and loudspeakers. Once more, thin wires, small strings, and larger-gauge wires (i.e., rods) were heard to be "singing," but in *Chanson pour instruments à vent* the sounds were much more robust, perhaps more coloured by the timbre of men's voices.

Since the late 1960s when I was an undergraduate, I had been familiar with some of Bertoncini's work, a chance visit to a record store in 1967 having prompted my discovery of an LP – with its then obligatory psychedelic, indeed, phantasmagorical album cover – entitled *The Private Sea of Dreams,* performed by an ensemble called "Il Gruppo." The immensely original contents of this vinyl record helped me to discern new sonic delicacies ranging from well-structured and startling improvisations to many uncommon and mysterious sounds. Since I had been a member of a composer's improvisation group for three years while I attended Wayne State University (Detroit), I could well appreciate the nature of these innovative and disquieting, at least to me, achievements. The performers on this album were all members of an Italian new music society known as Nuova Consonanza begun in Rome in 1959; as I was later to learn, Bertoncini had been one of the founding members. Performers included future film composers Ennio Morricone and Egisto Macchi and future agitprop composer Frederick Rzewski, who in 1966 was also a co-founder of Musica Elettronica Viva (Live Electronic Music) in Rome, another ensemble that shifted the paradigm for creative composition. In 1968, within the pages of *Source Magazine,* a large and oblong-shaped journal from California to which I was a subscriber, I discovered the astonishing graphic score to Bertoncini's *Cifre* [Ciphers, Collection of Numbers, Codes] (1964–67), scored for piano and prepared piano(s). It is in this work that he introduces the technique of bowing the piano strings with horsehair, a procedure that he first presented to the public in 1963 in a prototype for *Cifre,* and also included on the above-mentioned 1967 album. This technique would be copied by many other composers, including one who, during a lecture visit to the Faculty of Music in 1976, claimed he had invented this mode of playing several years earlier.[38] Bertoncini, who was sitting in the audience that afternoon, gently reminded the lecturer of the performances in Rome from a dozen years earlier and the publication of the score of *Cifre* in 1968 with its clear instructions for this bowing technique.

In addition to the fact that I had begun my second year of teaching at the Faculty, the autumn of 1974 remains in my memory not only for the announcement confirming the arrival of our first foreign visiting artist but also for two other singular events, each significant in its own special way. On 13 September 1974, exactly one hundred years after Arnold Schoenberg's birth, – which, as it also happened, was Friday the thirteenth, as was the day of his death on 13 July 1951 – the composition area decided to celebrate this important centenary with a commemorative dinner at a fine hotel restaurant organized by our colleague, Bruce Mather, a noted wine connoisseur and *fin gourmet.* Nothing could have been more meaningful, more final, I thought, than our affirmation as composers of the end of an epoch in the history of music. The only other great symbol of the passing of an era had occurred a few years earlier in 1971 with the death of Igor Stravinsky. Maybe now, I said to myself, music would be able to get on with its inevitable evolution, to begin to produce newer growth, since, after all, "Stravinsky et Schoenberg étaient morts," to paraphrase and expand upon an observation once made by a young and a very impatient Pierre Boulez.[39] One month later, in October 1974, during an inaugural speech at the Théâtre d'Orsay (Paris), the same Pierre Boulez, in his capacity as its new general director, described the orientation of a new state-supported institute to be called IRCAM (then, without a building) and spoke of "la nécessité pour les musiciens de travailler avec les scientifiques" [the necessity of musicians to work with scientists].[40]

From almost the beginning of his stay in Montreal a few short weeks later, Bertoncini often chatted with me, with other colleagues, and with our students about one of his most cherished ideas. For quite some time he had wanted to found what he described as a new *bottega d'arte* – with master composer-teachers and apprentice students – a novel kind of atelier-laboratory for the encouragement, promotion, and transformation of new music creation founded upon scientific principles, at once acoustical and constructivist. What is more, in 1968 when he was thirty-six years old, he had already proposed the establishment of such an enterprise to Peter Nestler, then director of the DAAD in Berlin, not imagining that five years hence, he would be invited there as an artist-in-residence. Bertoncini knew full well that in his home country such a project could never see the light of day due to the nature, since time immemorial, of Italy's decentralized cultural practices, reason enough to make a pitch to the new DAAD. But, *O tempora, o mores*, the political and cultural context of the former West Germany being what it was in the late and so revolutionary 1960s – so extremely complex and subject to so many other outside controlling forces – it is not surprising that such a radical artistic scheme with its inspiration originating in the South would not benefit from nourishment of the sun's rays emanating from the North. Only twenty-seven years later, in the summer of 1995, did the DAAD offer support for a trial run of the endeavour in the city of Trebnitz.

The principle features and broad outlines for the development of a new *bottega d'arte* were publicly announced for the first time in the program booklet of the Venice Biennale of 1970, during the world premiere of Bertoncini's important multimedia work *Spazio-Tempo* [Space-Time] (1967–69).[41] A succinct comparison between the plans for the early IRCAM project and those of the *nuova bottega d'arte* (see table 3.1) is not without interest.

Bertoncini's first effort for the new *bottega d'arte* project, however, was at McGill in the special project course entitled "Musical Design." Before he began his sojourn at McGill, Bertoncini had gained important experience teaching traditional composition at the Rossini Conservatory in Pesaro (1967–73), but at McGill in 1975–76 the pedagogical context was completely different. In order to offer the special project course, the University constructed, at the request of the Faculty of Music, a small laboratory space during the summer of 1975 (in what is now rehearsal room C-306 in the center block of the Strathcona Music Building). Here Bertoncini set up a large work table with many tools brought from his studio in Berlin (soldering equipment, drills, etc.), together with a few of his aeolian instruments, metal plaques, and musical objects of all shapes and sizes: a tam-tam, Chinese gongs, cymbals, wood blocks, various flutes and bird calls as well as his special horsehair strands, numerous mallets, and other playing devices. And so began seven months of intensive work and research dealing with, among other things, the resonant and vibratory properties of metal plates, rods, and wires, the amplification and diffusion of inaudible (small)

Table 3.1.
A comparison between the Institut de recherche et coordination acoustique-musique (IRCAM) and the Nuova Bottega d'Arte

IRCAM	*Nuova Bottega d'Arte*
Original departments 1974, 1978	*Gruppi di lavoro [Work groups] 1968, 1970*
Computer	Electroacoustics
Electroacoustics	Mechanical-constructive
Instruments and voice	Choreography/Theatre/Plastic Arts
Pedagogy	Didactics (teaching aids)
Diagonal (musical perception)	Music
In 1980, Boulez abolished the above departments and substituted a musical sector and a scientific sector. These two sectors were linked together by a "pedagogical group" coordinated by a psycho-acoustician assisted by tutors capable of, among other things, initiating a composer-in-residence to the workings of large computers and software.	In 1975–76, during his teaching at McGill University, Bertoncini developed a composition and performance sector and a construction sector (theoretical, practical) in unofficial collaboration with the Mechanical Laboratory, Faculty of Engineering. In 1995, at Trebnitz (former East Germany), during a special summer seminar, he tried a "paraphrase" (Bertoncini's description) of the original idea, with master composer and apprentice/composers-in-residence.

sounds, the aesthetic distinctiveness of past and present instrument making (*lutherie*), and the techniques and idioms for group improvisation derived from the internal acoustical properties of sound-producing objects linked with the notion of a unity between sound production and performance gesture.

With his research into sound, sound-producing objects, and sound diffusion, he had invented, and patented at the end of the 1960s, the "Bertoncini wheel," a small direct-current (variable speed) motor attached to a rubber wheel (variously sized) installed within his idiosyncratic piano preparations that, as described above, creates a spectrum of celestial harmonics more rich and subtle than anything produced by synthesizers or computers. In addition to *Scratch-a-matic* (1971), the wheels are heard in other works for piano – *An American Dream* (1974) and *Il Cimitero degli Elefanti* [The Elephant Graveyard] (1979) for multiple pianos and electronic processing – that today should also be considered as spectral compositions, but *avant la lettre*. Bertoncini's surprising use of violin, cello, and contrabass bow hair detached from the bow in order to set the strings of a "singing" piano in motion made its first appearance as early as 1963 amidst a host of astonishing piano preparations in *Cifre,* a work in which, unlike John Cage's practice for the prepared piano, keys are never struck! Bertoncini considers the piano as a string instrument rather than a percussion instrument; he is drawn to the evocative power of sustained sounds.[42]

On 29 March 1976, at the end of a semester that also witnessed nine other concerts of contemporary music, the first of two demonstration-performances was given in Pollack Hall by the newly formed McGill MUD Ensemble ("MUsical Design") featuring the accomplishments of our students. This event, dedicated to the pedagogue, polymath, cultural critic, and philosopher of conviviality Ivan Illich (1926–2002), director of the Centro Intercultural de Documentation in Cuernavaca, Mexico, whose books *Deschooling Society* (1971) and *Tools for Conviviality* (1973) circulated freely among Musical Design students, focused attention also on the ambiance of the concert hall itself; thanks to the various individual and collective projects of the MUD group, all the spaces of Pollack Hall were employed for the first time on behalf of daring and new expressive purposes. Musicians could be found throughout the evening making sounds in the back rows of the hall, offstage, in the center and side aisles, and even on the three catwalks.

The final year-end concert, presented on 3 May 1976, featured audiovisual projects and also included an exhibition in the east lounge of the Hall and a discussion of student works-in-progress, even though the special project course had already been completed. As in the previous event – for these concerts were truly events – the program booklet expressed gratitude for the help everyone had received from two important partners – the mechanical laboratory of the McGill Faculty of Engineering and the EMS[43] – but on this occasion the program also included a special announcement: "The Founding Members of the MUD Ensemble plan to continue their work in design and performance as an independent group, while establishing contact with other groups, individuals and institutions in the aim of future collaborations."

Eighteen months later, on 22 and 23 September 1977, long after Bertoncini had returned to Europe, and following at least seven other public presentations,[44] MUD presented two back-to-back concerts in Pollack Hall: one dedicated to a retrospective of the achievements from the initial course work, and the other centered on new directions and recent developments. By this time, with fewer members than had been in the course (Andrew Culver, Charles de Mestral, Pierre Dostie, Chris Howard, and Linda Pavelka), the autonomous student collective could now boast not only a new home-atelier (a large rented second-floor warehouse space on Beaubien Street near Park Avenue) but also collaborations with an electrical technician, a lighting specialist, and two stage movement consultants, in addition to advice from art gallery owners. And it could also boast of funding in the form of an Explorations Grant from the Canada Council. Ah, the good old days! Thirty years ago ...[45]

Since the 1970s Bertoncini has produced not only poetry – more than 450 *Sonetti* inspired by the satirical verse in Roman dialect of Giuseppe Gioacchino Belli (1791–1863) – but also many long essays inspired by the dialogues of Plato, some of which have been published.[46] As of 2005 he had completed nine dialogues in Italian dealing almost exclusively with contemporary music topics and featuring eloquent discussions between two distinguished *personae*: Menippo and Bremonte, the former, an old, skeptical professor, and the latter his enthusiastic former student. (It is not too far-fetched here to compare "M" and "B" with another well-known set of musical alter ego creations, Robert Schumann's Eusebius and Florestan.) Imbued with the stamp of a classical education as well as the capacity for wide-ranging references and critical thinking, the voices of both teacher and student move with great ease from topic to topic, often with references from texts in Greek and Latin, such ancient wisdom being the inevitable fount of much irony and humour when called forth to comment upon modern ideas and current events.

As the Faculty embarks upon a creative, scientific, and technological journey embodied both by the construction of a new building housing a library, a multimedia room, an opera rehearsal studio and by the dedication to music research in all of its ramifications, it remains to be seen whether the model for our version of a very modern alloy, musical creation/scientific research, will have been indeed inspired by the institute founded by Pierre Boulez. I am fond of imagining that perhaps one day in the future our edifice may in fact come to be known as the home of "IRCAM on the Saint Lawrence." Bertoncini's idea of a new *bottega d'arte* will not return because the composer-centred project was frankly too composition-centered, or in other words, "useless" as he says himself in the eighth dialogue of *Arpe eolie e altre cose inutili*

[Aeolian Harps and Other Useless Things] (1999–2000). I would like to believe, nonetheless, that his work thirty years ago as a researcher, a role-model, and a profoundly imaginative artist and teacher actually did help by laying part of the foundation for the new multi-disciplinary paradigm driving McGill's new Schulich School of Music.

NOTES

1 Japanese proverb.

2 An Internet search for terms such as "riots in 1967," "riots in 1968," "assassinations in 1967," and "assassinations in 1968" generates nothing less than a portrait of horror and societal disarray.

3 Canada Council for the Arts, www.canadacouncil.ca/grants/xr127234091658125000.htm.

4 Concordia University, www3.concordia.ca/about/history/sgw5.html.

5 McGill University. www.news-archive.mcgill.ca/s99/demoen.htm as well as www.reporter-archive.mcgill.ca/Rep/r3114/francais.html.

6 Here is a brief summary of the events.

5 October 1970: The "October crisis" begins with the kidnapping of James Cross, British Trade Commissioner at 8.15 a.m.

10 October: At 6.00 p.m., the latest deadline announced by the terrorists passes. Within an hour, Pierre Laporte, provincial Minister of Labour, is kidnapped at his house by two masked men from the Chénier cell, which includes Jacques Rose, Paul Rose, Francis Simard, and Bernard Lortie.

18 October: The body of Pierre Laporte is found in the trunk of a car near the airport at St-Hubert on the south shore of Montreal. It appears that he was killed on 17 October in retaliation for the invocation of the War Measures Act. Another interpretation of this event is that, sensing his position to be hopeless with the invocation of the War Measures Act, Pierre Laporte attempts to flee and is killed in the ensuing scuffle. Public reaction to the murder is one of revulsion and shock. Later that day warrants for the arrest of Marc Carbonneau and Paul Rose are issued.

20 October: Pierre Laporte is buried.

23 October: Warrants are issued for the arrest of Francis Simard, Bernard Lortie, and Jacques Rose.

7 Throughout the 1980, and especially in France, composers reinterpreted acoustical principles (linked to the harmonic spectrum) so that they might serve creative projects.

8 Shinohara's classmates included Carlos Roqué Alsina, Eberhard Blum, Cornelius Cardew, Joel Chadabe, Alvin Curran, Hans Joachim Hespos, Erhard Karkoschka, Helmut Lachenmann, Emmanuel Nuñes, Bernard Rands, Rolf Riehm, Frederic Rzewski, and Isang Yun, all of whom went on to enjoy notable careers in contemporary music.

9 The fellowship came from the Deutscher Akademischer Austauschdienst (DAAD; German Academic Exchange Service), a cultural organization established in 1963 by the Ford Foundation as part of NATO's *realpolitik* response to the construction of the Berlin Wall by Soviet forces in 1961.

10 Pollack Concert Hall concert program, 6 April 1978.

11 Other notable works with Japanese instruments include: *Kyudo A* (1973) for shakuhachi solo and *Kyudo B* (1973) for shakuhachi and harp; "kyudo" is the traditional art of Japanese archery; in version B, the harp resembles a gigantic bow while the flute suggests an arrow. *Nagare* (1981) is written for *samisen*, a long-necked lute played with *bachi* (plectra); "Nagare" is a Japanese word meaning flowing or sliding, in reference to a style of Japanese architecture associated with the recognizable sloping or inclined roofs of temples. *Turns* (1983) is scored for violin and koto (or solo violin without koto).

12 Mayuzumi, the first postwar Japanese composer to attract international attention, had also studied in Paris with Tony Aubin

13 At the time Traditions musicales du monde was founded Ramón Pelinsky was a professor of ethnomusicology at l'Université de Montréal, José Evangelista was a composer and future doctoral student at McGill, and Matilde Asencio was a Spanish language professor; Gilles Tremblay acted as honorary president.

14 Italian patriot and later parliamentarian Giovanni Ruffini (1807–81) wrote the libretto for Donizetti's *Don Pasquale* (1843) while he was in exile in Paris. He moved to England perhaps as early as 1837, where he wrote autobiographical novels in English under the name John Ruffini.

15 The Torcuato Di Tella Institute, founded in 1958, opened avenues for research and teaching in the Argentine social sciences, and has contributed to the education of generations of professionals who have become prominent in the field of social and economic sciences. In the music section, which was sponsored by the Rockefeller Foundation from 1963 to 1971, a concentration of artists working in the avant-garde and dedicated to experimentation in the visual arts, theatre, and music, provided training for young composers. Composer Alberto Ginastera (1916–83) founded the Centro Latinoamericano de Altos Estudios Musicales (CLAEM; (Latin American Centre for Advanced Musical Studies) in the Di Tella Institute, again with support from the Rockefeller Foundation.

16 Pollack Hall concert program, 2 March 1976.

17 Ibid.

18 John Winiarz has taught at McGill University (electronic music) and at Concordia University (history, theory, and musicianship). Recent works include musical tributes to Frédéric Chopin, Anna Pavlova, and Astor Piazzolla. Since his student years at McGill Andrew Culver has composed chamber and orchestral works, electronic and computer music, and has created sound sculpture and music sculpture, film, lighting, text pieces, and installations. As assistant to John Cage during the last decade of Cage's life, Culver programmed the chance operations central to Cage's work, most notably all five operas. Culver directed *Europeras 1* and *2* in Frankfurt, Purchase (New York), and Zurich, *Europeras 3* and *4* in London, Strasbourg, Berlin, Paris, and Long Beach, and *Europera 5* in the garden of the Museum of Modern Art, New York.

19 Pollack Concert Hall concert program, 29 April 1976.

20 Located in the new eight-storey building recently constructed for the McGill Faculty of Music CIRMMT brings together researchers and students from McGill University (faculties of music, science, engineering, and medicine), l'Université de Montréal (faculté de musique, faculté des arts et des sciences), l'Université de Sherbrooke (faculté de génie), and the CÉGEP de Drummondville, as well as administrative and technical staff, research associates, visiting scholars, musicians, and industrial associates.

21 Pollack Concert Hall concert program, 29 April 1976.

22 These masks were designed and constructed by Warsaw-born Tristan Wolski (1955–), a future visual artist who, at the time, was a student in the department of physics at McGill (1973–75). He eventually went on to study painting and sculpture.

23 Conrad Aiken (1889–1973) was born in the state of Georgia. At Harvard University he shared a class with T.S. Eliot, with whom he also edited a literary journal. Aiken graduated in 1912, around the same time as Eliot, Walter Lippman, and E.E. Cummings. Aiken's first collection of verse, *Earth Triumphant,* which appeared in 1914, established his reputation as a poet. During the First World War Aiken argued that, being a poet, he was in an "essential industry" and was in due course granted exemption from military service.

24 Considered the greatest poet of the Tang Dynasty, a middle period in Chinese history during which literature flourished, Li Po (700–762) wrote many verses associated with the images of the moon and wine; his best-known poem is entitled *Drinking Alone under the Moon.*

25 The aquamarimba was jointly designed and built by McAdams and Mark Knighton, who played percussion in McAdams's composition. Knighton is currently a professor of Russian in the department of German and Slavic studies at the University of Manitoba.

26 Guillermo Graetzer (1914–93), born "Wilhelm Grätzer" in Vienna, came to Buenos Aires in 1939 fleeing the Nazis. In 1947 he participated in the foundation of the League of Argentinean Composers together with, among others, Juan José Castro and Alberto Ginastera. In his own compositions he combined many distinctive sources of inspiration, including African choral music, Hebrew songs, and Spanish music of the sixteenth century.

27 Juan Carlos Paz, *Introducción a la música de nuestro tiempo* (Buenos Aires: Editorial Sudamericana, 1970).

28 Encyclopaedia *Riemann Musik-Lexikon* (Mainz: Schott, 1972); Tomás Marco, *Historia General de la Música. El siglo XX* (Madrid: Editorial Alpuerto, 1973); Mariano Etkin, "Reflexiones sobre la música de vanguardia en América Latina," *Diario La Opinión*, 16 January 1972 (Buenos Aires).

29 See Jean Baudrillard, *Simulacres et simulations* (Paris: Galilée, 1981).

30 Pollack Concert Hall concert program, 23 February 1977.

31 Pollack Concert Hall concert program, 5 April 1977.

32 Ibid.

33 *The Routledge Critical Dictionary of Postmodern Thought*, ed. Stuart Sim (London: Brunner-Routledge, 2001), 181.

34 See Etkin, "Acerca de la composición" for a special reference to this concept in so far as it relates to the teaching of composition.

35 Source of this quote is www.schlagquartett.de/repertoire/komponisten/etkin.html (accessed 7 December 2006).

36 Siren's address to Odysseus, Homer *Odyssey*, book XII.

37 Pollack Hall was inaugurated on 10 April 1975.

38 To this day C. Curtis-Smith, a professor at Western Michigan University (Kalamazoo), claims to have invented the bowing technique used by other composers. See www.wmich.edu/music/faculty/som_fac_curtis-smith-c.html (accessed November 2006).

39 See Pierre Boulez, "Schönberg is Dead," *The Score* 6 (May 1952): 18–22.

40 Dominique Jameux, *Pierre Boulez* (Paris: Fayard/SACEM, 1984), 222.

41 Bertoncini's 1970 text, "Proposta di construire un istituto sperimentale di ricerca sul suono" [A proposal to build an experimental institute for sonic research], is reproduced in Micaela Mollia, ed., *Autobiografia della musica contemporanea* (Cosenza: 1979), 81–9.

42 Other innovations within his "lutherie" include:

1 Aeolian harps (wind harps) in the outdoors, activated by natural air currents, and in concert halls, particularly harps and aeolian gongs (clock chime rods of various shapes) activated by hand-controlled jets of compressed air. Appears in *Chain Reaction* (1973), a music-theatre work realized in collaboration with light-kinetic painter Peter Sedgley; *Vele* (1974; veils,

sailcloth) for two seven-metre wind harps; *Chanson pour instruments à vent* (1974); *Venti* (1980–82; winds, or twenty) for twenty aeolian harps and forty performers together with two orchestra conductors.

2 Action of a grand piano (keys and hammers alone, that is, free-standing) played "normally" where the hammers strike one or more Japanese gongs as they rotate on a carousel placed above the action controlled by the performer.

3 Choreophone (patented 1986), a contactless transduction system for linking the gestures of dancers to sound production; appears in its first version in *Spazio-Tempo* (1970).

4 Stabdämpfer (patented in 1993), an aluminium mute for use with string instruments, consisting of four small vertical bronze rods, from which carrier signals are transformed; used in *Streichquartett Nr 2* (1993) and *Elementi di forma* (2000–01) for prepared cello and electronic treatment.

43 Jack Kelly, senior technician of the Mechanical Lab, and Prof. George Fekete of the Mechanical Engineering Department provided many services to Bertoncini and to his students, as did EMS technician Eric Johnstone.

44 These include: Galerie Média (Montreal), two concerts, July 1976; Montreal Museum of Fine Arts, October 1976; Galerie Véhicule Art (Montreal), January 1977; International Symposium for Young Composers (McGill University, Pollack Hall), March 1977; Galerie Média, two concerts, March 1977; Open Air Event-Sonic environment (Mount-Royal Park, Montreal), May 1977; Atelier Concerts of Musical Design course, 12 and 13 July 1977.

45 To this day the group – now performing under the name *SONDE* [probe] – continues to be active with diverse projects that also include recordings, sound installations in galleries, and soundtracks for film.

46 The general title for the collection of nine dialogues (1976 –2000) is *Ragionamenti musicali in forma di dialogo* [Musical Reasoning in the Form of Dialogues]. For a brief discussion of the dialogues together with an explanation of the names of the principle protagonists, see Christine Anderson, "Dialoge und andere 'nutzlose' Texte – Anmerkungen zu den Schriften von Mario Bertoncini," *MusikTexte* 96 (2003): 44–5.

4

McGill University Records, 1976–1990: A Brief History

Paul Pedersen, Toronto, Ontario

One year before he came to McGill in 1966, PAUL PEDERSEN completed the first fully computerized composition written in Canada: *Serial Composition* for violin, horn, bassoon and harp. This piece, although only six minutes long, had taken an IBM 7094 computer – the same model that was used by NASA for its lunar landing program – twenty-eight minutes to generate and was, in the words of Pedersen himself, "virtually un-performable." At the time, however, it was a feat that brought Pedersen immediate stature, launching a journey that was to lead him from the Electronic Music Studio through various departmental administrative roles to the office of the dean, a position he was to hold for a remarkable span of ten years (1976–86). Pedersen's career path often left little time for composition but allowed his pioneering spirit to champion the creative accomplishments of his colleagues while taking advantage of the university's recent growth and relative economic wealth to garner financial support for new initiatives. In this chapter he writes as founder of one of those initiatives, McGill Records, looking back through his subsequent experiences as the Dean of the Faculty of Music at the University of Toronto in the 1990s, where his attempts to initiate a similar venture were unsuccessful. His memories of place, consequently, are laced with a touch of nostalgia, the span of thirty years representing for him the life of an idea whose time has come and gone.

McGill Records owes its existence to a chance meeting at the Chopin Academy of Music in Warsaw, Poland. In the spring of 1974, on my way to Moscow and Japan, I stopped in Warsaw to see the electronic music studio at the Music Academy. I had not made prior arrangements for my visit and I had difficulty in getting the Academy concierge to understand what I wanted, since my Polish was non-existent and he spoke neither English nor French. He called over a group of passing students, one of whom spoke excellent English. This student not only showed me around the studios at the Academy but also took me to the Polish Radio Studios and introduced me to people at both institutions. We spent the whole day together and that evening went out for dinner at a restaurant in the city; I recall an excellent borsht. The student, Wieslaw Woszczyk, was taking a *Tonmeister* program at the Academy and was interested in coming to McGill University as a visiting student.

On my return to McGill that summer, I was able to arrange a visiting student scholarship for Woszczyk to take various graduate courses at McGill. He stayed at McGill for two academic sessions and in 1976 went to New York where he found work at one of the larger recording studios. He also worked as sound engineer for various artists, including Harry Belafonte and Philip Glass, when they were on tour. Woszczyk kept in touch with me at McGill and made trips back to Montreal to do the recording engineering for recordings we were producing for the newly established McGill Records label. At the same time, I asked him to design a graduate program in sound recording for McGill. In a short time, the new Master of Music program in sound recording was approved; a professional quality recording studio, equipped with the latest in multi-track recording equipment, was built in the west lounge of Pollack Hall; and beginning in the fall of 1978 Woszczyk was hired as a full-time lecturer at the Faculty of Music, teaching classes in sound recording.

THE UNIVERSITY, THE FACULTY, AND MCGILL RECORDS

When I joined the Faculty of Music as a lecturer in 1966 there were only 174 full-time music students. There was no graduate program, few full-time staff, and the Faculty rarely registered on the consciousness of the University at large except as a rather expensive operation when considered on a "per student" basis. Rather than succumb to the University's desire to close the place down, however, Helmut Blume, then dean, embarked on a campaign to substantially increase the number of music students. This was the period of the baby-boom expansion at universities in general, so the potential for growth was there. By the time I was appointed dean in 1976, the number of full-time undergraduate music students had increased to 314, the Faculty had a new home in the former Royal Victoria College, the new Pollack Concert Hall had been built for the Faculty, a considerable number of new full-time faculty members had been appointed, and a graduate program was well underway.

As dean, I saw one of my tasks to be consolidating the gains that had been made. The student body had grown substantially in both numbers and quality but the Faculty still had a reputation as a minor, second-rate music school. McGill Records was starting to demonstrate to prospective students and the world at large, in a concrete and highly tangible way, the quality of music produced by our staff and students. It also served as a publishing outlet for the excellent performers and composers on staff at the Faculty.

The attitude of much of the University towards the Faculty of Music was reflected in an exchange that occurred when, after my appointment as dean in 1976, I first met with the administration's Budget Planning Group. The deans of all the university's faculties met with this group each year to discuss their budgets for the coming academic year. I had barely been introduced when the vice-principal of administration (who was a professor of chemistry) asked me why the University should provide music training – would not that be better left to the conservatory? Usually I only think of sharp replies long after they are needed, but on this occasion I suggested that while some might consider that to be the case, we should remember that at a time when medicine was practised in barbershops and chemistry was in the basements of alchemy, music was part of the *quadrivium* at the university. The meeting erupted in laughter and there were no more questions concerning the place of music in the university. Before long the attitude of the university administration made a complete turnaround. Instead of wanting to shut it down, the administration came to consider the Faculty as a most valuable asset, because the high public profile created through concerts and recordings generated uniformly positive public relations for the whole university.

STARTING MCGILL RECORDS

The McGill Records project was initiated by Woszczyk, Donald Steven, and me during the academic year 1976–77: Woszczyk was the recording engineer, Donald Steven was the recording producer, and I was the

Left to right, Donald Steven and Wieslaw Woszczyk recording in 1977. Reproduced by permission of Schulich School of Music.

executive producer, a rather grandiose-sounding title that meant that I had to do everything else, including endless hours of tape editing, in the days when editing was done with a razor blade and splicing tape. As dean I had secretarial assistance, but the dean's secretary had more than enough regular Faculty business to occupy her time and so I talked my wife, Jean Pedersen, into serving as the volunteer, unpaid secretary for McGill Records. I also hired a graduate student, Ichiro Fujinaga (now a professor at McGill and member of CIRMMT) to write a computer program to keep track of inventory, sales, and finances. One major problem was that personal computers were slow and available database software was primitive and full of bugs. MURIS, the McGill University Records Information System, crashed with almost predictable regularity.

EARLY HISTORY AND FINANCES

Financially, McGill Records was founded with a small amount of money in the Faculty budget that had remained unspent at the end of the budget year. At that time, it cost less than $5000 to produce a recording, including printing and pressing 1,000 copies. During the first three years we had to rent a mixer and microphones for each recording session and borrow monitors and tape recorders from the Faculty's Electronic Music Studio. When our own recording studio became operational in 1980 we no longer had this equipment rental expense. The major expenses in producing a record included cutting the master disc, pressing the 1,000 copies, and designing and printing the record jackets. While we hired a commercial artist to produce the mechanicals for printing the jackets, I took the cover photographs for five discs and my wife Jean created the cover artwork for four more. A number of my photographs were also used on jacket backs and in CD booklets. This art work and photography was supplied at no cost, as was all the work that Woszczyk, Steven and I did for McGill Records.

For the most part, the musicians on the recordings were either teaching staff or students at the Faculty of Music. Students who performed on recordings were given a few copies of the finished disc but received no other payment. Most student performers were members of the Faculty's larger ensembles: orchestra, choirs and bands. They were not obligated to participate in the recordings, but none refused. They were aware that the opportunity to participate in a professional quality recording session was a valuable experience and took great pride in the excellent recordings that resulted. A number of the faculty who performed on the recordings were part-time staff and as such were not on salary but paid only for the hours that they worked teaching students. Since we did not have the funds to pay these musicians for the recording sessions directly, we made agreements with them to pay royalties on sales after the recovery of initial production costs. Since these costs were kept to a minimum, all staff performers earned royalties from their recordings.

PROBLEMS WITH THE MUSICIANS' UNION

Before beginning production of the first recordings, we contacted the Musicians' Union to obtain permission for their members to participate, making clear the educational and non-commercial aims of the individual projects. However, since all matters pertaining to recording were controlled from the Union's New York office, we did not receive the permission requested but instead were sent a standard commercial recording contract. Since it was obviously not possible to operate under those conditions, correspondence with the union ceased. Our solution was to list the participating Union musicians as "co-producers" who would receive a percentage of the sales income through a royalty agreement. Since the participating musicians wanted to do the recordings, and since several local Union officials were also teachers or former students at McGill, we had no further Union problems until a controversial matter arose that was unrelated to McGill Records.

In 1987–88 Professor Joel Wapnick and Frank Opolko (a graduate of the sound recording program) initiated a project called McGill University Master Samples (MUMS) to produce a series of eleven CDs containing sounds for sampling synthesizers. While such sample discs were already available commercially, these discs were to be much more comprehensive. They differed from commercial discs in that every note of every instrument was recorded, so that samplers in the future could use all of the samples; many variants of the instruments (for example, four or five types of clarinets) were recorded and professional musicians were employed. Opolko's expertise as a recording engineer was a major factor in the production of the high-quality sounds.

The problem lay in the fact that they had used professional musicians. MUMS had arranged to record samples using the string sections of the Montreal Symphony Orchestra, but the Musicians' Union was fighting against the use of such samples on an international scale, so the president of the Montreal Musicians' Union told the players that they could not take part in the recording. As a result, McGill Records was blacklisted and Union members were not allowed to perform on our recordings. The Union did not even inform us of the black-listing – a faculty member told us that it had been published in the union newspaper. We protested that these sample discs were not produced by McGill Records and that we could do nothing to prevent their distribution, but our protest was to no avail. The Union replied that since both projects were at McGill University, they were the University's responsibility, and the blacklisting would stand. As with many technological issues, however, the Union was fighting a losing battle. Soon there was a plethora of sample discs on the market and those produced by MUMS were of little commercial significance. After a change in the presidency of the Montreal Union, McGill Records was removed from the blacklist. In the end, the problem did not cause significant delays in our production.

REPERTOIRE

McGill Records was conceived with a number of goals in mind. First, it was a vehicle to promote the Faculty of Music through recordings of faculty performers and the music by faculty composers. Second, beyond the McGill connection, it was intended to feature other

Canadian performers and composers. In general, we sought repertoire that was not currently commercially available. Works by McGill composers comprise 35 percent of the total playing time of the thirty-six recordings issued between 1976 and 1990. Music by other Canadian composers accounts for another 10 percent. McGill staff and students perform 90 percent of the music. About two-thirds of all the music recorded on these McGill Records is not found on any other commercially released recording.

During this period, a performance degree program in jazz was started at the Faculty and extensive studies in early music performance were also initiated. The Faculty acquired a substantial number of baroque instruments – strings, woodwinds, brass, and keyboards – and a major French baroque pipe organ was installed in Redpath Hall. These developments are reflected in the repertoire on McGill Records. About 10 percent of the music on McGill Records is jazz and 23 percent is early music performed on period instruments. Considerably more jazz was recorded on the McGill Records released after 1990.

During my tenure as dean of the Faculty of Music (1976–86) the final decision as to which artists and which repertoire would be recorded by McGill Records rested with me. While I did consult with other faculty members, particularly with Steven and Woszczyk, the process may have appeared to be that of a benevolent (I hope) dictatorship. Much of the unique repertoire on McGill Records has been due to the wide range of musical interests of the composers and performers at the Faculty. For example, Bruce Mather had a long-standing interest in microtonal music, and put together two discs of this music for McGill Records, commissioning new works, assembling repertoire, finding performers, and directing rehearsals, performances, and recording sessions. Much of the McGill Records repertoire was chosen by the performers and conductors, who were well aware of our bias towards Canadian composers. While I insisted on excluding my own compositions, I did influence repertoire selection in a number of cases. For example, it was largely due to my personal interest in the choral works of Buxtehude that we recorded his Christmas and Easter cantatas; since few of his choral works were available on disc, the criterion of selecting otherwise unavailable music was fulfilled. In addition, our excellent choral director Fred Stoltzfus, who had an affinity for the German baroque, and our thriving early music performance program under the direction of Mary Cyr combined forces to produce two outstanding recordings of Buxtehude's cantatas.

Mather – LePage Piano Duo recording session in 1977. Reproduced by permission of Schulich School of Music.

TECHNICAL AND MUSICAL QUALITY

From the beginning, technical and acoustic excellence was a priority for McGill Records. During the first few years, before our recording studio was built, we rented top quality microphones and mixers for the recording sessions. Fortunately, equipment in our Electronic Music Studio included the best professional tape recorders with the latest noise-reduction technology. The Pollack Concert Hall provided a recording space that was well isolated from outside noise. The ventilation and air-conditioning system were generally satisfactory for concert purposes, but were not as quiet as we had specified in the original plans for the Hall. This problem was simply and effectively solved by turning the system off during recording sessions. The relatively long reverberation time of the hall also enhanced the recorded sound without us having to resort to artificial reverberation.

The McGill Recording Studio, which opened in 1980, was built to serve the needs of the newly established Master of Music program in sound recording. Since the Recording Studio is built in the former west lounge of Pollack Hall, there is excellent communication between the

Hall and the Studio via multiple microphone, audio, and video lines. Even though the front of the Hall is only a few steps from the Studio door, the isolation between the two spaces is so effective that recording and monitoring sessions can take place in the Studio without interference from concerts or rehearsals in Pollack Hall. The Studio was equipped with the finest equipment for both twenty-four-track and conventional two-track recording. It also had a wide selection of the best microphones available. While digital recording equipment was starting to be available at this time, digital technology was still in an early stage of development. The decision was made to equip the studio with the best in analogue recorders and to add digital equipment when its utility and quality exceeded that of the analogue equipment. The students from the Sound Recording program also worked on McGill Records. Senior students served as recording engineers and tape editors for some of the discs and the other students in the program assisted in the recording sessions. Since this work was an accredited part of their program of studies, no payment was necessary. Throughout the process, Woszczyk kept a close watch on the work of his students.

The combination of a good recording space and top-quality equipment was complemented by a recording engineer of exceptional technical skill and musical ability. Woszczyk brought to McGill Records the thorough training in music, acoustics, and classical recording techniques of the European *Tonmeister* combined with the technical knowledge and experience acquired in professional American popular music recording. The result has been the production of a series of recordings of outstanding technical merit. Many reviewers have commented on the excellent sound quality on McGill Records, with the result that *Sound Canada* selected Woszczyk as the recording engineer for their *Audio System Test Record,* which was produced in the McGill Recording Studio and released on McGill Records.

During the 1980s surround sound, which became common in movie theatres, was also beginning to appear on music CDs. The recording process for surround sound required the use of an encoder that imbedded the spatial information into the music tracks of the CD. To achieve the surround sound effect, the CDs were played back with a decoder through a multi-channel amplifier and speaker system. Woszczyk, who had been researching microphone techniques for a number of years, developed methods for encoding the surround information using special microphone techniques, without the need for a special encoder. The

Wieslaw Woszczyk in the McGill Recording Studio in 1980. Reproduced by permission of Schulich School of Music.

spatial information was extracted on playback using Dolby Surround or Prologic decoders, which were commonly built into consumer multi-channel amplifiers and receivers. This innovative technique, called Natural Surround, was a unique contribution to the recording and distribution of music in surround sound on CD. McGill Records releases that use Natural Surround include *Celebration* with the Gerald Danovitch Saxophone Quartet and *Kevin Dean – Minor Indiscretions*. Selections from these recordings were included on a promotional CD of surround sound recordings used by the Danish equipment manufacturer Bang and Olufsen to market high quality home theatre systems.

Another example of the recognition of the outstanding quality of McGill Records, both technical and musical, is reflected in the honours received by the recording *Dietrich Buxtehude – Cantatas for Advent, Christmas and Epiphany*. First released on LP format in 1983, it immediately acquired critical acclaim, receiving the Noah Greenberg Award for early music. In 1989 it was re-issued on CD under the title *Buxtehude Christmas Concert* with the addition of five Buxtehude organ works performed by John Grew, and in this format, entered the

Fanfare Classical Hall of Fame in 2004. The reviewer in the November/December 2004 issue of *Fanfare* wrote:

> I can state without reservation that the interpretations found here are certainly worthy of inclusion in the collection of any lover of the Baroque in general or choral music in particular... There is an exceptional level of enthusiasm on the part of all concerned, the quality is overwhelmingly exceptional, and...the musicians of McGill University...offer us interpretations that certainly augur well for Buxtehude's reputation... The superbly balanced choral works speak well of the university's associated programs by way of the choir's high quality, enunciation, and crisp but never antiseptic articulation; and John [Grew's] rendering of the organ works leaves nothing to be desired either... One will certainly have to search far and wide to find a recording that displays the sense of commitment found here.[1]

Recordings of works by Canadian composers have also received critical acclaim. *Percussion,* one of the first McGill Records releases, won first prize for the Best Chamber Music Recording in the 1979 Grand Prix du Disque – Canada. This recording, which consists entirely of Canadian compositions, including a work by a student composer, was performed by students in the McGill Percussion Ensemble. In 1985, Maureen Forrester and the McGill Symphony Orchestra recorded Donald Steven's *Pages of Solitary Delights,* Malcolm Forsyth's *Three Métis Songs from Saskatchewan,* and Edward Elgar's *Sea Pictures* for McGill Records. On the basis of this recording, *Pages of Solitary Delights* was awarded a JUNO in 1987 in the category Best Classical Composition. The recording was re-issued on CD in 1988.

The outstanding musical quality of McGill Records, while primarily reflecting the excellence of the performers, was also due to the expertise of Steven in his role as recording producer. In the 1960s, after a few years as a performer and arranger of folk and rock music, Steven completed a bachelor's degree in composition at McGill, followed by master's and PhD degrees at Princeton University. When we started McGill Records, Steven had recently returned to McGill as a composition professor. His time in the popular music field served him well as we recorded everything from jazz to symphony. After leaving McGill in the 1990s Steven went on to an administrative career at several universities in the United States, and he is now Provost and Dean of the College of the Citadel, in Charleston, South Carolina.

McGill Percussion Ensemble recording in Pollack Hall in 1977. Reproduced by permission of Schulich School of Music.

The history of *Tangos* is another example of the musical and technical excellence of McGill Records. The noted Argentinean pianist Arminda Canteros had been the teacher of McGill composer and pianist alcides lanza. In 1989 lanza persuaded Canteros, who was retired in New York and more than seventy years of age, to come to McGill to record a disc of the tangos for which she was famous. This CD, one of McGill Records' best sellers, was later licensed by PolyGram for international distribution. It had always been the goal of McGill Records to have the kind of technical and musical quality found in the best recordings of major international labels. This licensing agreement indicated that, at least on one occasion, that goal was reached.

ADVERTISING AND DISTRIBUTION OF MCGILL RECORDS

When one has produced a good-quality recording with interesting repertoire and fine performers, there remains the problem of finding the people who might be interested in purchasing the disc and informing them about it. This problem is compounded by the fact that the audience for McGill Records was quite small and very scattered. Most of the performers were not well known even to Canadian audiences, and were often completely unknown internationally. The cost of print advertising in larger-circulation national magazines was far beyond our budget and probably would not reach many of our potential customers in any case. We did advertise in specialty magazines such as *New Music, Canadian Music,* and *Early Music.* However, we felt that our best chance for reaching whatever audience there was for our discs was to have them reviewed by writers for specialty magazines that catered to our target audiences. We made an effort to send out review copies to the magazines that published record reviews and served a potential audience. We were most successful with *Fanfare,* a publication dedicated to reviews of new recordings. Fortunately, they were not averse to reviewing small labels and usually had knowledgeable reviewers.

From the beginning we used a commercial distributor, Distribution Fusion III in Montreal, to get our discs into record stores across Canada, but the success of such distribution was always limited. Sam the Record Man in Toronto was about the only store where one could reliably find our recordings. Sam Sniderman was a supporter of Canadian performers and composers, and would always have at least one copy of our discs, even the most esoteric repertoire, in his main Toronto store. While there might be a fair-sized audience around the world for our recording titled *Music for 3 Pianos in 6ths of Tones,* that audience would not likely be found by having stock of our discs in record stores in Moose Jaw.

Our main distribution avenue was via direct mail. Building a mailing list of potential and repeat customers is a long and painstaking process. We started with lists of libraries, composers, university music faculty, members of contemporary music societies, early music societies, and almost any other list of potential customers that we could locate. To this we continually added the names of all new customers. Mail distribution is labour intensive, both in building and maintaining the mailing lists and in physically packaging and mailing the orders. This was only possible financially with the volunteer labour of my wife, Jean Pedersen, who served as the unpaid secretary for McGill Records.

CHANGE IN ORGANIZATIONAL STRUCTURE

In early 1986, when my term as dean was coming to an end, at my request the University administration appointed me as Director of McGill University Records for a five-year term. An advisory committee was established consisting of the Vice-Principal Academic, the Dean of Music, Steven, and Woszczyk, plus myself as chair. After my sabbatical leave, the committee met in the fall of 1987 and took several actions: we approved the document "The Aims and Philosophy of McGill University Records (see Appendix 2); we made recommendations regarding the proposal for the expansion of McGill University Records (see the discussion below); and we established the structure and function of an artist and repertoire committee.

The principal changes envisioned in the "Aims and Philosophy" document were the scale of operation (which is discussed below) and a shift in focus for artist selection. While the criteria for repertoire selection was to remain much as before, the selection of artists would change. Up to this point most of the performers on our discs were McGill faculty and students, but our new aim was to make the whole of Canada our source for performers.

The artist and repertoire committee consisted of those members of the advisory committee who wished to serve, plus two members from outside the University. The original committee included me as chair, Dean John Rea, Woszczyk, Steven, and Sam Sniderman. I was pleased to note that Sniderman, who brought a businessman's experience to the committee, approved and promoted our philosophy of recording works that were deemed musically significant but that might not be commercially viable. I recall that in our discussions about what might be considered rather obscure and esoteric repertoire, Sniderman's opinion was that if we thought that it was important to record the music, this was exactly what a university record label should be doing.

On occasion, however, this arts and repertoire committee system could go off the rails, making me long for the good old days of benevolent dictatorship (my own, of course). One such occasion involved a major work by a McGill composer that we had previously recorded with the intention of releasing it on McGill Records. The recording sessions had taken place before the establishment of the committee. The composer was well known internationally and already had a fair number of commercial discs on the market as well as a couple of McGill Records releases. Some members of the committee argued that the composer didn't need another McGill disc and that our money should be spent on the works of composers who had fewer recordings. This argument carried the committee by a single vote (with several abstentions), so the disc was not issued. The composer was, of course, disappointed, but did not really suffer professionally since a foreign label was also interested in his works. We released the master tape to the composer and the recording was issued by the other label. In the end it was the administrative reputation of McGill Records that suffered – to say nothing of the personal animosity created between faculty members. By disregarding the guidelines established in our "Aims and Philosophy" statement, we had turned down a major work by an important McGill composer that had been commissioned and excellently performed by a McGill ensemble – an instructive example of how a committee, through professional jealousy of some members, could subvert even the most carefully constructed policies.

THE EXPANSION OF THE MCGILL RECORDS PROJECT

During the first twelve years McGill Records produced an average of three discs per year. As mentioned above, this had been done almost totally with volunteer labour on the part of the director, producers, recording engineers, tape editors, secretary, et cetera. In January 1988 I made a proposal to the University administration for the expansion of McGill Records to ten discs per year by 1990–91 and up to twenty by 1997–98. To accomplish this I proposed that the University provide interim financing of between $150,000 and $175,000, including a one-time equipment purchase grant of $50,000. According to our projections, this amount could be paid back to the University with interest by 1993 or 1994.

While we would continue to issue recordings by McGill performers and composers, an increasing number of productions would feature other Canadian performers and composers. As stated in the "Aims and Philosophy" document approved in 1988, the criteria for selecting repertoire would continue to emphasize works not otherwise available on disc and works by Canadian composers. All repertoire to be recorded should be judged as musically important, and the selection of performers would emphasize the quality of performance and their demonstrated commitment to a professional performing career.

Recording engineering, editing, and productions supervision would continue on an unpaid voluntary basis for McGill Faculty of Music recordings, but would be paid for other projects. We proposed that projects from outside McGill be charged 50 percent of the productions costs, to be paid by the individuals or institutions proposing the project, and that grants be sought for eligible McGill projects. No royalty payments would be needed for any projects funded by grants that provided for performer's fees. For me, as director of McGill Records, the project would provide funds for replacement of some of my teaching duties. Since we estimated that McGill Records could turn a profit by 1992–93, we suggested that one third of these profits should be divided among the founders of McGill Records, who by that time would have been working on the project without remuneration for more than sixteen years. Finally, to make the whole project viable, we proposed a major effort in advertising and marketing so that projected sales targets could be reached.

By the end of March 1988 the University administration had approved my proposal. A revised budget projected an accumulated deficit peaking at $194,000 by 1991, then rapidly decreasing to produce an annual profit that was to rise to $158,000 by 1998. Needless to say, these rosy projections were not realized! However, the Sound Recording program did benefit from the $50,000 capital equipment grant, which was used to purchase additional microphones, two digital recorders, a digital editing system, and various other pieces of equipment.

Since I left McGill in the summer of 1990 to take a position at the University of Toronto, I was only able to oversee the first two years of the expanded McGill Records project. However, I am certain that we were not meeting our projections for either the number of discs produced or the volume of sales expected. The number of outside projects was much smaller than anticipated. Grant money from agencies such as the Canada Council and the provincial arts councils was limited, and there were many competing applications. Individual artists were often most interested in recording standard repertoire, and performers from other educational institutions may have preferred to have discs issued by an organization other than a competing music school. In the early years of compact disc production, sales were brisk as people built up their collections of CDs, but it didn't take long for initial buying enthusiasm to wear down; as CD production expanded, prices dropped, with the result that the price we could charge for a disc was less than we had projected back in 1988. Lower prices, combined with the limited market for the kind of music we produced, meant that our income was considerably less than projected. In retrospect, it was undoubtedly naïve to believe that such a project could be self-sustaining, let alone actually make a profit.

THE VIABILITY OF A UNIVERSITY RECORD LABEL

McGill Records succeeded in its initial phase due to a number of factors. First, there were a number of staff members who had the expertise and interest to devote considerable time to the project. Second, the Faculty had a significant number of composers and performers who were producing music that was worth recording. Third, the Faculty also had, or was in the process of acquiring, the space and equipment necessary for doing the recording and producing master tapes. Finally, the University administration was sympathetic to the Faculty of Music in general and to McGill Records in particular. They permitted the use of University funds to start the project and advanced further funds for an attempted expansion. McGill Records was also able to use the University's translation and publications services without charge to prepare record jackets and labels for printing, and postage for direct-mail marketing was also paid by the University. In retrospect, I also think that the particular historical phase of development of the McGill Faculty of Music' was important to the success of McGill Records. The staff was, for the most part, relatively young and ambitious. The Faculty had grown in one short decade from a small, rather insignificant institution to one that wanted to make its mark on the national scene. In general, the Faculty saw McGill Records as a useful means of attracting good students and promoting both individual careers and the renown of the institution.

The importance of the particular historical phase of the institution was also evident when I was Dean of Music at the University of Toronto in the 1990s. At that time, the Toronto Faculty of Music certainly saw itself as the premier music school in the country, but it had an aging staff, many of whom were within a decade of retirement. Most senior staff felt that the emphasis should be placed on traditional and academic music disciplines, and there was an antipathy towards technologically oriented programs. In those times of budget cutbacks and academic staff reductions, the appetite for new ventures was modest. Towards the end of my term, however, we did build a modest digital recording studio in two rooms in the Electroacoustic Music Studio complex and started an undergraduate course in music recording. After stepping down from the deanship I suggested to the new dean that I would be willing to work on establishing a record label for the Faculty of Music, but there was no interest. A few other music schools in Canada have produced recordings under their own labels, but none have made the sustained effort required to produce and market the number of recordings necessary to attract national and international attention. To the best of my knowledge, no other university-level music school in Canada has the type of professional recording studios, equipment, and technical expertise that is found at McGill's Faculty of Music.

The model of the university press does not translate directly to a university record company. A book written by a scholar is a solo effort that is then edited and produced by the press. A composer who wants to produce a recording requires musicians to perform the work, an equipped recording studio, skilled recording engineers and editors, as well as specialized art and editorial services for the CD jacket and booklet, all of which must be coordinated and marketed by someone. A university press serves the whole university, or in the case of McGill-Queen's University Press, two universities, but a university record label only serves a single faculty or department – usually a small one comprising perhaps one or two percent of the university's student body.

While a university press expects to obtain some revenue from sales, it is generally assumed that the university will subsidize the operation in various ways. This was certainly true for McGill Records: there was no charge to the McGill Records budget for office space, furniture, or equipment, and the recordings were made in Faculty of Music concert halls, using Faculty equipment, again without charge. As described above, unless a grant was obtained, musicians were not paid directly but they received royalties on sales. Various Faculty professors spent large amounts of time working on recording projects with no payment beyond their regular University salaries. Thus any talk of a profit referred only to the possibility that sales revenue might exceed the limited expenses that McGill Records did have to pay. It was obvious that a record label featuring Canadian compositions and other esoteric music would never make a profit in the business sense of having revenues that exceed all actual expenses. After all, the average disc only sold about 1,000 copies; a few sold 2,000 but only rarely more. In view of all these factors, it seems to me that a university record label may only be viable under rather special and exceptional circumstances such as those I encountered at McGill during the period from 1976 to 1990.

Today, the rapidly changing music recording and distribution technology is also an important issue when considering the viability of a university record label. In the past few decades, finding that their classical catalogues often lose money, major record companies have drastically cut back on classical recordings. Even in the pop music field, mass-market CDs are dying as most young people download and share their music via the Internet. Instead of CDs they use miniature digital music players that can hold up to 1,000 hours of music. While the current generation of adults may still buy CDs, it's doubtful that the next generation will do the same. Given the absurdity of the current situation where multinational media companies are suing fourteen-year-olds for downloading songs from the Internet, new models of marketing and distribution are obviously required. Current proposals include making music and other media a freely available public service, like roads, where everyone pays a small fee or tax that is distributed to media creators. Director Joel Wapnick's proposal to make McGill Records – music, notes, and images – available for free download via the University's website, would seem to be the way of the future.

I believe that whatever success McGill Records had during the period from 1976 to 1990 was due in no small part to the fortunate coincidence of the right staff, students, facilities, and opportunity all coming together at a crucial time in the history of the Faculty of Music. Today, it is widely perceived that the McGill Faculty of Music has become the pre-eminent Canadian music school, and McGill Records probably helped to create and solidify that perception.

NOTES

When I offered to write this brief history of McGill Records from its start in 1976 to 1990 when I left McGill University, I had assumed that I would be able to consult the files from that period, but I discovered that most of these files had either been discarded or misplaced. I have been forced to rely on my memory for much of this account. For any inaccuracies, I apologize and take full responsibility.

1 "Review," *Fanfare* (Nov.–Dec. 2004): 348.

5

The Making of New Music: Composer as Collaborator

James Harley, University of Guelph

A composition and digital music professor at the University of Guelph, JAMES HARLEY is a seasoned composer and new music scholar whose works have been performed throughout Canada, as well as in Belgium, Japan, London, and Warsaw. Adopting an autobiographical stance, he provides a student's perspective on the pedagogical template that fed the compositional curriculum in the late 1980s and the 1990s. Using drafts of his early works, he explores the ways in which the collaborative composer-performer relationships he cultivated while at McGill influenced his musical language and compositional approach. His memories, consequently, often assume the form of lessons learned; but they are as revealing as an aerial photograph, detailing both the internal dynamism of the place as a composite of shared spaces and the myriad paths which, opening out into the larger Montreal new music community and beyond, tie the Faculty to exemplary conductors and musicians who continue to have distinguished careers.

The "ivory tower composer" trope identified by Richard Taruskin and Susan McCLary as underlying the downfall of modern music has its roots in the nineteenth-century image of the willful composer creating music in tortured but inspired isolation.[1] This stereotype has been sustained in the twentieth century by the dissolution of a prevailing common practice and the notion of an "academic" genius who, working alone in the studio, uses the computer to compose and make music unencumbered by the limitations and human realities of performance.[2] While such composers do exist, the examples set by others, such as Luciano Berio, John Cage, Brian Ferneyhough, and Karlheinz Stockhausen, suggest another model: that of a composer who collaborates with performers as mutual partners in an evolving process. The model is not new, of course.[3] Nor is it essential.[4] It has, however, become more important in our times; composers typically are not accomplished performers.[5] New music, for better or worse, has become increasingly a specialty in which composers must rely on the assistance of highly-trained musicians to further their exploration of extended performance techniques, complex rhythms, alternative tuning systems, and so forth. This essay explores the nature of the collaborative relationships that have shaped my own work, focusing in particular on how bonds formed while I was a doctoral student at McGill have influenced my compositional aesthetic and engendered career opportunities.

FORMATIVE EXPERIENCES AS A COMPOSER

My own formation as a composer began in earnest after I completed my undergraduate training at Western Washington University, with a move in 1982 to London, England, where I was able to immerse myself in new music full-time. In addition to attending concerts, lectures, and workshops organized by the Society for the Promotion of New Music (SPNM), I visited the library regularly, studying scores and reading all the books on and by composers that I could find. Since most major music publishers had offices in London, I was also able to browse their new scores. In my creative work, I tried to assimilate everything that I was experiencing and to develop ways of applying the ideas to my own music. As an undergraduate student I had written music primarily for myself and other students to perform. This approach provided good practical experience, but my imagination was to some extent constrained by the limits of our instrumental accomplishment. In London, on the other hand, I was continually exposed to music that had been written for world-class musicians. And, when I had music accepted for readings at the SPNM composer workshops, the musicians were all professional and, for the most part, specialists in performing new music.[6] These opportunities significantly boosted my development as a composer by opening up my imagination to the possibilities of extended performance techniques and instrumental and vocal virtuosity. The isolation from other student colleagues, however, was dangerous. While being able to work with specialists was inspiring, the opportunities were rare and did not sustain ongoing relationships or stimulate occasions needed for continued dialogue and interaction.[7]

CHAOTICS AND THE PATH TO MCGILL, FACULTY OF MUSIC

Following my stay in London, I spent two years, 1985–87, in Paris, where thanks to the Mendelssohn Scholarship of Great Britain, I was able to attend Iannis Xenakis's seminar on aesthetics at the Université de Paris and to work with the UPIC, the graphic computer music system at the Centre d'etudes de mathématique et automatique musicale (CEMAMu). This experience did much to shape my thinking with regard to compositional systems; Xenakis advised me, as he would most others, to study mathematics. I followed his advice but I could not become comfortable using probability functions as a basis for generating music. In 1988, however, while living in Warsaw, Poland, as a postgraduate composition student at the Fryderyk Chopin Academy of Music – and remaining in contact with Xenakis through discussions of a projected Master's thesis under his direction – I came across an article by Douglas Hofstadter on nonlinear functions that exhibited "chaotic" traits.[8] For me, a musician, these traits resembled variations on a theme as the iterative processes unfold in time; a clear coherence underlies the unpredictability of exactly what will come next. This kind of behaviour is very different from random or stochastic distributions, and I found it fascinating.

At this point, I started to work on developing ways to apply nonlinear functions to music composition. I started by mapping the numerical output of my programmable calculator to melodic structures, durational fields, and so forth, but I soon realized a need to develop more sophisticated procedures for generating and mapping compositional data. A state-of-the art computer, I realized, would enable me to print out the results of the function runs, while programming skills would allow me to project the numerical output of these mathematical functions onto musical sets.[9] The pursuit of both led me to the new computer music resources being developed by Bruce Pennycook at McGill University's Faculty of Music. When I began my doctoral studies in September 1988 I had no programming skills whatsoever. The computer music I had produced at CEMAMu in Paris had been carried out on the UPIC, which had a unique graphic interface requiring no knowledge of computer code.[10] In his graduate seminar, Bruce Pennycook advised us to learn the C programming language, as it had become the main development tool in the computer music community.

I embarked on this with the aim of developing my own chaotic composition algorithms, while also working with Pennycook to familiarize myself with Csound, the music programming language that traces its heritage back to the first efforts of Max Mathews to create digital sound.

The first piece I completed utilizing this computer-aided compositional approach, which I eventually titled CHAOTICS, was *Variations* (1989), a solo piano piece organized in sections (variations), each built from a specific resolution of a temporal unit, density (number of voices), degree of rhythmic independence of these voices, registral range, choice of dynamics and articulation, et cetera. I had written the piece for a festival being organized at Western Washington University. The pianist was to be Laurie Hartz, a friend from my undergraduate days. When she saw the score, three or four months before the concert date, she declared, with some consternation, that it would be impossible for her to learn (see example 5.1).

I was somewhat taken aback at this response, as I had taken care to make sure that the music would be playable; that is, that all notes could be played by one pianist with normal-sized hands and fingers. Whether all the notes could be played up to tempo, along with the specified articulations and dynamic graduations, was another matter – something to be striven for. Laurie's response forced me to realize that I had been dwelling for several years in a highly exclusive musical realm – the professional, new-music specialist world – and that I had lost some perspective on what the limitations might be for musicians who did not habitually breathe that rarefied air. I quickly wrote another piece for her, *Piano* (1989), which was based on similar musical principles but was technically much simpler (see example 5.2).[11]

This experience taught me much. While I may have been drawn to exploring the algorithmic compositional applications of chaos theory, and may have shown a predilection for unusual timbral sonorities and complex rhythmic structures, my intent was not to stress people out, but rather to communicate something of value and beauty. The performers are always part of this process, and they need to be able to find the value and beauty in a composition if they are to do their part in conveying the music to the listener.

THE NEW MUSIC COMMUNITY AT MCGILL

Over the next six years, while completing my doctoral degree, I had a number of additional opportunities to collaborate directly with

Example 5.1.
Variations for solo piano, mm. 25–38

Example 5.2.
Piano for solo piano, mm. 1–12

performers, both within the confines of the Faculty of Music and outside of it. In 1989 I was appointed Composer-in-Residence for the McGill Symphony Orchestra. After spending a semester observing the Orchestra prepare symphonies by Bruckner and Mahler (among others from the standard repertoire), I wrote *Windprints for Orchestra* (1989), which was subsequently performed at Pollack Hall in February 1990.[12] While I did not feel that the experience was particularly collaborative,[13] the time spent in rehearsals and sectionals prior to composing provided extremely valuable insight into a variety of practical considerations, including how to avoid rhythmic complexity wherever possible, to limit divisions within the string sections, and to shape the metric scheme to help the conductor articulate formal divisions rather than merely keep time. This experience is reflected in particular in two subsequent scores for symphony orchestra – *Kekula (Memories of a Landscape III)* for the Hamilton Philharmonic (1992), and *Old Rock* for the Oshawa-Durham Symphony (1996).

In the chamber-ensemble context, I had begun to learn the importance of some of these practical considerations in 1987, just before I came to McGill, when Lorraine Vaillancourt conducted my most ambitious ensemble score to that date, *Tapisse(rêve)rie* (1986), at the National Tribune for Young Composers presented by Les Événements de neuf. The music, scored for eleven players, has many layers, moving seamlessly from one instrument or instrument group to another, and using complex rhythms and quarter tones throughout (see example 5.3).

Not only did Vaillancourt give the impression that she understood very well the general intent of the music – the linear unfolding of contrapuntal textures in combination with evolving timbres and harmonies – but she used her limited rehearsal time efficiently to present a convincing performance. As I watched her prioritize details in the score, I realized that, given the constraints on rehearsal time that most ensembles face, I needed to do the same in the composition process in order to effectively convey to the conductor and the performers the most important aspects of the music.[14] As a result, two ensemble scores written in the years immediately following – *Memories of a Landscape II* for thirteen strings (1988) and *Neue Bilder* (1991) for eight players (1991) – while equally intricately layered or contrapuntal have proven to be more accessible to musicians, with successful performances in Canada, the United States, Mexico, and Poland.

In 1990, I served as Composer-in-Residence for the McGill Percussion Ensemble, under the direction of Pierre Béluse. As with my residency with the McGill Symphony Orchestra, I attended rehearsals for a semester before embarking on a new piece – this time gaining insight into the logistics of selecting instruments, organizing the placement of players and instruments, and ways of achieving rhythmic precision and dynamic balance, among other things. Having the opportunity to rehearse with the ensemble over a period of several weeks also allowed for dialogue with the performers as they were working on the score, and enabled me to hear and gather my own impressions of the music. Notation is always imperfect, and is even more so when instruments and sonorities cannot be specified with absolute precision. There are always many variables in performance practice, particularly if one is

Example 5.3.
Tapisse(rêve)rie for mixed ensemble, mm. 11–16

working with percussion or exploring extended techniques. In this instance the collaboration allowed me to refine my notation so as to better define the shape and colour of sonorities, fine tune dynamic balance, and determine appropriate tempo and phrasing. *Daring the Wilderness* (1991), for five percussionists (although performed at the premiere by eight players to facilitate rehearsal), was premiered at Pollack Hall in March 1991.

Out of these and other experiences at McGill, I went on to develop close musical relationships with individual performers who were studying there at the same time. One of the most important of these was with pianist Marc Couroux, whom I first met in 1990 when he was a soloist on the concert in which my *Windprints* was premiered. His interest in new music quickly became apparent, and he agreed to give the long delayed first performance of my *Variations* for solo piano at a McGill Music Graduate Society event in March 1994. For Couroux, the dauntingly complex rhythms, tempo shifts, layered articulations, and dynamics became part of the music's significant attractions.

Our continued collaboration led to a second piece, *flung loose into the stars* (1995). Couroux advised me to write whatever I wanted in terms of pianistic difficulties, and even to notate the music in a way that made sense structurally (where the contrapuntal strands of the texture could be differentiated) rather than in a way to facilitate performance (see example 5.4).[15] This advice proved highly liberating, enabling me to work out the musical conception of the piece without struggling with notational issues at the same time. The work is built from eight voices shown clearly at the beginning of the score (the open note heads indicate a second voice on each of the four staves). The score does not indicate how the pianist is to play these interweaving strands (voices often cross), but it does show the linear, polyphonic origins of the music. It is not that the score is not fully notated; rather in the first half, the music takes the performer along a path of gradually increasing speed that goes far beyond what would seem possible (at its most dense approaching forty notes per second). Prolonged experience with the work makes it possible to play more of it accurately. This is obviously a risky strategy requiring a strong sense of trust on the part of both composer and performer. Couroux has performed *flung loose into the stars* numerous times over a period of several years in an ongoing relationship with the music.[16] I have, however, subsequently used his initial learning experiences to prepare a performance version of the score for the benefit of other interested pianists.

Example 5.4.
flung loose into the stars, beats 1–47

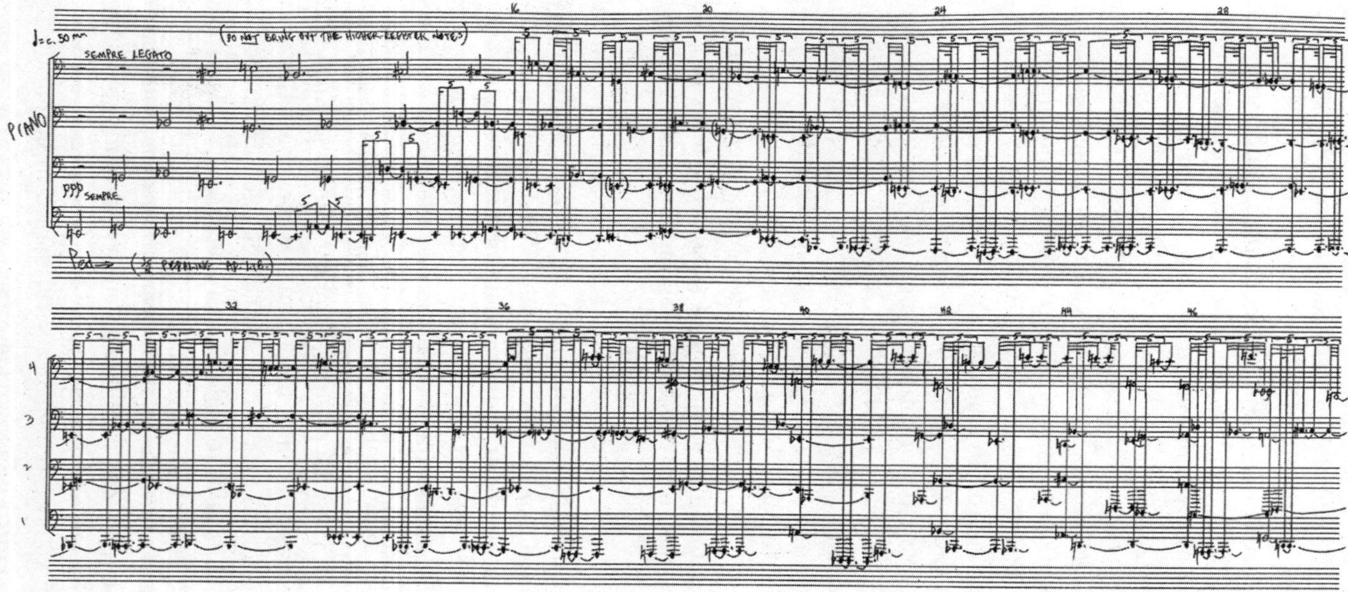

I first met percussionist D'Arcy Gray in 1990 during my residency with the McGill Percussion Ensemble. Gray and I were both involved with GEMS (Group of the Electronic Music Studio) during that time, and we discovered a shared interest in live electronic music.[17] His participation in a concert of music by Iannis Xenakis that I organized in April 1993 gave us opportunities to discuss issues relating to the performance of that difficult repertoire. Later, when he was director of the McGill Percussion Ensemble, he premiered two other percussion ensemble works of mine: *Tracings* (1988) for percussion trio and *Wine of Dragons* (1994) for nine players.

In 2001 Gray suggested that we do an interactive work for solo percussion and electronics. When our proposal was accepted for the 2002 Percussive Arts Society International Convention in Nashville, we set to work. *Chaotics* (2002) turned out to be one of my most collaborative works, as I knew Gray well enough to have confidence in his abilities to do more than just perform the notes. First, I gave Gray a series of rhythmic patterns that I had generated using my CHAOTICS algorithm. He recorded them as a series of sound files. I then used the recorded patterns as input for a Max/MSP patch I designed to re-sample and loop the audio. The output of this patch was recorded to CD for use in performance. In concert, the soloist plays the original patterns on a set of instruments and is free to change tempo, repeat *ad libitum*, impose dynamic changes, and switch the order of patterns. The live sounds, along with the prepared materials on CD, are sent into a second signal-processing patch on the computer, which granulates and vocodes the input. This processed sound is then mixed with the incoming signals (both live and pre-recorded) and sent to the house sound system. This design permitted Gray to perform the piece all on his own if a reliable partner at the console/computer was not available. (He has performed *Chaotics* on tour as far away as Brazil). It is perhaps surprising that such an idiosyncratically collaborative work as this should have been convincingly presented by a number of other percussionists over the past few years. I believe that the positive energy produced through creative cooperation finds its way into a work to be communicated beyond the immediate situation of the music's genesis.

In the summer of 1991 I was fortunate to be able to spend a period of time in residency at the Banff Centre. While there, I met violist Laura Wilcox and pianist Brigitte Poulin. As it turned out, both were in the process of moving to Montreal; Wilcox became a graduate student in performance at McGill that fall, and like me, also became a member of GEMS. The following year, I embarked on a new piece for viola and piano, *Here the Bird* (1993). I was particularly interested in exploring extended sonorities, microtones, and an extreme range of dynamics. The balance between the performers was critical to convey both the fragility and the violence of the music, and it was very productive for me (and for them) to be able to rehearse together a number of times. I was also able to explore with Wilcox the range of sonorities possible on the viola by means of adjusting bow pressure and vertical placement on the strings. The feedback I was able to pass along to them over the course of several performances was also an important part of the music-making process for us all.[18]

THE NEW MUSIC COMMUNITY IN MONTREAL

The larger new music community in Montreal has also been a source of lasting relationships and compositional opportunities that have shaped my development. When I moved to Montreal in 1988, I became involved in the Société des concerts alternatifs du Québec (SCAQ, renamed Codes d'accès in 1992), whose mandate is to present the music of young local composers performed by young local performers; I served on the conseil d'administration during 1992–93. Notice generated by performances of my music through SCAQ led in 1990 to a commission from the Société de musique contemporain à Québec (SMCQ) – *Étude pour une fête (Jazz II)* (1991). Scored for six players, it is primarily a study of rhythm and meter in which rhythmic patterns constantly shift, with only occasional repetitions (see example 5.5a).

Since the conductor plays an integral role in conveying musical structure and holding it all together, I worked extensively with conductor Véronique Lacroix as she prepared for rehearsals, discussing performance problems presented by the rapidly shifting meters and underlying pulse. When the piece was to be performed again, our discussions helped me to revise the score by simplifying notation so as to not compromise musical intent. As shown in example 5.5b, the revision lessens the rapidity of the changing pulse or meter without changing any other musical details. I have since collaborated with Lacroix on two commissions for her own group, the Ensemble contemporain de Montréal (ECM). *N(ouvelle)aissance* (1994), a work for chamber orchestra, utilizes microtones and a wide variety of extended performance techniques as well as layered and occasionally unsynchronized rhythms (see example 5.6). My earlier experiences working with Lacroix (and with Vaillancourt) made it much easier for me to create a score using as efficient a notation scheme as possible.[19]

Example 5.5.
Étude pour une fête (Jazz II) for mixed ensemble, mm. 1–19
(a) original score

Example 5.5. (*Continued*)
(b) revised score

Example 5.6.
N(ouvelle)aissance, mm. 12–16

The second commission, *Cachée* (2001) for guitar and cello with solo dancer, was completed in collaboration with the Van Grim de corps secrets dance company. The main challenge was to create a score that could be performed by the musicians onstage with the recumbent lighting and staging concerns required by the dance.

In 1992 an invitation from Philippe Keyser, director of the Big Band at CÉGEP de Saint-Laurent, also allowed me to extend my musical horizons. Although I had been very much involved in the jazz scene as an undergraduate, I had largely put jazz aside when I moved to Europe and became more and more immersed in notated new music. When Keyser expressed an interest in working on experimental repertoire, I dug out two progressive big band pieces from my earlier jazz days that had not been performed much.[20] These scores involve directed group improvisation, clusters, registral extremes, stylistic collages, and more. When I first went to see Keyser's students perform this music, I was amazed at the ensemble's precision, musicality, and willingness to experiment, and at their obvious enthusiasm for what was for them a completely new style of music. Earlier experiences presenting these scores to jazz musicians in London had been frustrating, given their unfamiliarity with the experimental idiom in which I was working, which combined jazz-style improvisation with avant-garde composition techniques. The resistance I encountered at that time was the main reason I had put the scores away and turned my attention to other concerns.

When Keyser went on to create his own ensemble, Kappa, he asked me to write a new piece for big band. I was reticent, not having had much involvement with jazz for about fifteen years, but knowing his dedication and his interest in all forms of new music, I was intrigued. Since improvisation and indeterminacy in a score implies, to me at least, a high degree of collaboration between the composer and the musicians, I was interested in reconsidering the relationships between notation, the composer's need to direct, and the performers' freedom of expression, and in finding ways to creatively address these issues. *bien serré* (1999), a work for sixteen players, turned out to be one of my most ambitious compositions. The music is highly structured with a fixed temporal plan, but there is also a great deal of controlled indeterminacy built into the score, ranging from solo improvisations using a given "mode" to free passages for the whole ensemble. For the musicians, the most difficult aspect of the score was the layered textures, sometimes with many strands unfolding simultaneously (see example 5.7).

Example 5.7.
bien serré for jazz ensemble, mm. 405–9

One layer may be pulse oriented, another arrhythmic, and yet another freely improvised. Kappa rehearsed for five months before the premiere, and the musicians' dedication was truly impressive. The group performed *bien serré* a number of times and later made a studio recording for CD release. This musical relationship has continued with a second commission, *KappaMusik* (2002), a work for twelve players that was premiered at the Open Ears Festival in 2003. This ongoing musical relationship has led me to conceive of music in ways that allow members of the ensemble to contribute new sonorities (especially through the use of electronic instruments) without compromising my conception of the music.

BEYOND MCGILL AND MONTREAL

After leaving Montreal in 1995, I spent a year teaching composition at Wilfrid Laurier University in Waterloo, Ontario. During that year, I worked very closely with Dianne Aitken (flute) and Trevor Tureski (percussion) on a new piece for bass flute and percussion, entitled *Tyee* (1995). The bass flute can produce multiphonics relatively easily, and I rehearsed with Aitken to fix a set of these sounds that would be consistent and reliable in performance. With Tureski we discussed possibilities for expanding the sonic possibilities of his instrument collection, including the construction of a unique marimba with non-equal-tempered tuning. The cooperation and involvement of both performers right from the beginning made it possible for me to create a composition that explores a variety of extended techniques. It also helped me to work with flexible notation schemes, knowing that the musicians understood the intent and would be capable of overcoming such issues as rhythmic coordination and dynamic balance.

That same year I also made contact with cellist Paul Pulford, then of the Penderecki String Quartet. A year later we had the opportunity to collaborate on the belated premiere of my chamber cello concerto, *Cuimhneachan Urramach* (1995), which he performed in March 1997 with the Canadian Chamber Ensemble.[21] The music was written but the material for the soloist was designed to take the performer to the edge of possibility, necessitating choices that go beyond what can be conveyed through notation. By working with Pulford, I was able to reassess certain rhythmically intricate passages, primarily in the extreme high register, where quick changes of fingering are impossible to execute with precision because the physical distance between notes is so small. When the opportunity for a second performance arose – this time with Simon Turner (then a graduate student in performance at McGill) and the McGill Contemporary Music Ensemble (CME) conducted by Denys Bouliane – I took the occasion to revise parts of the music to make the work more effective, primarily by delaying the ascent to the highest register until a later point, which heightens the drama and eases the difficulties for the soloist without lessening the musical or expressive impact of the passages involved. This performance at McGill was the first of many return visits to Montreal, as I continue friendships established while at McGill and forge new relationships with musicians in other places.[22]

CONCLUSION

The standard repertoire is replete with music written for particular musicians who have specific abilities and qualities. The same is true of new music. The connection between composers and performers is necessary and even obvious but it is often difficult for composers of new music who are drawn to innovative compositional ideas and interested in exploring the margins of accepted performance practice to find sympathetic and experienced musicians to share the journey. It is no help that the general public considers new music to be largely irrelevant, particularly when that same public demonstrates interest in live music and creative work in other disciplines. My experiences at McGill and in Montreal have proven highly fruitful, allowing me to build on my formative experiences in Europe and to explore the music of my imagination, a world filled out and inspired by collaborative relationships with adventurous performers.

NOTES

1 Richard Taruskin, "How Talented Composers Become Useless," *New York Times*, 10 March 1996); Susan McClary, "Terminal Prestige: The Case of Avant-Garde Music Composition," *Cultural Critique* 12 (1989): 57–81.

2 Cf., Milton Babbitt, "The Composer as Specialist," in *The Collected Essays of Milton Babbitt*, ed. M. Babbitt, S. Peles, et al. (Princeton: Princeton University Press, 2003), 48–54. This article was originally published in 1958 in *High Fidelity* as "Who Cares If You Listen," a more provocative title provided by the editors of the journal.

3 Gustav Mahler, for example, could not have written his incredibly detailed and refined orchestral scores without his deep experience as a conductor.

4 As I show in *Xenakis: His Life in Music* (New York: Routledge, 2004), for example, Xenakis had virtually no formal training as a performer, but became one of the most important composers of the twentieth century.

5 Nonetheless, a number of composers are also active as musicians, including Pierre Boulez, Heinz Hollinger, and Frederick Rzewski. Most of them, from Igor Stravinsky on, have tended to specialize in performing their own scores.

6 These works include *Soft Morning* (1983), for solo soprano, performed by Jane Manning; *singing a silence of stone* (1983), for soprano, harp, and two percussion, performed by the Nash Ensemble; *Stillness Dancing* (1984), for eleven players, performed by Lontano with conductor Odaline de la Martinez; and *Prelude (Under the Thin Rainfall)* (1985), for six players, performed by Circle with conductor Gregory Rose.

7 One exception to this was an on-going musical friendship with flutist Nancy Ruffer, for whom I wrote an ambitious work for flute/bass flute and tape, *Per Foramen Acus Transire* (1987). She recorded it for Metier Records in 2000.

8 Douglas Hofstadter, "Mathematical Chaos and Strange Attractors," in *Metamagical Themas: Questing for the Essence of Mind and Pattern* (New York: Basic Books, 1985), 364–95.

9 Cf., James Harley, "Generative Processes in Algorithmic Composition: Chaos and Music," *Leonardo* 28/3 (1995): 221–4.

10 Cf., Gérard Marino, Marie-Hélène Serra, and Jean-Michel Raczinski, "The UPIC System: Origins and Innovations," *Perspectives of New Music* 31/1 (1993): 258–69.

11 I myself, even though no longer a dedicated practicing pianist, performed *Piano* at a GEMS concert at McGill in February 1993.

12 *Windprints* was awarded a prize in the first Witold Lutoslawski International Composers Competition and was performed by the National Philharmonic of Warsaw, conducted by Kazimierz Kord, in April 1990.

13 Symphony orchestras, even within educational institutions, tend to follow a corporate model with a focus on product and marketing. Creative collaboration with living composers does not easily fit into this scenario.

14 It was gratifying that Vaillancourt choose to return to this score in 1996, performing it with Nouvel ensemble moderne in Montreal, Belgium, and Japan.

15 Couroux and I discussed some of these issues in a lecture-recital on *flung loose into the stars* at the 1999 conference of the Canadian University Music Society at Bishop's University, 10 June 1999.

16 Couroux has performed a number of my chamber works, and also commissioned a solo work, *Édifices (naturels)* (2000), which was broadcast in March 2000 by Ensemble Kore (a group that he co-founded).

17 GEMS, long directed by alcides lanza (and co-directed by Bruce Pennycook during the time that I was involved in it), is a good model for collaborative new music-making. Group members are graduate students, both composers and performers, and concerts are produced collectively. Friendships formed in GEMS have continued long beyond direct participation in the group's activities.

18 Brigitte Poulin has also performed my later work *Épanoui* (1995) for flute, cello, and piano on numerous occasions with Trio Phoenix, as well as my more recent solo piano work, *Édifices (naturels)* (2000), including a performance on her doctoral recital at l'Université de Montreal.

19 ECM performed *N(ouvelle)aissance* on a tour of Quebec and again two years later on a tour of the island of Montreal.

20 *Sabbath* (1981) and *The Tail of Pinky Oozegreen and the Mossbrains* (1983), both scored for big band.

21 *Cuimhneachan Urramach* was commissioned by Codes d'accès in Montreal for cellist Claude Lamothe and the Belgian ensemble, Champ d'action. In the event Lamothe decided he was not prepared to learn the piece and canceled the premiere intended for the Musiques échange festival in March 1996 in Montreal.

22 Examples include Marco Parisotto (Oshawa-Durham Symphony Orchestra), Elizabeth McNutt (Boulder, Colorado), Duo Kovalis (Edmonton/Montreal), NUMUS (Waterloo), Transit Festival (Belgium).

6

From Mixed Up to Mixin' It Up: Evolving Paradigms in Electronic Music Performance Practice

Laurie Radford, City University, London, England

While completing his doctoral studies (1992–97), composer LAURIE RADFORD was also teaching electroacoustic music at both McGill and Concordia Universities. It was one step of a continuing journey that has subsequently led him via the University of Alberta from his home province, Manitoba, to City University in London, England. At the same time, his music has been performed internationally and he has won coveted commissions from such esteemed ensembles as the Winnipeg Symphony Orchestra, Le Nouvel ensemble moderne, Esprit Orchestra, Trio Fibonacci, Trio Phoenix, the Molinari String Quartet, and the Penderecki String Quartet. Despite the taxing rigours of such success, however, Radford has on many occasions used travel as an excuse to stop by to share new directions, thoughts, and ideas with old friends. The following chapter represents one such "moment caught in time," it being a paper delivered first at the twentieth anniversary of the EMS (2000) and a few days later at a seminar held in the Marvin Duchow Library. Read in the wake of John Rea's reflections on the passage of time and the difference thirty or thirty-five years can make, it highlights some of the ideologies that composers are currently using to make sense of their ever-changing world and the possibilities for musical expression which that world offers.

Music making and artistic practice in general have undergone fundamental changes over the past half-century. Radical shifts in strategies for creating, presenting, and receiving have accompanied the introduction of new techniques and tools that facilitate innovative approaches to these actions and reactions. Voluminous and readily available documents of image and sound are plied, prodded, and mixed together to reflect the world's diverse cultures forcibly compressed by ubiquitous communication technologies. Methods for cultural appropriation of the aural and visual and the use of tools expressly created to serve and develop these methods have become common fare and are widely disseminated. A social impetus to engage in sound gathering and assembling has developed and has given rise to a new instrumentarium that, in its turn, has led to new artistic actions and objectives.

The present discussion will highlight and evaluate current directions in technological and artistic development involved in a global mixing of sounds. This activity is predominantly concentrated, given the technical means that it affords, in the many varieties and subgenres of electronic music that have ebbed and flowed over the past fifty or more years. We will consider several definitions for the term and concept of the "mix" in sound and music making. The evolving instrumentarium and attendant performance practice arising from the technique of "mixing," in a broad sense, will be discussed in the light of current trends towards an equalization of acoustic and electroacoustic performance practices.

The concept of the "mix" will also be evaluated within the framework of François Delalande's proposal of a threefold paradigm of present-day music making. Delalande proposes that current music practices may be understood through the paradigms of oral tradition, scored or written music, and electroacoustic music. Through reference to the work of Jacques Attali, a fourth paradigm is proposed, in which an emerging cultural imperative to "mix" and "remix" the sounds and images of the world erases the historic and aesthetic boundaries distinguishing Delalande's paradigms. Reference and context for this discussion are provided by the activities of the GEMS new music ensemble of McGill University, of which I was a member during the 1980s. The activities of GEMS exemplify the ongoing tendencies in electronic music performance practice towards an integration of a broad field of sound sources and instrumental forces.

MOTIVATIONS

Change takes place in a context, both personal and social. My alma mater, McGill University (Montreal), continues to act as a hub for significant activity and research in music and technology and will serve here as both a point of departure and an underlying context for a discussion of recent changes in the concepts and tools of music making. GEMS was founded in 1982 when a number of students at McGill University's Faculty of Music felt the need to explore the possibilities of combining contemporary concert music performance and evolving electroacoustic music practices. It seemed inevitable for these young composers and performers that the parallel innovations and investigations of instrumental composition and electronic studio production would converge into a unified practice of invention and performance.

I traversed Canada from west to east, and arrived in Montreal shortly after GEMS was founded. From its inception the rehearsal and performance atmosphere of GEMS neutralized the seemingly incompatible domains of traditional acoustic instrument practice, carefully sculpted studio-based audio work, and real-time electronic transformation of sounds in performance. Sound was sound and by extension was a source for music making regardless of its origin. GEMS explored improvisation, experiments with live electronics, and the processing of instrumentalists in performance, the combination of carefully crafted electroacoustic studio work with the temporal exigencies and acoustic realities of performance, sound poetry, and the theatrical element which is at the root of all concert performance. A belief arose from these experiences that any combination of sound-generating instruments and modes of sound production was credible; that it was a normative and necessary point of departure in contemporary performance practice to seek out and develop these types of combination. This experiment in mixing together modes of collective creation, combining studio and stage, and confounding composer and performer proved an accurate barometer of a much broader inclination in music and, in fact, most arts practices, to cross and erase categorical lines, to seek out the treasures of the impure and the hybrid, to draw upon the delightful and bewildering mixture of pan-global cultural ingredients.

Music does not appear out of thin air. More often than not, developments in music have been based upon styles, materials, and concepts of previous musical activities, adopted and adapted in part or in whole. Classical concert music experimented with quotation and pastiche during the 1960s and 1970s as a way to relieve the restrictions of serial procedures and reintroduce a broader range of languages and concepts. At the same time, after several decades of somewhat peripheral, experimental activities of *musique concrète* and electronic music, dance-oriented popular music began to develop strategies of production that either incorporated or were entirely based upon the mixing of fragments of previously recorded music. The distinguishing factor in this development was the use of the audio recording, the fixed document of music performance. Audio recordings served as fundamental material for further musical production, as building blocks, often in unmodified fashion, for a musical activity that employed it almost exclusively as "object."

The introduction of commercial audio products, such as samplers and computer-based audio recording and sound-transformation systems in the 1980s, provided readily-available tools for the application of a broad approach to "mixing" music and sound, from the traditional multi-channel audio mix to the automated remixing of components of pre-recorded audio documents. This inclination to mix readily available sights and sounds and the development of tools to facilitate this activity have continued unabated. It has now become the norm in many areas of popular music and has crossed the borders into world music, jazz, and experimental concert music. It has staked a substantial claim in the concert hall, the cinema, the radio wave, automobile, and earbud.

CONCEPT AND PRACTICE

A study of current sound and music practices involving the appropriation and mixing of audio recordings requires several lines of investigation that inevitably criss-cross and exchange. On one hand, the new approach to sound and music making has developed in a period that culturally and historically reaches towards the future and back into the past for materials and motivation. The weight of historical and cultural documents and the imperative to evaluate and come to terms with the meaning and ramifications of preceding actions and production has given rise to a variety of techniques and concepts, not the least of which has been the permutation and re-contextualization of unmodified audio and visual objects.

At the same time, this approach to the appropriation and use of the cultural object is fuelled and facilitated by the invention and development of new tools that have given birth to new modes of conceptualization, presentation, and reception, as well as the more obvious developments in the practices of finding, making, sounding, and showing. There is a reciprocal dynamic at work here between social intention and technical facilitation. We will first turn our attention to changes in the tools and instruments of music making, the agents of mediation that have pried open the past and promised the future.

THE CONTEMPORARY INSTRUMENTARIUM

Technologies born of a particular need in turn bring about changes in their maker and their maker's world. Artists-as-makers routinely sift through an array of technologies, old and new, in pursuit of the tools most appropriate for the task at hand with which to cradle and release their expressive intentions. Composers and sound artists working over the past century have been offered an ever-changing instrumentarium and, in turn, have foreseen and demanded many of these very implements. Confronted with new tools and environments for creation at the beginning of the twenty-first century, the clash of old and new resounds and blurs the accepted paradigms and approaches to music making. Sound is recast as "immaterial pleasure turned commodity,"[1] the composer refitted as archivist and curator, and the auditor reborn as consumer-arranger.

At the heart of recent tendencies towards appropriation and repurposing of existing cultural products are the evolving technical facilities to access, evaluate, fragment, and reshape sound and image documents in powerful and efficient yet relatively simple ways. These types of tools have long been embraced in the solitude of the sound and image studio, but recently they have emerged to take their place alongside the traditional instruments of the concert and theatre stage, the presentation mechanisms of the cinema and gallery, and the leisure activities of the family salon and recreation room. Our current instrumentarium, the acknowledged set of tools and instruments available to a given group of practitioners, has grown and been transformed by the introduction and acceptance of these new tools into live performance and music making in a broad sense.

The early 1980s represented a watershed in music technology and electroacoustic music as well as in notation, compositional methodology, and sonic design. The creation of the GEMS ensemble and its eager search for new tools for creation and new modes of performance coincided with the appearance of the first Apple Macintosh personal computer, the Yamaha DX7 synthesizer, the MIDI protocol, and the first commercially available audio editors and sequencers. The criteria of immediacy coupled with sophisticated parametric control, portability married to eloquent performability, were suddenly (if, at the time, only partially) met. The studio transformed into a powerful and manageable "instrument" that offered itself up to the experiments of sound seekers such as the GEMS ensemble and traded its traditional isolation for a place at centre stage.

The symbiotic relationship in the arts between need and tool, between artistic objective and material or conceptual facilitator, proffered by these new instruments accelerated the merging of creative methods, musical styles and performance practices. It empowered individuals to investigate new possibilities for music making and sonic design. Mike Berk has observed that "it's the electronic music studio – instruments, processing gear, and recording and editing equipment – that inaugurates a new sonic paradigm, confounding our standard definitions of what 'instruments,' 'composition,' and 'recording' are."[2] The recording studio, in moving beyond its function as a facility for documenting musical performance, became a place of creation, and moreover a new "instrument" that, once mastered, opened up new, exciting ways of making music and exploring sound. The rarefied electroacoustic studio, the hedonistic pop music studio, and the portable onstage studio developed and expanded into complex, flexible, "playable" instruments.

ACOUSTIC, ELECTROACOUSTIC AND ...

The emergence of audio culture, in which there is a growing emphasis on sound itself in music making, proceeded slowly but steadily throughout the twentieth century, at the margins of musical culture, in cinema, radio and innovative performance practice. The outcome of this development is that sound, from its most skeletal acoustic form to the complexities of a natural soundscape, has become the subject and object of music and sound art making. Defined as much by the media and facilities employed as by any stylistic or historical criteria, one can distinguish three practical approaches in this new technologically-driven musical terrain: acoustic music that employs traditional instruments and the voice; acousmatic audio art that employs every recordable sound, bound for aural scrutiny, repurposing and transformation in the electroacoustic studio; and a "mixed" approach to musical practice that combines and integrates acoustic instruments with electronic instrumentation and signal processing.

Consideration of the last category, the transformative mixing of old and new, acoustic and electroacoustic, brings us to a discussion of the growing inclination towards the alchemical mixing of cultural product as artistic material and experience. It is this activity that was the initial underlying motivation of the composers and instrumentalists of GEMS. Others have, of course, taken up this challenge of mixing media and materials, some of them many years before the fledgling essays of the GEMS collaborators and even many more since then. From the mid-twentieth century to today, composers have combined, in both improvised and scored music, in concert hall, gallery, studio and cyberlink, musicians performing on traditional acoustic instruments with prerecorded sound and electric sound.[3] This partnership has typically been referred to as "mixed" music, acknowledging the novelty of the required performance conditions as well as the resulting sonic product. From Stockhausen's *Kontakte* to Davidovsky's *Syncronisms*, from Denis Smalley's *Clarinet Threads* and alcides lanza's *Interferences III* through Jonathan Harvey's *Bhakti*, the "mixed" work has been the territory of choice for a unique range of expression and material exploration. The "mixed" work finds its home at the intersection of a human performer's skills and the sonic extensions of the electric current, where the transduction of sound and gesture and time lead to a feedback circuit between neuron and voltage, between synapse and data stream.

The acts of making music with an acoustic instrument and with an electronic instrument have until recently remained distinct in most histories and theories. The acoustic-electroacoustic distinction has served to support categories of style, to fortify the differences between music of a popular inclination and that of a more experimental bent, and to distinguish the instruments and practitioners of a revered acoustic tradition from the motley collection of inventions and *bricoleurs* that are identified with the electronic aspirations of the twentieth century.

Viewed from a more neutral perspective, where an instrument or tool for making music is simply that, regardless of the technology involved, the instrumental categories of acoustic and electronic have surprisingly similar histories, traditions, and modes of application and appreciation. Traditional acoustic instruments require idiosyncratic performance strategies that are rigidly fixed for the most part by the physical construction of the instrument. They produce a wide variety of sounds and require an extensive technical and sonic familiarity on the part of composer and performer in order to produce appropriate physical performance actions and resulting sounds. The acceptance or rejection of such instruments by public and practitioner is dependent on social, cultural, and economic factors, resulting in a long line of oddities and wonders left along the developmental roadside. Only a few refined and judiciously selected members remain on stages of the world and in homes alike.

Electroacoustic instruments require similar performance strategies, similar familiarity for employment, and offer a similarly vast and varied (one might too often add naively, or perhaps hopefully, the questionable adjective *limitless*) sonic output. The landfill of rejected electronic instruments is also vast, and today's rapid turnover of new and exciting models and versions of software and hardware interfaces maintains a focus on an equally select and limited number of basic instrumental types. In respect to performance practice today, the only characteristic of much electronic instrumentation – from physically daunting arrays of boxes and cables to the virtual modular studio housed within a single laptop computer – that differs fundamentally from most traditional instruments is its intrinsic malleability and modular character.

Much contemporary electronic music navigates between "two poles of postmodern referentiality and *musique concrète* re-creation."[4] The collapsing and condensation of the classic electroacoustic and recording studios into virtual software instruments wielded by individual laptop artists has provided a degree of flexibility and predictability never before available in live usage of electronic instrumentation. The ubiquitous availability of these tools and instruments has also contributed to a democratization of music making unparalleled since the introduction of the salon piano in the nineteenth century and the affordability of the guitar in the 1960s. The microchip has replaced the guitar as the urban music instrument of choice and serves both "brazen extravaganzas of sonic larceny"[5] and truly innovative sonic creation. It has, in fact, taken its place as the new folk instrument in the home, in the dance club, at laptop jams and at media festivals.

It is not difficult to assert at this point that the past several decades have seen the computer ascend to the rank of instrument proper. The computer operator-composer-programmer-creator has (re)gained the rank of performer for many composers and audio practitioners. The computer is the common source, environment, and tool of conception, design, composition, notation, capture, transformation, and of performance. (It continues its presence in the chain of music-related activities as a tool for analysis, criticism, discourse, and promotion.) It is now functionally integrated in live music practices and provides a unique link between the acts of inception, creation, and re-creation. It is a "mixer" of sound and pulse, of control impulse, and of creative impetus.

The integration of timbre, gesture, and motive has always been a point of departure for a variety of methodologies in electronic music production. Current tools provide accurate and faithful access to these vital parameters and methods during real-time performance. The computer has entered the hallowed instrumentarium as performance instrument, extending and transforming other live instruments with a considerable measure of parametric and temporal control, and, in addition, bringing its own distinct character, both sonically and physically, to the performance act. Recent computer music performance attempts to neutralize all contributing sources via confrontation with the temporal and morphological exigencies of improvisation. It also involves a return to the exploration of a unity of source that speaks to the origins of both the acousmatic and acoustic composition traditions. Instead of a single sound object or motivic cell giving rise to a wealth of sonic progeny and entire sound structures, the act of performance, the sonic and visual attributes of the performers and the place and space of performance are treated as unifying points from which issue all possible sights and sounds, mixed together for transformation and selection in the environment of the software interface.

FROM MIXED UP ...

Use of the term "mixed" to denote a combination of traditional acoustic performance with one of a variety of electroacoustic processes and scenarios continues today. The all-encompassing sonic experiences and activities of ensembles and sonic explorations like GEMS, in addition to fostering a type of music making in the general public that makes less and less distinction between the protocols of instrumental and stylistic combination, has perhaps, in fact, undermined the usefulness and legitimacy of the term "mixed." A much broader and more encompassing range of "mixing" has been embraced and developed in almost every area of sound and music making.

Let us survey a few definitions of this concept of the "mix" and the act of "mixing" in the sound and music domain. A "mix" is:

- the mixture of acoustic instrumental and electroacoustic instrumentation;
- the live mixing of various audio sources in performance (with or without amplification);
- the mixing of discrete tracks of a multi-track recording;

- the mixing of spectral components in search of unique timbral objects;
- the mix of associative (mimetic) and non-associative (abstract) sound materials (*objets sonores*) in classic *musique concrète* and, in fact, in all music which combines these elements, including film and television, neue hörspiel, radio art, etc.;
- a mix of music works for dancing, partying and listening, such as a personalized collection of music that defines an activity, relationship, event, or time;
- the (re)mix or "mash up," essentially a marriage of the age-old technique of variation with the deconstructive, bricolage and assembly techniques of classic *musique concrète* and the virtuosic tool kits and skills of contemporary electronica and dance music;
- a mix of live performance, pre-programmed response and cyberspace connectivity.

Most of these definitions indicate a positive, constructive amassing and combining of disparate elements and concepts for the purposes of creating something new. The classical use of the term "mixed" music would appear to continue to emphasize the combination of disparate sound sources and instruments and belies an entrenched attitude towards the infiltration of electronic instrumentation into the hallowed territory of the acoustic performer. The concept of a mix of acoustic and electroacoustic in performance is now a moot point. The "mix" of familiar instrumental and unfamiliar electronic sounds (or sounds not normally associated with musical expression) frequently explored in recent music may be the only remaining credit for this terminology. Even this is unlikely given that the palette of recorded sounds first daringly plundered by acousmatic and soundscape composers is now the field of choice for popular music, television, and film sound production. Indeed, many contemporary listeners will never hear the original acoustic source of many sounds, only their recording or emulation. Witness the explosion of high-quality, performable instrumental sample collections and the rebirth of virtual versions of acoustic and electroacoustic instruments from yesteryear, not to mention the wealth of indigenous acoustic instruments representative of the cultures of the world, as employed in the sequencer and audio software environments of music and media production. Many people may be familiar with the characteristic sonic signatures of Wurlitzer or Fender Rhodes pianos, or perhaps even the *oud* or *bodhran*, but fewer have seen or heard these instruments in live performance. The usefulness of the term "mixed" music is, for all intents and purposes, excepting historical reflection, exhausted.

We obviously cannot, in our enthusiasm for clarity and definition, completely abandon our use of the adjective "mixed" or the verb "to mix" in our queries about the art and activities of music. It is a fundamental concept and action in many if not most facets of music and production. In the domain of electroacoustic music, for instance, acousmatic performance mixes collected and selected sounds in the spatial confines of the concert experience and compensates for our loss of spatial control through the encoding involved in the recording process. It allows the listener to reach out and explore in a very specific fashion the farthest reaches of the listening space, to engage in a creative re-evaluation of that space via the choreography of sounds provided by the composer-performer mixing real and virtual space. The manipulated faders of the mixing console act like tentacles reaching out to the corners of the performance arena and by extension to the listening receptacle, the listener. The radio artist and broadcaster are the pioneers of this art of mixing material and space. Acousmatic and multimedia performers, as well as installation artists and sonic designers, continue to seek the poetry of moving sounds and of reconfigurable sonic spaces that mix the real and the imaginary.

In experimental electroacoustic music, as with much current electronica and popular music experience, it is the "break with the ideals of real-time interactive playing and natural acoustic space that still govern most music making."[6] In Western classical concert music tradition there has always been a reluctance to rectify the mixture of an amplified with an acoustic signal. Popular music immediately sought a solution to this rift by amplifying all the contributing signals to strengthen the perception of a unity of source. In the classic concept of "mixed" music, the proscenium stage and concert setting maintain, and to a certain extent exacerbate, a sense of division between the acoustic source at the centre and that of the "alien" loudspeakers flanking the performers. The unique character of much early "mixed" work is a result of this collision of two sound worlds: the pure acoustic source, filtered and coloured within the space of the concert hall; and the loudspeaker-distributed "imaginary space"[7] that seeks to mix with the real acoustic space as well as the performing space of the live instrumentalist.

... TO MIX'N IT UP

Modern popular music has enthusiastically embraced the "mixing" of acoustic and electronic, from simple amplification to extensive transformation. This crossroads of the acoustic and electronic signal is the common territory of popular music – or even, one might say, its area of expertise. The characteristic irreverence of popular music towards convention, combined with its eagerness to embrace new technologies, has made it a rich terrain for the exploration of new methods and modes of creativity. In recent popular music production, "instead of a finite entity ... the song is treated as a set of resources that can be endlessly adapted and rearranged ... the notion of music as a process rather than object."[8] Post-rock's ubiquitous strategies of the remix make of all recorded music and sound, as well as the tracks and minuscule audio components of which they are constructed, an endless feeding trough of bits and pieces, materials and resources, decimating concepts of authorship and copyright, the artist-as-star and the composer-as-originator in its wake. In the aesthetics of remixology, "there's no definitive version, no moment of completion; everything remains *in the mix*, always and forever."[9]

Classical music, with its highly developed dialectic between the authority of the musical document and the interpretative traditions that are its lifeblood, has maintained a haughty distance from recording technology and the powerful influences and gravitational pull of the market. Alex Ross, in an article on the effect of recording on music, observes that "throughout the twentieth century, classical musicians and listeners together indulged the fantasy that they were living outside the technological realm. They cultivated an atmosphere of timelessness, of detachment from the ordinary world." Yet, "recording has the unsettling power to transform any kind of music, no matter how unruly or how sublime, into a collectible object."[10]

Considered within a larger historical and sociological context of a "mixed" approach to instrumentation and compositional strategy, the admission of the electronic storehouse of sonic commodities, antiquities, and novelties into a standardized and narrowly defined acoustic instrumentarium appears to parallel the growing need to "mix it up," to "mix" and "remix" the sounds and images of the world. An inclination to appropriate and subsequently reconstitute all aural and visual experiences to date, to make subservient the raw sensorial stores built up in the audio world for more than a century (and in the visual domain for millennia) has become a fundamental operation in the making and remaking of culture. Artists seek out tools and new forms of mediation with which to bend, transform, and unleash these audible and visual markers of people and places, events and spaces. Confronted with overwhelming issues of artistic practice and the ubiquitous facility of appropriation, there is a growing desire to find means by which to release the amassed stockpiles of cultural sights and sounds from the codes and grooves and celluloid that hide their origins and erase their context.

The warehouses of media objects became unbearably full and exceeded their capacity some time in the early to mid-twentieth century. The sum of human experience and production burst its confines, flooding us with the fruits of countless soundings and sightings. The response was an entirely new genre of music that "assembled itself from the disregarded and degraded pop-culture detritus that the mainstream considered passé, disposable."[11] The objective of this music (and much digital art in general) is the exploration of deracination, fragmentation, and permutation. The software environments at the centre of much of this type of artistic creation, either literally or as models for creative methodology, "make it 'natural' to follow a different logic – that of selection ... with a model of authorship as selection from libraries of predefined objects."[12]

Digital stockpiles nourish the artist in search of material and conceptual sustenance; but they also feed one of the most widespread contemporary addictions: the collecting and gathering that afflicts a consumer lust for more and more of everything. This (re)turn towards a state of hunting and gathering, of foraging amongst the testimonies of absolutely every experience (witness the recent blog and video log phenomena, not to mention reality television!) belies a primal belief that these readily available sources of sound and sight offer (perhaps even guarantee?) a path to the mysteries and rewards of the creative act; that the transcendence associated with this act is somehow equivalent with the culture industry's feverish objectives of provision: the purchase of the complete human experience of our choice. Perhaps the destination of this "archivalism" is Arthur Kroker's "monstrous hybrids" and "digital recombinant culture"[13] where "the creation of a new music [is] out of shards of reified sound, an alchemical liberation of the magic trapped inside dead commodities."[14]

A recent advertisement for a commercial software product that facilitates the mixing of audio samples and recordings announced: "Be a pro musician. Or, just sound like one." The materials for creation are front-racked and sold at bargain-basement prices. The tools with which to sculpt these objects, with which to bend and refashion them into a highly convincing semblance of artistic expression, are but a purchase away. Media theorist Lev Manovitch observes that "by encoding the operations of selection and combination into the very interfaces of authoring and editing software, new media 'legitimizes' them" and that "rather than assembling more media recordings of reality, culture is now busy reworking, recombining and analyzing already accumulated media material."[15] Every object, both real and virtual, has now become not only a pawn in the age-old quest for longevity, the pursuit of the eternal manifest in that which we can hold, but also the object of cultural imperative, the mad hoarding and committing to ownership of every sensorial event.

The recent incarnation of the "mix" provides an ever-replenishable commodity for "a culture based on systematic incorporation of the recombinant production of media objects that are abstracted, layered, and infinitely customizable."[16] A cut-and-paste lifestyle is reflected by a cultural product based on appropriation (conscious or otherwise) and reconstitution, re-permutation, reassignment of the sights and sounds of the past, present, and imagined future, housed in a numeric code that equalizes the imprint of all sensorial experience, drawing upon digital catalogues, datascapes,[17] shuffleverses[18] and ring-tone repositories.

An existing abundance of readily accessible technologies allows and invites everyone to experiment with the concept of the "mix," with a global mixture of musics. From the multi-LP record changer of a bygone era through the multi-CD changer, to the digital play list and MP3 player, there is both genuine and invested interest at all levels of society in what people *can* or *will* do given pre-existing materials and the tools to reassemble them. From the microcosm of Stockhausen's *Tonmixtür* and DJ Spooky's remixes of Xenakis and Boulez to the global übermixes of squadrons of looping laptop and turntable DJ producers, everyone wants a crack at this "mixin'" thing.

Global communications systems have transformed the fervour of radiophonic broadcast from the early twentieth century into the music-blender mixes and podcasting of the twenty-first. From the tinkering and invention of electronic pioneers throughout the twentieth century, to the current "circuit bending" live-coding performances of live electronica, the circle would appear to have been completed. From the heights of ars electronica to the mom and pop show in the rec' room, everyone is mix'n it!

PERFORMANCE PARADIGMS

The work of French musicologist François Delalande exemplifies a renewed direction for musicology that expands the discipline's research towards a serious study of the aesthetics and theories of new music technologies, electroacoustic music, and the audio culture that has arisen and been shaped by current technological products, concepts, and modes of access. Delalande maintains that three paradigms of musical activity co-exist today: oral tradition, scored or written music, and electroacoustic music.[19] Delalande's three paradigms obviously imply a chronology that parallels historical changes in technology and society. There are also certain similarities and differences between one and the other that are important to note. All three involve a variety of approaches to the act of making musical sound where physical input is (either directly or indirectly) transduced into sonic output. A distinction arises between them when one considers the role and method of prescription involved, the code employed to trigger the act of performance. In oral tradition the trigger is memory, spoken word, time, and place. In written music it is the specialized abbreviations and visual symbols for time and effort, for physical precision and temporal shaping that guide the makers of the sounds. A combination of physical intervention, encoded response, and networks of carefully routed and organized impulses and actions are the prescription for the makers of electroacoustic music.

It is tempting to make a correlation between Delalande's three paradigms of music and Jacques Attali's "orders," in which music and musical activity are considered as reflections of a particular social, political, and economic state and, additionally, serve as auguries of future societal and economic development. Attali's "order" of forgetting through sacrifice and ritual equates with Delalande's vocal music of the Middle Ages and Renaissance; the "order" of belief through representation and enactment is that of the instrumental music of the hallowed classic and romantic eras; and the "order" of mass-produced, repetitive music that silences "all other human noises"[20] is that of the recorded and electronic music of the twentieth century. Music is viewed as a tool of power, employed to make one forget, to instill belief, or to force one to succumb in silence.

BEYOND THE MIX ... A NEW PARADIGM

Attali maintains that current musical activities foreshadow a fourth social paradigm and thus secure the role of music as both mirror and prophet of history and societal development. He calls this fourth category "composition," "in which music effects a re-appropriation of time and space."[21] Many of Attali's descriptions of music's role in this present and future "composed" world veer surprisingly close to descriptions of the methods and objectives of composers and musicians working the remix, the mash-up, the mixture of today's self-referential, sampled sonic creations. "Time no longer flows in a linear fashion; sometimes it crystallizes in stable codes *in which everyone's composition is compatible,* sometimes in a multifaceted time in which rhythms, styles, and codes diverge, interdependencies become more burdensome, and rules dissolve."[22]

Following Attali's lead, the author proposes that a fourth paradigm of music and music making has indeed begun to emerge in an environment where the historic, aesthetic, and technological boundaries between Delalande's aforementioned three paradigms of oral, written, and electroaoustic are consciously or unconsciously erased by artists who embrace and concatenate the similarities and the differences of the contemporary instrumentarium. These artists meld, borrow, and transform elements native to each of these paradigms into new methodologies for sound creation, into performance principles that neutralize the divisive instrumentarium of acoustic and electroacoustic, of time-honoured performance practice and new-found technical acuity and skill, that combine the visual codes of the written score, the digital codes of recording and signal processing, and the physical codes of intention and reaction. The resurrection of Attali's *jongleurs,* individuals who build their own instruments, compose with the tools of their time, travel in search of new performance venues and means of distribution, and adapt to the confluence of historical and global styles and practices, are the laptop-wielding members of an audio culture that has shifted the emphasis from "what the music 'means,' [to] how it *works.*"[23]

Audio culture has embraced the modus operandi of its producers, the studio-based and live electronic "techno-rhetoric"[24] of pop culture production. Current practices of electronica produce work that is deemed and perceived as artifact as much as or more so than personal experience. This is Attali's fourth historio-political order, "composition": "a music produced by each individual for himself, for pleasure outside of meaning, usage and exchange."[25] Simon Reynolds acknowledges as much in the inclinations and aspirations of contemporary electronica and electronic dance music.

The physical and electronic encoding and performance practices of Delalande's music paradigms now "mix" together to encompass the physical, tactile precision, and excitement of performance control, the refinement of real-time interaction between all "players" and "instruments" in the broadest sense, the continued extension and exploration of the sonic palette, and the introduction of new venues for performances that usher in new modes of reception. This fourth paradigm of musical practice, equipped with a vast, historically rich, and still expanding instrumentarium, has the potential to unify the places and spaces where disparate concepts can collide, coalesce, and congeal. This was the destination of the activities of the fledgling GEMS ensemble, as its young members probed and prodded a new instrumentarium from the studio towards the concert stage.

Much of our discussion has excitedly veered towards and taken its direction from the media offered and selected for music making today. Gear lust and the upgrade factor of current technologies must of course not preclude in-depth and far-reaching research into applications for these tools perhaps unbeknownst to their inventors. As Douglas Kahn has observed, "the emergence of digital recording, synthesis and transmission, and virtual audio in particular, will fundamentally transform the relationships among sound, technology, and art only if new ways of thinking also emerge."[26] This thinking has begun in earnest, along with overdue attempts at a truly unified theory of music making and instrumental performance practice. The continuing convergence of these energies towards an all-encompassing audio culture will very likely supersede the concept(s) of the "mix" as the legacy of its many trajectories is transformed into a normative activity.

NOTES

1 Jacques Attali, *Noise: The Political Economy of Music* (Minneapolis: University of Minnesota Press, 1992), 4.

2 Mike Berk, "Technology: Analog Fetishes and Digital Futures," in *Modulations: A History of Electronic Music*, ed. Peter Shapiro (New York: Caipirnha Productions, 2000), 199.

3 Joel Chababe, *Electric Sound: The Past and Promise of Electronic Music* (Upper Saddle River, NJ: Prentice Hall, 1997).

4 Simon Reynolds, *Generation Ecstasy: Into the World of Techno and Rave Culture* (New York: Routledge, 1999), 43.

5 Ibid., 42.

6 Ibid., 41.

7 Trevor Wishart, *On Sonic Art* (York: Imagineering Press, 1985).

8 Reynolds, *Generation Ecstasy*, 278

9 Ibid., 281 (emphasis in the original).

10 Ross, "The Record Effect: How Technology Has Transformed the Sound of Music," The Critic at Large, *New Yorker*, 6, no. 6 (2005): 6.

11 Reynolds, *Generation Ecstasy*, 24.

12 Lev Manevitch, *The Language of New Media* (Cambridge, MA: MIT Press, 2001), 129.

13 Arthur Kroker and Michael A. Weinstein, *Data Trash: The Theory of the Virtual Class* (New York: St Martin's Press, 1994), quoted in Reynolds, *Generation Ecstasy*, 45.

14 Reynolds, *Generation Ecstasy*, 47.

15 Manevitch, *The Language*, 130–1

16 Joel Slayton, "Foreword" to Matthew Fuller, *Media Ecologies: Materialist Energies in Art and Technoculture* (Cambridge, MA: MIT Press, 2005), ix.

17 Manevitch, *The Language*, 86.

18 Carl Wilson, "Shufflers versus List Makers," Overtones, *Globe and Mail*, 26 March 2005.

19 François Delalande, *Le Son des musiques: entre technologie et ésthetique* (Paris: Buchet/Chastel, 2001).

20 Attali, *Noise*, 19.

21 Ibid., 147.

22 Ibid., 147 (author's emphasis).

23 Reynolds, *Generation Ecstasy*, 9.

24 Ibid., 49.

25 Ibid., 46

26 Douglas Kahn, "Histories of Sound Once Removed," in *Wireless Imagination: Sound, Radio, and the Avant-Garde*, ed. Douglas Kahn and Gregory Whitehead (Cambridge, MA: MIT Press, 1992), 14.

PART TWO

Composer-Work Studies

Introduction

As at any crossroads, the languages spoken at the Faculty of Music are multiple and in constant evolution at its manifold visitors come and go. The conversation changes depending on the route taken through the building, with the presence of composers as teachers and the openness of the Faculty's institutional infrastructures encouraging chance meetings and casual exchanges that have their own inspirational value for the creative work of composers, conductors, and performers, and for the theoretical model-making and hermeneutical analyses of musicologists and theorists. Yet, like other crossroads, such as an airport or a train station, the conversations have a certain sameness, ultimately revolving around what Edward Casey describes as the "preoccupations of travellers":[1] – where are you coming from and where are you going? The answers are as revealing of place as the languages spoken. To this end, the following composer-work studies may be read not only for the value of their scholarly insights but also for the ways in which the various themes, ideas, and compositions discussed by the different authors recur, resonate, and interact as part of a larger ongoing conversation unfolding in both word and sound. While it would be impossible to convey the richness of that conversation, one thread might begin in the following way:

Bengt Hambræus is remembered by students who had the opportunity to take his now legendary twentieth-century performance-practice seminar as a man forever in search of inter-relationships.[2] His search often began with a fascination for words, not only for what they say but also for the surprises hidden deep within their histories.[3] "Chime," as a noun, means the rim of a cask; an apparatus for striking a bell; the sound produced by a bell; an agreement or accord. To "chime in" means to interrupt the speech of others, usually with an unsolicited opinion. The carillon – a stationary set of chromatically tuned bells in a tower, the first fully automatic or mechanical musical instrument – links technological advances in fourteenth-century watch design to developments in seventeenth- and eighteenth-century organ construction, nineteenth-century musical boxes, and the early twentieth-century "re-producing piano." The word "carillon" stems from the latin *quartern* meaning "by fours." Change ringing is a musical practice that, bound up with the intimacy of moving bodies in a reverberant space, creates music based not on melodies or themes but on methodical variation of the order in which bells are rung. It is a tradition that has remained largely unchanged since its development in the seventeenth century, but some consider it to be the origins of serialism. Hambræus's quest for the seeds of his own modernism as a spiritual and musical disciple of Scriabin took him to Paris in 1969 where, through a series of chance encounters, he discovered the quarter-tone music of Ivan Wyschnegradsky. Four years later, he introduced Bruce Mather to Wyshnegradsky, a meeting that was to have a profound impact on the development of Mather's own compositional voice.[4]

alcides lanza's interest in the tango, like Hambræus's fascination with the sound of bells, is the product of a childhood memory of a distant homeland that has left an indelible mark. For Hambraeus this memory remained silent or unconscious until he came to understand its musical influence later in life through his conception of "music as klang," inspired by hearing his own compositions against the backdrop of Montreal's world musical soundscape.[5] For lanza, the memory has been an explicit one that demands musical exploration, the evolution of his musical language in the early years of his career having focused primarily on technological applications and the development of what he described to musicologist Pamela Jones as an "international" sound. The exploration of that memory has unfolded against the backdrop of the tango achieving world popularity. In 1986, while in Paris receiving recognition for his re-invention of the language of the traditional tango, Argentinean composer Astor Piazzolla, having been told many years earlier by Nadia Boulanger that his voice was not to be found in the new but "in the rhythms of the soles of his feet," noted that the "tango is the sad thought danced."[6] That same year lanza composed *arghanum I*. Four years later at the premiere of *arghanum V*, the virtuosic performance of Joseph Petric, the soloist for whom both works were commissioned, was credited with having "emancipated the accordion from its historical past."[7] Ianza's work, in this sense, can be linked to a series of composer-performer collaborations – dating back to the mid-1970s with the emergence of early music ensembles in Montreal – that used the languages of the new to re-invent instruments once discarded as old.[8]

In *Die klingende Zeit,* Brian Cherney is concerned not so much with distinctions between old and new, past and present, as with the concept of time itself. Like many of his mature works, *Die klingende Zeit* is contemplative in character and is intricately bound with Cherney's memories of sounds and their relationship to time. His former student Neil Middleton explores these memories through Jean-Jacques Nattiez's semiotic theory of musical meaning, moving systematically between the physical "trace" of music as sound and the poetic and aesthetic processes of composer and listener.[9] In 1993, the year Cherney composed this work, Nattiez's theory represented one of the most significant "new" developments in North American musicological discourse. The work could also be heard through the various influences that have shaped Cherney's quest for voice over the years, including Bartók's sustained variation and arch-shaped forms, Ligeti's thick textures and obsession with time counting, particularly with respect to his capacity to develop wholes in which past, present, and future are explicit in every moment, and a cohesive harmonic language inspired by the music of Bruce Mather that, as Neil Middleton recognizes, allows the vertical and horizontal to be structured so that "accord" and "discord" are not merely the product of "chance collisions."[10] Middleton's analysis, in turn, can be heard as part of a continuing internal dialogue initiated in the early 1980s by Montreal composer Claude Vivier's statement that "time is a geometrically variable space in which different planes exist side by side, are intersected and transformed by the marvellous laws of celestial mechanics."[11] This dialogue embraces many of Cherney's earlier works as well as John Rea's *Time and Again* (1987) and *Les Raisons des forces mouvantes* (1984) (a work inspired by the title of a seventeenth-century book on the making of clocks, music boxes, and fountains), Middleton's *Fading Points* (2004), and recent compositions by Rea's former student Veronika Krausas. The emphasis on "sculpted sonic events that seem suspended outside time," in Krausas's works has led percussionist D'Arcy Gray to proclaim that "time has died."[12]

La Princesse blanche (1994), Bruce Mather's only opera to date, stands apart from operas written by McGill composers[13] in that, with the exception of John Rea's re-orchestration of Berg's *Wozzeck* (1995), all the others are bound to the tradition established in 1967 by Harry Somer's and Mavor Moore's *Louis Riel*, a tradition that, framing opera as a quest for identity, uses the artistic rendering of seminal events in the history of Canada to discover heroes and heroines through which we can define our own attributes as a people. La musique – "Naît du silence comme la couleur naît de la nuit" ([music] born of silence is like the colour born of night).[14] The themes of Mather's opera resonate with the preoccupations of the Québécois poets Ann Hébert, Gatien Lapointe, and Saint-Denis Garneau, whose works Mather has also set to music. There is, moreover, a real sense in which the work, while beginning with Rilke's turn-of-the-century play *Die weisse Fürsten*, was literally born of place, the ensemble for which the opera was written, Chants libres, having evolved initially from musical friendships formed within the French new music community in Montreal. Mather had written for and performed with Pauline Vaillancourt before, and the approach of Chants libres to chamber opera made it not a genre of economic necessity using a limited resources (as is often the case in Canada) but an outgrowth of the intricate and intimate relationships of chamber music itself. Interestingly, musicologist Steven Huebner's reading of those relationships as an extension of the symbolist aesthetics of Maeterlinck's "*Théâtre de l'âme*" (theatre of the soul) that initially inspired Rilke resonates with Hambræus's characterization of Mather's music more generally – music that "is increasingly transformed into a spiritual séance, evoking an irrational spirit in infinite space where sonorities float, at times ecstatically."[15]

John Rea describes both *Une Fleur du mal* (1992) and *Alma & Oskar* (1994) as "melodramas from beyond the grave," opening the first scene of the latter with the lines, "But I know that I could never sing again ... except in death." He prefaces *Objets perdus* (1991) with a series of quotes, one of which is from art historian Jacques Barzun: "Music, not being made of objects nor referring to objects, is intangible and ineffable; it can only be ... inhaled by the spirit: the rest is silence." Referring to *Music, according to Aquinas* (2000), Rea speaks about the privileged place of music in the thirteenth-century theologian's thought, remarking that Aquinas even had the foresight to consider quarter tones, a phenomenon generally considered the product of twentieth-century technological developments.[16] The title of his *Schattenwerk* (2003) is a German word that refers to the work and play of shadows, ghosts, and spirits. While each of these observations could be tied to Mather's *La Princesse blanche*, Jérôme Blais's interest in these five works is shaped by the context of the Nova Scotia Music Festival where they were performed in 2003. Bringing together what have typically been considered two distinct aesthetic orientations, his analysis frames Rea's compositional process as a complex dialogue with the history of music, a dialogue in which memory assembles, dismantles, and reconstructs its own past through a constant re-evaluation of history's shifting grounds.

This poetic process recalls Laurie Radford's reference to Attali's "orders of forgetting" (chapter 6) and links Rea's works with those of Denys Bouliane.[17] But for Bouliane, the history, the sense of there being a past, is itself an illusion, an aural mirage in which the shadows and ghostly apparitions recede with each effort to grasp them. Bouliane's perspective shares a close affinity with magic realism and the transformative elements of contemporary Québécois theatre where, as exemplified by the works of Robert Le Page, Larry Tremblay, and others, cultural identity is tied to the sense of a dying language, "une culture perdue dans la nuit des mots" (a culture lost in the darkness of its language).[18] For Bouliane as a second-generation Québécois composer, though, it is more about there never having been a cultural tradition in the first place, as he has no memories of new music from his youth that he can link to a sense of his homeland as a birthright. His compositions, consequently, seem intricately bound up with Baudrillard's notion of simulacrum as the "the generation by models of a real without origins or reality, a hyper-real."[19] And, in the end, Patrick Levesque intimates, it is seemingly "the map that engenders the territory."[20]

NOTES

1 Edward Casey, "How to Get from Space to Place in a Fairly Short Stretch of Time: Phenomenological Prolegomena," in *Senses of Place*, ed. Steven Feld and Keith Basso (New York: School of American Research Press, 1996).

2 See, for example, Per Broman, Nora Engebretsen, and Bo Alphonce, eds., *Crosscurrents and Counterpoints: Offerings in Honor of Bengt Hambraeus* (Gothenburg: University of Gothenburg, 1998).

3 This can be seen even in Bengt Hambræus, *Aspects of Twentieth-Century Performance Practice* (Uppsala: Royal Swedish Academy of Music, 1997).

4 Bruce Mather recounts this story in the liner notes of the recording of *Carillon* performed by Mather with his wife Pierrette LePage on McGill Records. This recording also includes works by Ivan Wyschnegradsky.

5 Per Broman, *Back to the Future: Towards an Aesthetic Theory of Bengt Hambraeus* (Gothenburg: University of Gothenburg, 1999).

6 Gorin, Natalio, *Astor Piazzolla: A Memoir*, trans. Fernando Gonzalez (Portland, Oregon: Amadeus Press, 2001).

7 Courtesy of Joseph Petric from the archives of the Canadian Electronic Music Ensemble. Petric is responsible for commissioning more than forty works for this ensemble and more than 110 for the accordion in general.

8 Other McGill and Montreal composers who have also written specifically for Petric include Bengt Hambræus, Brian Cherney, Mariano Etkin, James Harley, Claude Vivier, Denis Gougeon, and Normand Forget. Another example of the rediscovery of old instruments through the languages of the new can be seen in a series of compositions written for harpsichordist Vivienne Spiteri by John Rea, Brian Cherney, and Bengt Hambræus. Donald Patriquin's revitilization of Jean Carignan's fiddle music as a ballet – capturing and holding that which has been considered to be lost or on the verge of being lost – might also be included in this list. Around the same time, jazz was discovered to have a "history."

9 Jean-Jacques Nattiez, *Music and Discourse: Toward a Semiology of Music* (Princeton: Princeton University Press, 1990).

10 Brian Cherney, email correspondence with Neil Middleton, 1 October 2005. See, also Jacques Desjardins, "Brian Cherney et Bruce Mather: la clairvoyance du compositeur solitaire," *Circuit* 10 (February 1999): 17–28.

11 John Rea refers to this discussion in the program notes for his *Time and Again* (1987). A number of composition students over the years remember hearing the statement on multiple occasions during seminar discussions and personal meetings with John Rea.

12 See, D'Arcy Philip Gray, "Time Has Died: The Music of Veronika Krausas," *Musicworks*, 83 (Summer 2002): 36–41.

13 Operas by McGill composers include István Anhalt's *La Tourangelle* (1975), which is based on the experiences of Marie de l'Incarnation; Bengt Hambræus's *L'oui dire* (1986), which is based on Jacques Cartier; and *Evangelina Revisited*, a recent work by Julian Wachner and Alexis Nouss which is based on Nova Scotia history. *La Tourangelle* was not completed until after Anhalt left McGill and is the first of four works exploring themes relevant to Canadian history and the immigrant's experience of finding voice within Canada's borders. John Rea's children's opera, *The Prisoners Play* (1967), is not included because it was written before he came to McGill.

14 Stage director, Guy Beausoleil, program notes for the re-staging of *La princesse blanche* at McGill in 1998.

15 Bengt Hambræus, *Compositeurs au Québec: Bruce Mather* (Montreal: Canadian Music Centre, 1974).

16 Composer's Forum preceding the first performance of *Music, according to Aquinas*, Vancouver, 2000.

17 The process may also be linked to the works of McGill composer Jean Lesage and Montreal composer Gilles Tremblay.

18 The quote is from Québécois singer/songwriter Gilles Vigneault's "Dans la nuit des mots." For more about magic realism and Québécois contemporary theatre, see Hélène Beauchamp, *Les théâtres de création au Québec, en Acadie, et au Canada français* (Montréal: VLB, 2005).

19 Jean Baudrillard, "The Procession of Simulacra," in *A Postmodern Reader*, ed. Joseph Natoli and Linda Hutcheon (Albany, N.Y.: State University of New York Press, 1993), 343.

20 Ibid.

7

The Lost Recital: An Analysis of Bengt Hambræus' *Carillon for Two Pianos*

Bruce Mather, McGill University

Recently retired from the Faculty of Music, BRUCE MATHER is respected throughout Canada for his work as both composer and pianist. Before coming to McGill University in 1966 he studied at the University of Toronto and at Stanford University, as well as in Paris and Darmstadt where he worked with Darius Milhaud, Olivier Messiaen, and Pierre Boulez, among others. As director of the Contemporary Music Ensemble from 1986 to 1995 he developed a reputation for the detailed attention of his analytic mind and the fine tuning of his musical ear. Hambræus dedicated *Carillon* to Mather and his wife, Pierrette LePage, who also teaches musicianship and ear-training at the Faculty of Music. Mather's analysis of the work here commemorates his friendship with Hambræus and reciprocates the high praise Hambraeus showered on Mather's own music when he described it as "the product of a musician-poet who is aware of the innermost values of the poets he has chosen."

I have always liked the sound of bells and chimes – evident from many of my scores! – and have long been interested in the principles of classic English "Changing Ringing." In *Carillon*, the two pianos placed a great distance from each other, provide that illusion of spatial reverberation which one observes when listening to bells from a tower. In this soundscape of bells, I had a nostalgic vision of some sort of "forgotten recital," similar to the vision of Liszt in his *Valse oubliée*. In my piece, the two musicians try to remember fragments of an earlier repertoire. Thus, my original French title explains itself: "Carillon les cloches, les souvenirs fugitives de quelqùes oeuvres de

Beethoven, Chopin, Scriabin, le récital oublié." The work was finished on 26 July 1974, and is dedicated to my friends Pierrette LePage and Bruce Mather.

Bengt Hambræus[1]

Since the early 1960s composers have often experimented with a collage technique that integrates musical quotations from the past into their music. In many cases, the result is simply a work without stylistic unity, an incoherent "mish-mash." In Bengt Hambræus's *Carillon*, however, the historical quotations emerge in and through a musical environment of bells that is central to the personal language of the composer. The work, as such, is a coherent whole that is both structurally complex and musically expressive.[2] This paper tracks the natural and subtle manner in which the quotations emerge from the bell environment, and, through an analysis of the ways in which the original texts are modified, explores the different relationships established between the quotations and Hambræus's personal language.

INTRODUCTION: SECTIONS 1 TO 4 – ESTABLISHING THE BELL ENVIRONMENT

In the first thirty-six measures of *Carillon* there are no quotations. Instead an environment of imitative ringing bells is created through three basic motives (see example 7.1): motive "a" is formed by two minor ninths in extreme registers; motive "b" is defined by its sixteenth-note rhythm and by its symmetrical design around G. The first four notes of the upper line form a whole-tone sonority: D–F-sharp–A-flat–C. The lower line doubles the upper line in major or minor sixths. The first four notes of the lower line form a dominant seventh chord: F–A–C–E-flat. Motive "c" is a whole-tone chord in which the two tritones – E–B-flat and G-sharp–D – are similar in content to the upper line of motive "b."

The thirty-six measures developing these thematic motives are divided into four sections. In the first section (see example 7.2) the basic rhythm consists of an iambic foot (quarter note, half note) followed by three quarter notes. In measure four, the rhythm of motive "b" is on a repeated note. The second section, mm. 9–14, resonates with motive "a." Again, as seen in example 7.3, the basic rhythm consists of an iambic foot followed by three quarter notes. Motive "a" also dominates the third section, mm. 15–22; although motive "b" appears once and motive "c" is introduced in mm. 19 and 22. On the down beat of m. 15 (see example 7.4a), four middle-register notes – C (doubled with a

Example 7.1.
Motivic construction of bell environment

Example 7.2.
Basic rhythm, mm. 1–8

Example 7.3.
Basic rhythm, 9–14.

Example 7.4.
Section 3
(a) motivic structure, m. 15

(b) basic rhythm, mm. 15–22

Example 7.5.
Motivic structure in relation to underlying basic rhythm, mm. 23–36

major sixth) and B (doubled with a minor sixth) – are added to motive "a." On the second beat of the same measure, a transposed version of motive "b" is stated and then expanded to a density of four, then five notes. Note the elaboration of the basic rhythm in example 7.4b.

The fourth section, mm. 23–36, has three elements: (1) in the middle register motive "c" and then motive "b" are stated ending on B or on G (original position); (2) in the extreme registers motive "a" is heard, as well as (3) a high trill on a perfect twelfth (from m. 29). The rhythmic placement of the first two elements is shown in example 7.5.

ELABORATION OF THE BELL ENVIRONMENT: INTRODUCING THE QUOTATIONS

Having established the bell environment, the remaining sections of the work gradually introduce quotations from various works by Beethoven, Chopin, and Scriabin.

Section 5 (mm. 37–62)

The first brief quotations from Beethoven's Piano Sonata, op. 106 (see example 7.6) appear almost imperceptibly out of the surrounding context. The section starts with bold chords that prepare us for the traditional harmonic language of the quotations. The widely spaced chord in m. 37 opposes the A (with a major tenth) in the bass against a B-flat with a perfect fifth in the high register (see example 7.7a). In m. 39 (see example 7.7b), the chord marked "X" is introduced. This chord is similar to motive "c" with one added note (D), and appears several times in the work. At the end of m. 39, the perfect twelfth trill on F and C, first heard in section 4 (m. 29) returns. Following a brief appearance of motives "c" and "b" in measure 40 (an echo of m. 36), there is a

Example 7.6.
Quotations from Beethoven's Piano Sonata, op. 106

Example 7.7.
Harmonic materials preparing Beethoven quotations
(a) chords in m. 37 and m. 39

(b) relationship between motive "c" and the chord in m. 39

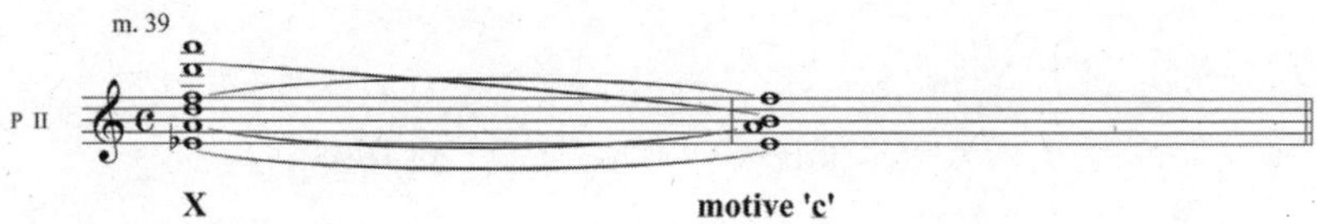

passage in the high register that continues until the end of m. 48. To the F and C of the trill are added major thirds, creating two augmented triads – F–A–C-sharp and C–E–G-sharp – which, articulated in regular eighth notes, rhythmically prepare the first quotation.

In mm. 48–50, there are many upbeat figures with doublings inspired by organ registration. These include the first four notes of motive "b" in major tenths, two superimposed diminished triads, and the first notes of motive "b" doubled a major sixth, major sixth, minor sixth, minor sixth in m. 48 (see example 7.8), as well as the scale passage doubled in major triads in m. 49. The first quotation, m. 50 (see example 7.9a), is disguised by the last interval, a minor third (C–A), instead of the major third of the original (D–B-flat), and by the harmonization in parallel diminished triads (see example 7.6). The continuation of the quotation in m. 51 (see example 7.9b) is even more disguised by modified intervals – G-sharp–A-natural (instead of

Example 7.8.
Section 5, doublings inspired by the organ

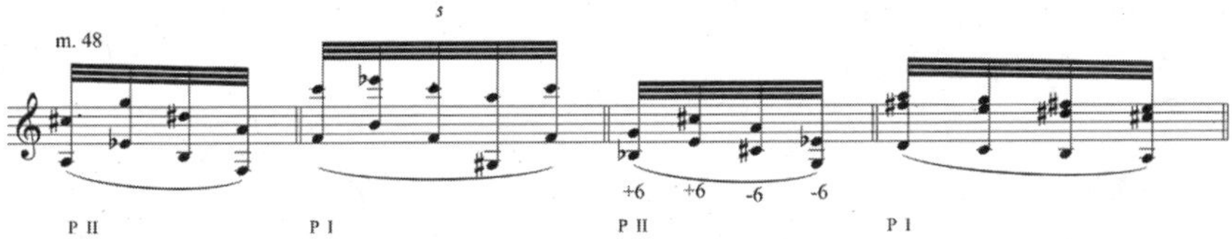

Example 7.9.
Section 5, quotations from Beethoven's Piano Sonata, op. 106

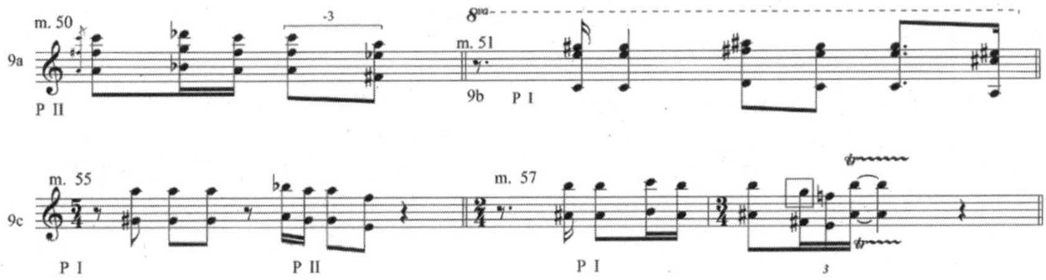

Example 7.10.
Section 6, basic rhythm

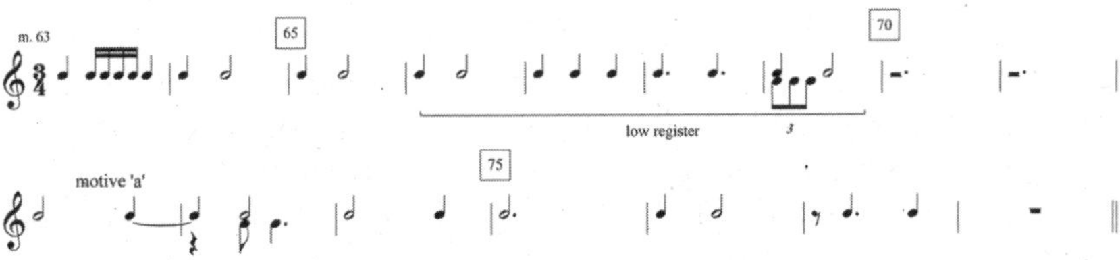

G-natural–A-flat), G-sharp–E-sharp (instead of G-sharp–E-flat) – and by the harmonization in widely spaced augmented triads. In mm. 55–56 (see example 7.9c) it is fused with motive "a" using the doubling of a minor ninth. In the following two measures it is disguised by the ornamentation of the final G articulated on the second half of the first beat in m. 58.

Section 6 (mm. 63–78)

Starting with motives "a" and "b" from the introduction, section 6 has the character of a recapitulation. The basic rhythm is shown in example 7.10. In m. 63, motives "a" amd "b" are present in both pianos. The

Example 7.11.
Section 6, transposition of chords from example 7

upper part of motive "b" is doubled at a minor ninth, and the lower part at a perfect twelfth. Measure 64 is m. 37 transposed down a semitone, except that the original chord from m. 37 (see example 7.7a) is spread over two beats; the major tenth is on the first beat, and the perfect twelfth on the second beat. In a similar manner the three chords of m. 39 are rearranged and transposed in mm. 65–6 (see example 7.11a). The pitch content of the low passage (mm. 66–9) is an ornamentation on C and G doubled at the minor sixth. The inversion of motive "a" – that is, two major sevenths in extreme registers – is introduced in mm. 72–5. From the second beat of m. 76, and overlapping with the beginning of the quotation in m. 79, the classified harmonic elements from mm. 64–66 and before are used to once again seamlessly prepare the harmonic language of the ensuing Beethoven quotations in section 7 (see example 7.11b).

Section 7 (mm. 80–104)

The Beethoven quotations in this section are longer than those in section 5. The first quotation from op. 106 in m. 79 (see example 7.12a and cf. the original in example 7.6) is in augmentation and in D major, instead of the original B-flat major. The second half of the phrase (mm. 82–4) is delayed and appears in D-flat major with slight rhythmic alterations (see example 7.12b). In m. 81 Piano II makes a modulation to D-flat major through the bass notes B-flat and C. In mm. 82–7 Piano II exploits the two tritones of motive "c" – B-flat–E and D–G-sharp, plus an added tritone B–F (see example 7.12a).

Example 7.12.

Section 7, quotations from Beethoven's Piano Sonata, op. 106

(a) quotations from op. 106, mm. 79–88

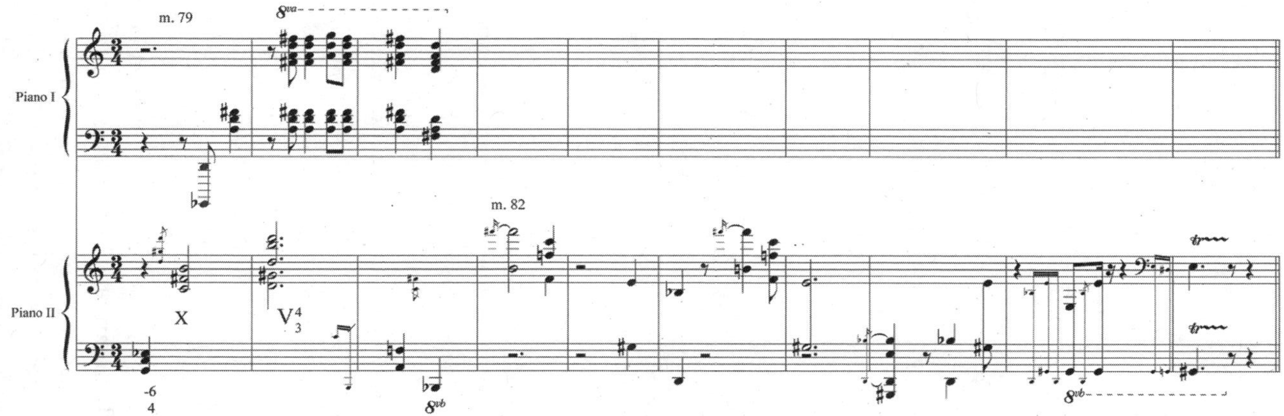

(b) quotation in Piano II (m. 82) and Beethoven's original

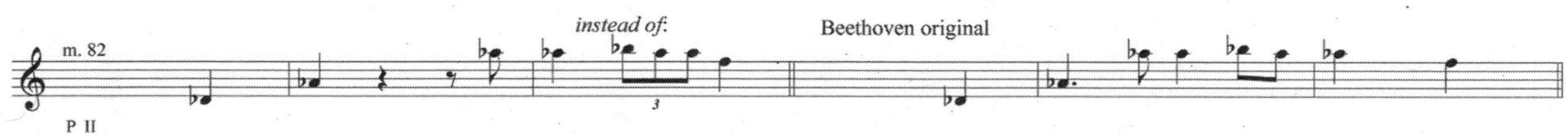

Example 7.13.
Section 7, introduction of quotations from Beethoven's Piano Sonata, op. 111
(a) quotation from op. 111, mm. 88–92

(b) original quotation

The second phrase of the op. 106 quotation at m. 88 (cf. the original in example 7.6, mm. 5–6) is in G major (instead of B-flat major) and is rhythmically augmented with elongations in mm. 88, 90 and 91. These elongations accommodate the insertion of the quotations from op. 111 in mm. 89 and 91 (Piano II) (see example 7.13a, and cf. the original in example 7.13b). At the end of the second beat of m. 92 the quotation is interrupted abruptly. Measures 93–4 contain elements of the op. 111 quotation, namely the diminished seventh chord (m. 93, beat 1), the diminished seventh chord with the trill (m. 93, beat 2), and motive "a" (m. 92, beat 3; m. 93, beats 2–3; m. 94, beat 1). In m. 95 the quotation from the second phrase of op. 106 appears again, this time starting on the downbeat instead of the upbeat and *not* in augmentation. After only six notes it is abruptly interrupted by a "pause" of three measures (mm. 96–8) on the note C, which is introduced by a minor second inversion chord on the first beat of measure 96 (E–A–C). Also appearing during this "pause" (m. 96) is a premonition of the first two chords of a five-chord sequence that will play an important role in section 10 (see example 7.17b).

In m. 99 the quotation attempts to continue in Piano I but hesitates again. Instead of the original rhythm – two eighths followed by a quarter – there is a triplet eighth rest followed by two triplet eighths, followed by a quarter rest, followed by an eighth. The last attack of m. 99 is accompanied by the continuation of the quotation in Piano II. In other words, two successive notes of the quotation are superimposed (see example 7.14). This continuation of the quotation by Piano II (see example 7.13b) stops short of the final note of the phrase and overlaps onto the quotation of the first phrase of op. 106 in augmentation, harmonized in parallel second inversion dominant seventh chords. This, in turn, is superimposed on the op. 111 quotation (m. 102), which is subsequently interrupted by the second phrase of op. 106 quoted in F-sharp major and then in G major. The final chord of the op. 111 quotation is extended through a trill on the diminished seventh which links it to the next section. The three asterisks in example 7.14 identify rhythmic alterations needed for the layering of materials. The last of these alterations is a dephasing of the original rhythm by one sixteenth note.

Section 8 (mm. 104–133)

The trill on E from the diminished seventh chord of the op. 111 quotation acts as a pedal point for the first twenty-three measures of this section. Example 7.15 shows the original melody from Chopin's *Grande valse brillante* and Hambræus's modification of it. As can be seen, there are shifts of tonality to A major in m. 112, a sudden short return to A-flat major at the end of m. 117, and then again to A major in m. 119. There are "pauses" of various lengths (six quarter notes at m. 110, two quarter notes at m. 113, three quarter notes at m. 116, an eighth note in m. 117, and two quarter notes in m. 118). These "pauses" occur at the end of measures (referring to the original) (mm. 110, 113, and 118) or in the middle of measures (mm. 116–17). Some notes of the original are omitted (in m. 109, 122) and some are lengthened (in m. 114 a dotted half replaces a half note; in m. 115 a half note replaces a quarter note). In mm. 117–18, there is an interesting mixture of tonalities in Piano II, first with the right hand in A major and the left hand in A-flat major, and then with hands reversed.

The Chopin quotation repeats in m. 121 but is interrupted two measures later by the Beethoven op. 111 quotation (mm. 123–33; see example 7.16a), but this time, the op. 111 quotation is a major third higher

Example 7.14.
Section 7, superimposed quotations from Beethoven's op. 106 and op. 111

Example 7.15.
Modification of melody from Chopin's *Grande valse brillante*

Example 7.16.
Section 8, Beethoven's Piano Sonata, op. 111 and Chopin modification
(a) quotation from Beethoven's Piano Sonata, op. 111, m. 123

(b) Chopin modification, m. 128

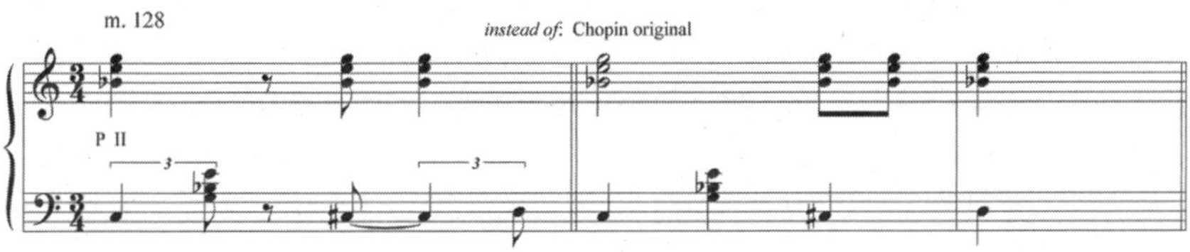

than the original and there are many interruptions to accommodate superimposed material from motive "a" (in mm. 124–5 and 130–1) and a two-measure quotation from the *Grande valse brillante*, here transposed to C major so as to fit with the descending major sixth (C, E-flat) of the op. 111 quotation. Where the C was originally a quick upbeat to the E-flat, it is now in m. 128 prolonged for three beats. The Chopin quotation in the same measure is also rhythmically compressed so that the bass line (C–C-sharp–D) can lead to the E-flat in m. 129 (see example 7.16b). In m. 131 Hambræus also furtively anticipates the two chords of the op. 111 quotation that enter on the offbeat in measure 132.

Section 9 (mm. 134–160)

Like section 6, this section affects a return to the bell environment. It resembles the opening four sections in its basic rhythm, the use of motives "b" and "c," the grace-note groupings spanning one to five notes, and the major and minor sixth doublings. However, up to m. 155, only the low register is utilized.

Section 10 (mm 161–192)

This slow section features five bell-like chords, each having six notes. They resonate with a quotation from Scriabin's Piano Sonata No. 6 (see example 7.17a). The first, third, fourth and fifth chords (see example 7.17b) are constructed from two three-note groups consisting of m (perfect fourth, augmented fourth) and m' (perfect fifth, augmented fourth), and may accordingly be represented as follows:

1	3	4	5
m	m'	m	m'
m	m	m'	m

The second chord opposes consonances on C and D-flat, a first inversion C major triad (with the fifth missing) and a first inversion D-flat major triad. The five chords are played four times in this section with varying durations. As shown in example 7.17c, the Scriabin quotation starts simultaneously with the third appearance of the fifth chord (m. 180).

Section 11 (mm. 194–217)

The long resonances created by the pedal in section 10 are starkly contrasted in this section by the fast sextuplets of Piano II, a sort of *perpetuum mobile.* There are no less than forty permutations of the basic twelve-note row. The first five notes (m. 195) of the row are very similar to motive "b" – two tritones A–D-sharp and F–B, followed by a central pitch E – a pattern which is then used to form a sequence of six tritones (see example 7.18a). The first note (A) is the *third* note of a chromatic scale from G to F-sharp (see example 7.18b). The second note (D-sharp) is the *ninth* note of that chromatic scale. The third note (B) is the *fifth* note of that scale, and so on. In this way one obtains the series 3, 9, 5, 11, 10, 4, 8, 2, 1, 12, 6, 7. By applying this series to permutation I, one obtains permutation II (B, G, E, C, F-sharp etc.) and by applying it to permutation II one obtains permutation III (E, A, F-sharp, B-flat, D-flat, etc.). The process continues until permutation IX, the chromatic scale from G to F-sharp (with notes 2, 3, 5, 10, 11, 12 filtered out; see m. 200,

Example 7.17.
Section 10, bell-like chords and Scriabin quotations
(a) Scriabin, Piano Sonata No. 6, opening

(b) bell-like chords

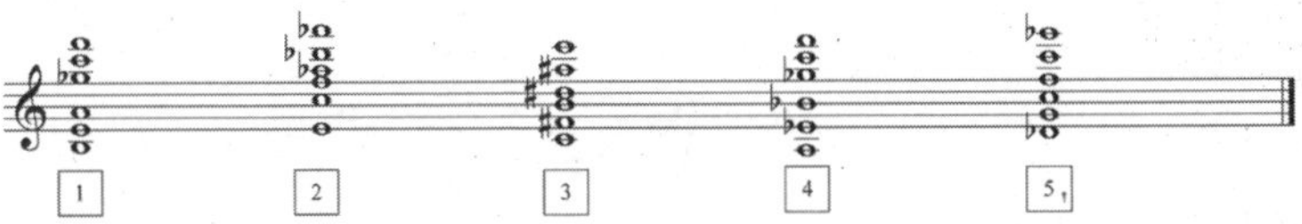

(c) quotation from Scriabin's Piano Sonata No. 6, mm. 179–85

beat 3). Since the next step, permutation X would reproduce permutation I, Hambræus creates a new series by applying the series 3, 9, 5, 11 … to itself. The third number is 5, the ninth number is 1, the fifth is 10, and so on. The new series is 5, 1, 10, 6, 12, 11, 2, 9, 3, 7, 4, 8.

Applied to permutation IX, this new series produces permutation X (B, G, E, C, F-sharp, etc.). As permutation XVIII would yield the chromatic scale, it is again necessary to find another series. Hambræus does this by applying the numbers of series one to series two, to produce series three – 10, 3, 12, 4, 7, 6, 9, 1, 5, 8, 11, 2. When this is applied to permutation IX, the result is permutation X (B, G, E, C, F-sharp, etc.). As permutation XVIII again yields another chromatic scale Hambræus

Example 7.18.
Section 11, derivation of row
(a) derivation of row

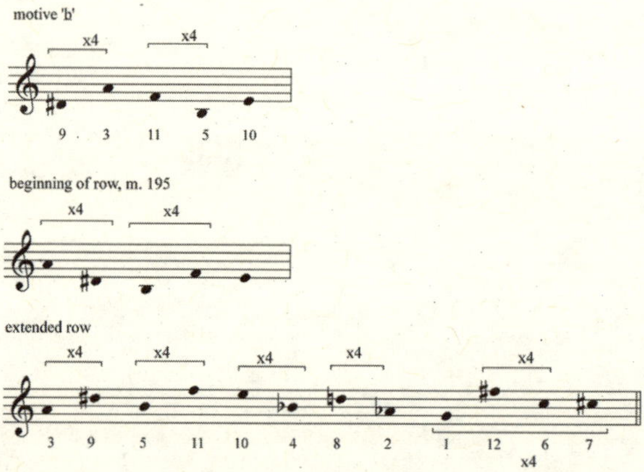

applies series one to series three, producing series four – 10, 3, 12, 4, 7, 6, 9, 1, 5, 8, 11, 2 – which is subsequently used for permutations XIX, XX and XXI. For permutation XXII, series one is applied to series six to produce series seven – 8, 12, 2, 4, 9, 6, 5, 10, 7, 1, 11, 3. When the application of series seven for permutation XL would again produce a chromatic scale, Hambræus creates a new series by another method, extremes to centre – 8, 3, 12, 11, 1, 2, 7, 4, 9, 10, 5, 6.

What is remarkable is the variety obtained in the realization of this long passage in Piano II. The basic line of forty permutations is doubled at major or minor sixths, like motive "b." From permutation I to IX, the motion is in the low register, staccato, and the doublings are varied, major or minor sixth plus one or two octaves more (see example 7.19a). From permutation X to XXI (that is, starting at the end of m. 200) the motion is legato, in the middle register, and doubled exclusively in major or minor sixths. From permutation XXII, the two hands alternate major and minor sixths, staccato, in patterns of six like an opening fan (see example 7.19b). In permutations XXVI and XXVII, the patterns are more complex, alternating high and low within the sixteenth note sextuplet in a constantly changing order. In permutation XXVIII the alternating hands are in close range (see example 7.19c). In permutation XXIX, they alternate in extreme registers in patterns of four (see example 7.19d). In permutation XXX, the two hands are separated by major or minor sixths plus two, three or four octaves

Example 7.18. (*Continued*)
(b) series permutations

Example 7.19.
Section 11, treatment of permutations in Piano II

Example 7.20.
Section 11, rhythmic patterns of five chords and continued evolution of patterns

(see example 7.19e). From permutation XXXI to XXXIX, the motion is in the middle register with a separation of the two parts by major or minor sixths or one octave more.

As a counterpoint to this *perpetuum mobile,* Piano I adds various elements. As a link with section 10 it plays the five high register chords (see example 7.17b) in various rhythmic patterns (see example 7.20, mm. 194, 196, 199). At m. 200 the chords fill in the filtered elements of the chromatic scale from permutation IX, giving the sequence of rhythms shown in example 7.20 (mm. 200, 202, 209, 211, 214).

But Hambræus is not yet finished, for in m. 203 he introduces yet another quotation from Beethoven's op. 106. A rhythmic pattern recalling the four sixteenth notes of motive "b" is introduced in m. 205, and then rearticulated "off-phase" in m. 206 (see example 7.21).

Example 7.21.
Section 11, off-phase presentation of rhythmic cell

Example 7.22.
Coda, final quotations.
(a) Chopin's *Grande valse brillante*

(b) appearance with Scriabin quotation, mm. 218–22

THE CODA

The coda, marked *Adagio molto,* uses the middle section of Chopin's *Grande valse brillante* (see example 7.22a) an octave lower and at a very slow tempo, combined with a fleeting glimpse of the Scriabin quotation (m. 220; see example 7.22b). The work ends *Presto* with a quick recall of the bell motives "a" and "b."

NOTES

1 Hambræus, liner notes for recording *Carillon for Two Pianos,* performed by Bruce Mather and Pierette LePage, McGill Records, 77002.

2 Hambræus uses quotations in a number of other works. *Diptychon* (1952), for flute, oboe, viola harpsichord, and celesta contains quotations from the "signore, alutami a caminare" in Dallapiccola's *Il Prigioniero. Motetum Archangeli Michaelis* (1967), for mixed choir and organ (dedicated to the memory of Varèse), uses short quotations from Varèse's *Deserts. Rencontres pour orchestre* (1968–71) contains quotations from works by Beethoven, Wagner, Bartók, Scriabin, Reger (and also Hambraeus's *Rota* [1956–63], for three orchestras) as well as Mahler and Vietnamese folk music. *Extempore* (1975) for organ uses various transformed quotations from Gregorian chant, medieval proportional notation symbols, Bach, Middelschulte (in much disguised form!), Varèse, and Stockhausen. *Continuo – A Partire da Pachelbel* (1975), for organ and orchestra, uses different quotations from Pachelbel's organ music, including the big D minor prelude, a D minor fugue, and two *Ciaconas* (F minor and G major), as well as his *Aria Sebaldina. Toccato – Monumentum per Max Reger* (1973), for organ, employs various quotations from Reger's works, opp. 16, 33, 60, 63: 5, 69: 9, 73, 127, 132, 135b. *Parade* (1977), for wind orchestra, contains quotations from Spanish procession music for Holy Week, and from tribal music among Navajo Indians in Ecuador (relics of conquistador military music from the sixteenth century). *Cappriccio* (1981), for harpsichord, contains quotations from Reger's op. 69: 9. The movement "Ronde des tierces en couple" from *Livre d'orgue* (1980–81), contains quotations from Bach, Brahms, and Reger (and is rhythmically inspired by a popular tune from the 1930s, the rumba Ti-pi-tin!). *Three Dances* (1986), for free bass accordion and percussion, contains quotations from Bach, Buxtehude, Mozart, and Prokofiev (all very disguised!). *Litanies* (1988–89), for orchestra, contains quotations from an Indian mantra and an Anglican Easter hymn. *Concerto per corno principale ed orchestra* (1996) uses short transformed quotations from old Swedish herding signals. *Fm 643765* für grosso Orgel (1997)

uses transformed quotations from the Mendelssohn Festival in Bad Homburg, Germany, Sept. 1997. See also John Mackay "*Les Jeux Sont Faits!*: Ensemble Strategies and Historical 'Borrowing' in the Music of Bengt Hambræus," in *Crosscurrents and Counterpoints: Offerings in Honor of Bengt Hambraeus at 70*, ed. Per Broman, Nora Engebretsen, and Bo Alphonce (Gothenburg: University of Gothenburg, 1998), 227–45.

8

The Soles of the Feet: alcides lanza Reconnects with his Roots

Pamela Jones, Montreal

Musicologist PAMELA JONES has had a lifelong passion for both music and dance. The journey spawned by this passion has included undergraduate studies at McGill University, Faculty of Music, doctoral studies in musicology at King's College, University of London, early dance studies at the Julliard School and the New England Conservatory, and appearances as a member of the Nonsuch Historical Dance Company in England. She currently teaches at the National Theatre School of Canada, Ballet *Divertimento,* and Bishop's University in Sherbrooke, Quebec, and has published widely in journals and reference books, including *Studi Musicali, Early Music, Perspectives of New Music,* the Montreal new music journal *Circuit,* and the *International Encyclopedia of Dance.* Her interest in alcides lanza was sparked when she heard his music at a McGill new music concert and has led a recently published book, *alcides lanza: Portrait of a Composer* (McGill Queen's University Press), from which this essay is taken. Her husband, composer Robert Jones, has also collaborated with lanza in numerous duo piano recitals.

> For many years I [had been] writing music that I described as city, urban music – non-folkloric, non-nationalistic. Then, something prompted me to open the door and let some of those things enter my music ... I don't know what caused it. It just happened. I think it was there building up pressure inside me and finally it burst through.[1]

Thus lanza describes an evolution in his thinking. It is always interesting to a biographer when a subject does something wholly unexpected, especially when it is something he has previously opposed. For decades lanza had been determined to write music with an "international" sound, unconnected with his native Argentina, and bearing no trace of folkloric elements or nationalism, but during the late 1970s he broke with this practice and began to create works that have specific connections to Latin American culture. He does this in many ways: he might evoke the atmosphere of a place (such as a café in Buenos Aires), imitate the sound of indigenous instruments, include recognizable tango melodies and rhythms, or use a well-known tango as scaffolding for entire sections of a work.

BACKGROUND

Before we enter into a discussion of lanza's works that contain overt quotations from traditional Latin American styles, it is important to consider the context in which these works were written. From the late 1960s through the 1980s composers from many different countries and from extremely varied backgrounds began to insert quotations from older tonal music into their compositions. What seems clear in retrospect is that this reinvestigation of mainly diatonic sounds was a first step taken by many atonal composers toward including significant diatonicism in their works, or even adopting a "neotonal" language. By the late 1970s a significant number of composers were writing some form of neotonal music. In North America – where most faculties, institutions, and award committees were dominated by composers who wrote and taught some brand of atonal music – it was a brave thing to do. There was a great deal of vitriolic and pointless invective between the atonal and neotonal camps, each arguing in favour of their own place in history. The debate drew together as allies composers who had little in common – for not all atonal composers respect each other's brand of atonalism, and the same is true of the tonal set. What many failed to grasp, however, was that for some time contemporary music had not been limited to one or even two universally accepted languages. Composers were now living in an era of multiplicity and idiosyncratic compositional languages. As an indefatigable concert-goer and participant in numerous contemporary music festivals world wide, lanza was cognizant of the different and overlapping trends, and was well aware of the outburst of quotation pieces, polystylistic pieces, and neotonal works.

In the 1970s lanza was not in favour of neotonal composition. He thought it "regressive" (and he still does). However, he was not vindictive about his opinion, and sometimes played the neotonal compositions of his friends and students in concerts. When it came to the use of tonal quotation, however, lanza was less hostile. He was not against quotation per se, and, as far as his own music was concerned, he believed that quotation had a place in theatre music for programmatic purposes. But when it came to concert music, he felt that quotation was "something other composers did." He couldn't see himself doing it. lanza has said that if I had interviewed him in the early 1970s and asked if he would ever use extensive quotation or significant amounts of diatonicism in his atonal compositions, he would have replied with a resounding "No, never,"[2] – which only goes to show that composers, like everyone else, are often blissfully unaware of where they are heading.

By the late 1970s, it had been more than a decade since lanza had lived in Argentina. Although he loved his adopted country of Canada and had a successful career there, he began to feel nostalgic about his homeland. It was not the kind of nostalgia that makes one want to pack up and return home, but rather a realization that certain people, places, and sounds of the old country have left an indelible mark on one's character and art. *ekphonesis V* (1979) and *acúfenos III* (1977) both reflect this nostalgia. *ekphonesis V*, the opening movement of *trilogy*, is an intensely personal portrait of lanza's family in Argentina, and the singer's part consists of a series of tender vignettes about his grandmother, grandfather, and first son. None of the music, however, sounds particularly Latin American: the family could be anywhere. *acúfenos III*, for flute, piano, and tape, was inspired by an image of a native playing a *quena* (a native flute) on the wind-swept high mesas of the Andes. The tape component contains recordings of indigenous Latin-American flutes, while the solo flute and piano imitate the sounds of Andean folk instruments. It is important to note, however, that it is only the tone colours of the instruments that are recalled, not any specific indigenous musical style.

It is possible to listen to *ekphonesis V* and *acúfenos III* without recognizing any references to Argentina, but when we consider these two pieces, it is clear that lanza was reconnecting, however obliquely, with his cultural roots by recalling people, places, and instrumental colours. Some years later he went a step further and established a direct connection by using the actual music of his homeland in his works. *arghanum I* (1986) and *arghanum V* (1990) illustrate this change in musical focus.

ARGHANUM I (1986)

lanza has said that the desire to use traditional Argentinean material in his music was ready to "burst out" of him, but it was not until 1986 that we get a vivid aural connection with Argentina. It took the right kind of commission from the right kind of performer to make this a reality. Joseph Petric, a first-rate Canadian concert accordionist, tirelessly champions the accordion as an instrument capable of interpreting serious music, and to this end, has commissioned a number of new works from Canadian composers. When he approached lanza about a commission in 1984, lanza replied that he wasn't interested; he has since admitted that at the time he had a rather low opinion of the accordion. Petric, who was quite used to negative reactions from composers on a first approach, sent lanza a few recordings of his previous commissions.[3] After listening to them, lanza realized that Petric was an excellent musician and that his own thinking vis-à-vis the accordion had been limited: "I had been thinking of the piano accordion, *canzonetta napolitana,* someone trying to accompany *O sole mio*. The tapes made me realize that Petric was a concert musician."[4]

The timbral qualities of the accordion stirred old memories, and lanza began to recall the sound of the bandoneon, a type of accordion used in popular tango music in Argentina. With the link from accordion to bandoneon to tango to Argentina, he was more than happy, even excited, to write for Petric. The result is *arghanum I,* scored for accordion, clarinet, bass clarinet, vibraphone, and synthesizer.[5] In the score, lanza indicates that the soloist can play either accordion or bandoneon: "What I'm actually doing is writing for bandoneon, but the bandoneon players haven't commissioned me." In Argentina, tango is ever present: in streets, restaurants, stores, dance halls, theatres, and most especially in cafés. lanza had vivid memories of the bandoneon players playing tangos in the cafés of Buenos Aires, and with this image in mind, chose a well-known tango melody – Angel Gregorio Villoldo's *El choclo* [The Corncob] – to underpin his new composition (see example 8.1).

The accordion enters at the end of the first page of *arghanum I* and, after an brief flourish, immediately introduces the first twelve notes of *El choclo* in a version that is rhythmically spasmodic with stuttering repetitions and atonal interruptions. Example 8.2 shows the accordion part of this passage with the tango fragments indicated below. Here the tango melody is used somewhat like a cantus firmus. lanza has not hidden the tango references, and in fact takes care to thin out the texture

Joseph Petric, photograph by Warren Beck. Reproduced by kind permission of Joseph Petric.

when they appear so they can be easily recognized. For example, the initial two- and three-note motives in the accordion, which prepare the ear for the longer quotations to come, are played either solo or with light accompaniment. Without a program note, and with the frequent atonal interruptions, we may not yet be quite sure we are hearing snatches of tango, but because the instrument is an accordion and the tune is so well known, we surely suspect it. Our suspicions are confirmed a few moments later when, after so much teasing of our ears with brief glimpses of *El choclo*, lanza finally provides us with a full twelve-note phrase (see example 8.3). From this moment on our ears are primed to catch the tango quotes and rhythms that appear

Example 8.1.
Angel Gregorio Villoldo, *El choclo,* opening

Example 8.2.
arghanum I, accordion part, opening

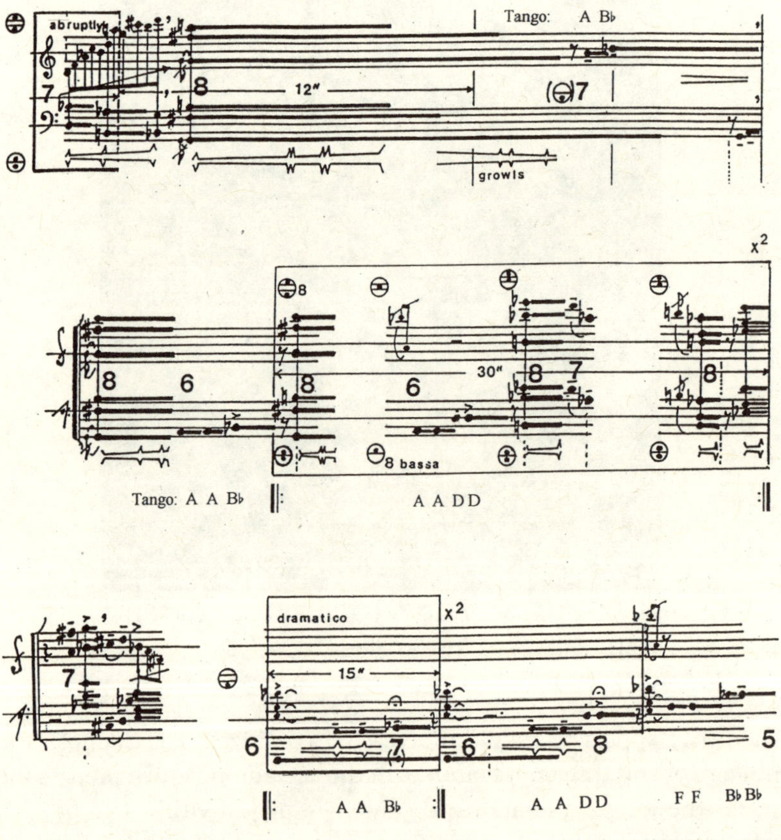

throughout the rest of the score. For example, on page 3 of the score motives of the tango are interspersed among a wild series of tone clusters (see example 8.4). The music is hectic, but now that our ears are sensitized to tango references, we recognize them in spite of the surrounding mayhem.

Toward the end of the work, after so much teasing of our ears with hints, allusions, and distortions, lanza finally shines a musical spotlight

Example 8.3.
arghanum I, accordion part from figure *d*, p. 3

Example 8.4.
arghanum I, accordion part from figure *e*, p. 3

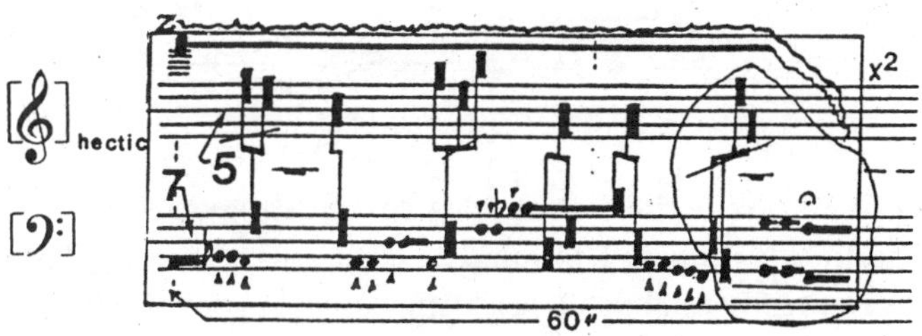

Example 8.5.
arghanum I, accordion part from figure *k*, p. 6

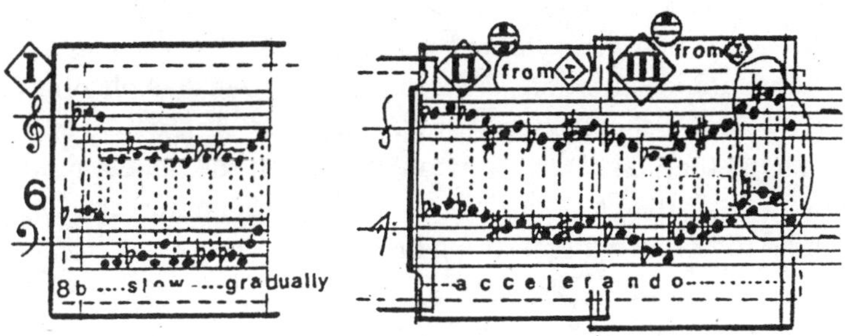

on *El choclo*. In a vivid cadenza passage, the accordionist plays an unadorned quotation of several phrases of the tango melody, but even here lanza cannot resist playing with us by removing the tango rhythm (see example 8.5).

The harmonic language of *arghanum I* is eclectic. In addition to the frequent embedding of tonal tango fragments in an overall atonal texture, there are a number of diatonic passages that have little or no relationship to tango. At the opening of the work (see example 8.6) every note is taken from the pitch collection of F minor (including both

Example 8.6.
arghanum I, opening, reduction showing pitches only

natural and raised sixth and seventh degrees) creating an impressionistic blur of sounds hinting at F minor. However, this and other diatonic passages do not really establish a key – they are not goal oriented – but instead give a certain harmonic colour to the music. In earlier works that contain tonal episodes, such as *ekphonesis V,* lanza keeps the tonal and atonal worlds quite separate: one does not intrude on the other. But in *arghanum I,* there is a constant blurring of boundaries. We shift back and forth between café and concert hall, between almost tonal and almost atonal, in a sort of dreamlike haze. lanza is playing with our perceptions. Schoenberg's *Pierrot Lunaire* has been described as "a Lieder recital that has taken the wrong turn."[6] In the same way, *arghanum I* sounds a little like a café concert heard through the ears of someone under the influence of a strong hallucinogenic.

ARGHANUM V (1990)

Petric knew that in order to raise awareness of the accordion as a concert instrument, he needed a repertoire of strong solo works. With this in mind, he commissioned lanza to write a second accordion piece. This time he requested a solo. *arghanum V* (1990)[7] is a four-page work scored for accordion and tape. While the accordion plays throughout, the tape is heard only on the second and fourth pages. Petric was unhappy that performances of the work would require a technician to start, stop, and restart the tape at the appropriate moments – apparently he had had bad experiences when he had to rely on assistants – and he asked lanza to rework the piece so that the tape part would be continuous from beginning to end. lanza does not often rework a piece once it is finished, but Petric's argument must have been convincing. In the revised tape part, rather than simply splicing in blank tape to connect the two original sections, lanza added additional electroacoustic music.[8]

When Petric commissioned the work, he told lanza that it would be premiered at a sound symposium in Newfoundland. lanza had never visited the island, but he had seen photographs and films of Canada's rainy, wind-swept, maritime province. He felt that these images reminded him of a place back home in Argentina. At first he thought of Patagonia, but soon realized the two places were not really similar. Then, in a moment of inspiration, he thought of the Islas Malvinas (Falkland Islands), dramatically situated in the South Atlantic Ocean off the eastern coast of Argentina.[9] He immediately saw a similarity of climate, vegetation, and quirky national character. He knew the analogy could not be taken too far, but it served as an image, a connection between Canada and his homeland that made the new work more personal to him. lanza had been reading about industrial pollution in areas of Newfoundland. *arghanum V* reflects his feelings of frustration at the continuous destruction of nature by man. The work is subtitled "sobre la belleza de lo salvaje" [on the beauty of the wild], and the opening is marked, "agitated and wild, with repressed anger," a rubric that gives the flavour of the entire work. It is a piece of protest music: wild anger contrasting with lamentation.

arghanum V is made up of a series of programmatic gestures that are listed in the preface with explanations of their meaning (see example 8.7). Each gesture has its own distinctive rhythmic, melodic, registral, and timbral characteristics: the bird chant always has repeated notes with a chirping grace note upbeat; the glimmering lake is always a low tremolo; and the ceremonial ritual is a repeated gong-like low note or interval. lanza provides each gesture with an individual harmonic character: the "fading memory" gesture is essentially whole tone; the bird chant is usually accompanied by a pentatonic bass line; the glimmering lake always begins with suggestions of the dominant of F minor; and several gestures highlight diminished triads.

The language of *arghanum V* is eclectic, with atonal, diatonic, pentatonic, and whole tone passages appearing side by side, but the piece most definitely does not sound like a bit of this and a bit of that; instead it is strikingly organic.[10] lanza has fashioned his family of sound

Example 8.7.
arghanum V, excerpt from prefatory instructions

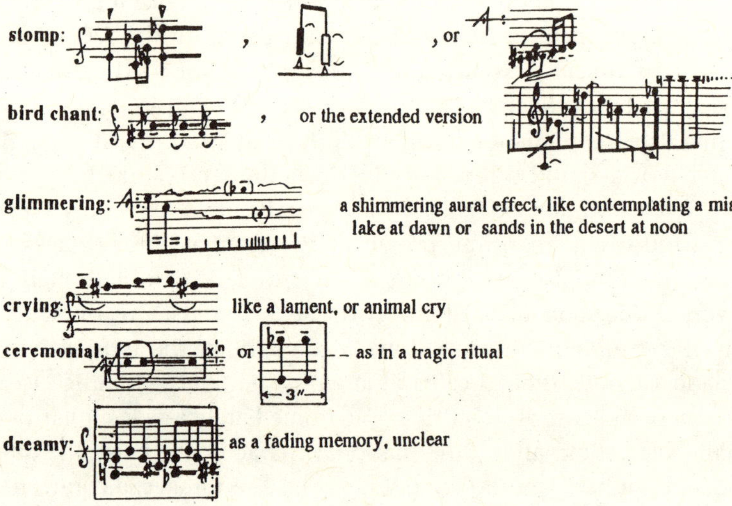

gestures so that one flows into another with deceptive ease. The extended bird chant ending on a high repeated B-natural leads easily into the animal cry that begins on the same note (see example 8.8). Similarly, the grace note of the bird chant, usually a major or minor third, flows seamlessly into the low tremolo third that begins the glimmering lake motive. The most important feature uniting these disparate gestures, however, is the association with tango. In the preface lanza informs us that a number of the melodic, harmonic, and gestural features are derived from *El monito* [The Little Monkey], a popular Argentinean tango by Julio de Caro. These tango associations are seldom obvious; while there are places where almost everyone in the audience will recognize a tango quotation, the greater part of the piece exploits *El monito* in a more subtle manner. lanza uses melodic and harmonic fragments from the original piece but often strips them of their tango character, smoothing out a syncopated tango rhythm, or selecting a series of pitches from unrelated bars of *El monito*, so that the listener is unaware of the tango reference.

Let us examine a few of these references. *arghanum V* opens with two aggressive tone clusters (like gunshots setting the action in motion) followed by a repeating white key/black key (right hand/left hand) clustery ostinato (see example 8.9a, and note that both hands are notated on bass clef). The right-hand part outlines the diminished triad F–B–D–B–F

Example 8.8.
arghanum V, excerpt from p. 1, second system

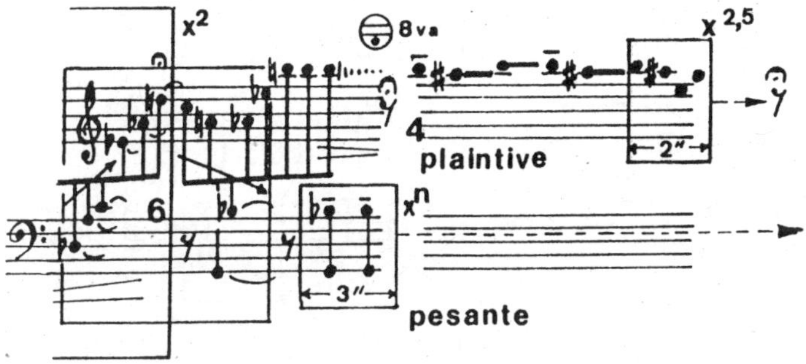

Example 8.9.
(a) *arghanum V,* opening ostinato

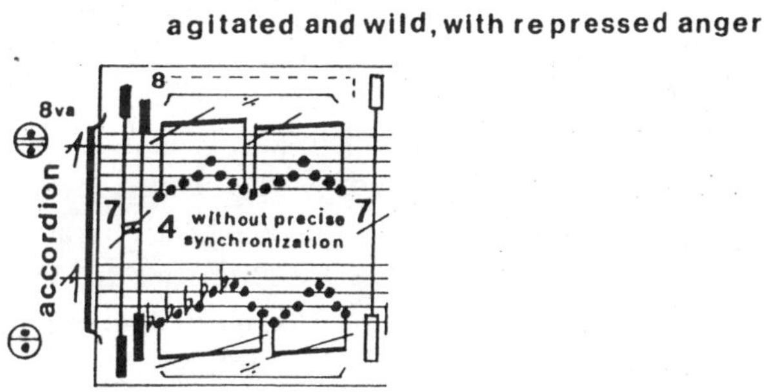

(b) Julio de Caro, *El monito,* m. 1

with passing notes connecting the F and the B, a configuration of notes that corresponds to the opening measure of *El monito* (see example 8.9b). From the very beginning lanza takes his inspiration from the tango, but we would not likely have discovered this if he had not informed us.[11]

Example 8.10 shows a longer excerpt from the second system of the score featuring multiple associations with *El monito*. The passage opens with a repeated weeping semitone, B–A-sharp (labelled [a]) that is described in the preface as "an animal cry, like a lament." The descending

Example 8.10.
arghanum V, excerpt from p. 1, second system

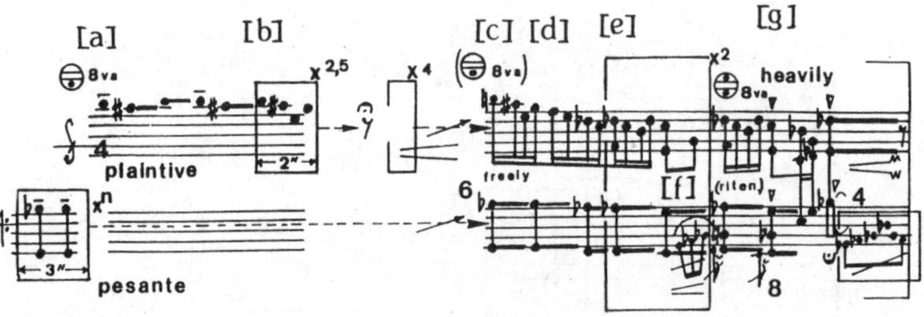

semitone grows into a plaintive four-note motive, B–A-sharp–E–G (labelled [b]), that is repeated six and a half times before it initiates a sixteenth-note flourish [labelled c]. The four-note lament motive [b] is derived from measure 27 of *El monito* (see example 8.11; the arrows highlight the motive F–E–B-flat–D-flat that lanza transposes to begin on B so it can evolve out of the weeping animal cry, B–A-sharp. The continuation of the sixteenth-note flourish ([d] in figure 8.10) is also derived from bar 27 of the tango (see figure 8.12). The next gesture ([e] in example 8.10) is not a direct quotation from *El monito* but rather a conflation of bars 21–23 (see example 8.13). Its continuation ([g] in example 8.10) resoundingly reminds us of tango with a direct quotation of measure 22 of *El monito* (see example 8.14). To reinforce the gesture, lanza adds a typical tango flourish in the left hand ([f] in example 8.10) and heavy foot stomps by the accordionist (indicated by small triangles in the score). Thus almost everything in example 8.10 is derived in some way from passages of *El monito*.

In the previous paragraph we examined excerpts from the first two systems of *arghanum V.* If we put the entire work under the same magnifying glass we will find that more than 90 per cent of the piece is connected either directly or obliquely to *El monito*. With the exception of the closing dreamlike coda, practically no new material is introduced in the remainder of the work. Instead, lanza uses the motivic gestures introduced in the first page as building blocks, arranging and rearranging the various discrete components in different orders and combinations, as if he is shuffling a deck of musical cards.

Example 8.15 shows an intimate passage about halfway through the piece in which lanza recycles a number of gestures familiar to the listener from their appearances earlier in the work: the "ceremonial ritual" interval (labelled [t]), the "animal cry" [u], the lament motive [v]

Example 8.11.
El monito, m. 27, and lament motive from *arghanum V*

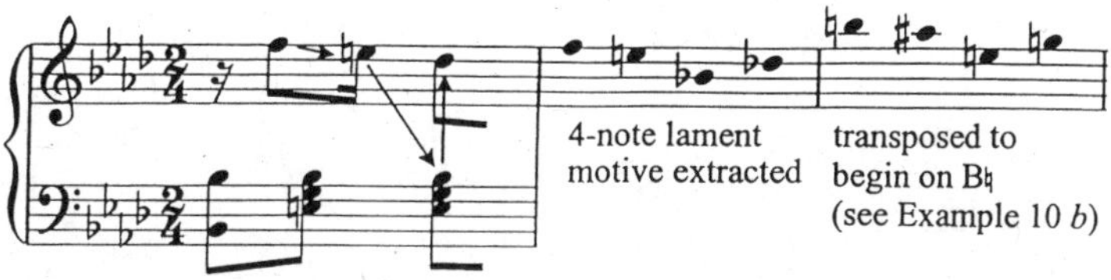

Example 8.12.
El monito, mm. 26–7, and excerpt from *arghanum V* (see example 8.10 "[d]")

Example 8.13.
El monito, mm. 21–3, and excerpt from *arghanum V* (see example 8.10 "[e]")

Example 8.14.
El monito, m. 22, and excerpt from *arghanum V* (see example 8.10 "[g]")

El monito *arghanum V*

Example 8.15.
arghanum V, end of p. 2 and beginning of p. 3

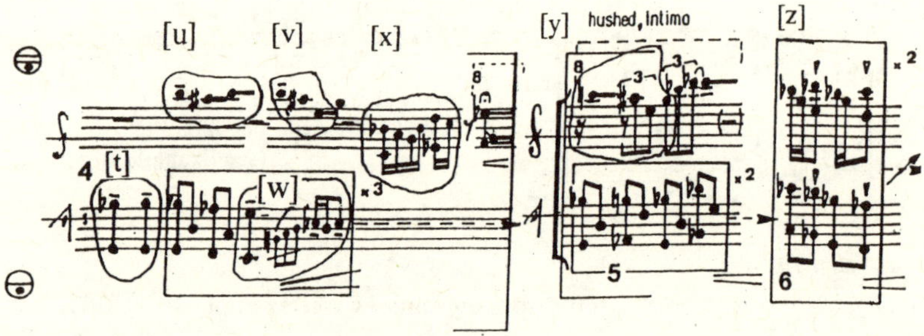

accompanied by a tango flourish [w], a direct tango quote [x], the lament motive once again [y], and finally several repetitions of the direct tango quote emphasized by foot stomps [z]. lanza follows the same process through almost the entire work, paring down material to a few precise and strikingly recognizable gestures that are repeated and developed like leitmotivs. As a result, *arghanum V* is an approachable work. Because of the network of memories and associations, listeners become so familiar with the components that they absorb the larger structure without struggle. lanza also twists our heartstrings with plaintive, evocative echoes of the past.

Considering the amount of material derived from tango, we would expect *arghanum V* to sound Argentinean. But does it? The answer is both yes and no. While the accordion music sounds Latin American in many places, the tape component has a somewhat "northern" feel to it. The reason for this is that the tape part contains only minimal references to tango and is replete with realistic sounds of nature: bird cries, icy winds blowing through vast empty spaces, huge waves crashing against rocky shores – the sounds of nature in Newfoundland. lanza took many of these "real" sounds from special effects records. It seems to me, however, that the contrast between the accordion and tape parts is not "south" versus "north," but rather "humanity" versus "nature." The accordion part, with its tango fragments and "artificial" animal sounds, represents the human element; the tape depicts the real world of nature. As such, the tape component has no sense of musical development or emotional manipulation. Nature is simply there. It is the accordion that reacts and counter-reacts; it is humanity that experiences anger, regrets, and dreams.

lanza later made a piano version of *arghanum V* (entitled *arghanum Vπ*) that he recorded and performed extensively in concert.[12] At a performance of *arghanum Vπ* that I attended in Buenos Aires in October 1996 lanza was asked to speak briefly about his composition before the work was played. He explained that the work was essentially his protest against the destruction of nature in Newfoundland. He also said that the work contained a series of musical gestures depicting various aspects of nature, but did not explain the meaning of any of these gestures. I spoke with several members of the audience afterwards. Some had recognized the tango quotations, others had not. Each had felt the composer's anger and understood that nature was the main protagonist in the drama, but each had interpreted the musical gestures differently and were convinced of their own interpretations. One person heard the opening tone clusters and running ostinati as the composer's raging anger, while another heard animals fleeing the destruction of their habitat. The low "murmuring lake" tremolo was to some an anxious mother nature brooding over the loss of her domain. Some heard the "lament motive" as the composer's sense of loss, but to others, it was the despair of an animal that can endure no more. Of course, for an Argentinean audience, the subject matter of *arghanum V* touches a nerve, because so many of the natural habitats in Argentina are under attack from the corporate world. Nevertheless, the fact that people can have such different vivid images indicates to me that the work can cut through the consciousness to tap deep emotions.

lanza uses tango quite differently in *arghanum I* and *arghanum V*. In *arghanum I* we are meant to hear the quotations from *El choclo*. The melody is left relatively intact and lanza often gives us enough of the tune for our ears to grasp it easily. Also, the melody is so well known – it is almost a catchphrase for tango in the world at large – that we assume a programmatic intent. Fragments of this melody played on an accordion trigger certain associations even for listeners with no Argentinean background: we automatically think of cafés, tango, and Latin America. Even though lanza obscures the Latin flavour with atonal interruptions, other tonal passages, and general mayhem, the colourful programmatic effects are still easily perceived. In *Arghanum V*, on the other hand, lanza uses tango more as scaffolding than as a source of recognizable quotations. The tango he chose, *El monito*, is less well-known in North America than *El choclo*, and he takes as source material not only its melody but also its harmonies, rests, rhythms, and intervals. *El monito* serves as a quarry to furnish building material for large portions of the composition. Some quotations we recognize as tango, but most are so embedded in the texture that we are unaware of them. Why, then, does lanza use this material throughout the work? There may be purely musical reasons: in a work with such a plurality of harmonic languages, lanza may have sought an underlying musical glue that would bind the disparate elements together. But it is an oversimplification to think that the tango quotations are there solely for technical reasons. In my opinion, there are philosophical issues at play. Composers often use quotation extensively because the quoted music has a powerful personal significance. The medieval monks used Gregorian chant to underlie polyphonic mass movements, not simply as abstract source material, but because the chant melodies connected them to their faith and to their God. lanza chose tango for much the same reason: it connects him to his essence – to the music of his youth, the dances and dance songs of Argentina, to a symbol of his native land, to both the soles of his feet and his inner soul.

CONCERTO FOR MIDI PIANO AND ORCHESTRA (1993)

lanza used the *arghanum V* music in one other major work. In 1993 Argentinean pianist Hugo Goldenzweig commissioned him to compose a piano concerto. lanza recalls, "Hugo specifically requested a piano concerto with electronics but stipulated that since he knew nothing about electronics, everything would have to happen automatically."[13] lanza had in mind a piece with considerable ebb and flow between pianist and orchestra, and wanted to avoid situations where the musicians had to coordinate with a tape. With this in mind he decided to score his concerto for MIDI piano. The MIDI piano, first developed by Yamaha in the late 1980s, is a hybrid instrument, a normal grand piano with a keyboard modified so that the keys activate not only the hammers that strike the strings but also the triggers that send MIDI signals which can be received and processed by synthesizers or other electronic devices. In addition to the keyboard, there are a number of buttons that can transmit other signals to the receiving devices. If the MIDI outputs are not connected to external devices, the instrument functions as a conventional grand piano.

lanza could see the potential of this instrument. The electroacoustic elements of the work could be pre-programmed in synthesizer modules that the pianist could trigger from the instrument. When playing with a tape, performers have to synchronize their live music with the predetermined and unvarying music on the tape. With the MIDI piano, however, the performer can trigger the electronic effects at exactly the right moment. This leaves the pianist free to "interpret" the music, vary the tempo, and introduce dramatic pauses, without worrying about coordination with an inflexible tape part. The live musician, rather than the electronics, controls the musical agenda.

When lanza received the commission in February 1993, the premiere with the Orquesta Municipal de Rosario was scheduled for December of that year. lanza was occupied with teaching, performing, and composing during the winter and early spring, so he planned to write the concerto in the summer after his university work was complete for the academic year. He had just begun work in June, believing he had ample time, when he received a telephone call from the conductor to say that the premiere had been advanced to October. lanza didn't panic – after all, October was four months away – but the next week he received a second call saying that the concerto was now scheduled for September. The pressure was beginning to mount when, like the third act in a comedy of errors, he received yet another call changing the date to August! At this point the premiere was in jeopardy: there were only six weeks for lanza to compose the work and for Goldenzweig to learn it.

After pondering his predicament for a few days, lanza suddenly saw a solution. Goldenzweig was a champion of *arghanum Vπ* (the version for piano and tape), and had performed the piece in several concerts. lanza decided to use the piano part of *arghanum Vπ* as the third movement of the concerto. It was an inspired idea. *arghanum Vπ* is a work of protest, replete with colourful programmatic and sonic images. Its energetic, fast moving, and rhythmically decisive character is much in keeping with the finales of classic piano concertos. But most importantly, Goldenzweig already knew the music, and he reacted positively to the idea.

lanza's MIDI piano concerto is scored for piano and a large chamber orchestra. When lanza reworked *arghanum V* as the third movement of the concerto, he made the important decision to retain only the piano part. In place of the unambiguous imitations of nature on the tape, he composed new orchestral music, drawing heavily on the intervals, motives, and harmonies of the piano part, with only minimal references to the original tape sounds. In *arghanum V* the sounds of nature on the tape sometimes soften the intensity of the piano part, but in the concerto both the solo and the orchestral parts have the passionate quality

Example 8.16.
arghanum V, excerpt from p. 1, second system,
and opening of piano part from lanza's *piano concerto*

(a) *arghanum V*

(b) piano concerto

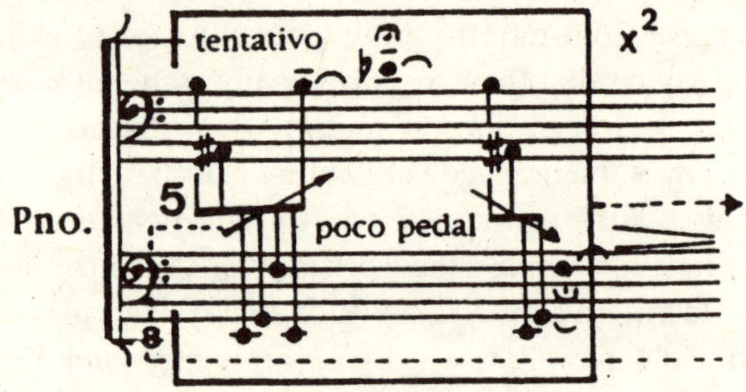

of protest. The concerto has a more universal character – it is a piece of protest music *per se* – but the nature of the protest is left to the imagination of the listeners.

lanza composed the third movement of the concerto first. He then linked the first and second movements to the third by quoting a few musical gestures from *arghanum V* in the earlier movements. But lanza often transforms the quotations to give them a new character. For example, the high, lyrical, narrow-range lament motive is stripped of its lamenting character to become the ominous and threatening widely-spaced, low-register minor-ninth motive that opens the concerto (see example 8.16). In *arghanum V* lanza used *El monito* as a quarry for building material; in the concerto *arghanum V* itself is the quarry. Since listeners are introduced to elements based on *arghanum V* before the third movement, the concerto is a little like a musical detective story:

the vivid, disparate "characters" of the first two movements are only tied together when the listeners hear the final movement, the music that generated so much of what came before.

Each movement of the concerto has its own character and timbral quality but, it is important to note that the first two movements are carefully planned to lead to the final protest. We have the impression that an underlying drama is taking place, that we are experiencing a musical play. The piano part of the first movement contains a number of repeated melodic fragments in frame notation. These repetitions serve to establish pools of harmonic and melodic stability that are reinforced in the orchestra with repeated or sustained chords drawn from the piano part. At a certain point, all of this obsessive repetition becomes almost oppressive. Musically, the players exhibit a certain frustration, almost as if they are trying to break free of the confines of the frames. At two points a single cellist manages to escape and plays tender solos; lanza has described the solo that closes the movement as "a love duet between the cellist and the pianist."

The second movement, a strong contrast to the first, is scored for a small chamber ensemble (two flutes, two oboes, two clarinets, two bassoons, trombone, and solo piano). This movement is more improvisatory, with a certain amount of graphic notation, and is very unstructured. The musicians are quite independent of each other, and their mobile-like music creates a succession of seemingly random arrangements, like hanging objects turning in the wind. It is almost as if this small group, having broken free of the strictures of the first movement, escapes into aleatoric unpredictability and delicate special effects. The third movement breaks the spell; here the composer is angry. It doesn't really matter what he is angry about. The drama has evolved from oppression, to freedom, to rage, and this momentum is reinforced by the manner in which the orchestra supports the pianist: sometimes moving hand in hand at the pace of the soloist, other times pushing the pianist forward even more forcefully in his rage.

It is magical how lanza supports the drama of the moment in each movement with musical effects created by electronic processing of the MIDI piano. Sometimes the instrument sounds like a gamelan, giving the music a quasi-Oriental quality, other times, like a marimba. All of this adds subtle colour to the musical palate, but the MIDI "effects" represent a small proportion of the music, perhaps as little as 10 per cent. Knowing that few musicians or concert halls possess a MIDI piano, lanza composed the work so that it could be effectively played on a traditional piano. After the premiere in Rosario, the concerto was performed by the Orquesta Sinfónica Nacional (Buenos Aires), the Orquestra Simfónica de Ribeirão Preto (Brazil), the Orquestra de Cámara de Santos (Brazil), and the Aarhus Symphony Orchestra (Denmark). Of a total of ten performances, only the Danish performance used a MIDI piano; the soloist on that occasion was British pianist Philip Mead. lanza is the only Canadian ever to perform the concerto, but he has never played it in Canada, and no Canadian orchestra has ever programmed the work. On the other hand, when we consider how few contemporary experimental works are played by Canadian orchestras, lanza is in good company.

VÔO (1992)

The tango-related works discussed above demonstrate lanza's deep connection to the culture of South America. It is embedded in the pores of his skin. His most moving work about this culture – and arguably the best work he has written – is *vôo*. Like *arghanum V* it is a work that cries out against man's destructive side, but in *vôo* it is not nature but peoples and cultures that are under attack. It is a work concerned with Columbus's discovery of America, and with the death of the New World at the hands of the Old.

In 1990 lanza was commissioned by the Centro para la promoción de la música Contemporánea of Madrid, Spain, to write a work commemorating the 500th anniversary of the first voyage of Christopher Columbus to the New World, to be premiered at the Festival de Alicante in 1992. The commission was controversial. In Spain Columbus is seen as a hero who ushered in a new and positive era in Spanish history, a courageous and farseeing individual who, against great odds, discovered a new land full of promise, space, and opportunity. But many in the New World, particularly First Peoples, have a negative view of Columbus, remembering the annihilation of millions through disease, exploitation, and slavery. lanza admired Columbus in the same way he admires discoverers of all types, knowing that such explorations require not only daring but also imagination, but he was equally aware of the horrors brought by the Old World to the New.[14] (We should note that lanza is of Guaraní ancestry on his mother's side.)

lanza wanted to write a piece that would somehow heal the wounds between the Old and New Worlds, and as we shall see, the healing effect of *vôo* works in a way that he could not have imagined when he first thought about the work. In 1990 he began to look for a text that was poetic but economical, a text that would tell the tale simply and directly. He considered writing it himself, but then remembered *No olvido do tempo / No ouvido do tempo*[15] by the Brazilian composer-poet Gil Nuno Vaz. lanza had attended the launch of this book three years previously in Brazil, and the author had inscribed a copy to him. This extraordinary work, written in Portuguese, relates the history of the world from the viewpoint of two imaginary poets, Raul and Leônidas. The two poets' work appears on facing pages of the printed book. Raul's text (printed on the right-hand pages) reads from the top to the bottom of the page, while Leônidas's text (printed on the left-hand pages) reads from bottom to top, so that the book can be turned either up or down. Readers can follow Raul's work from beginning to end, or turn the book upside down to read Leônidas's contribution. The two fictional poets confront each other on each set of facing pages, with each one's work upside down relative to the other's.

This poem fascinated lanza. The text is replete with word games: Nuno Vaz is fond of words that when reversed spell a second word, and of the subtle associations of palindromes and anagrams. lanza had pored over the poem for many days, and eventually put it away in his library. Three years later, when he received the commission from Spain, he took it down from the shelf, vaguely remembering that there was something in the work he could use. Soon his eyes fell on two facing pages that dealt with his subject matter. One page describes an Eden, a world where *columbinas* [doves] fly overhead; the facing page begins, "Os pés de Colombo pisam o Novo Mundo" [the feet of Columbus stepped onto the new world]. lanza felt, however, that for the purpose of his composition, the Nuno Vaz poem was too uncritical of Columbus. He wanted to add a few lines of his own to address this issue, and contacted Nuno Vaz; the poet had no objection.

vôo,[16] scored for voice, tape, and electronic modification of the voice, was composed with the voice of Meg Sheppard in mind; she sang the premiere and has performed it more than forty times since. The title is a Portuguese word meaning "flight." The work opens with the sounds of wind, waves, and seabirds on the tape. The singer enters immediately with the words, "Asas Columbinas" [the wings of the dove]. It is a land at peace, where life is evolving at its own natural pace, a world replete with angels, reptiles, and a long flight of eagles ("ser anjo, ser réptil e o vôo largo das águias"). At the line "o vôo largo" [a long

Example 8.17.
vôo, excerpt from p. 1

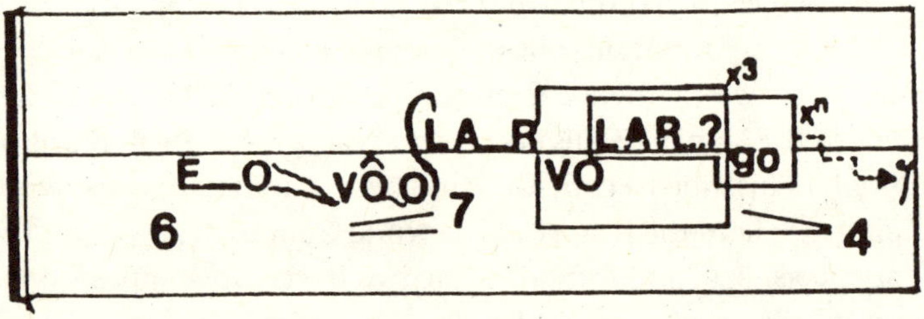

flight], lanza embarks on a series of word games in which the text shifts between *ovo* [egg], *vôo* [flight], *volar* [to fly], and *largo* [long] (see example 8.17). In the text, "E-OVÔOLAR-VOLAR-GO," the palindromic word *ovo* becomes *vôo* which elides into *vôolar*, followed by *volar*, which in turn elides into *largo*. lanza chose the syllables for sonic reasons – he is always thinking of timbral qualities (combining the same phonemes in different ways) – but he is also making a statement: he is telling us that Columbus's voyage was not only a flight of imagination but also an egg that would give birth to long-range (*largo*) consequences. At this point the tape part introduces rhythmic drumming, telling the listener that this world now contains human beings. There is something heightened in the music, a feeling of suspense. Something is about to happen. In the next line, "O ovo levanta o vôo: asas da imaginação" [the egg lifts in flight: the wings of imagination], the poet tells us of a flight – a voyage – of imagination. lanza accompanies the line with an ominous, dark cluster loop that becomes louder and louder until the appearance of a disturbing G-minor ostinato with the words, "Os pés de Colombo pisam o Novo Mundo" [the feet of Columbus stepped onto the new world]. In a hushed voice the singer whispers, "então" [then]. It is a fearful presentment.

She proceeds to tell the tale of a world now surrounded by ambushes ["envolven-nos ciladas"], and we hear the words *oro* [gold], *prata* [silver], *lanceros* [soldiers], *con crucis, con armas* [with crosses, with weapons], all accompanied by ethnic percussion, cymbals, gongs, and deeply tolling church bells. Eventually the tension subsides and the soloist, shadowed electronically in parallel lines, sings plaintively of "A linha leviana" [the heedless path]. After a five-second silence, lanza introduces a plaintive minor-mode melody composed by the native-born Peruvian composer, José de Orejón y Aparicio

Example 8.18.
vôo, excerpt from p. 4

(1706–65), taken from his *Cantada a Sola Mariposa*, one of the most beautiful works composed in the New World during the eighteenth century.[17] lanza has skilfully reworked the Baroque tune to give it a more timeless flavour (see example 8.18), creating a melody to break the heart. To it he adds words of his own that speak of the infinite ideas of imagination slowly disappearing ("largo, vaporlas alturas ideas infinitas de imaginación"). The opening words of the work, "asas columbinas," now return reminding us of what has disappeared and how. As the music fades away we again hear the gentle sound of seabirds and water, along with a half-whispered reminder, "asas – asas da imaginação" [wings – wings of imagination].

vôo is an overwhelmingly moving work that brings tears to the eyes. Sheppard views the singer as a storyteller, a shaman relating the story of her people around a campfire at night,[18] but like all shamans, she is also a healer. When lanza began to compose the work he had an idea that he could somehow reconcile the opposing attitudes to Columbus. *vôo* does not do this, but it achieves something better. It is a cathartic work in which we relive the tragedy in order to heal from within. Perhaps it is not surprising that *vôo* was not popular in Spain: the subject matter is too incriminating. The New World, on the other hand, has embraced the work wholeheartedly, recognizing its need to relive the tragedy and be healed. lanza, who has spent much of his career composing works about memory, instinctively understood that the emotional scars of a nation can only be healed by accepting reality. As an old Jewish saying tells us, "Deliverance comes through memory. Forgiveness is only possible through memory. And he who suppresses, he who forgets, lengthens our imprisonment."

CLOSING THOUGHTS

vôo is essentially about memories, a theme that since 1972 has been ubiquitous in lanza's output, like a thread winding its way from one work to another. lanza remembers world history in *penetrations VII* (1972) with the woman crushed by memories of humanity; in *ekphonesis IV* (1971) with the bombing of Guernica; in *vôo* with the memories of genocide. He remembers South America in *acúfenos III* with the sounds of Andean instruments; in *arghanum I* and *arghanum V* with the memories of tango, cafés, and bandoneons. He remembers personal history in *ekphonesis V* with his family in Argentina; in *bourdrones* (1985) with a friend who has died; in *un mundo imaginario* (1989) with the life and death of a beloved son. It could be said that this exploration is part of lanza's approach to life. Some people remember through family photographs, letters, or knick-knacks; lanza remembers through sounds. And more importantly, he wants us, as listeners, to participate in the memory experience so that these people, events, and sounds will live again in our ears and minds.

It is lanza's good fortune that his focus on memories coincided with the period of postmodernism in which the use of musical memories was once again acceptable. He has often been able to link psychological and historical memories to musical memories, bringing back melodic motives associated with a specific person, or using the same passage of music to introduce each new section of a work. This is especially apparent in *ekphonesis VI* (1988) , the final movement of *trilogy,* where all the dramatis personae reappear with their musical tags.

The idea of musical recollection is present not only in lanza's programmatic works but also in his more abstract pieces, such as *sensors III* (1982) and the MIDI piano concerto. Since 1979 lanza has often constructed works out of small motivic cells that expand incrementally, contract, and then expand again to form cellular variations of the original motive. He also uses referential blocks of sound – melodic, motivic, intervallic, or harmonic – that keep returning. Whether the piece is completely atonal, partly tonal, or a mixture of musical languages, the building method is the same, and the result is strikingly different from his works of the 1950s and 1960s, in which sonics come first and pitch is almost incidental. Since the 1950s lanza has travelled along a path from a music that sought unpredictability and instability at all costs to one full of musical recollection at many levels – one of the major historical paths of the late twentieth century that a number of serialist and aleatoric composers have also followed.

When it comes to sonic exploration, however, lanza has never deviated from his original path. The sonic effects in *plectros I* (1962) – where two pianists explore the colours created by touching the strings of a piano with fingers and various objects – come out of the same mindframe as the timbral effects produced by the MIDI piano in his second piano concerto twenty years later. And indeed the waves of sonic energy in *eidesis II* (1967) – where thirteen instrumentalists create an ever-changing landscape of seemingly electronic sounds – are closely related to the rapidly changing textures of *un mundo imaginario* written in the late 1980s. Throughout his life, more than anything else, it has been instrumental colour and timbre that have directed lanza's musical decisions.

Some composers reflect a school of thought in which the actual physical sound of a musical work is, to a certain extent, considered to be of a lesser order of significance than the abstract relationships of pitches and rhythms, a position summed up in a jocular remark attributed to Schoenberg that great music is music that would sound great even played on a zither. lanza's philosophy is quite the opposite: for him the sound *is* the musical work. lanza's compositions would not make good zither solos; they would lose their identity. Each one is wholly connected to specific and carefully chosen sonic landscapes – it is this soundscape that is the soul of the composition.

When I began my research I had the impression that lanza had been fortunate to live in interesting places in interesting times, but as my research progressed I began to realize that luck had little to do with it. I now believe that it is lanza's energetic, passionate, and outgoing personality that has enabled him to take advantage of each step, from Buenos Aires, to New York, to Berlin, to Quebec. In an address at the ceremony in which lanza was presented with the lifetime achievement award of the Organization of American States, Gilles Tremblay spoke of lanza's passionate nature: "His works with their evocative titles – *penetrations, eidesis, acúfenos, plectros* – testify to meticulous research and, at the same time, to a mode of thinking that is very intuitive, even frantic: a kind of organized frenzy. If I had to associate him with one of the four elements – earth, air, water, and fire – it is certainly fire that I would choose."[19] During the reception after the award presentation, when I was introduced to Tremblay as lanza's biographer, Tremblay commented perceptively, "You are fortunate, for quite apart from the music, [lanza] is such an interesting person." Tremblay proved to be right. lanza is formidably intelligent, fiercely original, courageous in the face of criticism, and resolutely optimistic.

alcides lanza at the Akademie der Kunste, Berlin, 1973. Photograph by Werner Berthsold, reproduced by kind permission of alcides lanza.

It is sadly true that many composers and performers lose their joy in music as they grow older: whether it is because they are disappointed in their careers, or feel that their style is becoming passé, or simply grow too tired, there is a sense of bitterness. This is definitely not the case with lanza. In terms of sheer joy in music, it is almost as if his biological clock stopped at the age of thirty. He still exhibits the same enthusiasm and youthful curiosity about music as a young man setting out on his career. So, with this character trait in mind, I would like to conclude by adding to Tremblay's choice of element. Yes, "fire" very much describes lanza's passionate music and energetic personality, but I also think that one could equally choose "water" – the element associated with life, growth, and above all, endurance.

NOTES

1 Interview with alcides lanza, Montreal, 14 June 1999.

2 Interview with alcides lanza, Montreal, 15 May 2005.

3 Interview with Joseph Petric, Montreal, 9 June 2001.

4 Interview with alcides lanza, Montreal, 14 June 1999.

5 lanza discusses *arghanum I* in interview, Montreal, 14 June 1999; all quotations from lanza in this section are from that interview. lanza found the word "arghanum" in Sibyl Marcuse's dictionary, *Musical Instruments*, where she defines it as an "Arabic name for the Byzantine organ ... It had bellows of skin and iron, and the word arghanum was interpreted as meaning 1000 voices ... The Byzantines reputedly used the arghanum to disconcert their enemies, and it is reported to have been audible sixty miles away." Sibyl Marcuse, *Musical Instruments: A Comprehensive Dictionary*, corrected edition (NY: Norton, 1975), p. 21.

6 Constant Lambert, *Music ho!* (London: Faber, 1934), p. 213.

7 lanza discusses *arghanum V* in interview, Montreal, 14 June 1999; all quotations from lanza in this section are from that interview.

8 Petric recorded the second version of *arghanum V* on his CD, *Orbiting Garden* (Centrediscs CMCCD 7802, 2002).

9 To lanza, the Islas Malvinas are Argentinean.

10 In my interview with Petric (Montreal, 9 June 2001) he describes the work as "amazingly organic."

11 In a 1997 lecture on his MIDI piano concerto (a work that incorporates much of *arghanum V*) lanza pointed out many of the connections with *El monito*. Much "inside information" in the following discussion comes from his notes for this lecture.

12 In order to distinguish between the different versions of *arghanum V* lanza added suffixes to the roman numeral: the second version for Petric is called *arghanum pet* (*pet* for *Pet*ric), and the piano version is called *arghanum Vπ* (π for *piano*). lanza recorded *arghanum Vπ* for his CD, *Music of the Americas, 1* (Shelan eSp-9301-CD, 1993).

13 lanza discusses his *concerto for MIDI piano and orchestra* in interview, Montreal, 22 Oct. 1999; all quotations from lanza in this section are from that interview.

14 lanza discusses his feelings about Columbus in interview, Montreal, 15 Dec. 1997.

15 Gil Nuno Vaz, *No olvido do tempo / No ouvido do tempo* (Santos, Brazil: private publication, 1984).

16 *vôo* is discussed in three interviews: lanza and Sheppard, Montreal, 15 Dec. 1997; lanza, Montreal, 15 Dec. 1997; and lanza, Montreal, 22 Apr. 1998.

17 lanza used the excerpt found in Gerard Béhague, *Music in Latin America: An Introduction* (Englewood Cliffs, NJ: Prentice-Hall, 1979), 49. The original is in E minor, but lanza reworked the music in C-sharp minor. The text of the original aria begins with the words, "*Con las alas*" [with wings]. lanza was attracted to both the music and the flight imagery of the text.

18 Interview with Meg Sheppard, Montreal, 15 Dec. 1997.

19 "Ses oeuvres aux titres évocateurs – penetrations, eidesis, acúfenos, plectros – témoignent à la fois de recherches poussées et d'un mode de pensée très intuitif, voire frénétique: une sorte de frénésie organisée. Si j'avais à l'associer à l'un des quatre éléments que sont la terre, l'air, l'eau et le feu, c'est sûrement le feu que je choisirais." Address given at McGill University, Montreal, 9 Dec. 1996.

9

Hidden Meaning in Brian Cherney's *Die klingende Zeit*

Neil Middleton, McGill University

As conversation, this study of *Die klingende Zeit* may be read as a "lesson with the master," since it was initially motivated by NEIL MIDDLETON's admiration for and desire to better understand his mentor's capacity to control and shape the intricate complexities of large scale formal structures across time. Originally from Saskatchewan, Middleton travelled to Montreal in 2001 with an already impressive record for his youth, in that several of his compositions had already been performed by the Saskatoon Composers Society and broadcast on the CBC. While at McGill, he studied with Brian Cherney, he was composer-in-residence for the Wind Symphony, and he was an involved member of the Electronic Music Studio and the ensemble GEMS, participating in the latter as composer, performer, producer, and historical archivist. Since his graduation (2004) he has written compositions for film and for solo oboe as well as various vocal-instrumental duets with and without electronics. All reflect his interest in the perception of time and its expansion and contraction as a specious present, evident in his thesis project, *Fading Points,* for large wind ensemble.

The works of Brian Cherney have long been recognized for their exquisite pacing and beauty. What is not immediately evident to the listener is the intricate web of musical reference lying beneath the surface. After much thought and examination, Cherney creates pieces that are full of layered and subtle references to a central theme, drawn from such diverse disciplines as poetry, painting, mysticism, or even other music. In *Die klingende Zeit* (1993), a mini-concerto for flute and orchestra dedicated to the Pierrot Ensemble and its director, flautist Robert Cram, Cherney explores the relationship between music and time. In his own words, "on one level, the piece is about time made 'audible' but on another level it is about the way we experience music during the passing of chronological time."[1] To develop a better appreciation of this work, it is necessary to explore the many layers of reference that Cherney weaves together.

The narrative of *Die klingende Zeit* follows the passing of the twenty-four hours of a day through the form of a timeline that is divided into four quarters: afternoon (noon to 18:00 hours), evening (18:00 hours to midnight), night (midnight to 06:00 hours) and morning (06:00 hours to noon). Each six-hour quarter is reduced to six and a half minutes of *Die klingende Zeit*. The four quarters ought to add up to twenty-six minutes of music but a note in the score indicates that the fourth section, "morning," is absent from the work: "The fourth quarter – 06:00 hours to noon – does not exist in the piece, only in the imagination."

THE SOUNDS OF TIME

Central to the language of *Die klingende Zeit* is the sound of bells. Originally used to call people to prayer, the practice of ringing bells at regular intervals has made them an important symbol of time in the western world. Cherney borrows this symbology by using the sound of bells to indicate the time of day, the passing of musical time, and by making reference to music about bells in order to create temporal distinctions such as past and present.

The work opens with the sound of twelve bell chimes, indicating 12:00 noon. Bell chimes occur next at 15:00 and then at 18:00 and can be heard faintly ringing twelve times at midnight. These times correspond to the canonic hours of prayer: *sext, none, vespers* and the start of *vigils*, which Cherney indicated at appropriate points in sketches of *Die klingende Zeit*. When asked about the significance of including the names of the prayer times in sketches, but not in the score, Cherney stated that "these merely created a kind of additional link in my mind to the history of the chiming clock in Europe, which was first of all intended to chime out the times for these prayers."[2]

By chiming specific hours in *Die klingende Zeit*, Cherney creates immediately perceptible time symbols that help to articulate the narrative flow. As the work progresses, though, the role of the chiming bells becomes less and less important. The opening chimes are very loud and involve the whole ensemble, but each subsequent bell figure is quieter, in a lower tessitura, with longer intervals between bell "tolls," marking

Example 9.1.
The development of the bell-like chord

Time	Interval between "tolls"	Pitches	Dynamic level	Instrumentation
12:00 PM			*ff*	glockenspiel, vibraphone, piano, violin, viola, cello
3:00 PM	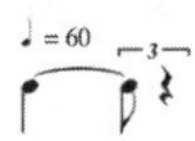		*mf*	vibraphone, piano
6:00 PM	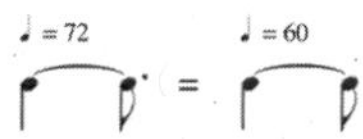		*mp*	3 gongs, piano
12:00 AM	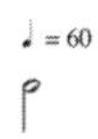	Changing single pitches in piano.	*mp* - gongs *pp* - piano	3 gongs, single pitches in low register piano

a reduction in instrumental numbers. The final chime, at midnight, is a subdued, nostalgic gesture. The progression from clearly perceptible time markers in the opening to their disappearance in the latter part of the work suggests that the flow of time is slowly unravelling.

It is also important to note that church bells as such are not included in the instrumentation in that the work is scored for flute (doubling alto flute), clarinet (doubling bass clarinet), percussion (marimba, vibraphone, glockenspiel, crotales, gongs, triangles, tubular chimes, glass, wood and metal chimes, sistrum, sleighbells and bass drum), piano, violin, viola, and cello. Cherney deftly mixes the piano with metallic percussion instruments to create the illusion of large church bells, an illusion supported by the similarity of the attack and decay envelopes between large bells and metallic percussion instruments in combination with held piano notes. Another aspect is the design of the piano chords; as shown in example 9.1, Cherney creates harmonies that sound like the inharmonic resonance of large church bells. These harmonies are part of a larger harmonic language based on the interplay between relative levels of consonance and dissonance. Two temporal layers are created through the orchestration: the piano and percussion recreate clock time, while the flute, clarinet, and strings articulate the flow of musical time.

Example 9.2.
The minute repeater rhythm in the glockenspiel, m. 50

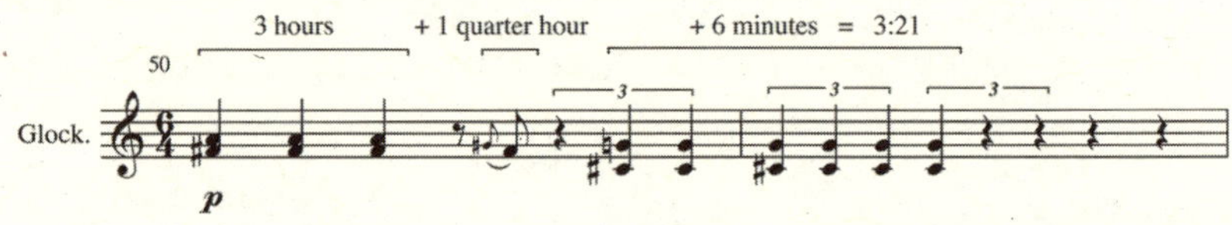

A second, less obvious, reference to the sound of bells is Cherney's use of rhythms taken from the repeater watch, an ingenious mechanism invented in 1680. This watch originally chimed only on the hour and the quarter-hour when activated, but with later advances in technology, it sounded the minutes of the day as well. In the twentieth century the mechanism was sufficiently miniaturized to fit into a wristwatch. The chimes in a repeater watch consist of two steel bands in the body of the watch that when struck mimic small bells. Numerous rhythmic patterns can be created on these two bands, so that chimes for the hour, quarter-hour, and minute each have a distinctive rhythmic pattern. Cherney was intrigued by the sophisticated mechanism of the repeater watch and the detailed engineering necessary to transform it into a wristwatch, and he includes a detailed description in the notes to *Die klingende Zeit*. Indeed, the title is a direct reference to the ability of the repeater watch to "sound" time. Cherney used the hour, quarter-hour, and minute patterns to articulate a more precise "current time" between the chiming bell figures. The repeater-watch figures usually have one second between hour chimes; the quarter-hours are indicated by grace notes, and individual minutes are separated by less than a second (see example 9.2).

The minute repeater rhythm is not immediately obvious for two reasons. First, such a rhythm is not automatically associated with the indication of a specific clock time. The repeater watch has never been a mainstream timekeeper and its rhythms are virtually unknown in the latter twentieth and early twenty-first centuries. Second, in sharp contrast to the sound of the chiming bells marking 12:00, 15:00, and 18:00, the rhythms of the repeater watch are always marked *piano*, placing them in the background of the local texture. Why obscure such a musical artefact? While this rhythm is obviously important to Cherney, it is not necessarily important that the listener immediately perceive its significance as a marker of current time. Though the rhythms are placed at important structural points in the piece, they are seldom noticeable because they are worked into the overall rhythmic texture of the piece, becoming an inseparable element of *Die klingende*

Example 9.3.
Short-long and down-up patterns of ticking music

Zeit. In this manner Cherney intertwines clock time with the flow of musical time, creating a sense that one disappears into the other.

Related to the sound of the hour chimes is "ticking music," which represents the actual mechanical sounds of clocks. Cherney describes "ticking music" as an archetype, a set of parameters that create a type of music without actually defining its contents. He often reuses archetypes in his works, recasting them each time in a different context with different content. In *Die klingende Zeit* the "ticking music" is defined by musical lines made up of short, repeated rhythmic cells, creating the image of many clocks ticking together. The layering of lines with different rhythmic cells results in a texture full of "many minute differences and complexities," which Cherney likens to many small mechanical parts sounding at the same time.[3] The short cells are either a single rhythmic duration, such as an eighth note, or a pattern of short and long durations such as those illustrated in example 9.3. The short-long rhythmic cells are usually combined with a down-up melodic pattern to create a sense of cycle or periodicity, lending credibility to the idea of mechanized music. The different rhythms present in "ticking music" also create a context for rhythmic elements that come later in the piece.

In m. 69 Cherney uses the sound of ringing bells to link the perception of time with place through a reference to Ravel's *La Vallée des cloches,* a title that for Cherney also evoked a reference to the Vallée des Joux, a famous watch-making region in Switzerland. Cherney often works quotations and allusions to other music into the texture of his works. References are selected both for their topical relevance to the piece at hand and for their ability to integrate well with the surrounding music. Often, a musical reference is not revealed immediately, if at all. "Rather than direct quotation, I much more often make allusions to other music (i.e. pieces) – this means that I use certain features of the original, such as texture and rhythm, but alter the pitch structure to fit the context."[4]

In this instance, Cherney tries to capture the overall texture of the piece, created by wide-ranging dyads and a sextuplet accompaniment

Example 9.4.
A comparison of *La Vallée des cloches,* mm. 3–4 and *Die klingende Zeit,* mm. 69–70

pattern, going so far as to include Ravel's indication "*très doux et sans accentuation*" [very softly and without accent] in the score. The reference is first anticipated by an octave C-sharp in m. 57, but it is not actually unveiled until m. 69. Dense mid-register chords in the piano, foreign to the Ravel texture, follow the initial octave C-sharp. In m. 65 the register shifts to that of the *La Vallée des cloches* reference, and in m. 67 we finally hear its defining octave dyads, though they are C-sharps instead of G-sharps. In the latter part of m. 69, Cherney reveals the full texture. This rhythm appears as a naturally occurring element in *Die klingende Zeit* since it is prefigured by the clarinet starting in m. 23, during the first instance of "ticking music." As such, the reference to *La Vallée des cloches* is not an obvious quotation but rather seems an indigenous part of the texture of *Die klingende Zeit,* creating a connection to both time and place through its double allusion to the Vallée des Joux and the sound of bells. From m. 69 on Cherney quickly starts to alter the referenced music. Instead of condensing the intervals of the accompaniment pattern from fourths to thirds, as in the original, the intervals are expanded from fourths to fifths. The chords in the left hand also have altered intervals. The fourth, which descends a third in Ravel's version, for example, becomes a second (see example 9.4).

Example 9.5.
Non-retrogradable rhythms and predetermined chord progressions

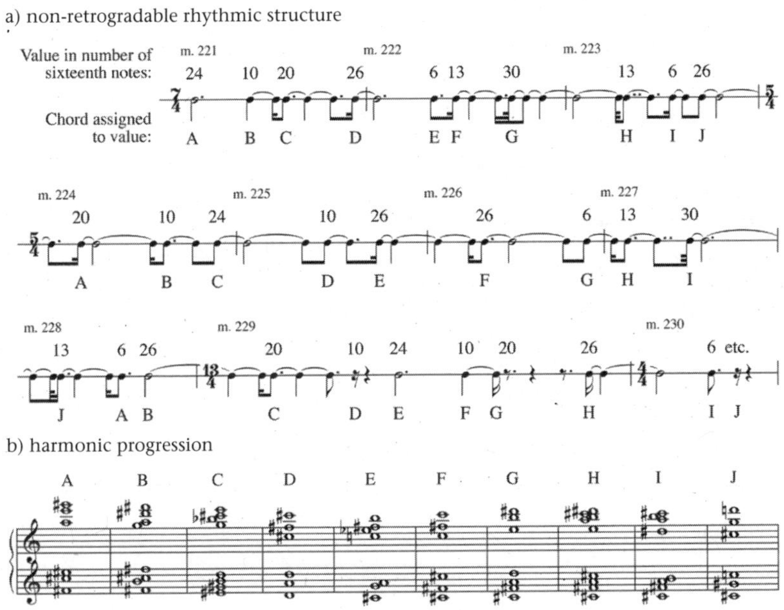

Another reference to bells is "tolling bell music," an archetype borrowed from Cherney's *In Stillness Ascending* (1986). This music is quite different from the chiming bell sounds previously discussed. In Cherney's words, "(it is) a multi-layered complex of chords based on a long 'non-retrogradable' rhythmic structure."[5] In *Die klingende Zeit*, the complex takes the form of a repeating chord progression (labelled A to J in example 9.5b). The "non-retrogradable" rhythmic structure[6] also repeats, though at a different interval from the chord progression (see example 9.5). The term "tolling bell music" is derived from the timbres of the chords, which resemble the inharmonic timbres of bells. Given the important role of bell-like chords in the piece, and Cherney's explicit reference to *La Vallée des cloches*, how could he not include a reference to his own tolling bell music? This autoquotation re-initiates music from Cherney's past in that of the present, creating a personal link between music of the past and present.

STRUCTURING TIME

The structure of *Die klingende Zeit* was created using a technique described by Cherney as "breathing rhythms." At the core of breathing

Example 9.6.
Basic phrase shape

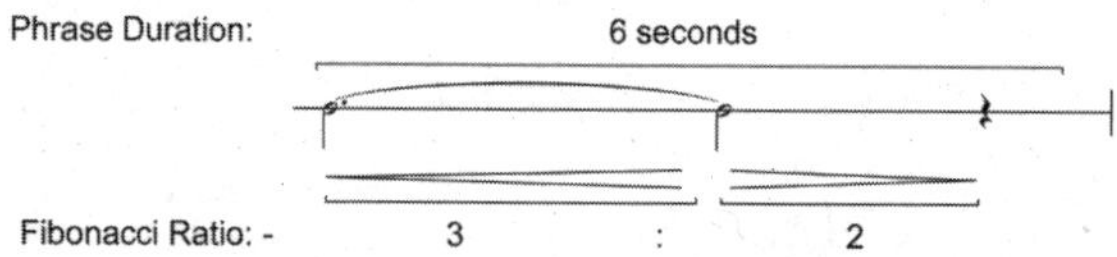

Example 9.7.
Layered rhythmic lines

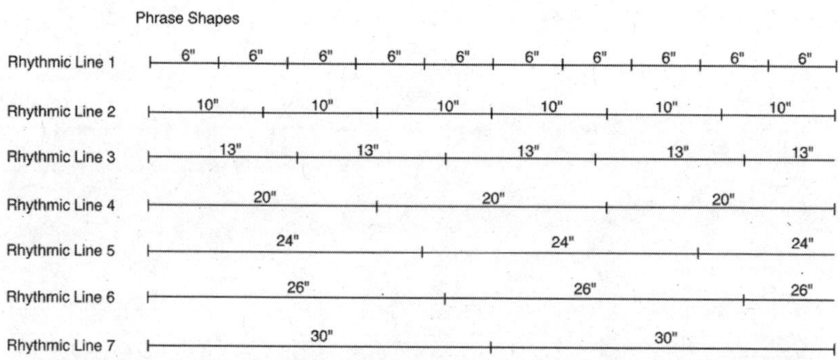

rhythms is a simple phrase shape modelled on the act of breathing, which Cherney demonstrated in an interview by slowly breathing in (analogous to crescendo), then out (analogous to diminuendo), and then pausing for a few seconds. The proportion of crescendo to diminuendo within each phrase shape is determined by ratios taken from the Fibonacci sequence.[7]

This phrase shape, along with its specific duration, is then repeated to create a long rhythmic line, a single "breathing rhythm" that extends the entire length of the piece. Within that line a larger layered structure of breathing rhythms is created when different rhythmic lines, each having a unique basic phrase duration (6, 10, 13, 20, 24, and 30 seconds) are layered one on top of the other (see example 9.7). This structure extends the entire length of *Die klingende Zeit.* This layering was originally inspired by Bernd Aloys Zimmermann's *Photoptosis* (1968). In the opening section of *Photoptosis* two rhythmic patterns made from two different repeated durations are out of phase with each other, which suggested to Cherney the "use of two basic durations which I thought of as breathing rhythms."[8] This layered structure defines a substructure or rhythmic backbone over which the rest of *Die klingende Zeit* is laid out. Cherney wrote the substructure in advance of

Example 9.8.
Breathing rhythms and phrase structure, mm. 122–5

Example 9.9.
Breathing rhythms, ratios, and sectional durations

BR duration:	6"	10"	13"	20"	24"	26"	30"
Ratio:	6/129	10/129	13/129	20/129	24/129	26/129	30/129
Section durations:	54"	90"	117"	181"	217"	235"	272"

the rest of the music and composed the actual pitches and surface rhythms while making constant reference to it. The lengths of phrases, rhythms, and larger arches are therefore all subordinate to the breathing rhythms. The substructure is not, however, a hard rhythmic rule. Rather, it is treated more as a guide that is sometimes clearly evident in the surface structure, while at other times remains unnoticeable. Example 9.8 shows a section where the layered breathing rhythms clearly control the phrase structures of most instrumental lines. The flute, however, is only vaguely attentive to the substructure, displaying phrases that often extend beyond the phrase shape suggested by its breathing rhythm.

It is no coincidence that the rhythmic backbone is divided into seven sections, seven also being the number of layered breathing rhythms. Cherney has always been intrigued by the mystical implications of the number seven, and uses it in most of his works. Further, the durations of the subsections are determined by the ratio of the basic duration (6 seconds, 10 seconds, 13 seconds, etc.) of the breathing rhythm to the sum of all the basic durations (129 seconds). This ratio, multiplied by the duration of the entire piece (1170 seconds) gives the duration of each individual subsection of the backbone (see example 9.9). These same numbers were also used in the non-retrogradable surface rhythms of the tolling-bell music. By reusing these numbers to determine surface rhythms, larger phrase durations, and large-scale structural ratios, Cherney creates a rhythmic connection among all these levels.

MAKING SENSE OF TIME

What then is the correlation between the subdivisions of the rhythmic backbone and the three sections of the narrative form indicated by the chiming bells – afternoon, evening, and night? In preliminary sketches of the work Cherney assigned musical characteristics to each of these three sections. Afternoon is described as "bright, high, intense," evening is described with the words "colour darkens, twilight," and the terms "Nachtstück, misterioso" [nocturne, mysterious] are ascribed to

Example 9.10.
Narrative form, substructure, and registral form

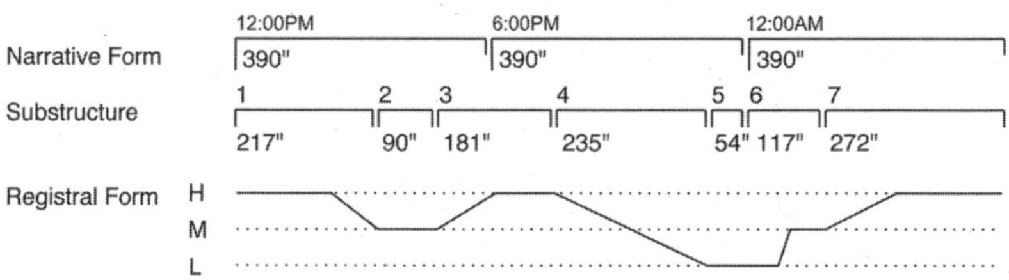

night. Though the narrative form of *Die klingende Zeit* is drawn from the poetic idea of the passing of a day, the substructure is by contrast a purely functional form, creating containers of time into which Cherney places the various events and processes of *Die klingende Zeit.* It is in the subdivisions of the substructure that Cherney's musical arguments supporting the narrative are to be found. The nature of that narrative is revealed, in between the simple hour chimes that mark the passing of time, as a long descent into the darkness of night, followed by a rise into the light of morning.

The descent begins with large-scale registral changes which, linked to the overall trajectory of the solo flute, are governed by the subdivisions of the rhythmic backbone (see example 9.10). The piece begins in a very high register in all instruments, in line with Cherney's words "bright, high, intense." The flute first emerges as a clear soloist towards the end of the opening subdivision, playing in a virtuosic style that covers its entire range. In the second subdivision of the backbone, the flute is exchanged for the alto flute and the clarinet for the bass clarinet, instruments that introduce a register approximately three octaves lower than the opening measures of the piece. This section develops into a multi-instrument duet between the alto flute and the viola in their lowest registers, and the bass clarinet and cello in their middle registers, slightly higher than the flute and viola to maintain an overall middle register.

The third subdivision starts with the reference to *La Vallée des cloches.* The alto flute and bass clarinet are traded for flute and clarinet as the music returns to the high opening register. In the middle of this subdivision the second section of the narrative form, evening, is signalled by the sound of bells chiming six o'clock. The fourth section of the substructure, the second longest of the piece, presents the listener with a long, slow descent in register, again in line with Cherney's description "colour darkens, twilight," coupled with a long acceleration and deceleration. In the midst of this rhythmic motion there is a brief flute cadenza, the only cadenza in the piece.

In sketches of *Die klingende Zeit* Cherney linked this descent with *Dark Night of the Soul,* a mystical text by St John of the Cross that describes the soul's descent towards earthly pleasures and away from union with God. Cherney carefully develops this powerful image, which is by no means immediately perceptible to the idle listener, as a subtle subtext within *Die klingende Zeit.* The predominance of the high register in the first section is used to highlight the long descent, and the flute, which reminds us of its role as soloist in the cadenza, represents the soul.

The fifth and shortest subdivision, the ultimate goal of the descent, contains a strange pseudoreference in the form of a melody, obviously foreign to *Die klingende Zeit,* that is described by Cherney as an "imaginary East-European" sounding melody. This highly ornamented tune is played by the alto flute and the bass clarinet in parallel, a twelfth apart, and is accompanied by a rhythmic underpinning suggestive of folk percussion instruments. The cello plays a pizzicato low C-sharp while the viola plays an offbeat, left-hand pizzicato A; the left-hand pizzicato ensures that the offbeat is weaker than the onbeat, helping the listener to clearly identify the beat. Over this rhythmic pedal the melody shifts back and forth between onbeat and offbeat patterns. By giving the cello a low C-sharp pizzicato instead of a resonant, low open-string C, Cherney creates a more percussive pizzicato with a much quicker decay, emphasized intermittently by muted notes in the piano. Cherney instructs the pianist to mute the bottom A and C strings at the approximate halfway point in order to create a "rich, gong-like sound." This rich mix of percussive sounds evokes the simple percussion instruments of a folk band. Described by Cherney as "an exotic, unexpected occurrence," this visceral, almost dance-like music evokes a sense of the body as a distraction on the path to enlightenment, a suggestion emphasized by the clear contrast between this section and the rest of *Die klingende Zeit,* making it seem almost a diversion from the musical path of the piece.

The sixth subdivision starts at the midnight point with an extensive reference to "Nacht" [night] from Arnold Schoenberg's *Pierrot Lunaire.* Cherney borrows texture, rhythm, and instrumentation from the opening of "Nacht" (see example 9.11a) and adds significance by overlapping the reference with the midnight chime in the percussion and the piano in m. 176 (see example 9.11b). The chiming has now

Example 9.11a. Opening measure of Schoenberg's "Nacht" from *Pierrot Lunaire*

Example 9.11b. *Die klingende Zeit*, mm. 176–9

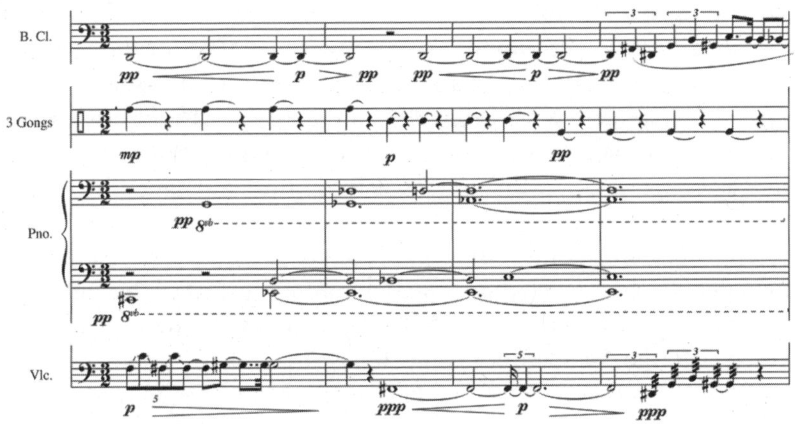

lost all of its original force; the piano only participates in the first eight chimes, leaving a lone gong to sound the last four. The text of "Nacht" describes giant moths killing the brightness of the sun and the descent of monsters on giant pinions (*Schwingen*) into human hearts. Schoenberg's setting of the text is full of undulating, descending musical lines made more eerie and furtive by the tremolo near the bridge in the cello and flutter tonguing in the bass clarinet. In *Die klingende Zeit* Cherney reorders and extends these elements so that it takes some time for the full texture to develop.

After presenting the opening of "Nacht," with altered intervals and with the cello and bass clarinet entrances inverted at m. 176, Cherney

Example 9.12.
Comparison of the bass clarinet in Schoenberg's "Nacht" and in Cherney's *Die klingende Zeit.* Courtesy of Belmont Music Publishers, Pacific Palisades, CA 90272

gives the first descending, flutter tongue line to the alto flute in m. 178. By employing the alto flute, an instrument not used in "Nacht", and presenting the material in a higher tessitura, Cherney suggests that the descending, flutter tongue line is in fact indigenous to *Die klingende Zeit.* In m.180 the alto flute starts an exact quotation of the opening vocal phrase from m. 4 of "Nacht". The text to this phrase is "Finstre, schwarze Riesenfalter – Töteten der Sonne Glanz" [Dark, black giant moths; killed the brightness of the sun].[9] The end of the phrase (m. 6 of "Nacht") overlaps with the descending, flutter tongue line in the bass clarinet (see example 9.12). This exact material is not actually found in "Nacht," but it is similar in terms of register, instrumentation, and effect to the bass clarinet material found in m. 13 of "Nacht." The powerful musical imagery of "Nacht" illustrates the dark night into which the soul has descended, an image that Cherney places at the nadir of *Die klingende Zeit* to underline and clarify his allusion to the St John text: the soul is lost.

Immediately following the "Nacht" reference is a reference to Gustav Mahler's setting of Friedrich Rückert's poem "Um Mitternacht" [Midnight]. Again the reference is disguised by slight alterations to the rhythms, pitches, and instrumentation. Two different motifs from "Um Mitternacht" are heard in m.188 (see example 9.13). One is a descending diatonic line played by the bass clarinet; while it is not an exact replica of the descending bassoon line in "Um Mitternacht," it is devoid of the chromaticism of the descending motif used in "Nacht," and is thus identified with this new material. The alto flute and viola repeat the short opening motif of "Um Mitternacht," which the listener can easily identify. Two measures later the violin plays an almost exact quotation of Mahler's setting of the first two lines of "Um

Example 9.13.
Comparison of motives in *Die klingende Zeit* and Ravel's *Um Mitternacht*

Mitternacht." The text, "Um Mitternacht / Hab' ich gewacht / Und aufgeblickt zum Himmel" [At midnight I awoke and gazed up to heaven][10] presents an antithesis to the dark imagery of the Schoenberg reference. The music, transposed up two octaves and played by harmonics on the violin, creates a startling contrast to the dark, low register of the preceding reference to "Nacht."

The vocal line in "Um Mitternacht" rises, in direct contrast to the vocal line in "Nacht." By placing allusions to two such different descriptions of night side by side and by using allusions to motifs from the works rather than large, cumbersome quotations, Cherney skillfully works the not dissimilar musical motifs into a larger texture that portrays first the darkness and despair of a lost soul, followed by the hope that humans must rely on in their darkest hour. This amazing juxtaposition turns the piece away from the mundane and towards the spiritual.

The "Um Mitternacht" reference is followed directly by the final and longest subdivision of *Die klingende Zeit*, the beginning of which is subtitled "In the Garden of Time," a reference to *The Garden of Earthly Delights*, a work from the 1970s that Cherney never completed; this piece, based on the painting of the same title by Hieronymous Bosch, was intended to be an involved piece of *Augenmusik*, a term used to describe a style of symbolic notation, the effects of which are apparent to the eye, not the ear.[11] Cherney notes: "The idea of a garden of time appealed to me, since it took a very abstract notion such as time and made it sound as if it could somehow have attributes which would be found in a garden, such as flowers and trees."[12] In *Die klingende Zeit* this idea is literally transposed into the score through a collage inserted into the music, starting at m. 196, the beginning of the last subdivision, where we hear the repeater watch rhythm for the last time, now in the piano, indicating that it is 1:49. The primary element of the collage is a large watch with the four inner dials replaced by snippets of music (see example 9.14). Behind the inserted music, we can just make out the time on the watch, which is 1:50, one minute after the repeater watch. The inserted music is to be played by the percussionist who is instructed to "improvise a very soft tapestry of sound using the material in the circles. Begin with any circle and proceed clockwise or counter-clockwise to each circle in turn."[13] Brief motives taken from throughout *Die klingende Zeit* recall the references to *La Vallée des cloches,* "Um Mitternacht," and the "ticking music" archetype, among others, but Cherney obscures these references by placing them in the crotales and the glockenspiel, necessitating their transposition up several octaves. The improvised percussion texture is underpinned by static pitches that fade in and out in the rest of the ensemble. A walking path drawn into the score leads from the watch at m. 196, across three systems, to a picture of a repeater watch at m. 205 with its faceplate removed to show its inner workings. This image coincides with the start of the last instance of ticking music. Placed along the path are pictures of people walking and standing idly, trees, a duck, a robin, a butterfly, and a donkey, as well as small pictures of chronometers.

What then are the conductor and performers to make of this large, complex, and somewhat humorous collage? The key is in the instructions to the percussionist. The option to move clockwise or counter-clockwise through the snippets of music suggests that time has now

Example 9.14.
Watch faceplate with inserted music; © Les Éditions Doberman-Yppan, 2002

been transcended or simply dissolved. In this garden of time the listener hears snippets of music from earlier in the piece, and from much earlier in the past century. The images of people standing idly, looking at the various objects around them, seems a response to the static nature of the music that the ensemble is playing. The music does not develop, but is rather at a point of repose and reflection after the grand image presented in the previous subdivision.

The musical action starts again at the end of the collage with the "ticking music" followed by an ascent in the flute part, indicative of the awakened soul's rise toward God, in parallel with the sunrise of a new dawn. The end of the ascent meets the "tolling bell" archetype, suggesting stasis and the soul's achievement of enlightenment. This ascension towards stasis is a form Cherney often uses in his more mystical works, where the idea of ascension is literally translated into long, rising harmonic lines that eventually arrive at a musical plateau or point of stasis symbolizing enlightenment. While the piano plays the "tolling bell" music in a high register, the flute and clarinet are given fast, active gestures mimicking morning birdsong, also in their highest registers.

Near the end of the "tolling bell" music, a descending gesture (six quarter notes) starts in the vibraphone and is picked up by the wind and string instruments, each with a different rhythmic value. The performers are instructed to repeat this gesture a set number of times, getting softer each time, even though the original dynamic marking is *ppp*. In the brief coda-like section that follows all instruments hold long sustained notes or trills beneath the solo flute melody, which is an elaboration of the preceding descending gesture. Then the music fades out into a quiet flurry of wind chimes. In the aleatoric section Cherney effectively splits the flow of time into a number of individual streams. We become aware of a number of individual instruments, instead of a unified ensemble. As the music fades out this final impression is left with the listeners who are now to imagine their own fourth quarter, the new day. The music fades into silence but the flow of time fades into the infinity of countless imaginations.

The subtle, almost humble references that illustrate the narrative and subtext of *Die klingende Zeit* are drawn from music and sounds that Cherney knows and loves. The musical images resulting from these layers of reference, both musical and otherwise, are both convincing and compelling. Often inaudible to the unaware listener, their true significance must be explored in order to gain a deeper understanding of Cherney's impressive composition.

NOTES

1 Introductory notes to the score of *Die klingende Zeit.*

2 Electronic correspondence between the author and Brian Cherney, 1 October 2005.

3 Cherney, interview with the author, 30 May 2005.

4 Brian Cherney, quoted in Sandy Thorburn, "Like Ghosts from an Enchanter Fleeing: Melodic Quotations as Recognizable Signifiers in the Works of Brian Cherney," *ICM Newsletter* 1 (Jan. 2003): 3–7.

5 Liner notes for *In Stillness Ascending*, CD, McGill Records: 750036-2

6 A "non-retrogradable" rhythm is one in which the retrograde produces the same sequence of durations as itself.

7 The Fibonacci sequence is a series of numbers in which each number, except the first two, is the sum of the preceding two numbers (0 1 1 2 3 5 8 ...).

8 Cherney, interview with the author, 15 June 2005.

9 Poetry by Albert Giraud (trans. from German, Stanley Applebaum).

10 English translation by Emily Ezust.

11 This type of subtle musical ornamentation flourished in the sixteenth and seventeenth centuries.

12 Electronic correspondence between the author and Brian Cherney, 1 October 2005.

13 Introductory notes to the score of *Die klingende Zeit.*

10

Bruce Mather's Symbolist *Théâtre de l'âme*

Steven Huebner, McGill University

STEVEN HUEBNER currently holds the prestigious James McGill Chair in Musicology. Born and bred in Montreal, he returned to his alma mater in 1985 after completing doctoral studies at Princeton University. His internationally celebrated research focuses on French and Italian music of the nineteenth and early twentieth centuries and he has written extensively on opera, including *French Opera at the Fin de Siècle: Wagnerism, Nationalism and Style* (1999) and *The Operas of Charles Gounod* (1990). Moving effortlessly back and forth between the libretto, the poetic significance of various musical elements, and broader questions of identity, his interest in *La Princesse blanche* and Bruce Mather's seemingly French soul reflects both the hermeneutical rigour of his scholarly intellect and the curiosity of a colleague who, himself routinely travelling back and forth between Montreal and France, also leads a *vie bifurqué* of sorts.

TWO FRANCOPHILES

Canada, two solitudes: clichés are inevitably paper-thin. McGill has long nurtured an interaction between composers from *le Canada anglais* [English Canada] and the Québécois milieu. Hired in 1966, Bruce Mather may well be the ur-Francophile among McGill Anglo composers. An admirer of French culture generally, he has also been committed to – and, in turn, celebrated by – the Québec new music community. Studies at the Paris Conservatoire and early settings of French texts were followed by sabbaticals and teaching in France, the purchase of property there, a *vie bifurqué* [bifurcated life] between two countries, and even a predilection for French wines that have supplied titles for his compositions. And Mather's one-act opera *La Princesse blanche* (1994) was commissioned by Chants Libres, a Montreal-based music theatre company created in 1990 by "chantactrice" Pauline Vaillancourt, metteur-en-scène Joseph St-Gelais, and writer Renald Tremblay.[1]

Mather's opera rearticulates Rainer Maria Rilke's early and rarely performed play *Die weisse Fürstin; Eine Szene am Meer* [The White Princess; A Scene by the Sea], via a compact translation and adaptation by Tremblay. Rilke commands attention here not because of his central position in twentieth-century German letters or the popularity of his German verse with other composers, but a little more obliquely because his enthusiasm for French culture resonates with Mather's own expatriate Francophile tastes. Following a peripatetic existence with his mistress Lou Andreas-Salomé, a brief marriage to the sculptor Clara Westhoff, and the drying up of his funds, Rilke settled in Paris in 1902, initially to collect material for a book on Rodin that had been commissioned by his German publisher. This stay stretched into twelve years. The French capital became Rilke's base during a period of wide-ranging travel and, as has often been argued, the focal point of his understanding of urban modernity and alienation. Well versed in French literature from a young age and an accomplished translator, he would even make his own contribution to his adopted homeland with a substantial number of French poems that occupy a relatively unexplored corner of his prolific output.

Rilke completed the first version of *Die weisse Fürstin* at the end of 1898, when he was only twenty-four years old. Although the play predates the Paris period it manifestly shares some of the major Parisian theatrical enthusiasms of the 1890s – a little Ibsen, a lot of Maeterlinck. Nurturing the hope that the great Italian actress Eleonora Duse would take an interest in the title role, Rilke greatly expanded the play in 1904, developing more fully the relationship between the Princess and her sister, Monna Lara.[2] It is this version that Renald Tremblay reduced, often tapering Rilke's elaborate free-verse metaphors into succinct and evocative aphorisms to produce a libretto that Mather crafted into one hour of music. Yet in both abbreviated and complete form, the pedigree of Rilke's play as a turn-of-the-century symbolist drama remains clear, and a fundamental *point d'appui* [starting place] for critical reflection on Mather's chamber opera.

SYMBOLIST POETICS

Plot summaries inherently shortchange the operas they represent, but perhaps no more so than in symbolist works that cultivate an aesthetic of suggestion over narrative. With pointed reference to the texture of the play itself, Rilke's (but not Tremblay's) Princess tells her sister that in the dream world "die Zeit ist Raum" [time is space], surely an intended echo of Gurnemanz's famous words to Parsifal, "Du siehst, mein Sohn, zum Raum wird hier die Zeit" [You see, my son, here space becomes transformed into time], as the last half of the first act of Wagner's opera becomes suspended in ritual. To recount the sequence of stage events in *La Princesse blanche*, then, is radically to flatten the perspective. Rilke's setting is a villa on the Italian seashore during the late sixteenth century; the Italian seashore emerges as the location in the musical and verbal text of *La Princesse blanche*, but the time is less precisely identified. The Prince has left the castle for the first time in eleven years. The Princess (soprano) awaits a lover about whom she has dreamed since her marriage. She wishes to send both the old servant Amadéo (bass) and her younger sister Monna Lara (coloratura soprano) away. When Monna Lara insists on staying, the Princess draws her into her dream world. Amadéo introduces a messenger (baritone) who bears a letter for the Princess, the contents of which she already knows: her dream lover will appear that very night. She is to wave to him from the shore to signal her readiness. The messenger also informs the sisters that he has witnessed the devastating spread of bubonic plague elsewhere in Italy. He warns them to be wary of sinister monks who remove bodies from houses but who themselves are infected and deadly. The Princess, given to ever more extended descriptions and fantasies about her lover, comforts Monna Lara, who is horrified and frightened by the messenger's account. At last a sound is heard from the sea. Monna Lara leaves the Princess to her own thoughts. But the lover does not disembark. The verbal text in both the play and opera breaks off at this point, giving way to precisely described gestures in the Rilke play and an extended solo for the Princess in Mather's opera.

The question of what actually happens at the final curtain – shrouded in mystery in both works – is best held in abeyance. I will return to it only at the end, and turn for the moment to a more extended reflection upon the aesthetics of symbolist theatre. In his mid-twenties, Rilke made no secret of his enthusiasm for Maurice Maeterlinck's plays in a series of reviews of the Belgian writer's work.[3] He rightly identified the centrality of simple external action having the effect of drawing spectators into a "grossen, primären Gefühl"[4] [a large primal feeling] that lay behind the spoken word. Veritable marionettes, the psychologies of individual characters count for little. Nor was it Maeterlinck's aim to create fragmented, individuated reactions in the attending public. Rilke recognized that this dank, dark *théâtre de l'âme* seemed engineered to elicit a collective response, like that which ties people together in the face of natural catastrophes as they share their inner anxieties. In many of the earlier plays – *L'Intruse, Les Aveugles,* or *Pelléas et Mélisande* for example – the primal feeling arises from *malheur,* and the most cogent vehicle to project that condition, death. Rilke suggested that: "One might group all of these plays together under the name of "death dramas" because they contain nothing but dying-hours and reflect the belief [Bekenntnis] of a poet who sees in death ... the only disconsolate certainty felt every day of our lives [tägliche trostlose Sicherheit unseres Lebens]."[5]

This summary remark touches on important elements of Maeterlinck's art: inner anguish and fatalism, the recognition of fear as a dark spiritual condition in contradistinction to Christian faith, and the omnipresence of *malheur* even in the midst of daily affairs.[6] For although Maeterlinck's plays tend to be set in distant and gloomy chateaux – an effect heightened in performance by the use of scrims and the dreamlike enunciation of the players – a quotidian quality emerges in their plainness of syntax and diction. Characters using everyday language suggest, but do not name. This quintessentially symbolist trait has a corollary in Maeterlinck's cultivation of dialogue replete with successions of non sequiturs. Reduced teleology on the large-scale level of plot, then, seems mirrored on the local level in the attenuated teleology of dialogue among characters, almost suggesting the limitations of verbal communication itself. They typically "talk around" their concerns, skirt the absences in their visible lives, and allow primal feeling (and the quality of those absences) to emerge in pregnant silences.

More space than time, one might say. *Die weisse Fürstin* seems tributary to Maeterlinck's approach to drama in its stasis, isolated palatial setting (Renaissance rather than Gothic, however), strong lapsed-Christian undertone, evocation of general feeling behind the word, numerous pauses in the dialogue, preoccupation of its title character with her destiny, nagging presence of *malheur* clothed as death, and a general unresolved sense of an absence (in this case of the lover, at least in body). To this enumeration we might add the figure of the *princesse lointaine* cultivated by the English pre-Raphaelites and so admired by French symbolists. Mélisande, princess Maleine, and other Maeterlinck heroines, sisters of Dante Gabriel Rossetti's Blessed Damozel, participate in a vision of distant and idealized purity. "Therefore it is, perhaps, that ... all women have communications with the unknown that are denied to us," wrote

Maeterlinck in *Le Trésor des humbles*, a variation of the hoary woman/body cliché that replaces the second term with the "spirit." "For women are indeed the veiled sisters of all the great things we do not see," Maeterlinck continues. "They are indeed nearest of kin to the infinite that is about us."[7] Similarly, draped in white and a virgin in body (but not in thought), the Princess has a prescience that extends to death. Whereas the messenger's account of the plague is more emphatic on the surface than we would expect from Maeterlinck, the Princess herself often gives subtle voice to the ubiquity of death in a manner reminiscent of the Belgian playwright. Following a passage in which she describes her dreams of both union and separation from her lover, she tells Monna Lara: "Sieh, so ist Tod im Leben. Beides läuft / so durcheinander, wie in einem Teppich di Fäden laufen" [Behold, thus there is death in life. / They both run entwined, / as threads overlap in a carpet"].[8] In Tremblay's libretto this becomes "La mort vois-tu petite sœur est derrière tout ce qui bat et respire / Le fil de nos jours, la vie le tisse sur la trame de nos morts" which, as an aside, provides a fair representation of the poetic liberties taken in the translation and adaptation.

But all the similarities to Maeterlinck's approach and style in *Die weisse Fürstin*, should not be overstated. The thematics of Rilke's play also deserve attention on their own terms. Although Rilke's free poetry is often relatively plain in syntax and diction, as in Maeterlinck's early plays, it is much richer in metaphor. Instead of pithy non sequiturs, the characters give voice to more extended thoughts. The messenger spins out a horrific image of the plague and a grotesque description of a cathedral service that utterly mocks the impotence of Christian faith before the scourge. Monna Lara voices empathy for the victims. And, more elaborately, the Princess describes her dream world. Indeed, she often assumes the role of a mentor preparing to induct her younger sister into a life consumed by interiority. This relationship not only leaves a strong impression of the author's own voice behind the Princess's didactic stance (perhaps with the spectator taking Monna Lara's position), but, as literary critic Anthony Stephens has observed, it also tinges the Princess with narcissism.[9] Monna Lara acts as a resonant sounding board, responding both with transport and tenderness to her sister's words. In the play, somewhat more than the opera, she also eagerly attends to the Princess like a maid, arranging her hair and praising her beauty. At the end of play (not the opera, perhaps regrettably) the Princess kisses her sister on the mouth; Monna Lara breaks away and returns with a silver mirror that she holds up for the Princess to arrange her hair. Much as in Mallarmé's *Hérodiade* fragment, the pairing of two characters serves principally to highlight the self-absorption of one of them. Yet death looms as well. Rilke's play taken as a whole exhales not a *single* primal feeling, but rather negotiates between two states of being: anxiety, *malheur,* and death on the one hand and the self-absorbed dream world on the other – or, more succinctly, reality and the unreal.

That symbolist aesthetics privilege primal feelings behind the text of the work naturally fostered questions early on about the appropriateness of music as an adjunct to symbolist literary texts. Such was Mallarmé's response to Maeterlinck's *Pelléas et Mélisande* when he saw the play at its premiere in 1893. He called it a "superior variation" on melodrama, executed "Almost silently and abstractly to the point that in this art, where everything becomes music in the real sense, even the addition of a single, pensive violin part would be unnecessary."[10] The music is, paradoxically, silent, a neo-platonic shroud for the soul. In setting *Pelléas et Mélisande,* Debussy obviously could not endorse this interpretation literally, but criticism of his opera has always underlined its responsiveness to mystery and evocative use of silence. Against the foil of Wagner's operas, the relatively discreet orchestra and controlled vocal declamation of Debussy's *Pelléas* have served as markers of symbolist poetics.

In a critical view more obviously congenial to composers than Mallarmé's, music might be portrayed as an enrichment of the symbolist text, one that adds depth to create a sense of limitless interiority (or scarcely fathomable *pureté,* as Mallarmé might have it). But to understand music in any symbolist opera as merely responsive to a primary level of meaning is not without its problems, for the notes themselves surely partake of primary "meaning" as well, or at least are experienced as primary in a phenomenological sense. A pragmatic critical orientation might shift incessantly between thin foreground and deep background, say between the immediacy of verbal and vocal expression and a role of the orchestra as a resonator. This too, however, is open to a similar commonplace critique in opera criticism that words do not act as mere triggers in the final aesthetic result (although they may have functioned that way during compositional genesis) but form part of an expressive whole. Nevertheless, a distinction between vocal line/verbal text and an orchestral resonator does have limited applicability to Debussy's *Pelléas,* both because voice and orchestra rarely share material and because the vocal part is set off by its relatively restrained declamation.

The textures of *La Princesse blanche* are much different. Mather's voices often have the character of instrumental parts and interact with the other (real) instruments in close interchanges of gestures and motives. The effect is much like traditional chamber music, in which the musical lines – now instrumental *and* vocal – cavort as equal partners. Remarkably, the counterpoint is transparent enough to ensure clarity in the projection of the words on a par with Debussy, a level of comprehensibility nourished further by skilful prosody that (unlike Debussy) avoids articulating the mute "e" at the ends of words.

DREAM'S FLESH

Despite all the provisos that might be mustered, the perspective of Maeterlinckean symbolism remains viable in a critical appreciation of *La Princesse blanche* – and even with respect to the construct of the orchestral resonator. Such is the case with the unfolding of the music heard in the instrumental prologue during the remainder of the opera. Mather begins *ex nihilo* in a very low register with eerie glissandi on timpani, harp, double bass, and trombone. This *ex nihilo* beginning belongs to a venerable pedigree stretching back to Debussy's *La Mer* and Ravel's *La Valse* and, far beyond to Beethoven's *Ninth Symphony*, and has often invited metaphysical exegesis. Literary lineage matters here, for to challenge the border between sound and soundlessness in this way at the beginning of the opera hearkens to the attention generated by silence in symbolist theatre. The opening texture recurs a few times later in the opera, most conspicuously when the messenger begins his account of the plague: "Vous venez de Lucca ... Comment est la ville?" inquires the Princess. "Grise comme cette poussière," he responds, "Grise et silencieuse." (mm. 469ff)[11] [You have come from Lucca ... How is the city? / Grey as this dust, Grey and silent]. Sounding music paradoxically evokes silence here through forbidding pianissimo colour. Later, the low glissandi return at the beginning of the second great dialogue between the Princess and Monna Lara: "Ma petite, tu as peur? (mm. 661ff) [Little one, are you afraid?]," the Princess asks. The beginning of the opera appeals to the same anxiety in all listeners, creating a primal feeling out of which the specifics of the story emerge.

In the instrumental prologue, the sinister glissandi merge seamlessly with a more extended passage in which the texture becomes filled out with rising figuration. The effect across the first fifty measures is of a succession of expanding phrases. Cellos and basses begin at the registral nadir and return to it at progressively longer time intervals, first after four measures, then after five-, six-, seven-, and eight-measure intervals, after which process the music reaches a twelve measure stasis in harmony and texture that articulates the end of the prologue. With each successive dip to, and subsequent rise from, the nadir, more instruments join the texture, and (generally) new pitch classes become the target of the upward surge. Within the overall rising context, individual instrumental parts retain their own gestural, rhythmic, and intervallic character: cellos and basses largely arpeggiate in triplets; brass instruments move at slightly slower note values in conjunct motion; flutes and oboes execute fast scales; and the piano plays wide and quick arpeggios. Single phrases in the parts, even those with many notes, avoid the complete chromatic aggregate: pentads characteristic of the octatonic scale emerge frequently and the interval of the seventh (most often major) defines the outer limits of passagework on the local level. "Eine Scene am Meer" [A Scene by the Sea], Rilke (but not Tremblay) writes as the generic marker of his play: an analogy to waves is difficult to avoid even in a relatively technical description of Mather's music. As a metaphor for the soul, the image of the sea in the opera (and play) might be spun out in any number of ways: for its connotations of depth, or its sense of an imposing timeless mass, or its suggestions of buoyant freedom from social constraints, like that eloquently embodied in the relationship of the heroine to the ocean in Ibsen's *The Lady from the Sea*.

With its framework of discrete rising phrases, the music of the prologue also has a striving, even yearning, quality. An abbreviated reprise of the full texture from the prologue produces the conclusion to the first scene of the opera, the dialogue between the Princess and her servant Amadéo. With the impending arrival of her lover (as the other characters later learn but which the Princess already intuits), she wants to send Amadéo away. She no longer requires a servant. "Ouvrez les armoires et prenez, prenez tout ce qu'il vous plaira" [Open the cupboards and take, take all that you want,] she instructs him, as her material needs seem to evaporate before the dream. What she yearns for above all is to break loose, to be cast adrift: "Me laisser glisser Amadéo comme un navire au gré du temps, au fil de l'eau, au gré du vent, au fil du jour, laisser gonfler mes voiles et puis partir" [To let me glide Amadéo like a ship wherever time takes me, drifting in the current, wherever the day takes me, to let my sails billow and then to depart]. Example 10.1 reproduces a short excerpt from the passage to illustrate the texture I have described above, but now with the addition of the voice.

Example 10.1.
La Princesse blanche, scene 1 (page 1 of 3)

The chamber-music-like treatment of the Princess's line blends with the evocative maritime imagery of both the orchestra and the verbal text. Her ascent from D to B-flat in the fourth measure of example 10.1 is mirrored immediately in the violins. Runs in the other instruments echo the major seventh ambitus of the entire phrase from D to C-sharp ("Comme un navire au gré du temps"). On a measure-to-measure level, the pitch vocabulary is mainly produced by major seventh transpositions of pitch classes (for example, C-sharp, E, G, A in the cello at

Example 10.1. (*Continued*)
La Princesse blanche, scene 1 (page 2 of 3)

measure 3 "generate" C, E-flat, F-sharp, G-sharp above). My point is that the Princess's voice organically blends with the entire maritime texture – with its suggestions of depth, timeless mass, and freedom. The music of the prologue is revealed to be no mere atmospheric foil, or even responsive resonator, but the very essence of the soul behind the words, the primal matter that is exposed first. To be sure, the opera employs other textures as it unfolds, but fragments from the maritime prologue reverberate throughout – often in the guise of the woodwind

Example 10.1. (*Continued*)
La Princesse blanche, scene 1 (page 3 of 3)

runs seen in example 10.1 – to perpetuate the subliminal presence of the sea and its confluence with the Princess's inner world.

The music in example 10.1 quickly leads to an accumulation of sound and harmonic stasis to articulate the end of the scene. For a brief instance after the expression "et puis partir" the Princess drifts up to high B-flat (mm. 168–70) with a vocalise, another strategy in Mather's *théâtre de l'âme* – now with deep historical roots – for reaching to essences of affect beyond the verbal text. This is because the passage anticipates more extended textless vocalizing later in the work, in each instance communicating the rapture produced by the dream lover.

The next, and much longer, vocalise brings the Princess and Monna Lara together in a duet at the end of the second scene (mm. 380–90), their first extended scene together – a moment that seems to magnify the dramatic role of Monna Lara as a vehicle for the Princess's self-absorption. But to understand this passage – a culminating gesture, after all – we need to look back earlier in the dialogue. Monna Lara's strong identification with her sister emerges from her first appearance a few minutes before: she sings of feeling older than the Princess: "Si tu savais comme je me sens plus âgé que toi!" (m 208) [If you only knew how much I feel older than you]. Of course, this cannot be true according to the clock of real life, and Monna Lara goes on to justify her feeling by singing that it arises in her dreams: "Moi dans mes rêves je me sens toujours plus âgée" (m. 217) [As for myself, in my dreams I always feel older]. The musical language at this point slips into quarter tones, initiated by the harp, the C, E, and G strings of which are tuned a quarter tone flat, and followed by the sinuous entwinement of microtonal music by other instruments. Although the Princess emits a distant pre-Raphaelite glow *throughout* the work, quarter-tone music always occurs when the verbal text *explicitly* refers to dreams. This makes for an important element of her musical language: she has already sung quarter-tone music in the first scene with Amadéo – "Je veux rester seule enfermée dans mes songes" (m. 103) [I want to remain alone enclosed within my dreams] – and will return to it many times later. As it happens, the only time that Monna Lara sings on her own with the Princess's quarter tones is the very passage in which she imagines herself as her senior (in her dreams), in effect assuming the role of the older sister. That is, from her first appearance Monna Lara defines herself as an empathetic recipient of the Princess's poetic images, a kind of embodied resonator. (Here, it is worth recalling the image of the mirror that Monna Lara holds up to her sister at the end of Rilke's play.) As the long dialogue continues, the Princess reveals details about the lover who has inhabited her dreams. Her description builds to the impassioned avowal: "Devant lui, je me sens comme un puits sans fond où vont s'éteindre tous les feux de la nuit" (m. 371) and "Il est mon rêve et mon rêve est ma chair" (m. 376) [Before him I feel like a bottomless well where are all nocturnal fire becomes extinguished / He is my dream and my dream is my flesh]. The Princess sings in quarter tones here and, well before she completes her text, is joined by Monna Lara

Pauline Vaillancourt (soprano) as la princesse blanche and Ethel Guéret (soprano coloratura) as Monna Lara in the Chants Libres production of *La Princesse blanche*, April 1998. Reproduced by permission of Chants libres, www.chantslibres.org/site.htlm.

with the extended vocalises mentioned above, each phrase aiming towards a higher pitch in the stratosphere of the coloratura's range. By abandoning words, Monna Lara seems even more carried away than her sister. Encouraged by this vocal refraction of her own yearnings, the Princess soon joins Monna Lara's wordless music over static harmony to bring the scene to its conclusion, an updating of the technique well known from nineteenth-century opera of saving vocal efflorescence for the coda of set pieces.

Today, just as conventionally, operatic criticism celebrates such passagework as irrational exuberance, instantiations of *jouissance*, extravagance, a focus on the body through the sensuality of the voice unencumbered by explicit meaning. This seems right for "Mon rêve est ma chair" [My dream is my flesh]. But we may also want to linger on the paradox of this line. The orchestral and wordless vocal texture of this passage occurs again later in the opera, in the fifth scene when the Princess describes her imagined nights of carnal bliss with her lover: "Je m'allongeais dans l'herbe tiède à ses côtés et nous partagions notre ivresse" (m. 783) [I stretched out in the warm grass beside him and we shared our rapture]. With an immediacy that the spoken play does not achieve, these long melismas come close to suggesting that the Princess may actually experience real sexual fulfillment in her reverie, a symbolist impossibility.

Carnal disappointment inhabits the fifth scene as well, for just after telling of her tryst, the Princess reflects on the times her lover did not appear by imagining a petrifaction of her own body: "Alors je devenais tombeau de pierre" (m. 798) [Then I became a stone tomb]. Here the music takes up the tolling heard earlier in the fifth scene at the moment Princess reflected dolefully on the grim news brought by the messenger – "La mort, oui, la mort" (m. 673) [death, yes death] – with bell-like chords distilled from the stringent harmonies that punctuated his report about the plague in the previous scene. At their fullest and most terrifying manifestation (see example 10.2) during the messenger's account, these harmonies relentlessly hammer nine pitch classes of the conventional twelve-note aggregate, a repeated orchestral shriek of terror interpolated into music that relentlessly presses the baritone voice to its upper limit.

Mather's music captures Rilke's essential contrast more cogently than is possible in a spoken text. The reality of the bubonic plague is to the Princess's dream as hammered dissonant chords are to the sinuous quarter-tone music and oceanic textures. Yet – to return to the Princess's self-representation as a sarcophagus – even when it comes to death, it is not clear that a distinction between the real and unreal has any meaning for her. After the evocation of her own corpse without her lover, she slips seamlessly into that passage mentioned above, in which she admonishes Monna Lara that death, after all, is omnipresent in daily life.

The action of the play taken at face value might suggest that the Princess does indeed distinguish between dream and reality and that the action moves inexorably forward to the intrusion of reality. Her lover has filled her dreams. Then he announces his arrival. His boat appears. She waves, as instructed. He passes by. Although such a

Example 10.2.
La Princesse blanche, scene 4

common-sense reading has a good deal to recommend it, as the play and opera unfold plot teleology is not unassailable. For one, it is not very clear whether the Princess has indeed *ever* actually met her lover in real life, for there is little to suggest this other than a fleeting reference to him holding Monna Lara's hand as a child. Is this a real or imagined past? The Princess knows the contents of the messenger's letter before he arrives. Her lover putatively appears on the sea: but the sea has been mapped on to the Princess's inner world to such an extent, particularly in the opera, that it is difficult to see beyond its metaphoric role, not to mention the Princess's conspicuous assimilation of space and time (in the play), or Monna Lara as an embodiment of her interiority instead of as a fully independent character.

So, what to make of the conclusion? As I intimated earlier, play and opera diverge at this point. Rilke's version contains an extended description of action. The Princess sees something and reaches into her sash pocket as if getting ready to wave a cloth. Oars sound. Then monks with black masks appear, whispering among themselves. The Princess sees them and from that moment remains fixated upon the brothers. Frozen, she cannot signal and the boat moves past. From one of the high windows a barely discernible figure appears, almost like that of child, and waves. The gestures first seem to beckon, and then turn more ponderous and slow, as if waving goodbye. The curtain falls. Why can't the Princess bring herself to continue in this sequence of events? On the level of plot, the intrusion into her life of the black monks whom the messenger had earlier described creates sudden panic and paralysis, surprising in light of her earlier self-possessed counsel to Monna Lara about the ubiquity of death. To speak as a dreamer is one thing, to wave another, for it is the latter action that truly engages reality. On the level of her soul, the crush of reality becomes too great when terms heretofore presented as binary opposites – true-to-life plague and the dream lover – are redefined because the lover, in effect, verges on becoming as real as the disease. Yearning too urgently for the embodiment of her lover while the plague festers around her, the Princess freezes. Put more succinctly, in terms of the "death drama" that Rilke identified in Maeterlinck, the flesh of the lover who emerges on the cusp of the real becomes subsumed by flesh that is diseased and deadly. It is Monna Lara, her younger alter ego and less invested in the dream world, who is left to wave to the passing boat and sustain the dream world.

The score of the opera removes Monna Lara from the concluding scene and provides much less explicit gestural detail. The eerie glissandi heard at the beginning of the opera initiate the final sequence of events and, once again, transmute into wave-like swells. *Ma fin est mon commencement* [my end is my beginning]: this very circularity suggests an enclosed space, more space than time. Now, however, the implicit fear evoked by the glissandi is trumped by the nine-note chords from the messenger's scene that interrupt the roiling orchestral textures. Death cuts through her soul as the Princess abandons verbal text for the most extended vocalise of the opera. The monks do not actually appear, but a small addition to the messenger's scene in the original orchestral score (that is, the autograph facsimile at the Canadian Music Centre) reflects self-consciousness about plot clarity at the level of creative intent. Whereas in the original sequence of the messenger's earlier report he merely warns the sisters about the roaming monks of death, in the longer revision Mather adds: "Dès que par la fenêtre on leur fait signe de la main, ils viennent et emportent tout" [From the moment that one signals to them from the window, they come and take everything away]. This seems motivated by a desire during the creative process to better prepare the terror of the dissonant chords during the opera's concluding scene. Yet despite this ostensible preparation, the score and libretto are silent on whether the Princess actually attempts to wave. Notwithstanding production decisions, one might entertain the argument that physical gesture is quite superfluous in light of the expressive impact of the orchestra. Either way, the lover does not disembark. And when fear seizes the Princess, it seems that the dream world cannot provide consolation, for the oceanic music during the final vocalise culminates in a sharp augmented triad on the brass, a sonority used a few times earlier in the opera to etch a border between reality and the dream. Quarter-tone music follows. The Princess continues her vocalise, now accompanied by textures that had earlier culminated in her avowal: "Il est mon rêve et mon rêve est ma chair" [He is my dream and my dream is my flesh]. But both the vocal line and orchestra become progressively fragmented as the opera ends, thinning out into pianissimo, and silence. Soft staccato singing intrudes upon the legato delivery of the melisma, almost as if the very life breath were being sucked out of the Princess. Fear gives way not to fulfillment, but to disembodiment, hollowness, absence, the watery volume of the sea dissipated into thin wisps of sound.

Such, perhaps, is the result of obsession. The Princess should have known better than to force the dream lover too close to the light of day, or even perhaps to intone his existence in the first place. The opera retreats into the silence from which it emerged, and beyond the Princess's condition to touch our collective experience. After reading Maeterlinck, and around the time he wrote *Die weisse Fürstin*, Rilke noted in his diary: "Perhaps it is not a good thing that you pay so much attention to your dreams. You often awake with difficulty and live the entire morning looking backwards ... Only now that I know how much I love this state of being I realize its great danger."[12] An object lesson seems to lurk over Mather's final measures, a final reminder of the impossibility, perhaps even dangers, of equating "le rêve" and "la chair."

NOTES

1 For a brief overview of the history of the company, see Réjean Beaucage, "Chants Libres présente *L'Archange*," *Scena musicale*, 10 (April 2005): 44. Musicians of the Nouvel ensemble moderne supplied the chamber orchestra (requiring sixteen players) in 1994, and once again when *La Princesse blanche* was revived by Chants Libres in 1998. A performance of the opera announced by L'Opéra de Montréal for the season of 1995–96 never materialized.

2 The text of the second version of *Die weisse Fürstin* may be found in Rainer Maria Rilke, *Sämtliche Werke* (Frankfurt am Main: Insel Verlag, 1955), 1: 203–31. For an English translation as *The White Princess*, see Rainer Maria Rilke, *Rilke: Nine Plays*, trans. Klaus Phillips and John Locke (New York: Frederick Ungar, 1979), 165–87. For the first version, see Rilke, *Sämtliche Werke* 3: 267–87. For a summary background to the play and relevant criticism, see Monika Ritzer, "*Die weisse Fürstin (2. Fassung, 1904)*," in *Rilke-Handbuch: Leben, Werk, Wirkung*, ed. Manfred Engel (Stuttgart: Verlag J.B. Metzler, 2004), 283–90. Also valuable is the first volume of a newer fully annotated complete edition of Rilke's work: *Gedichte 1895 bis 1910*, ed. Manfred Engel and Ulrich Fülleborn (Frankfurt am Main: Insel Verlag, 1996), 688–704. For a brief English summary of context and meaning, see Wolfgang Leppmann, *Rilke: A Life*, trans. Russell M. Stockman (New York: Fromm International, 1984), 97–100.

3 The two most important essays are "Das Theater des Maeterlinck," (published 1901) in *Sämtliche Werke* (Frankfurt am Main: Insel Verlag, 1965), 5: 479–82; and "Maurice Maeterlinck" (published 1902), ibid., 527–49.

4 Rilke, "Das Theater des Maeterlinck," 480.

5 Rilke, "Maurice Maeterlinck," 536.

6 For a thorough study of Maeterlinck's theatre, see G. Compère, *Le Théâtre de Maurice Maeterlinck* (Brussels, Palais des Académies, 1955).

7 Cited by Roger Nichols and Richard Langham Smith, *Claude Debussy: Pelléas et Mélisande* (Cambridge: Cambridge University Press, 1989), 26.

8 *Die weisse Fürstin*, 225; *The White Princess*, 182.

9 See Anthony Stephens, "Das Janusgesicht des Momentanen: Rilkes Einakter 'Die weisse Fürstin,'" *Hofmannstahl Jahrbuch* 1 (1993) [Zur Europäischen Moderne], 263–86.

10 Cited by Nichols and Langham Smith, *Claude Debussy: Pelléas et Mélisande*, 4.

11 In Rilke the messenger's text reads in English translation: "Your Highness, / the town is gray. Gray as this dust. It seemed as if no joy could enter there. The town was without voice," *The White Princess*, 174.

12 Entry of April 1900, cited by Erich Simenauer, "R.M. Rilke's Dreams and His Conception of Dream," in *Rilke: The Alchemy of Alienation*, ed. Frank Baron, Ernst S. Dick, and Warren R. Maurer (Lawrence: Regents Press of Kansas, 1980), 248.

11

"Music under the Influence": On *la nécessité extérieure* in the Music of John Rea

Jérôme Blais, Dalhousie University

JÉRÔME BLAIS teaches composition and music theory at Dalhousie University in Halifax. After studying music theory at McGill University he completed doctoral studies in composition at l'Université de Montréal under the supervision of Michel Longtin and Reno De Stefano. His works have been performed by a variety of new music ensembles, including the Ensemble contemporain de Montréal, the Quasar Saxophone Quartet, the Quatuor Bozzini, Bradyworks, and Array Music. His interest in John Rea's compositional languages seemingly provides a perspective on place from the outside, in that his insights are a result of having heard five works through the programming choices and discourse of the 2003 Scotia Festival of Music. However, since the essay was originally written in French ("Une musique sous influence: Au sujet de la 'nécessité extérieure' dans l'oeuvre de John Rea), and is woven together with the words of Rea himself – words that slip effortlessly from French to English, English to French – its expression remains firmly grounded in place.

My first contact with John Rea goes back to autumn 1986 when I was enrolled as an undergraduate at the Faculty of Music of McGill University. Rea being one of the most prominent figures in the musical life of McGill and Montreal, his compositions were regularly performed and his enthusiasm for teaching was manifest, not only in the classroom, but also in numerous articles and public lectures. Although I never had an opportunity to study with Rea, I quickly made his acquaintance – he was dean of the Faculty at the time – because we worked together on various committees and because my provincial background had spawned a hunger to discover, which drove me to go to as many public events as I could attend.

The first composition of Rea's that I heard was *Vanishing Points* (1983). Applying various principles of pictorial symmetry to musical parameters such as pitch content, rhythm, and orchestration, the music has a repetitive quality which I, at the time, associated with the music of American minimalists. Shortly after, I heard *Offenes Lied* (1986), a theatrical "melodrama" that includes many references to nineteenth-century music. The two works sounded so different that I thought Rea was "an eclectic composer." It is true that each of these works belongs to one of the two approaches or manners which Rea identifies when he speaks of his own compositional process:

> I'm attracted to one type of music that could be called narratological, that has some type of intrigue, or human element, that involves human destinies ... There's a whole other part of my work that I would say, for lack of a better word, might be called geometrical, or structural, figurative. Not that it's inhuman, but it involves musical elements for their own sake, and for their own relationships, probable or improbable among themselves.[1]

However, although the two approaches are distinct from one another, they also have something in common: both are strongly influenced by what I would call *la nécessité extérieure* or external forces – that is, Rea's "geometric" or structurally-motivated approach is inspired by visual phenomena, while his "narrative" approach is marked by prominent use of literary or theatrical elements and includes musical quotations that, without being literally "outside" music, are nevertheless extrinsic to the composition itself. In this essay, I will show how these external forces serve to unify his œuvre by giving it, not an eclectic character, but a rather profound coherence. I will focus on five representative compositions: *Alma & Oskar* (1994), *Une Fleur du mal* (1992), *Music, according to Aquinas* (2000), *Objets perdus* (1991), and *Schattenwerk* (2003). All five works were performed in 2003 at the Scotia Festival of Music in Halifax, where I currently live. They also combine various pictorial, literary, and theatrical elements to create the impression of a "total" artistic expression more typically associated with opera than with chamber music.

THE SCOTIA FESTIVAL OF MUSIC

Founded in 1981, the Scotia Festival has hosted many internationally recognized artists, often within the framework of a composer-in-residence program. The first composer, Pierre Boulez (1991), was followed by Alexina Louie (1992), R. Murray Schafer (1993), Oliver Knussen (1996), Joan Tower (1997), Christos Hatzis (1998), and Philip Glass (1999); before Rea's visit in 2003, the Festival invited two local composers, Scott Macmillan in 2000 and Emily Doolittle in 2001.

While at the Festival in 2003, Rea gave a lecture and a master class to young composers, and attended the public performances of his five compositions mentioned above, one of which, *Schattenwerk,* had been specifically commissioned by the Festival. The repertoire was collaboratively chosen by Rea, the Festival's artistic director, Christopher Wilcox, and violinist Mark Fewer (who has since become the Festival's artistic director). As explained by Fewer, they sought to integrate Rea's work with the long-term programming strategies of the Festival by selecting compositions "that were related to some themes of performance that [had] been developing over the last four to five years ... [which] included theatre inside musical performance (rather than musical back-up to a theatrical event) and hyper-romanticism."[2] Rea's string quartet *Objets perdus* was also connected to the cycle of late Beethoven quartets that the Supernova quartet had been performing, one per year, over the previous four years.

THE WORKS

Each of these five works is rooted in one or the other of Rea's two approaches or manners; the three vocal works, *Alma & Oskar, Une Fleur du mal* and *Music, according to Aquinas* represent the narrative approach, while the two instrumental works, *Objets perdus* and *Schattenwerk,* represent the geometric or structurally-motivated approach. However, the two approaches are not mutually exclusive, in that external forces play an important role in all five works. These factors are most quickly detected in the vocal works simply because they appear in a concrete and tangible way through the theatrical use of literary texts and musical quotations easily identified as coming from "elsewhere." They are less obvious in the instrumental works because, as geometric or structurally-motivated works, they have a more abstract character. That said, as the word "geometric" itself suggests, the approach often stems from external visual and pictorial phenomena that have a decisive, albeit more subterranean, effect on the music.

Alma & Oskar

The centrepiece around which Rea's works were programmed for the Festival was *Alma & Oskar*.[3] This work, based on the text *Alma Mahler ou l'art d'être aimée* by Françoise Giroud, is a "beyond-the-grave melodrama" that "describes in music the love story between Alma Schindler Mahler and the writer and expressionist painter Oskar Kokoschka."[4] It was commissioned by Radio-Canada as the imposed eight-minute composition for the semifinal round of its young performers' competition. Since it was impossible to predict the voice types of the contestants in advance, the work had to be scored so that it could be performed by either a female or a male voice, low or high, and the language of the text chosen so as not to favour any one finalist.[5] Commenting on the challenges posed by such external constraints, Rea writes: "I firmly believe that music associated with vocal tessituras, and therefore with sexuality, cannot be transposed ... [and] that poetic texts cannot be translated. Music written for a soprano who sings in Russian is not music written for an English tenor."[6]

Consequently, instead of setting a poem that would later be used to generate various translated and transposed versions, Rea decided to structurally cast the work more as an opera than a lied. Three separate scenes present the story or plot as if there were two actors – Alma and Oskar – and embellish the storytelling with theatrical elements such as a gunshot evoking the assassination of the Archduke Ferdinand at Sarajevo in 1914. When the solo part is performed by a woman, she sings not only her own music as Alma but also the role of Oskar –in the third person – when it comes to his turn to tell the story. Likewise, when the solo part is sung by a man, he sings the part of Oskar in the first person and the role of Alma in the third person. For instance, in the version for soprano or alto, the first lines of text, meant for Alma, read: "Mais je savais que je ne chanterais plus ... que dans la mort [But I knew that I would no longer sing again ... except in death]."[7] In the version for tenor or baritone, the same lines read: "Mais elle savait maintenant qu'elle ne chanterait ... plus que dans la mort [But she now knew that she could never sing again ... except in death]." The work may also be performed by two soloists of opposite sex, each assuming the appropriate part. In order not to inadvertently favour a contestant by using a text in his or her mother tongue, Rea also ingeniously wrote both roles so that they contain spoken passages that can be rendered in either of Canada's two official languages; the sung parts are delivered in German – a requirement that is quite normal for a voice competition.

Like many of Rea's other narrative works, *Alma & Oskar* also contains many references to musical works of the past, each one playing a specific role in the unfolding of the story and the weaving of a musical backcloth against which the characters come to life. In his article "Nashville ou Darmstadt: le masque mortuaire de la postmodernité," Rea himself provides the key to some of these quotations.[8] He confirms, for example, that "the very first music heard in Scene 1 is a small citation from the last of Gustav Mahler's *Kindertotenlieder* ... Thus we have the image of Alma who, while alluding to the end of her relationship with Oskar, also seems to recall not only her 'servitude' to her husband Gustav but also the rage that seized her when he wrote this tragic music about dying children in 1904 shortly after the birth of their own children."[9] With reference to a later passage, Rea notes: "A quotation from Wagner's *Tristan* suggests that she is thinking back to their first meeting [with Oskar] at her house, where she perhaps played and sang some of this music for him. But now, everything is dead and war is on the verge of breaking out in Europe, as emphasized by a reference to the lugubrious *March* that Alban Berg completed in August 1914."[10]

All of the musical quotations are very carefully chosen, not only for the mood they create but also for their intrinsic meaning and relationship to the plot, with the composers being treated much like characters. Berg's *March*, for example, reflects both a connection to the text that it highlights – it is a funeral march, and Berg had gone in search of new musical languages and modes of expression to replace the traditions of the past, which he now believed to be dead – and the composer's close friendship with Alma.[11] Rea's compositional process thus clearly goes well beyond strictly musical parameters, and when he describes the genesis of the work's narrative approach, he even notes this himself: "The idea of narration obviously suggests the form of a novel or short story, and I do indeed operate essentially like a novelist because I use the descriptions of plot as imagined by the writer Françoise Giroud as much as original text that I reconstitute into virtual dialogues."[12] And he adds: "But I also behave like a film-maker, because I have to compress into eight minutes the experiences, real and imagined, of two passionate beings, experiences that occurred over the span of three very turbulent years."[13] Novel, film, song: "total" art reveals itself here unequivocally.

Une Fleur du mal

Total art also emerges, albeit in a different way, in *Une fleur du mal,* for soprano, clarinet, cello, and percussion.[14] Another melodrama revolving around the omnipresence of death, this work has many features in common with *Alma & Oskar,* but it is also distinct in a number ways. On the literary side, where *Alma & Oskar* was cast as a dialogue between two characters and uses a single text as its literary source,[15] the story of *Une fleur du mal* is delivered by a single character and unfolds in poetic verse, which seems to give the work a dream-like character. The text consists of excerpts drawn from Charles Baudelaire's translation of Edgar Allan Poe's short story *Morella.*[16] Poe's story concerns the strange relationship between a man and his wife, the mysterious Morella, who, after a long illness, dies while revealing to her husband that she is carrying a child who will survive her. The child grows up bearing an uncanny resemblance to her mother, whose eternally damned soul now seems to inhabit her daughter. Baptized several years after her birth, the daughter dies at the very instant she receives the name Morella. As her father buries her, he breaks into laughter, long and bitter, when he discovers no trace in the family tomb of his wife, Morella. In Poe's original the tale is told in the first person by the husband, but Rea chose to invert the roles, giving the narrative role to Morella, who continues to tell the story even after her death: thus the subtitle of the work "*melodramas from beyond the grave*"; the plural "melodramas" likely refers to the duality of the Morella character as both mother and daughter.

Grafted onto the text are excerpts drawn from two other classics which the performer alternately sings and declaims. The first, *Correspondances,* a sonnet from Baudelaire's *Fleurs du mal,* suggests the resonance between natural and supernatural worlds and explores synaesthesia. The second consists of two extracts from Robert Brassilach's translation of two poems by the Greek poet Sappho (seventh century BC): *À une aimée,* which deals with the corporeal effects of love, and *Les Adieux,* which describes the poet's lesbian heartache.[17] The complete texts of these three poems are given in table 11.1; the excerpts used by Rea appear in bold.

Although the form and lyric character of these poems contrasts with Poe's prose, Rea coherently sequences the excerpts so that certain words and themes, such as nature, the senses, death and childhood, interact and resonate with one another in a way that poetically underscores the dramatic plot line. As seen in table 11.2, for example, in mm. 187–210, the Baudelaire and Poe excerpts meld in their descriptions of nature,

Table 11.1.
Poetic sources for the libretto of *Une fleur du mal*

*Charles Baudelaire: Correspondances**	
La Nature est un temple où de vivants piliers **Laissent parfois sortir de confuses paroles;** L'homme y passe à travers des forêts de symboles Qui l'observent avec des regards familiers.	Nature is a temple in which living pillars Sometimes give voice to confused words; Man passes there through forests of symbols Which look at him with understanding eyes.
Comme de longs échos qui de loin se confondent **Dans une ténébreuse et profonde unité,** **Vaste comme la nuit et comme la clarté,** **Les parfums, les couleurs et les sons se répondent.**	Like prolonged echoes mingling in the distance In a deep and tenebrous unity, Vast as the dark of night and as the light of day. Perfumes, sounds, and colours correspond.
Il est des parfums frais comme des chairs d'enfants, Doux comme les hautbois, verts comme les prairies, – Et d'autres, corrompus, riches et triomphants,	There are perfumes as cool as the flesh of children, Sweet as oboes, green as meadows – And others are corrupt, and rich, triumphant,
Ayant l'expansion des choses infinies, **Comme l'ambre, le musc, le benjoin et l'encens** **Qui chantent les transports de l'esprit et des sens.**	With power to expand into infinity, Like amber and incense, musk, benzoin That sing the ecstasy of the soul and senses.
Sappho: À une aimée / To a Loved One†	
Il goûte le bonheur que connaissent les dieux Celui qui peut auprès de toi Se tenir et te regarder, Celui qui peut goûter la douceur de ta voix,	He appears to me like unto the gods, That man, who opposite to you, Sits and to you speaking a sweet word,

Table 11.1.
Poetic sources for the libretto of *Une fleur du mal* (*Continued*)

Celui que peut toucher la magie de ton rire, Mais moi, ce rire, je le sais, Il fait fondre mon coeur en moi.	He replies to your lovely laughter. Truly that flutters my heart in my breast.
Ah! moi, sais-tu, si je te vois, Fût-ce une seconde aussi brève, Tout à coup alors sur mes lèvres, Expire sans force ma joie.	For when I look at you for a moment, I can not speak.
Ma langue est là comme brisée, Et soudain, au coeur de ma chair, Un feu invisible a glissé. Mes yeux ne voient plus rien de clair, A mon oreille un bruit a bourdonné.	But, my tongue is broken, [I have lost my language] Right then, over my skin a light fire races, I see nothing with my eyes, my ears rumble,
Je suis de sueur inondée, Tout mon corps se met à trembler, Je deviens plus verte que l'herbe, Et presque rien ne manque encore Pour me sentir comme une morte.	And sweat pours over me a trembling, Seizes me entire, greener than grass I am, just about to die I seem to me.[1]
Sappho: Les Adieux / The Departed	
Atthis n'est point sur ses pas retournée. Vraiment, je voudrais être morte. En me quittant, elle pleurait,	"I … really wish I were dead." She, shedding many tears, was leaving me And she said to me:

Table 11.1.
Poetic sources for the libretto of *Une fleur du mal* (*Continued*)

Elle pleurait et me disait: **"Ah ! Saphô, terrible est ma peine.** **C'est malgré moi que je m'en vais ..."**	"Oh my! What awful things we have had to endure, Sappho. It is really unwillingly that I leave you now"
Et je lui répondais moi-même: "Pars en joie, souviens-toi de moi. Ah! tu sais bien comme je t'aime!	And I answered her with these words: "Go away in happiness, remembering me, for you know how I cared for you.
Sinon, je veux te rappeler Nos heures si belles, si chères, (Les as-tu vraiment oubliées?)	And if you don't know, I want to Remind you ... (if) And we felt lovely things
Les couronnes de violettes Et la rose avec la saphran. Près de moi, tressées sur la tête,	With many garlands of violets And roses and crocus for you And, ... you set down beside me
Les guirlandes entrelacées, Autour de ta gorge fragile, Les fleurs adorables mêlées,	And sweet scented garlands with many Braids around your lovely neck You threw, of flowers fashioned,
Et le parfum mystérieux, Les flacons de parfum royal, Qui inondaient tes beaux cheveux,	And with much ... myrrh The royal run Then desire ... nidón
Et l'heure, où, sur un lit couchée, Mollement et entre mes bras, Tu calmais ta soif altérée...	

Table 11.1.

Poetic sources for the libretto of *Une fleur du mal* (*Continued*)

	"And nobody or nothing Holy nor … Was there, from which we were lacking Nor grove dance Instruments Song …"

* Charles Baudelaire, *Correspondances*, from *Une fleur du mal*, in *Oeuvres complètes* (Paris: Gallimard, 1961), 11. English translation by William Aggeler, *The Flowers of Evil* (Fresno, CA: Academy Library Guild, 1954); available at http://fleursdumal.org/poem/103 (accessed 15 November 2006).

† The English translations of *À une aimée* and *Les Adieux* are by William Harris and reproduced here by permission of the translator; they are available on pp. 109 and 123 at http://community.middlebury.edu/~harris/Sappho.pdf (accessed 15 November 2006). Sappho's poems are fragments, and translations into different languages vary markedly. This one was selected for the importance it attaches to the passages selected by Rea and for the measure of the poetic rhythm, which plays an important role in Rea's setting of the text. The French translations are by Robert Brasillach, *Anthologie de la poésie grecque* (Paris: Stock, 1950), 127–30. The differences between the French and English translations illustrate the importance language plays in one's reading of these poems and Rea's decision to be inspired by French translations of the text.

Table 11.2.
Libretto for *Une fleur du mal*

Measures	*Author*	*Text*	*Translation*
Program notes read in front of the audience by a man.	Poe	First two paragraphs of the novella in their original form, i.e., told in the first person by Morella's husband: Morella's description, her wedding with the narrator.	
FIRST PART			
1–3	Sappho	[Spoken without accompaniment]	I can not speak.
		Ma langue est là comme brisée, *Et soudain, au coeur de ma chair,* *Un feu invisible a glissé.* *Mes yeux ne voient plus rien de clair,* *A mon oreille un bruit a bourdonné.*	But, my tongue is broken, [Ed. note: meaning, I have lost my language] Right then, over my skin a light fire races, I see nothing with my eyes, my ears rumble,
		Je suis de sueur inondée, *Tout mon corps se met à trembler,* *Je deviens plus verte que l'herbe,* *Et presque rien ne manque encore* *Pour me sentir comme une morte.*	And sweat pours over me a trembling, Seizes me entire, greener than grass I am, just about to die I seem to me. (See Table 11.1)
13–23	Baudelaire	[Spoken] *La Nature est un temple où de vivants piliers* *Laissent parfois sortir de confuses paroles;*	Nature is a temple in which living pillars Sometimes give voice to confused words; (See Table 11.1)

Table 11.2.
Libretto for *Une fleur du mal* (*Continued*)

24–186	Poe	[Sometimes spoken, sometimes sung] From the novella, this time told by Morella herself: her relationship with her husband, her declining health.	
187–96	Baudelaire	[Spoken] *Comme de longs échos qui de loin se confondent* *Dans une ténébreuse et profonde unité,* *Vaste comme la nuit et comme la clarté,* *Les parfums, les couleurs et les sons se répondent.*	 Like prolonged echoes mingling in the distance In a deep and tenebrous unity, Vast as the dark of night and as the light of day. Perfumes, sounds, and colours correspond. (See Table 11.1)
197–210	Poe	[Spoken] *Mais un soir d'automne, comme l'air dormait immobile dans le ciel, je l'appelai à mon chevet. Il y avait un voile de brume sur toute la terre, et un chaud embrasement sur les eaux, et à voir les splendeurs d'octobre dans le feuillage de la forêt, on eût dit qu'un bel arc-en-ciel s'était laissé choir du firmament.*	 But on an autumn night, as the air was sleeping, immobile in the sky, I called him to the foot of my bed. There was a hazy veil over the earth and a warm glow over the water, and looking at the leaves in the forest, in the splendour of October, one could have thought that a rainbow had fallen from the sky.
211–66	Poe	[Sometimes spoken, sometimes sung] Morella announces that she is going to die and that she is carrying a baby that will survive her.	
267–70	Poe	[Spoken] *Mais je retournai mon visage sur l'oreiller; un léger tremblement courut sur mes membres, je mourus, et il n'entendit plus ma voix.*	 I turned over on my pillow; a light tremor went all over my body, I died and he did not hear my voice any more.

Table 11.2.
Libretto for *Une fleur du mal* (*Continued*)

272–6	Sappho	[Spoken without accompaniment] *Ah! Sappho, terrible est ma peine. C'est malgré moi que je m'en vais…*	Oh my! What awful things we have had to endure, Sappho. It is really unwillingly that I leave you now … (See Table 11.1)
SECOND PART			
290–7	Baudelaire	[Spoken] Il est des parfums… Il est des parfums frais comme des chairs d'enfants…	There are perfumes… There are perfumes as cool as the flesh of children… (See Table 11.1)
305–19	Poe	[Spoken] *Comme je l'avais prédit, mon enfant, – auquel en mourant j'avais donné naissance, et qui ne respira qu'après que la mère eut cessé de respirer, – mon enfant, une fille, vécut.*	As I predicted it, my child – to whom I gave birth just before dying and who breathed only after her mother ceased to breathe – my child, a girl, lived.
320–400	Poe	[Sometimes spoken, sometimes sung] The child's first years (from the novella).	
401–7	Baudelaire	[Spoken] *Il est des parfums…* *Ayant l'expansion des choses infinies,* *Comme l'ambre, le musc, le benjoin et l'encens,* *Qui chantent les transports de l'esprit et des sens.*	There are perfumes… With power to expand into infinity, Like amber and incense, musk, benzoin, That sing the ecstasy of the soul and senses. (See Table 11.1)

Table 11.2.
Libretto for *Une fleur du mal* (*Continued*)

408–530	Poe	[Sometimes spoken, sometimes sung] The baptism of Morella's daughter, her death.	
531	Sappho	[Spoken] *Ma langue est là comme brisée,* *Et soudain, au coeur àde ma chair,* *Un feu invisible a glissé.* *Mes yeux ne voient plus rien de clair,* *A mon oreille un bruit a bourdonné.*	 But, my tongue is broken, [Ed. note: meaning, I have lost my language] Right then, over my skin a light fire races, I see nothing with my eyes, my ears rumble. (See Table 11.1)

light, and sounds. Later, at the moment that Morella tells her husband that she is about to die (mm. 267–319), the themes of death and childhood, already present in the main story, find poetic reverberations in the subsequent excerpts from Baudelaire and Sappho.

The great care with which Rea fashions his musical materials also works to fuse the texts. Where *Alma & Oskar* is almost entirely assembled from musical quotations, *Une fleur du mal* is structured around autonomous musical materials that suggest the economy of means more redolent of the composer's geometric or structurally-motivated approach. Granted the vocal part in certain places obviously refers to the lyric song of the nineteenth and twentieth centuries: for example, an *aria di bravura* (at m. 423) and a *recitativo quasi Sprechgesang* (at m. 128), not to mention a short quotation from Schubert (a fragment from *Gute Nacht*, the first song of the cycle *Winterreise*, mm. 391–6). But in general, the music is spun from a few original musical motives. Take, for example, the clarinet's opening motif shown in example 11.1, an upward, fan-like unfolding wherein intervals grow systematically larger, from an initial minor second to a terminal perfect fourth.

Not unlike Rea's approach to pitch content in his other geometric or structurally-motivated works, this motive sounds five times in the instrumental introduction, but, it is shorter by one note at each occurrence: the initial presentation has six pitches, the final one only two. At each return, the first note is dropped, so that the end always remains unchanged. The only exception occurs when the major and minor thirds change places at m. 6, in order to retain the D sharp, which, as evidenced by its rhythmic value in example 11.1, is an important referential pitch in the passage.[18]

The reduction in example 11.2 showing only the high pitches at the end of each appearance of the motive reveals that this pattern also manifests itself in the contour of the melody as it unfolds through time. Only here the process has been inverted so that melody's registral highpoints descend downward from the major third to the minor second, instead of upward from the minor second to the perfect fourth, as seen in example 11.1. Rea's economy of musical means is further illustrated when the voice enters for the first time in m. 106 (see example 11.3). Here, the word *mélodie* is embellished through other musical material introduced at the beginning of the work by the cello. This material, woven from alternating descending minor thirds and minor seconds, is taken up by the voice much as it was initially stated by the cello. The voice then balances its downward motion (mm. 111–16) by using the clarinet's first motive to ascend back into the upper register.

Example 11.1.
Une Fleur du mal, first motive, articulated by the clarinet

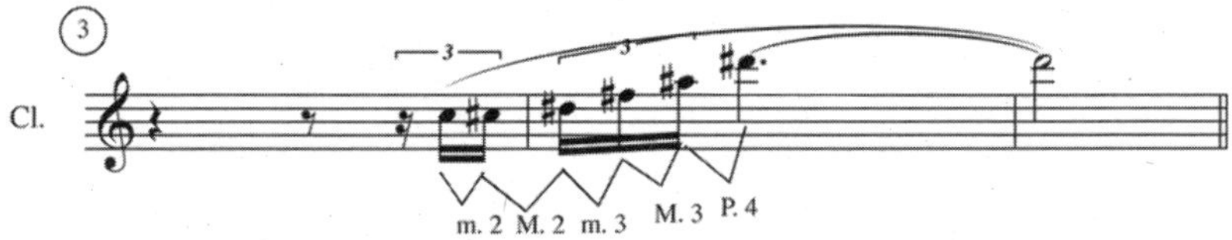

Example 11.2.
Une Fleur du mal, reduction of registral highpoints in the melody

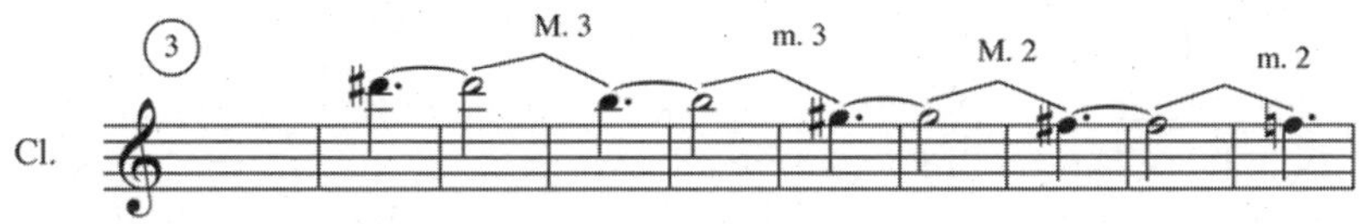

Example 11.3.
Une Fleur du mal, relationship between the introductory cello material and the entrance of the voice
(a) introductory cello material

(b) entrance of the voice at m. 106

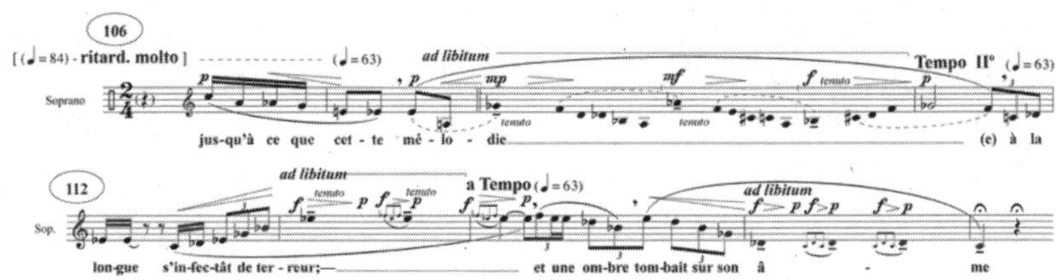

Example 11.4.
Une Fleur du mal, second motive played by the clarinet and the cello, mm. 524–30

The degree to which the cello and clarinet motives permeate the whole work can be illustrated by a final example, drawn from just before the end of the work (see example 11.4). Here the clarinet and cello play the first motive in a mirror image to each other, the clarinet giving it as an expansion from a minor second to a perfect fifth, and the cello as a contraction from a perfect fifth to a minor second. The work closes with a reiteration of the same words spoken by Sappho at the opening (see table 11.2).

The geometric design of the work in this way has a pictorial symmetry that reinforces the theatricality of Rea's libretto as a melodrama. In forging a work from literary sources drawn from three markedly different contexts – the love song of Sappho's ancient Greece, the macabre drama of Poe's early nineteenth-century United States, and the symbolist poetics of Baudelaire's late nineteenth-century France – Rea fashions a total art that explores how the sensibilities of someone from the twentieth and early twenty-first centuries might reflect on the more universal human condition.

Music, according to Aquinas

Such striving for an all-compassing vision that pushes beyond the frame of the notes themselves also occurs in *Music, according to Aquinas*, a work for chamber choir, two clarinets, and cello.[19] Although the piece is essentially narrative in that it, by title, purports to present an account of music according to the thirteenth-century scholar Saint Thomas Aquinas, its construction is highly geometric. As shown in table 11.3, the libretto consists of excerpts drawn from Aquinas' *Summa Theologiae* and his *Commentarium in Aristotelis Librum de Anima.*

Table 11.3.
Literary sources for *Music, according to Aquinas*

Measures	*Latin Text*	*English Translation*
1–26	Universum …	The universe … cannot be better than it is; its good consists in the world order, most handsome it is and bestowed by God.
27–42	non potest esse melius propter decentissimum ordinem his rebus attributum a Deo in quo bonum universi consistit.	
43–58	Quorum si unum aliquod esset melius corrumperetur proportio ordinis; sicut si una chorda plus debito intenderetur, corrumperetur citharae melodia. [*Summa Theologiae,* I, 25, 6-3.]	For one part to be improved out of recognition would spoil the proportions of the whole design; overstretch one lute string and the melody is lost.
58–67	Constat quod harmonia proprie dicta est consonantia in sonis. [*Commentarium in Aristotelis Librum de Anima,* I, 9, 135.]	It is well known that harmony, properly speaking, means consonance in sounds.
67–76	Homo autem delectatur secundum alios sensus … propter convenientiam sensibilium … sicut cum delectatur homo in sono bene harmonizato. [*Summa Theologiae,* II-II, 141, 4-3.]	Human beings get pleasure from their senses … because of a suitability that things have for sensation … Thus, they take pleasure in nicely harmonized sound.
75–89	Huiusmodi enim musica instrumenta magis animum movent ad delectationem quam per ea formetur interius bona dispositio. [*Summa Theologiae,* II-II, 91, 2-4.]	Musical instruments usually move the soul to pleasure and delight rather than creating a good disposition in it.

Table 11.3.
Literary sources for *Music, according to Aquinas* (*Continued*)

90–123	Et dicit quod cum symphonia, id est vox consonans et proportionata, sit vox quaedam, et vox quodammodo sit idem quod auditus, et symphonia sit quaedam proportio, necesse est quod auditus sit quaedam proportio. [*Commentarium,* III, 2, 597.]	And [Aristotle] says that, since harmony – i.e., a consonant and well-proportioned voice – is a kind of voice, and since voice, in some sense, is the same as that heard, and since harmony is a kind of proportion, it necessarily follows that what is heard is a kind of proportion.
125–61	Et ideo salubritur fuit institutum ut in divinas laudes cantus assumerentur, ut animi infirmorum magis provocarentur ad devotionem. [*Summa Theologiae,* II-II, 91, 2c.]	Wisely, therefore, song has been used in praising God, so that the minds of the fainthearted may be incited to devotion.

Example 11.5.
Music, according to Aquinas, choral rendition of "Universum," mm. 1–14

Rea selected only passages that address Aquinas's reflections on beauty, balanced proportions, and the "consonance of sound," and based the structure of the work on the interval of the perfect fifth, with respect to both the choice of individual chords and the succession of harmonies through the entire composition. At the beginning of the work (see example 11.5) the pitches C–G on the open strings of the cello are followed by a choral rendition of the word "Universum" consisting of tranquil melodic lines in the C Dorian mode, which, through the gradual accumulation of vertical sonorities, expands from the perfect fifth to sevenths and ninths (m. 7) and then to elevenths and thirteenths (mm. 10–12).

Example 11.6.
Music, according to Aquinas, tonal ground plan

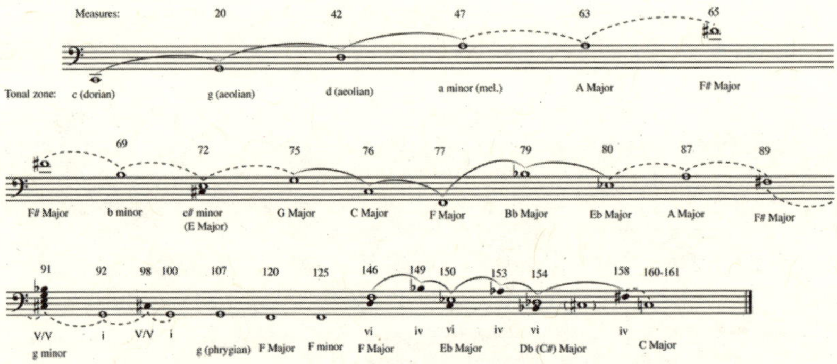

Two events in mm. 19–20 make it clear that the music actually progresses in a gradual upward curve around the circle of fifths. First, the cello sounds the fifths G–D and D–A, still on open strings. Then, in the backwash of the prevailing C Dorian sound, the entry of the clarinets (m. 20) surprisingly introduces E natural (in the high register of the E-flat clarinet, notated at pitch). In m. 42 the E-flat belonging to C Dorian is excised, and in m. 47 the B-flat disappears, to imply A minor. After m. 58 the music continues to progress around the circle of fifths by leaping from A minor to its parallel major in m. 63 (an increase of three sharps in the key signature and therefore three steps around the circle). From A major the harmony moves swiftly another three steps by means of relative keys and modal mixture to F-sharp major in m. 65. At this point, as shown in the tonal ground plan for the entire work presented in example 11.6, the music reverses direction and starts back around the circle of fifths, this time in a less predictable, more sinuous way. Solid lines indicate progressions that follow the circle of fifths, such as mm. 75–80 where the harmonies move from G major to E-flat major, via C, F, and B flat. Dotted lines show progressions involving chromatic alterations.

This systematic development of a single interval recalls the paintings of Vasarely, which were the pictorial stimulus for Rea's first truly geometric work, *Hommage à Vasarely* (1977), a work that, like the paintings themselves, seems to replicate a single figure almost into infinity. In *Music according to Aquinas* the geometrical logic driving the underlying ground plan can also be seen as representative of Rea's narrative approach in that, as the work progresses, the chords increasingly stray from the natural circle of fifths, thereby encapsulating the historical evolution of harmony. That is, progressions are diatonic at the beginning, much as with medieval and renaissance music, but become more and more chromatic in the manner of nineteenth-century music, where progressions to more distant tonal regions are normative (for example, movement by thirds in mm. 64–5 and 88–9 and by tritones in mm. 73–4 and 86–7).

This narrative thread is further reinforced by the different textures Rea uses. The mellifluous modal lines at the beginning hearken back to the period of Thomas Aquinas himself and to later renaissance polyphony involving parallel thirds and sixths. The words *musica instrumenta* (see example 11.7) in mm. 73–8, in turn, invoke the romantic era through wide spacings and arpeggiated passagework in the clarinets and cello typical of nineteenth-century instrumental textures, as well as the chromatic inflections of the movement from a suggested C-sharp minor (or E major) to G major. In suggesting a journey through time radiating outward from the opening word, "Universum," Rea seemingly underscores the universality of Thomas Aquinas's philosophy by showing its relevance in different periods and styles. And, in so doing, Rea seems to reflect not only on the evolution of music but also on our own century – much like opera, which so often reflects the present with plots situated in the past.

Objets perdus

Even though its structure mainly suggests Rea's geometric approach, *Objets perdus,* for string quartet, is also strongly influenced by literature and theatre.[20] The work consists of twelve movements arranged in order of increasing duration, the first barely fifteen seconds long, the last extending to more than three minutes. As shown in table 11.4, the course of other musical parameters is similarly charted, only sometimes in reverse. Rea elaborated this table himself and uses it to systematically map out what he defines as the "trajectories" of each musical parameter. The intrinsic symmetry of the work revealed in the table is so pronounced that the table itself has a pictorial quality, which, given the composer's passion for the visual arts, could be framed as an external force.

The twelve staves of the table show the pitch-classes and registers for all 12 movements, from bottom to top. The first column on the right indicates the number of structural pitch-classes used in each movement; these numbers go from twelve in the very first movement, to

Example 11.7.
Music, according to Aquinas, romantic textures on "musica instrumenta," mm. 73–8

one in the twelfth movement. The figures in the second column indicate the number of "registral pitch-classes." Table 11.4 details the register(s) in which a pitch-class is used; the work was written in a "fixed register" fashion such that each pitch-class shown is used only in the register indicated on the table (in other words, the only transpositions used are the ones shown in the table). For example, the first movement is organized around or utilizes twelve pitch-classes, but one of them, the C, occurs twice because of octave transposition, which brings the total number of registral pitch-classes used in the movement to

Table 11.4.
Trajectories governing the structure of *Objets perdus*.

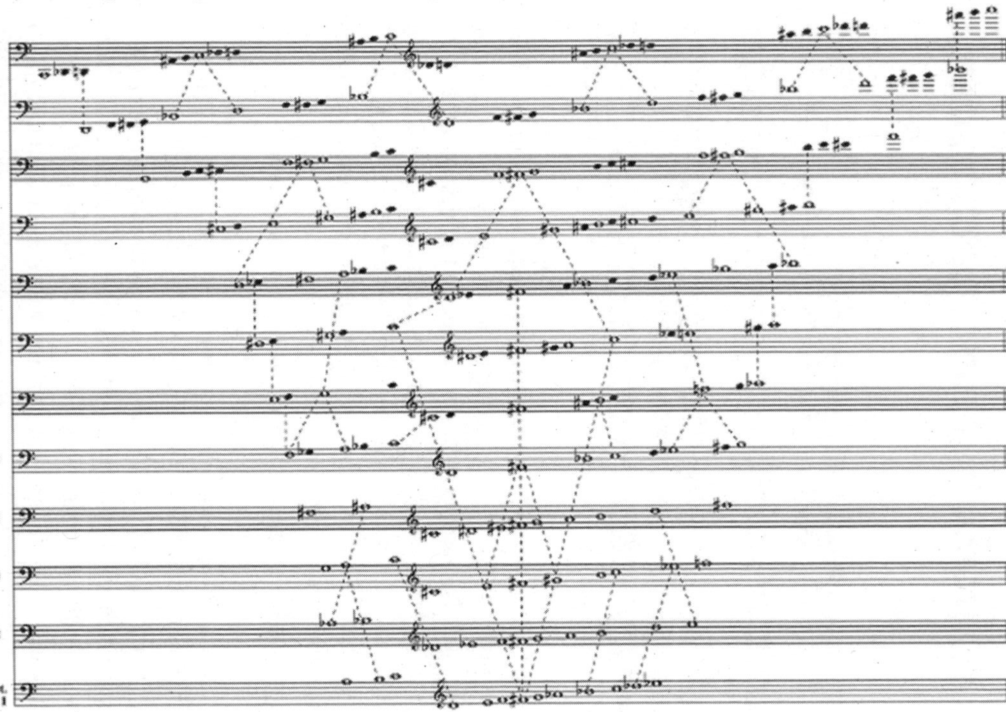

mvt.	Structural pitch-classes	Registral pitch-classes	Quantity of pitches	"Pulse"	Duration
12	1	6	26	♩ = 45	3′12″
					pause
11	2	10	25	♩ = 80	2′12″
10	3	11	23	♩ = 90	2′00″
					pause
9	4	12	20	♩ = 120	1′48″
8	5	9	17	♪ = 160	1′36″
					pause
7	6	9	15	♪ = 180	1′24″
6	7	7	13	𝅘𝅥𝅯 = 240	1′12″
5	8	9	13	𝅘𝅥𝅯 = 300	1′00″
4	9	11	11	𝅘𝅥𝅯 = 360	0′48″
3	10	11	11	𝅘𝅥𝅯 = 420	0′36″
2	11	11	11	𝅘𝅥𝅰 = 480	0′24″
mvt. 1	12	13	13	𝅘𝅥𝅯 = 540 (5 or 6)	0′12″

Example 11.8.
Objets perdus, first movement, mm. 1–7

thirteen. The second movement contains eleven pitch-classes, but since none of these pitch-classes is transposed, the number of pitch-classes and the number of pitches noted in the third column is the same (eleven in both cases). Rea uses the third column to define the pitch content of each movement by combining the structural pitch-classes and the registers in which they are used, showing each as a whole note. Starting with the fifth movement, Rea uses some black notes to represent subordinate pitch-classes that have an ornamental function. The last two columns on the right side of the table show how the tempi have also been systematically organized to produce the impression of a gradual *rallentando* from the first to the last movement.

Let's now look at the details of pitch organization, starting with an extract from the first movement shown in example 11.8. Because the music of this movement evolves within a limited range that does not go beyond a diminished twelfth, the movement contains much crossing among the parts; it also features polymetre (6/8 in the first violin and viola, 3/4 in the second violin and cello), extremely rapid surface rhythms, phrasing that rubs against the grain of the metre, and

Example 11.9.
Objets perdus, organization of structural pitch classes in the first and second movements

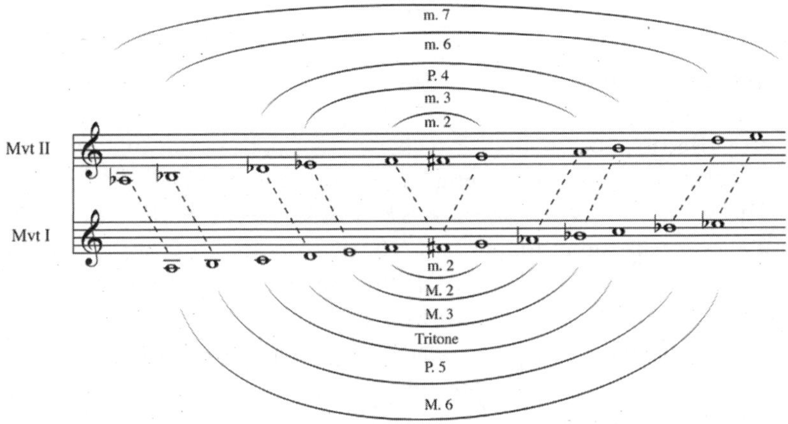

extremely soft dynamic levels (*ppp*). The net effect prefigures later movements in the skillful entanglement of melodic lines that make for a *trompe l'œil* counterpoint where we are not sure who is playing what. I call it a *trompe l'oeil* because the musical or aural impact of the counterpoint is not unlike optical illusions found in many twentieth-century paintings, especially those of Vasarely, where the addition of many geometrical figures has a global effect that is misleading. This movement contains twelve structural pitch-classes, one for each note of the chromatic scale with C occurring twice because of the octave transposition noted above. As can be seen in example 11.9, the organization of these notes may be seen as a mirror in which the last six notes (the second half) are a symmetrical inversion or reflection of the first six notes around the axis F-sharp.

The second movement employs only eleven structural pitches, also grouped around F-sharp. Example 11.9 shows that the organization of the pitches in this movement also involves a mirror reflection around F-sharp. The dotted lines detailing how the pitch-content evolves from the first to the second movement show pitches being "pushed outward" from the F-sharp axis: the high E-flat in the first movement goes up to E-natural in the second movement; its mirror pitch, the low A-natural, is pushed down to the A-flat. In this process, both the C^4 and C^5 in the first movement disappear, so that the second movement contains only eleven structural pitch-classes instead of twelve. The same process leads to ten pitch-classes in the third movement, nine in the fourth, and so on. While the number of pitch-classes is reduced from one movement to the next, however, the registral field is sequentially expanded or pushed outward. Where the total range for the first movement is only a diminished twelfth (from A^3 to E-flat^5), it is an augmented twelfth for the second, a minor fourteenth for the third, and so forth, to a span of five octaves for the last movement. In other words, the expansion of the registral field across movements is inversely proportional to the number of pitch-classes used.

The organization of this work is not only spectacularly geometrical but also details something of plot. The *objets perdus* (lost objects) in the title refer to the musical materials themselves, which, beginning with the C from the first movement, seem to disappear as the work unfolds. In the performance note included in the score Rea requests that this loss be experienced by the performers as a dramatic event: "As the composition 'runs out' of material, a continuous if not greater intensity in the performance energy must be assured, so that there be conveyed, by the eleventh movement, a desperate sense of hysteria at having had less and less 'material' to play." Example 11.10 shows a passage from the eleventh movement where this sense of hysteria is expressed, first by obsessive repetition of the remaining two structural pitch-classes (B-flat and D) splayed vertiginously across five octaves, then by incessant tremolos, and finally by passagework through three octaves that highlights the subordinate pitch-classes (represented by the black notes in table 11.4): F, F-sharp, G (m. 426 in the second violin).

It is also worth noting that, as seen in the first movement, although the four instruments now each span a large range, they are again constantly overlapping to create the contrapuntal *trompe l'oeil* effect to which I alluded above. After this climax, although only a single object remains, the pitch-class C, the last movement brings calm, perhaps suggesting acceptance and resignation in the wake of the drama that has just taken place. It is tempting to interpret this moment in the context of Rea's comment concerning the plight of modern culture after the end of Alma's and Oskar's relationship and the outbreak of the First World War: "now all is dead."[21] However, the passage in mm. 462–70 quotes an extract from Beethoven's String Quartet in C major, op. 59, no. 3 (second movement, mm. 25–30) together with this surprising notation, "Objets trouvés," in the score. Consequently, just as in the three other works I have discussed where Rea reflects upon the present by looking at the past, he seems here to seek solace from the drama of today's music in a masterpiece from the past.

Example 11.10.
Objets perdus, expression of hysteria in eleventh movement, mm. 425–34

In this way, both the geometric design and the "plot" of *Objets perdus* appear to reflect a musical working out of the five epigrams quoting five different artists, philosophers, and art historians which appear on the first page of the score:

Reconnaître un objet usuel consiste surtout à savoir s'en servir. [Recognizing a common object consists above all in knowing how to make use of it.] – Henri Bergson

Chaque objet est le miroir de tous les autres. [Each object is the mirror of all the others.] – Maurice Merleau-Ponty

C'est en rentrant dans l'objet qu'on rentre dans sa propre peau. [It is in entering the object that one enters one's very own skin.] – Henri Matisse

Je regarde ce que je perds et ne vois point ce qui me reste. [I look at what I am losing and do not see what remains.] – Molière

La musique est intangible et ineffable, n'étant pas faite d'objets et se référant pas à des objets; elle ne peut qu'être ... inhalée par l'esprit: le reste est silence. [Music, not being made of objects nor referring to objects, is intangible and ineffable; it can only be ... inhaled by the spirit: the rest is silence.] – Jacques Barzun

Objects perdus is not Rea's first work to include such extra-musical literary additions. The score of *Alma & Oskar,* for example, quotes a passage from Roland Barthes: "We now know that a text is not a line of words releasing a single 'theological' meaning (the 'message' of the Author-God) but a multi-dimensional space in which a variety of writings, none of them original, blend and clash. The text is a tissue of quotations drawn from the innumerable centres of culture ... (*The Death of the Author,* 1968)." In *Alma & Oskar* this text has a particularly valuable explanatory function for a work unfolding mostly through quotation; in *Objets perdus* the combination of words and music, especially given the "visual" inspiration of its geometric structure, creates an instrumental opera of sorts, that seems to invite not only listening (and performance), but silent reading, and as such represents yet another step in Rea's quest for a total art.[22]

Schattenwerk

Also driven by a visually inspired, musical-geometric logic, *Schattenwerk,* for two violins, is like *Objets perdus* in that it has a prominent theatrical dimension and uses extended references to the past in a narrative way.[23] The program note indicates that *Schattenwerk* is a German word that refers "to the work and play of shadows, silhouettes, images, even shades (ghosts), phantoms and spirits." This play of shadows is translated into music by a mirroring strategy where musicians invert the image of each other's musical materials in some way. Example 11.11a demonstrates a passage in which the pitch content is inverted: in mm. 9–15 each instrument plays a series chords based on the open strings G (violin 2) and D (violin 1). The melodic line of the higher part (violin 2) ascends by semitones from D-sharp to F-sharp whereas the lower part (violin 1) descends chromatically from C-sharp to B-flat.

In the first six measures of example 11.11a, the strategy is also applied to articulation, with the instruments alternating between normal bowing and tremolo opposite to one another. This alternation is rapid at first, with changes occurring on each beat (quarter = 152), but then becomes slower at m. 20 with changes occurring every four beats. In other places in the work, the mirroring strategy involves the exchange of both thematic and functional roles. Example 11.11b shows the violins switching roles. In mm. 213–29 one plays a sustained and lyrical melody, the other accompanies with detached, rhythmic figuration. At m. 230, the musicians repeatedly trade places as if one were the shadow of the other.

Rea, however, does not intend the effect to be a simple aural translation of a visual phenomenon, but rather to engage the performers in a ludic play that has its own drama. Urging the performers to exaggerate certain effects, he writes in his performance notes: "This composition is to be played with a light touch. Many passages are "mysterious" in their mood. In some other passages, the piece also may be played faster than the metronome mark indicates, but always with care to maximize colour changes, and to enhance the idea that, at any moment, one instrument may be the "shadow" of the other."[24] Rea then goes on to create a veritable *mise en scène* with concrete performance instructions, such as the directive for the musicians to play facing one another. This visual use of space obviously exaggerates the mirror effect of the work, but it also gives the audience the impression that it is witnessing a joust, a duel between two protagonists in a drama, particularly when the directives instruct the performers to go beyond their role as musicians to become actors; for example, at m. 319 Rea asks the musicians to realize the full stop or hiatus in the music in a physical way by freezing their gestures.

Example 11.11.
Mirror strategy in *Schattenwerk*
(a) mm. 1–27

(b) mm. 213–46

The musicians' theatre, moreover, is bound up with pointed references to past virtuosic repertoires. Example 11.11b above, for example, recalls Bartók's string quartets, and more generally the gypsy music of Eastern Europe, in a variety of ways: the intensity of melody brought out by use of the G string (violin 2, m. 214; violin 1, m. 236) and percussive accompaniments; the modal writing, particularly the suggestion of the mixolydian mode and the augmented fourth (m. 214–29) much cherished by Bartók; and other features of rhapsodic and idiomatic string writing, including varied articulations, glissando, and chords on open strings. The combination of virtuosic reminiscence and rhapsodic musical lines encourages the performers to let go of their musical inhibitions, to forget about the audience and the stiffness of concert hall decorum, and to show without embarrassment their own pleasure, as musicians, in performing the traditions that define their own past or heritage as performers. In this respect, the theatrical dimension of *Schattenwerk* is just like the other works performed at the Scotia Festival, although it certainly reveals a much lighter side of Rea.

A TOTAL ART

The five Scotia Festival works thus make for a coherent corpus, first for the ways in which the geometric and narrative aspects of their design are integrated and interwoven, second for the way in which various external forces (for example, conditions of commission, literary sources, visual phenomena, history and tradition, theatricality of performance, plight of modern music) function as the unifying agents to create an art that is much more than "music." During an email interview that he granted for this article, I asked Rea to reflect on the notion of music as "pure music" and the reason that external forces have played such an important role for him – in other words, why music, in his art, is never "alone." He responded first in French.

Que la musique puisse être seule, en tant que véhicule d'expression, revient au concept de la musique dite absolue, notion très chère à la philosophie allemande et, évidemment, aux compositeurs allemands. Enfin, ce concept (malgré sa volonté d'être autonome ou objectif – "seul" si vous voulez) n'est rien d'autre qu'une construction épistémologique qui sépare la musique germanique de toutes les autres musiques européennes, surtout de la musique française, par la volonté même des philosophes et compositeurs germaniques! [That music can stand alone as a vehicle of expression is a legacy of the concept of absolute music, a notion close to the heart of German philosophy and, quite obviously, German composers. But in the final analysis this concept (despite its drive to remain autonomous and objective – "pure" if you will) is nothing but an epistemological construction that separates German music from all other European music, especially French music, through the explicit will of German philosophers and composers!]

He then continued in English:

That being said, I'm reminded of something Morton Feldman once told me many years ago (in Montreal, where he visited very frequently): "Virtually all of the music ever written has been program music; it's very difficult to write absolute music." So, anyone who knows Feldman's music knows that he himself tried very hard to compose absolute music! And, I think, he succeeded quite well at it![25]

Without denying the importance of external forces for his music, Rea situates his approach in a larger context where the notion of "pure music" is no longer of little importance. It is true that the post-war music current to which he belongs (modernism of the 1950s and 1960s, postmodernism of the 1980s and 1990s) has attached more explicit value to external forces as a source of inspiration than has been the case in other historical periods, and has almost completely abandoned forms traditionally associated with "pure" music, such as sonatas and symphonies. Nevertheless, the way in which musical, literary, theatrical, and visual forces or stimuli intersect in his work and the erudition with which he manipulates them are, to my mind, unique. He has succeeded in creating a total artistic expression combining many disciplines. Indeed, Rea has even declared that he has not always been sure whether he is really a composer. Even though this assertion is likely intended to be more provocative than anything else,[26] it does underline an important side of his creative personality, which is that Rea is *not only* a composer: by the nature of his work, he has made himself into a writer, a *metteur en scène*, a visual artist.

It might therefore seem quite natural that opera, a total art that encompasses many artistic disciplines, would be his preferred medium of expression. But, even though he has shown interest in opera in his writing about Wagner,[27] in his casting aspects of *Alma & Oskar* as opera, and in his reorchestration of Berg's *Wozzeck*,[28] Rea has composed only one opera – *The Prisoners Play* – and it is a chamber opera for children, written early in his career while he was a graduate student at Princeton University.[29] When I asked him why he has not explored a genre for which he has so many affinities, he answered: "I've followed the 'evolution' of opera pretty closely, both in Canada and abroad, and I know that, in our country, we are neither equipped nor disposed to spending taxpayers' money on experimentation. In general, all of our best singers want to leave Canada to sing in Europe and the US; if they do stay, they only want to sing in productions that make their careers meaningful."[30]

It is a response that echoes the often open criticism of the Canadian and Québécois music scenes expressed in John Rea's writings and public lectures.[31] So it was not surprising, in the interview, when he went on to comment on the vulnerability of events as modest as the Scotia Festival with this eloquent, but nonetheless cutting, horticultural analogy:

> "In general, but especially in Canada, cultural initiatives of this nature are always subject to a precarious existence: the terrain is dry and there are few if any nutrients in the soil which, sadly, is also wholly resistant to the infiltration of a genuine system of roots. So, to the uninitiated amateur of cultural products, it is never quite clear whether the beautiful flowers on display – and being admired – actually spring from perennials or whether they are simply the fruit of annuals."[32]

It seems, then, that the realities of the current Canadian music scene and the contingencies that it imposes for its composers have been the ultimate *nécessité extérieure* or external force for John Rea, leading him to express his total art in musical genres other than opera. I believe that if he had lived at another time, or in another country, his œuvre (or at least a part of it) would have taken on a completely different appearance. His melodramas would probably never have seen the light of day in a time or place where he could let his extra-musical inclinations flower as opera; nor would his instrumental works have had the same colour if his taste for literature and visual art had been channelled towards the art of Wagner. But necessity being the mother of invention, the plight of contemporary music in Canada has rendered Rea's art more complex and polymorphous, so that his œuvre has become characterized by original and personal forms that have few equivalents in today's music.

NOTES

It was the publisher's decision, rather than my choice or that of the editor of this volume, to print this article in English. The original French version may be obtained by contacting me directly at Jerome.blais@dal.ca.

I constructed the title of this essay in the same way that John Rea constructs many of his works, that is, by means of quotations and borrowings. The first part, "Music under the Influence," alludes to the title of a 1974 work by John Cassavetes, *A Woman under the Influence*. The expression "nécessité extérieure" in the second part is borrowed from Rea, who used it in reference to Kandinsky's "nécessité intérieure," during a lecture titled "Postmodernity: 'que me veux-tu / what do you want of me'," first given on 15 May 1995 at the Chapelle historique du Bon-Pasteur in Montréal. The text of this lecture is published in *Circuit: Revue nord-américaine de musique du XXe siècle* 8 (1977): 55–69. The reference to Kandinsky is on p. 58.

I would like to thank the following people whose help and advice were most valuable to me in the research for this article: Simon Docking, Mark Fewer, Janice Jackson, Juliette Valcke, Christopher Wilcox, Steven Huebner, and Eleanor Stubley. I would also like to warmly thank John Rea for having generously answered my questions and for supplying several useful documents.

1 Paul Steenhuisen, "Interview with John Rea," *Whole Note* (March 2004).

2 Email exchange with Mark Fewer conducted between 9 and 19 September 2005.

3 The original version of *Alma & Oskar* is for voices (soprano, mezzo, tenor or baritone) and piano. The version presented at the Festival was for soprano, baritone and orchestra. The performers at the Scotia Festival were Janice Jackson, soprano, Olivier Laquerre, baritone, and Alain Trudel, conductor. The concert took place at the Sir James Dunn Theatre, 8 June 2003.

4 From the program note included with the score.

5 John Rea, "Nashville ou Darmstadt: Le Masque mortuaire de la postmodernité," *Circuit: Revue nord-américaine de musique du XXe siècle* 9, no. 2 (1998): 66.

6 Ibid., 66.

7 This sentence suggests that Alma is telling her story after her death and explains the "outre-tombe" [beyond the grave] of the title.

8 John Rea, "Nashville ou Darmstadt," 61–73.

9 Ibid., 70.

10 Ibid., 71.

11 Berg's *Violin Concerto* was written in memory of Alma's daughter, Manon Gropius, who died of polio at age eighteen.

12 John Rea, "Nashville ou Darmstadt," 68.

13 Ibid., 68.

14 Performed by Janice Jackson, soprano, François Houle, clarinet, Mark Duggan, percussion, and Denise Djokic, cello, at the Sir James Dunn Theatre, 5 June 2003.

15 Even though Rea employed other texts ("Nashville ou Darmstadt," 68) such as Alma Mahler's journal or her correspondence with Kokoschka, all of these focus on the same story as Giroud's work.

16 Poe's original version was used at the Scotia Festival.

17 Robert Brasillach, *Anthologie de la poésie grecque* (Paris: Stock, 1950), 127–30.

18 In order to keep the original order of the intervals, that is the major second to minor third then major third, the D should have been natural.

19 Performed by the choir of the Church of Saint-George, conducted by Alain Trudel and David Buley, at the Sir James Dunn Theatre, 6 June 2003.

20 Performed by the Supernova quartet (Mark Fewer and Scott St. John, violins, Douglas McNabney, viola, and Denise Djokic, cello) at the Sir James Dunn Theatre, 27 May 2003.

21 John Rea, "Nashville ou Darmstadt," 71.

22 In fact, because of the richness of the texts that accompany Rea's score – be they quotations or explanatory notes – it seems as if many of his works invite silent reading as much as performance. This is the case with both *Objets perdus* and *Alma & Oskar*, but also with the other three works discussed in this article, each of which contain literary elements in program notes or epigraphs that are meant to enrich the musical discourse or simply to explain the nature of the extramusical elements. But the most striking example of a score that is meant to be read as much as heard is Rea's *Las Meninas*. Each variation in the work is dedicated to – and often written in the style of – a musical figure, usually a composer, including José Evangelista, Alexina Louie, Anton Webern, and Frédéric Chopin. These dedications are explained by a series of fascinating texts that, when read while listening to the music, considerably augment the listener's appreciation. For example, the choice of paraphrasing the *Gymnopédies* for the variation "À la mémoire d'Érik Satie" does not seem very original at first hearing, but the text provided by Rea is, to say the least, enlightening: "In this variation, one needs only to imagine Érik Satie, grown old and tired, sitting 'by the fireside' ... trying to recall the first of his *Trois Gymnopédies* (1888) but somehow, involuntarily, hearing Schumann's music." The score also bears a quotation from Satie's writings: "How lucky to be old. When I was young, people pestered me: 'You'll see one day! Just wait, you'll see!' Well, here I am, and I've seen nothing. Nothing."

23 Premiered by Mark Fewer and Scott St John (violins) at the Sir James Dunn Theatre, 30 May 2003.

24 John Rea, Score, *Schattenwerk*, performance notes.

25 Text provided by John Rea during an email interview between 13 and 27 September 2005.

26 In an interview with Paul Steenhuisen in 2004, Rea provided this gloss on his statement: "The answer is designed to be provocative, and asks the interlocutor to question the answer" (Paul Steenhuisen, "Interview with John Rea," *Whole Note* (March 2004).

27 John Rea, "Richard Wagner and R. Murray Schafer: Two Revolutionary and Religious Poets," *Cahiers canadiens de musique / Canadian Music Book, Canada* 8 (Spring-Summer, 1974): 37–51.

28 Rea's re-orchestration for twenty-one instruments was premiered in 1995 by the Nouvel ensemble moderne, conducted by Lorraine Vaillancourt.

29 Rea's doctoral dissertation is titled "Franz Liszt's 'New Path of Composition:' The Sonata in B Minor as Paradigm" (Princeton University, 1978). It contains the following note: "This essay and a composition, *The Prisoners Play*, together constitute the dissertation but are otherwise unrelated."

30 Email interview with John Rea between 13 and 27 September 2005.

31 For example, in his previously cited article "Postmodernité," Rea comments on the lack of vision and culture on the part of decision-makers in Ottawa and Quebec City. For Rea, writing articles and presenting public lectures at conferences is not simply an academic exercise but constitutes a vehicle for expression that is part of his total art. For each article and lecture he works with the same care and sense of form that infuses his compositional process, so much so that I have come to use the expression "troisième manière" [third approach] to describe this aspect of his work.

32 Email interview with John Rea, 13 to 27 September 2005.

12

Illusions, Collapsing Worlds, and Magic Realism: The Music of Denys Bouliane

Patrick Levesque, Université de Montréal

PATRICK LEVESQUE picks up the conversation where Jérôme Blais leaves off, but he writes from a vantage point at the Université de Montréal, on the other side of the mountain that once isolated McGill "as a seat of wisdom well worth taking in." The bleak despair of John Rea's assessment of the new music scene in Canada has also been replaced by a sense of hope. The analyses comprising this chapter in turn represent the voice of the sceptic former student, motivated by a need to reconcile Denys Bouliane's own description of his compositional processes with apparent stylistic changes and seemingly different approach to orchestration in his most recent works. The conversation between composer and student initially took the form of a silent interrogation, with the scores of Bouliane's works providing both answers to questions and the measure through which their truth across time might be established; so it was with some surprise that Levesque discovered that the differences did not chart a new course per se, but rather reflected a mastery of technique and an increasing capacity to play with complex formal structures. Like Bouliane, Levesque is accomplished in a variety of musical languages and discourses: his thesis for the MA degree in music theory at McGill (completed 2004) explored various musical and linguistic aspects of the late Claude Vivier's music, and his undergraduate studies in composition were completed under the watchful eyes (and ears) of alcides lanza and Jean Lesage.

Je suis un musicien sans culture, sans tradition en quelque sorte.
(I am a musician without culture, without tradition so to speak.)[1]

These are intriguing words, especially given that they are the words of Denys Bouliane, a musician who has emerged over the last two decades as one of the propelling forces of the Canadian musical avant-garde. One can not help but wonder what it means to be a musician without "culture or tradition." For Bouliane, it is first and foremost a matter of lacking a tradition of concert or "creative" art music that is collectively recognized, appreciated and encouraged as one's own and through which one can visualize oneself and one's history. Since our society does not believe that it may express itself originally and forcefully in (pure) music, Bouliane asserts, contemporary Canadian and Québécois composers have no body of works, musical models, or collectively celebrated musical figures through whom to explore their own artistic individuality or from whom to draw inspiration.[2] Neither is there a local critical discourse that is open to and identifies itself with avant-garde music:

même dans le foyer de la création, le discours critique sur la musique a rarement lieu. Et je parle d'un discours fondé sur une analyse comparée sérieuse au-delà des vociférations exacerbées. [... even in the fortresses of musical creation, a critical discourse on music is rarely heard. And I mean a discourse based on serious comparative analysis that goes beyond exaggerated cries of rage].[3]

Bouliane came to understand the importance of this critical cultural void for his own artistic motivation and aesthetic in the 1980s while studying with Ligeti in Germany. There, in Ligeti's famous composition classes, he met composers from around the world, all of whom were asking the same fundamental questions: "Que puis-je bien avoir à dire? Dois-je vraiment dire quoi que ce soit?" [What can I have to say? Must I really say anything?][4] With the majority rejecting the positivistic notion of progress and its musical incarnation in serialism that had characterized the formal abstraction of the 1950s and 1960s, the common denominator seemed to Bouliane "être ce besoin de se situer, avec force ou maladresse, de vérifier l'état ou la présence de racines" [to be a need to situate oneself, to forcefully or clumsily verify the state or the presence of one's roots].[5] And, perceiving himself to have no musical culture in which to find his roots, Bouliane could only conclude: "Tout ce qu'il me reste à faire, c'est de jouer avec la tradition, de devenir un illusioniste, de me donner l'impression de posséder une culture, d'inventer une pseudo-tradition, de jouer au caméléon pour tout dire." [All that I can do is to play with tradition, to become an illusionist, to make myself believe I do have a culture, to invent a pseudo-tradition, in sum to play the part of the chameleon.][6]

This last observation and others like it have led many to associate Bouliane's music with the literary movement known as magic realism, but the only serious studies in this regard have focused on works completed early in Bouliane's career. Since then his writing style has changed considerably. Through a detailed examination of selected works spanning Bouliane's career, this study explores how his aesthetic orientation and personal style continue to reflect the preoccupations of magic realism.

MAGIC REALISM

Art critic Franz Roh originally coined the expression "magic realism" in the 1920s to describe the work of German post-expressionist painters. The term was later adopted by literary critics to refer to the work of a select group of Latin-American writers, who like Bouliane, experienced themselves as lacking (in their case as a result of poverty and economic exile) a cultural tradition in which to ground their creativity. The genre, however, is not confined to Latin-Americans; it includes not only its well known proponents – Jorge Luis Borges, Gabriel García Márquez, and Alejo Carpentier – but also Salman Rushdie, Gunter Grass, and others.

Just as Bouliane speaks of his own aesthetic as a matter of becoming an illusionist or chameleon, magic realism is typically understood to "combine realism and the fantastic in such a way that magical elements grow organically out of the reality portrayed."[7] To briefly summarize Wendy Faris' description of the genre in literature, it depends on a plot that is grounded in detailed descriptions that provide or create "a strong presence of the phenomenal world" of the reader.[8] The text then introduces "an 'irreducible element' of magic, something [that the reader] cannot explain according to the laws" of that reality as he or she knows them.[9] The process usually involves the introduction of a fantastical or magic object, the incorporation of mythic worlds as if they were real, and/or the juxtaposition of conflicting value and belief structures. As a result, Faris continues, "The reader may hesitate (at one point or another) between two contradictory understandings of an event."[10] Because the author has used subtle effects of language and syntax to negotiate contradictions, the reader begins to "experience the closeness or near-merging of two realms, two worlds,"[11] such that a new reality, seemingly as real as the reader's original, begins to emerge. And the logic of the unfolding narrative seems so plausible that the reader is forced to question his or her own culturally "received ideas about time, space and identity."[12]

For example, Jorge Luis Borges' *Tlön, Uqbar and Orbis Tertius* depicts how one ordered and logical view of the world is defeated by the view of another world that is just as ordered, just as logical, but wholly fictitious. The narrator finds a banal reference to an imaginary country named Uqbar in a counterfeit encyclopedia. He can find no other reference to the country anywhere and would have totally forgotten about the place and his discovery of it had he not come upon another reference to it two years later in the Encyclopedia of Tlön, an imaginary planet existing solely in the culture of Uqbar. As the narrator learns more about this planet, some of its artifacts – a trinket, compass, language, concept, etc. – gradually begin to invade the narrator's perceptual reality of his own world until that reality collapses and is replaced by the reality of Tlön. The accretion is so slow and done in such a way that the story at any given moment seems believable.

In Gabriel García Márquez's *One Hundred Years of Solitude,* the process works through largely hidden temporal shifts in the narrative, the cumulative effects of which create a reality that seemingly stands outside of time as we know and understand it. The story is about the birth, growth, and ultimate disappearance of the village of Macondo. The last surviving character, Aureliáno Babilonia, is carried away in a hurricane with the remnants of his village as he deciphers a prophecy written years earlier by a gypsy elder. The prophecy refers to the very events that the story narrates – the growth and decline of the village and its last survivor being swept away by a hurricane. In order to decipher the prophecy, however, it is necessary to know the context of its creation and the intervening history. Past, present, and future are seemingly made to coexist in the same instant. The prophecy is also redacted in Sanskrit and the storytelling includes references to various biblical miracles, tales from *A Thousand and One Nights*, and South American folklore that, although involving different cultural values and beliefs often seemingly at odds with each other in our reality, appear to exist simultaneously without discord.

Salman Rushdie creates a similar effect at the beginning of *Satanic Verses*. Opening quite abruptly midway through the plunge of two skydivers towards British soil, the disjunct narrative jumps back in forth in time and space; only considerably later is it explained that the skydivers have survived the explosion of their hijacked airplane. The narrative strategy creates a sense of atemporality for the reader such that: "The Millenarian explosion of terrorist activity is, then, itself blasted out of its own sense of place in time."[13] In addition, the narrative is strung together with elements taken from Islamic mythology and Middle-Eastern folklore, as well as staples of British culture presented in an incongruous fashion (for example a character's bowler hat remains firmly stuck on his head throughout his descent). In context the effect is unsettling in that it is not immediately obvious to which set of cultural values readers should relate themselves. [14]

MAGIC REALISM AND ITS EARLY MANIFESTATIONS IN THE MUSIC OF DENYS BOULIANE

Although music typically lacks the semantic content or representational power of literature, Bouliane emulates the effects of magic realism by twisting and manipulating various melodic, rhythmic, harmonic, and formal elements, which, as continuous processes not unlike plot, have temporal implications that Bouliane believes will be recognized and responded to by the vast majority of concert goers. But having no particular cultural tradition or musical language of his own on which to draw per se, Bouliane creates the impression of an underlying syntax by using what he describes as a "pseudo-functional tonality."[15] The backbone of this syntax is the diatonic major scale, but Bouliane does not use it as such. Rather he systematically compresses or stretches it to create seven different modes spanning a pitch space of seven to thirteen semitones. Using Bouliane's nomenclature, Peter Niklas Wilson identifies these modes as +I (13 semitones), 0 (12 semitones), –I (11 semitones), –II, –III, –IV and –V (ten, nine, eight and seven semitones, respectively). Two of the modes are illustrated in example 12.1. The first, mode 0, is the diatonic major scale; the second, mode –IV, is the diatonic scale compressed into the pitch space of a minor sixth.

What Wilson does not explain is that each of the modes, while not a diatonic scale, maintains the allusion to a diatonic scale because, like that scale, each is built from two asymmetrical tetrachords.[16] The

Example 12.1.
Examples of modes forming backbone of syntax

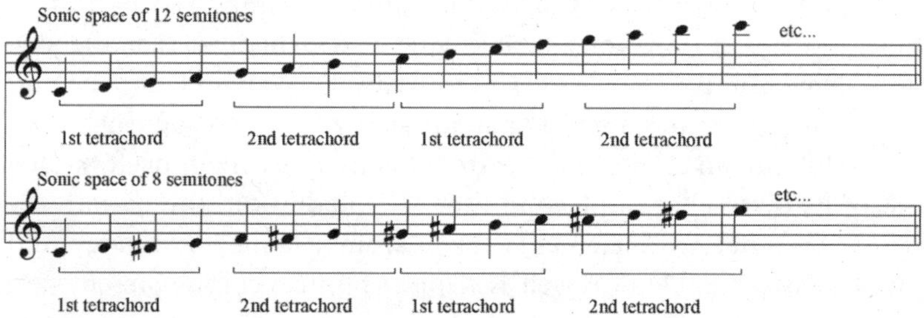

power of this allusion is particularly apparent when a mode is repeated. In example 12.1, for instance, while a mode covering twelve semitones repeats at the octave, a mode covering the pitch space of eight semitones repeats at the minor sixth in order to avoid any distortion of the last interval of the second tetrachord. The syntactical functions of each scale degree and of their repetitions, whether at the octave or at a different interval, remain the same no matter the pitch space (number of semitones) to which the scale has been confined. This has a peculiar consequence: chords constructed from one of the compressed modes may, by coincidence, sound identical to diatonic chords. They will however resolve in completely unexpected ways, thereby disturbing conventional listening habits.

For instance, the original chord in the first part of example 12.2 could be perceived in a diatonic context as a tonic chord in first inversion. One possible continuation would be a dominant seventh in second inversion, followed by its resolution in A-flat minor. When interpreted in mode –IV, as in the second part of the example, the same notes spell a tonic chord without the fifth that, when continued in the same mode, produces a different I–IV–V–I progression. The seemingly clear tonal "world" or "reality" evoked by the initial chord does not survive the progression in this new mode. The enharmonically respelled G-sharp major chord in first inversion is followed by an F-sharp diminished fifth chord in fourth inversion with an added ninth sonority. While it is tonally difficult for listeners to situate this two-chord progression, there are two common tones (C and G-sharp) and some conjunct motion that might be interpretable as a passing sonority. Such an interpretation, however, is made untenable by the following stack of fifths (A–E–B–F) that subsequently progresses to the pitch-class

Example 12.2.
Syntactical implications of chords resulting from modes 0 and –IV

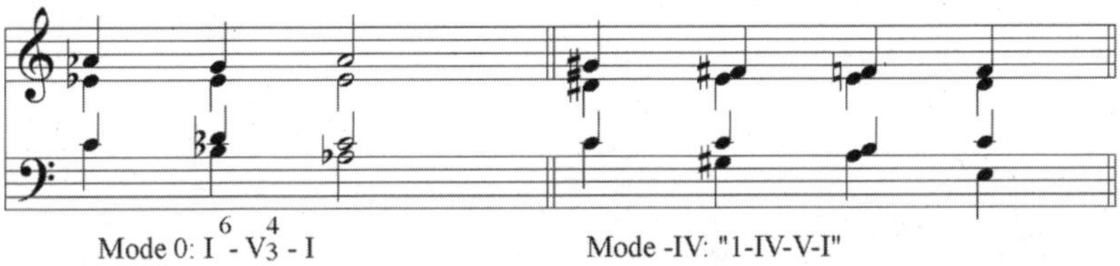

set [0,1,2,5]. In other words, despite the hints of chromatic voice leading, there is no clear tonal focus that can be sustained throughout the whole progression.

In this way, Bouliane uses the modes to create the illusion of tonal syntax, but then routinely foils it with small distortions that present listeners with two or more contradictory readings or interpretations of a musical progression as it unfolds. As processes, these small distortions have an effect similar to the "irreducible" magical elements identified by Faris. They are intentional modifications that cannot be explained by any audible rules of tonal harmony and voice leading. They are "irreducible" because they emerge from outside listeners' normally constituted sense of a tonal "reality," and while not necessarily experienced as being "unreal," are heard as "invented" or "fantastic" in the magic realism sense of having come from the composer's imagination.

This effect is central to the aesthetic intent of Bouliane's early work *Douze tiroirs de demi-vérités pour alléger votre descente* (1982), a concerto for piano and chamber orchestra that is divided into twelve stylistically different sections or "drawers." The tenth drawer is the only one in which the orchestra does not appear. The writing for solo piano in this drawer is energetic, technically demanding, and, given its position near the end of the work, reminiscent of a classical piano cadenza. However, the piano begins with what sounds like a jazz tune in F: a turn figure followed by a major ninth chord (see example 12.3). What makes this opening somewhat unsettling is that the harmony and melodic writing style do not, in context, fit the expected form. If this were indeed a cadenza, listeners would likely expect the sixteenth notes of the turn to develop into a virtuosic display, as they do; but listeners would also anticipate the virtuosic display to be followed by a dominant chord in the orchestra, rather than a major ninth played by the piano alone.

Example 12.3.
Douze tiroirs de demi-vérités pour alléger votre descente, conclusion of ninth drawer and opening of tenth drawer, mm. 1–3

Of course this is a very brief excerpt; in the context of the movement as a whole, the passage might be more comprehensive if interpreted through the mantle of jazz. But just as the F-sharp chord which follows did not fit the classical cadenza model, it does not quite realize an expected jazz harmonic pattern; and while its sonority is plausible (a minor chord with an added sharp eleventh in the bass), in a jazz idiom this chord would more likely be heard as a passing chord, not as a sustained fermata, as is the case here. As the music unfolds, moreover, the illusion of jazz continues to dissipate until the end of the drawer, where an excerpt from J.S. Bach's Chorale no. 140 appears, as if representing yet another musical style or "world."

What is particularly striking is that the Bach reference seems to develop effortlessly out of the jazz. For listeners it is not a matter of whether one musical world – baroque or jazz – constitutes a reality and the other fantasy; rather listeners, remembering the influence of medieval chant in a previous drawer, hear the formal sequence as disrupting the traditional historical narrative of Western music. Of course, what initially sounded like a Bach chorale turns out not to be right either. Listeners familiar with Bach chorales will recognize the chorale, but will also note subtle differences, including the change in tone between the legato chorale style of the antecedent phrase and the short, soft notes, à la Schumann, of the consequent phrase, as well as the unusual metric arrangement (5/4 + 4/4 + 6/4) of the passage.

Furthermore, elements of the chorale theme undergo rhythmic transformation as they are rewritten in each mode.[17] The original pattern, as seen in example 12.4a, is divided into two distinct rhythmic groups, each consisting of five quarter notes, one half note, and one quarter note with a fermata. In the first reference to the tune in the opening turn of the drawer, however, this rhythmic pattern appears to be twisted.[18] As illustrated in example 12.3 Bouliane initially eliminates one of the first five notes and articulates the remaining four notes as anacrusic sixteenths to the two longer final notes, the durations of which have been exaggeratedly increased. Several measures later, as detailed in example 12.5, there are six short scattered notes preceding the two longer notes, and the anacrusis involves only the first four short notes. By the end of the passage (example 12.4b) the pattern has been slowly brought back to its original form by stretching the metric organization to overcome or neutralize the effect of the delayed anacrusis.

Example 12.4.
Comparison of original Bach chorale with its appearance in *Douze tiroirs de demi-vérités pour alléger votre descente*
(a) J.S. Bach, Chorale no. 140, mm. 1–2

(b) *Douze tiroirs*, number 71, mm. 34–8

Example 12.5.
Douze tiroirs de demi-vérités pour alléger votre descente, rhythmic evolution of chorale reference, number 71, mm. 15–17

It could be argued that my analysis up to this point is not an accurate depiction of the music heard. For example, I initially described the harmony of the opening turn (example 12.3) in terms of jazz sonorities. In example 12.5 I could have described the chords of its rhythmic elaboration using such terms as French sixth, [0,1,6], dominant seventh with an added ninth. But such an interpretation would not take into consideration the formal expectations of the role of the drawer within the context of the previous nine drawers. Furthermore, the syntactic implications or expectations generated by these chords alone are not realized by the harmony. In literary magic realism the "reader may hesitate between two contradictory understandings of [an] event"; here listeners face a similar aural dilemma. Elements of the Bach chorale are transformed through Bouliane's pseudo-syntax from its most remote incarnation at the beginning of the drawer (technically, a rhythmic variation in mode –V, although not a transposition of the chorale to that mode) to one in mode 0 by the end of the drawer, closer to the Bach version, but with a piano style that, as alluded to earlier, opens up onto another "Schumannesque" world. This "turn" has a humorous effect in that the anticipated final or half-cadence at the end of a cadenza is suddenly interrupted by a cluster. The sonority may be funny in its own right, regardless of the evoked context, but functionally its playfulness punctuates or encapsulates what its overt character makes explicit: the same mischievous toying with expectations of syntax and formal designs that has been occurring throughout the movement. It is as if Bouliane, by presenting the baroque as an offspring of jazz, wants to evoke a relationship with the traditional historical narrative, but then indicates his intention to not fully realize it by using humour to disassociate himself, as a composer, from that narrative.

In ... *Comme un silène entr'ouvert* ... this disassociation plays an even more significant role. In this work seven instruments are divided into two groups – piccolo, oboe, bass clarinet; and trombone, piano, double bass, and synthesizer – each of which is matched by a recorded track. As seen in example 12.6 polyrhythmic motives blur the background over which various transformations of a source motive (marked with brackets and wavy lines) are played by the clarinet, piano, trombone, and tape in a quasi-imitative texture. The imitation, though, is far from rhythmically perfect and the constantly shifting metric position of the accents gives the melodic lines a staggering contour.

The recorded tracks and instrumental ensembles also perform at different tempi. At rehearsal letter B, where all instrumental forces and tapes are sounding for the first time, tempi markings are 87, 58, 116 and 92 beats per minute. At rehearsal letter O, the tempi markings for the same respective groups are 77, 57, 70 and 45 beats per minute. In this way, and through increasing and decreasing rhythmic activity, the four sonic entities evolve through time and register in a manner reminiscent of, yet not identical to, Conlon Nancarrow's famous "X" player-piano study.[19] Where Nancarrow only involved two lines varying in tempi and register, Bouliane extends the technique by also playing with the evolving sense of metric and motivic cohesion as the centre of "X" is approached.

Once the centre of the "X" is reached, at rehearsal letter S (example 12.7), the source motive of the piece is revealed to the audience in metric and rhythmic unison. As shown in example 12.7, it has a

Example 12.6.
... *Comme un silène entr'ouvert* ..., rehearsal letter C, mm. 12–14

Example 12.7.
... *Comme un silène entr'ouvert* ..., rehearsal letter S, mm. 1–2

melodic outline similar to the imitated motives detailed in example 12.6. Yet Bouliane does not immediately continue the rhythmic consolidation, registral displacement, and motivic elaboration that would complete the "X" shape as might be expected if the work is heard as a literal replication of Nancarrow's study. Instead, the now metrically stable motive is repeated and varied for twelve more measures (until rehearsal letter T). Then, the process of metric displacement begins again and the "X" shape potential of the piece does appear to realize itself. The impression only lasts for a few measures because the instruments merge to articulate an exact quotation from *Douze tiroirs de demi-vérités pour alléger votre descente*.[20] In that work Bouliane used the gradual accretion of pervasive minute changes to create an atemporality that would disassociate his work from the historical narrative of Western music; here he uses the same process to disassociate himself from the music closer to his own time.

It is at this point that an understanding of the term "demi-vérités" in the title *Douze tiroirs de demi-vérités pour alléger votre descente* becomes relevant, for, as explained by Bouliane, it clarifies the relationship between these two works.

> Je parle de "demi-vérités" en référence au caractère subjectif et purement ludique de l'art. Pour reprendre Max Ernst, la "création" de l'Artiste est plutôt affaire de révélation, d'établissements de liens nouveaux aux confins du plausible et du possible entre les êtres et les choses. [I mean "half-truths" in reference to the subjective and purely playful character of art. To quote Max Ernst, the artist's "creativity" is rather a matter of revelation, of forging new links at the limits of the plausible and the possible, between beings and things.][21]

While Ernst was not referring specifically to magic realism, his words are an apt description of what happens in this literary style, as well as in Bouliane's music. Bouliane does not claim inspiration from or affiliation with the canon works (musical or literary, past or present) on which he draws, as they clearly belong to a culture, historic or modern, not his own. Instead, he toys around playfully with their structural components and, by using the same thematic or harmonic generative material from one work to another, seemingly quotes himself.[22] Since one cannot identify by listening alone the piece in which a quotation or generative material originates, the quotations are intended to be experienced as false reminiscences. For all listeners know, *Douze tiroirs de demi-vérités pour alléger votre descente* could be quoting or heralding

... *Comme un silène entr'ouvert* ... And given the self-referentiality, to even raise the question is to chart a downward course (*descente,* author's italics) or spiral that can know no end.

LATER MANIFESTATIONS OF MAGIC REALISM

The sound of Bouliane's more recent works is noticeably different from that of the earlier pieces. Where, in his early works he used "pseudo-functional tonality" or illusory syntax to string together what might be described as a medley of textures, quotations, and stylistic pastiches, more recent works appear to have an almost romantic approach to form. This does not mean, however, that Bouliane has abandoned his earlier aesthetic ideals. On the contrary, the conceptual links to magic realism have become more pervasive and sophisticated in both depth and subtlety.

In *Qualia Sui,* a work commissioned by the Fibonacci Trio in 2001, the generative material is based not on one but two harmonic progressions in C, marked in the composer's drafts as "a" and "c." [23] As illustrated in example 12.8, the pitches in the first progression are taken from a tonic chord with an added sixth, and those in the second from a dominant seventh chord. When spelled out in ascending order the notes sound the diatonic major scale of Bouliane's mode 0.

In *Douze tiroirs de demi-vérités pour alléger votre descente* modes could be used only in their original octave registration; here Bouliane drops the necessity for octave correspondence so that modes can be transposed from one appearance to the next to provide greater flexibility in melodic writing and orchestration. In example 12.9, for instance, transposition allows the composer to use C-sharp^4 instead of C-sharp^6 when using the third repetition of the altered diatonic scale in the –II mode.

Bouliane subsequently expands his system for identifying modes to include letters and numbers, letters indicating the mode and the progression ("a" or "c"), and numbers the octave and chord displacement within the progression.[24] In most cases the composer does not alternate randomly between octave transpositions, but only proceeds sequentially from one transposition to the preceding or following one. Material extracted from the –IIa 3.1 (mode –II, progression "a," third transposition level, first chord of the progression) can connect with –IIa 2.1 or –IIa 4.1, but not –IIa 6.1. Also contrasting with the early works, the rate of modal change through the cycle of compression or expansion is typically much faster. For example, in *Douze tiroirs de demi-vérités pour alléger votre*

Example 12.8.
Two basic progressions from *Qualia Sui*

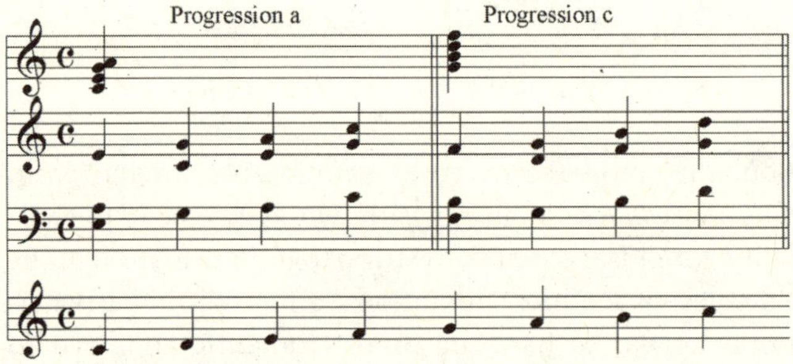

descente a change from mode –V to –IV occurs after twelve measures, and from mode –IV to –III after ten measures; in *Qualia Sui* it can change as frequently as every other note (see example 12.10a).[25] Furthermore, as seen in the two passages from the first movement in example 12.10, which alternate the "a" and "c" progressions with or within each change of mode, the modes are presented not only successively but also simultaneously: one for the piano and one for the strings. This is reminiscent of the unfolding plotline of *Tlön, Uqbar and Orbis Tertius,* where the alternate reality of Tlön at first punctures and then gradually replaces that of the narrator. But in Borges's novella the change works at the level of the plotline; in Bouliane's music, it targets the primary constituents of his own musical discourse.[26]

Of course, both passages in example 12.10 could be described using other analytical paradigms. The left and right hands of the piano part in example 12.10a could be read as two separate descending motions: D–C–B–B-flat–A-flat–F in the right hand and B-flat–A–G-sharp–G–F–G in the left hand. Alternately, this passage could be explained as a movement from a diatonic tetrachord in m. 7 (A–B-flat–C–D) to two [0,1,3,4] tetrachords in m. 8 (G–G-sharp–B-flat–B) and in mm. 8–9 (E–F–G–A-flat). Given that the [0,1,3,4] tetrachord alludes to the harmonic minor scale, listeners might be tempted to attribute a clear tonal underpinning to the movement.

Later in the movement, however, as was the case in *Douze tiroirs de demi-vérités pour alléger votre descente,* tonal theory is not sufficient to explain what happens (see the second part of example 12.10b). While the [0,1,2,5,8] sonority in m. 147 is in fact a C minor chord with a sharp eleventh and a flat thirteenth, this cannot in any sense be linked

Example 12.9.
Numbering of octave transpositions in *Qualia Sui*

Example 12.10.
Generative material in *Qualia Sui.*
(a) first movement, piano part, mm. 7–9

(b) first movement, trio, mm. 147–50

with the following six-tone sonority [0,1,2,3,6,8]. A foray into set theory, while highlighting that mode +I and mode –I share the same prime form [all sonorities will form subsets of six different prime forms (7-1, 7-2, 7-8, 7-23, 7-33, 7-35 corresponding to modes –V, –IV, –III, –II, –I and 0)], is not helpful when we consider the harmonic syntax over a longer time span as the transposition of pre-established material. In fact, all of these diverse acoustic phenomena are results of Bouliane's pseudo-syntax. The fact that isolated elements or passages may appear to be comprehensible using pre-existing harmonic theories or analytical paradigms is exactly what the composer wants to achieve. And when seen in this way, it is virtually impossible to concentrate only on the episodic nature of discrete passages. To understand the work, in other words, it is necessary to contemplate it as a whole.

The complexity of Bouliane's inventiveness also extends to conceptual discordances. In *La neige est blanche mais l'eau est noire,* a work for full orchestra commissioned by the National Centre for the Arts in 2003, this begins with the title itself – a semantic labyrinth framed by the Greek sceptic Empiricus in which the insertion of the word "but" leaves listeners to wonder why the whiteness of snow should have any incidence on the colour of water. Bouliane writes:

> On accepte généralement d'emblée que la neige est blanche... l'idée d'eau noire est une forme de distorsion de l'expérience courante ou alors une métaphore. Mais le véritable "court-circuit logique" apparait dans la mise en relation de ces deux parties par leur positionnement autour de la particule *mais.* D'une part *neige* semble être en relation avec *eau...* Et *blanche...* semble correspondre à noire... On a donc tendance à chercher une relation de "cause à effet"... Et cette quête s'avère bien illusoire... le *mais* ne peut s'expliquer que dans un vertige de liens de causalités tous plus hypothétiques les uns que les autres. [We generally accept as a fact that snow is white... the idea that water is black is either a kind of distortion of everyday experience, or a metaphor. The real "logical short circuit" appears in the relationship between these two statements by the word "but." On one side snow seems to be related to water...White seems to correspond to black ...We thus try to find a causal relationship...And this quest reveals itself to be illusory...The "but" can only be explained in a vertigo of causal links, every one more hypothetical than the next.][27]

While for Bouliane sound does not have the semantic function of words, he creates logical and syntactical short-circuits by suggesting to listeners formal paths that are then developed in improbable or unexpected ways that seem to have their own logic. The third movement introduces a solo violin passage (example 12.11) not unlike the twisted cadenza in *Douze tiroirs de demi-vérités pour alléger votre descente.* Where the cadenza in that work seemingly emerged naturally from the general design of the work as a concerto for piano, here listeners will not likely expect a classical violin cadenza, since the work has not thus far been considered as a concerto – at best, given the titles of each movement, listeners will likely conceive it as a tone poem. The violin interruption is thus perceived to be a cadenza only because it emerges from an orchestral tutti chord and becomes a technically challenging, virtuosic, unaccompanied instrumental line. However, just as listeners begin to accept this possibility, the cadenza is aborted as the rest of the string quartet joins the violin with their own virtuoso counterpoint, giving the movement new impetus. This new rhythmic drive, alternating fluid melodic lines with rapid successions of disjunct chords, propels the string quartet for a while until it ignites the rest of the orchestra.

While the violin cadenza was surprising at first, particularly given the fact that the movement has yet to reach its midpoint, its metamorphosis into a string quartet and then a full orchestral tutti gradually gains credibility in the second half of the movement as the causal link, the thematic manipulations of which prepare and connect motivic materials presented in the first half of the piece with their inversion in the subsequent furious melody of the second half.[28] In other words, the cadenza is in effect reinterpreted *a posteriori* as an emerging thematic unit or as an introduction to varied material. The "short-circuit" manifests itself even more noticeably when listeners hear the movement again: the appearance of the solo violin is so startling, and in the specific context of its appearance, so characteristic of a cadenza as to once more assault the credibility of the entire movement until it is once more validated by subsequent developments. This brings about the vertigo of causal links alluded to by Bouliane.

But does it defeat the purpose of the music? Not necessarily. Listeners who hear this piece for the first time obviously have no prior impression. The ending becomes paramount and alters their recollections of the beginning. For both first-time and experienced listeners the significance of the aural trap can be grasped only when listeners metaphorically, and from a distance, relate the music to the title of the piece. The formal function of the cadenza, acting like the word "but," links the two halves of the movement such that the expectations initially invoked by its appearance are at odds with the way in which the music subsequently unfolds, although the two halves of the movement, are, like the two parts of the original sentence, logical in and of themselves.

In the first movement, the "short circuit" evolves so as to give the impression of a music that moves but does not go anywhere. In mm. 303 and 304, for instance, a long fortississimo trill in the flutes, oboes, clarinets, and violins marks the end of a rhythmically frantic, polymetric development that has dominated the movement up to this point. This is followed by the shrill blow of a whistle that introduces the

Example 12.11.
La neige est blanche mais l'eau est noire, third movement, solo violin, mm. 104–10

timpani. Thus far, it has only been used to punctuate formal articulations, but here, quite unexpectedly, it proceeds with a solo that slowly fades in intensity. What comes next? Nothing. Contrary to what listeners might expect after the formal exposition and development of a musical idea, the new element thrown into the discourse is not developed any further. The music moves, but does not go anywhere. It simply stops.

How then can the formal design of a work or movement be conceived in such cases? Formal design in Bouliane's early works, as previously shown, depends closely on the gradual revelation of a pre-established source: a Bach chorale in *Douze tiroirs de demi-vérités pour alléger votre descente*; the source motive described above in ...*Comme un silène entr'ouvert...*[29] Although Bouliane may still model later works on pre-existing works or musical styles and genres from the Western concert music tradition, the sources themselves generally remain hidden.

The fourth movement of *Tetrapharmakos* (2004), a massive triple concerto for violin, cello, piano, and full orchestra is a case in point. In typical concerto fashion it opposes solo and orchestral textures. The orchestral writing is rhythmically square with dramatic, dense chords. The solo writing is flowing and melismatic. The timpani serves as a link between the soloists and the orchestra, playing rhythmic variations of the opening bass drum line (example 12.12), which is derived from two different sources: the opening theme of the second movement of Beethoven's *Seventh Symphony* (first four notes of mm. 1 and 2), and the funeral march from Chopin's Sonata no. 2, op. 35 (the remainder of m. 2 up to the end of m. 4).

Rather than revealing the two sources, the form of the movement is driven by the narrative content of the title of the movement – "Cette mort qui ne nous concerne guère: marches, dé-marches et vrilles de vie" – which, notwithstanding the pun on "démarches," may be translated as "Death, which is not of our concern: marches, un-marches, and swirls of life."[30] Bouliane's inventive and transformative play unfolds on a variety of different thematic, harmonic, rhythmic, and formal levels such that the alternation of soloists and orchestra associated with the concerto form is gradually fused into a fast, dance-like movement featuring the soloists with string (and sometimes brass) accompaniment, over which the rest of the orchestral instruments are gradually added. What began as a funeral march finally resolves into a wild *danse macabre* that fades away in the last six measures as the quiet beat of the timpani (accompanied by string harmonics) resounds once more. The

Example 12.12.
Tetrapharmakos, fourth movement, source material, mm. 1–4

very fact that the original sources are not revealed carries its own message: there is no point in fearing death, ignoring death, or trying to defeat it; death, like the sources themselves, always remains "beyond our grasp."

Detailing a narrative through musical constructs imbued with a pre-established social meaning, such as death (as in the case of the funeral march and the *danse macabre*), is another method by which Bouliane borrows elements of formal design from earlier musical forms. But where elements of the classical concerto were recuperated in *Douze tiroirs de demi-vérités pour alléger votre descente* to articulate formal design, or in *La neige est blanche mais l'eau est noire* to sap the syntactical foundations of that design, in *Tetrapharmakos* these elements are used to nihilistically evade the need for design itself. By basing all three works on similar sources but giving them in each instance a different twist, Bouliane seems to be mocking not only the classical concerto tradition but also previous and potential subsequent uses of it in his own works. And just as was the case with the decoding of the prophecy in Gabriel García Márquez's *One Hundred Years of Solitude,* distinctions distinguishing past, present, and future collapse and the chronological sequence of Bouliane's individual works becomes unimportant and irrelevant. All of Bouliane's compositions are meant to be understood as components of a larger, all-encompassing whole, which, however, remains incomplete.

> "All I've got left to do is to play with tradition, to become an illusionist, to make myself believe I do have a culture, to invent a pseudo-tradition ..."

This is why Bouliane associates himself with the ethos and technical tools of magic realism.[31] Far from innocent, the inventive play from one work to another with shared materials that hint at an underlying but willfully hidden logic and the subsequent self-referentiality and atemporality that it suggests are definite assaults on the notion of musical progress itself. As in literature, consequently, magic realism "reveals itself as a ruse to invade and take over dominant discourse(s)."[32] As Maria-Elena Angulo explains, magic realists "portray social conflict and implicitly criticize injustice and oppression" by presenting in each work "a closed world with its own laws" which reflects the artists' "*own vision of a problematic reality and a deep pre-occupation for his/her native culture and tradition.*"[33]

Typically, literary artists do this by using folk traditions to highlight the irregularities and identity crises precipitated by a perceived need to re-enact the behaviour and traditions of a dominant discourse or authority. Bouliane frames his identity crisis as the conflict between Western concert culture and his Canadian/Québécois culture, a culture that remains without its own traditions. Hence, instead of using folk traditions he relies on a mock syntax which allows him to freely and effortlessly pilfer musical styles and genres and through which he can interrogate and criticize the problematic reality that he confronts as a composer in a way that actively engages listeners. When a passage is reminiscent of Keith Jarrett or of a romantic concerto, it is because Bouliane manipulates his material to create this impression; but it is also because listeners habitually classify musical material according to prior models. Since these reminiscences tend to be short and fleeting and are never fully concretized, listeners are forced to question their musical culture. Why are they taken aback by such and such progression? What is it invoking, and how? These questions in turn nudge willing audiences to develop a greater cultural awareness.[34]

Bouliane's musical aesthetic in this sense may be viewed as another facet of his quest as teacher and conductor to foster awareness of contemporary musical culture and to engage the critical discourse that he believes is essential to the development of just such a contemporary musical culture. Although he cannot create the missing tradition by himself, he can incite others to reflect on their own musical heritage, its constituent styles and genres, and the intricate manners by which they not only co-exist but also ultimately depend on one another. The ideological parallel with García Márquez's *One Hundred Years of Solitude* and the impact it had on Colombian national consciousness is striking in that Márquez was able to intensify a nation's prevailing sense of social failure and fragmentation, such that the casual attitudes and matter-of-fact reactions of his fictional characters are transposed to the Columbian population at large to become a new "foundational myth of the nation and a narration of identity."[35]

Bouliane is attempting a similar process of re-identification, so to speak. His hope is that listeners will not only recognize that they are, in a way, disconnected from the elements of Western concert music present in his works, but also that they will identify with his solution, the play through which he processes these materials to create something unique that gives them new meaning. While I am not asserting that the impact of Bouliane's music on Canadian society has been as profound as García Márquez' writings in Colombia, the need to redefine oneself and one's culture is central to both artists.

NOTES

The scores by Denys Bouliane cited in this article include: ... *Comme un silène entrouvert ...* (Montréal, Canadian Music Centre, 1986); *Douze tiroirs de demi-vérités pour alléger votre descente* (Montréal, Canadian Music Centre, 1984); *La neige est blanche mais l'eau est noire (Snow is white but water is black)* (Montreal, Canadian Music Centre, 2003); *Qualia sui: Partition avec esquisses et analyse* (Montreal, 2001); *Tetrapharmakos, Quatre remèdes d'après Epicure* (Montreal, Canadian Music Centre, 2004). I must acknowledge Denys Bouliane's collaboration to the preparation of this article. In addition to the many hours of interviews, he has given me access to all the scores, recordings, and working notes relevant to his works, without which the analyses presented above would have been considerably harder to achieve. He also lent me copies of all the articles, press releases, and press clippings relevant to his music and career. I also thank Professor Eleanor Stubley, whose arduous task it was to help me to clarify my ideas and organize the text.

1 Peter N. Wilson, "La musique du réalisme magique," *Sonances* 7/2 (1988): 32. This and all further English translations are by the author.

2 Jean Boivin and Denys Bouliane. "Écrire sur la création musicale québécoise: Dialogue virtuel entre Jean Boivin et Denys Bouliane," *Cahiers de la Société Québécoise de Recherche en Musique,* 6 (2002): 17.

3 Ibid., 18.

4 Wilson, "La musique," 32.

5 Denys Bouliane, "L'image fécondante du silène: D'une incursion du doute, du rire et de l'ironie dans le musical: souvenirs, réflexions, 'autoréfléxions,'" *Circuit* 9/2 (1998): 32.

6 Wilson, "La musique," 32.

7 Wendy B. Faris. "Scheherazade's Children: Magical Realism and the Postmodern Fiction," in *Magical Realism: Theory, History, Community*, ed. Lois Parkinson Zamora and Wendy B. Faris (Duke University Press, London, 1995), 163. Magic realism should not be confused with surrealism; the latter style tends instead to eschew reality completely, replacing it with subconscious inspiration and *onirique* [dream-like] subjects.

8 Ibid., 169.

9 Ibid., 167.

10 Ibid., 171.

11 Ibid., 172.

12 Ibid., 173.

13 Stephanie Jones, "Of Numerology and Butterflies: Magical Realism in Salman Rushdie's *The Satanic Verses*," in *A Companion to Magical Realism*, ed. Stephen M. Hart and Wen-chin Ouyang (Tamesis, Woodbridge, 2005), 256.

14 For a more exhaustive study of the genre, its narrative techniques, and their uses in other art forms, see Lois Parkinson Zamora and Wendy B. Faris, eds, *Magical Realism: Theory, History, Community* (London, Duke University Press, 1995).

15 Wilson, "La musique," 26.

16 Wilson hints at this concept in music example 1.a (p. 23) of his article, but does not elucidate it in the text.

17 Wilson sketches out the different variations of the chorale using all seven of Denys Bouliane's modes, "La musique," 26.

18 Some minor editing modifications have been added to clarify the examples used in this paper. Preceding and continuing materials have been removed to focus the discussion on specific rhythmic examples. For the same reason, score indications and dynamic markings have in some cases also been omitted.

19 In Nancarrow's work melodic lines are set in the upper and lower registers of the instrument, at a very quick or a slow pace respectively. As the work unfolds the lines move towards a median register and tempo, reach it, and then continue on their course towards the opposite register and tempo. Bouliane's use of the technique is not as straightforward as Nancarrow's; for example, tempi progressions may be halted or repeated.

20 For more detailed information about the formal design of this work, see Denys Bouliane, "*Wie ein aufesprungener Silen*, eine Schappschuß Analyse," *MusikTexte* 21 (October 1987): 22–8.

21 Denys Bouliane, *Douze tiroirs de demi-vérités pour alléger votre descente*, program notes, 2.

22 This self-referential process is by no means exceptional in Bouliane's works. *Le cactus rieur et la demoiselle qui souffrait d'une soif insatiable*, *À-propos…et le*

baron perché?, and *A Certain Chinese Cyclopaedia*, all completed between 1985 and 1986, share the same harmonic generative material and often quote one another.

23 It is unknown to this author whether a progression "b" was dropped in the initial stages of the work.

24 It should be observed that in Example 12.9 the original register is numbered as transposition level one, the first octave transposition as level two, and so forth, following the indications in the composer's drafts.

25 The single instance in tenth drawer of *Douze tiroirs*, where five modes are used one after the other, changing every four notes, is a clear exception.

26 The rate of change on occasion can also be sharply interrupted. In the third movement, for example, a long segment built on alternating –Va and –Vc progressions spans mm. 34–60. It is interrupted by a shorter segment based on progressions –Ia and –Ic, with –Vc and –Va only to resume again at m. 73.

27 Denys Bouliane, *La neige est blanche mais l'eau est noire*, program notes.

28 Compare, for example, the motivic similarities in mm. 127–35 and 187–90 with those in mm. 69 and 94.

29 Bouliane's use of Chopin's Étude, op. 10, no. 8, in *Jeux de société* might also be included.

30 Denys Bouliane, *Tetrapharmakos*, program notes.

31 For more information on Bouliane's perception of the notion of identity and the act of composing, see Bouliane, "*Wie ein aufesprungener Silen*," 26–7.

32 Theo L. D'Haen, "Magic Realism and Postmodernism: Decentering Privileged Centers," in *Magic Realism: Theory, History, Community*, 195.

33 María-Elena Angulo, *Magic Realism: Social Context and Discourse* (Garland, New York, 1995), 106, italics added.

34 These techniques, however, are not unique to magic realism. Other composers have favoured approaches that use pastiches of pre-existing musical styles: Schnittke and Rochberg come to mind immediately. In both cases, unfortunately, affiliations to magic realism do not appear to have been explicitly researched in published articles, although such an endeavour would probably uncover interesting relationships between music and literature.

35 Erna Von der Walde, "El macondismo como latinoamericanismo," *Cuadermos Americanos, Nueva época*, 223–37, quoted in Ana María Ochoa, "García Márquez, Macondismo and the Soundscapes of Vallenato," *Popular Music* 24: 207–22.

EPILOGUE

The Schulich School of Music: Hearing the Future

30 September 2005: The Schulich School of Music, with its new building (designed by the architectural firms Menkès Shooner Dagenais LeTourneux and Saucier + Perrotte), stands ready. The transformation celebrates 100 years of music at McGill. Spawned at the intersection where technology, science, and music meet, it also "represents the dawning of a new era," an era in which, according to Dean Don McLean, "a world-wide cultural and educational revolution is finding in the practices of the arts a paradigm for re-imagining the purposes and dynamics of the university as an institution dedicated to the advancement of knowledge."[1] "Created by creators for creators,"[2] the eight-floor building is itself a testament to the meeting of minds which its very design serves to engender. The west wall, for example, is a representation in black stone and glass of the code used to program player pianos at the turn of the twentieth century. Like a mirror or a musical quotation in the music of John Rea, it carries within its glossy surfaces a reflection of the Strathcona Music Building, the play of light as day passes into night and again into day speaking to the vitality of the old and the manifest ways in which its traditions and evolving practices will be carried into the new. At the front of the building, the marble sculpture created by Marie-France Brière is both a scientific rendering of a sound wave and a constantly changing expression of its possibilities for music. The lofty view from the spacious glass windows of the Marvin Duchow Library, like the building's hidden state-of-the-art information network, on the third, fourth, and fifth floors, in turn, frames Sherbrooke Street, as author Nicole Brossard's "endless street," where "one slips, transparent and multiplied, from world to world" without ever seemingly having travelled.[3]

The Schulich School of Music and the Strathcona Music Building, McGill University. Reproduced by permission of the McGill Schulich School of Music.

Standing alone in the lobby, though, I am struck only by the silence. It is a technologically engineered silence, designed to ensure that the Tanna Schulich Recital Hall and the scoring stage that will be in the bottom of the building are acoustically sealed. And it will no doubt be the envy of recording studios world wide, and part of our draw as a crossroads. But, as the silence wraps itself around me, it seems somehow surreal, an echo of Arthur Danto's assertion that art as we have long known it is dead,[4] and a reminder that, while the building is a long-anticipated dream planned out in every detail, it represents, like "the stairs which spiral up through its center ... a journey through space-time [that has] only just begun."[5] I cannot help but wonder how the music of young composers recently hired at McGill will resonate in this place and what role their works will play in charting our future.

The questions, according to Edward Casey, are as important to an understanding of place as the documentation of its past, place being defined not only by the ways in which it "gathers people" and "holds" memories but also by the ways in which it looks to the future. Such looking is by definition intricately bound up "with the body and voice of the one who looks."[6] I, Eleanor Stubley, therefore introduce myself as the silent but omnipresent editor who in her efforts to hear the voices of place and the ways in which they resonate as a community is also a traveller in search of voice.[7] I look to the future, much like a composer, by beginning with the work whose title seemingly embodies many of the recurring themes that have shaped this journey, the *Wreath of Stone* (2001) by theorist-composer Jonathan Wild. Its text, a poem marking the passing of Henri IV of France, was written by the seventeenth-century physicist-mathematician Marin Mersenne as part of an enquiry into the nature of echo.[8] Through careful measurement and analysis, Mersenne noted that sounds when taken up by place do not return unchanged, and that the length of the silence between a sound and its return can vary. His poem was an effort to determine whether an echo could return speech in a different language from that originally spoken. The Greek words ending each line were carefully selected so that when the poem is read at the right tempo in the right acoustic, the echoes in the silences between lines would give rise to a shorter, complementary poem in French. Wild's setting avoids literal echo effects, using instead lengthy strands of Greek monody and curious dissonances from Mersenne's *Book of Dissonances* to create a web of internal musical relationships that play with Mersenne's other questions about echo: can it store sound indefinitely to be released at a later time? and can it return music at different pitches or otherwise transformed? As I listen to Wild's music in the silence of this place, I am struck by two thoughts: that while the music sounds new and I have no knowledge of either archaic Greek or Old French, I hear it as a lament from the past, the echo of another people's expression of grief; and that it was the bat's use of echo that inspired Stephen Hawking to define time as curved space.[9]

Out of the silence of my thoughts emerge the opening measures of Christoph Neidhöfer's *Schichtung* (1993), a colourful and complex hocket created by juxtapositioning and continually mediating overlapping layers of sound, seemingly static in and of themselves. I marvel, as I did the first time I heard the piece, at the technical craftsmanship, for although the motivic materials articulated in any given sound layer are rhythmically short and often ragged, I have no sense of brokenness, no sense of the music as fragmented. While I am constantly tuned to its timbre, I hear it not as a function of instrument but as the very impulse through which forward momentum is generated. As the piece progresses and the textures become more varied, however, I find myself increasingly fascinated by what Neidhöfer describes as the "unheard."[10] Sometimes it is the way in which the scoring of vocalized vowels and consonants seems to turn them inside out, stripping them of their linguistic associations so that I hear them simply as the sounds they are. Other times it is more a function of structure and of my own expectations and anticipations as a listener, change, surprise, twist, subtle rhythmic abbreviations or elongations creating what I can only describe as a "wrinkle in time" where the music seemingly becomes an acoustic mirror in which I hear myself listening. But unlike a visual mirror, the image is not in the music per se but a matter of that which was literally "unheard." I experience it, moreover, not as a continual thwarting of expectation in the fashion of L.B. Meyer but as a type of forgetting that leaves me open to hearing new possibilities. And, here in this place, I can't help but wonder what role "forgetting" will play in our future understanding of memory, listening, and music learning more generally, the focus of the cognitive sciences to date having largely been that which needs to be remembered, that which should not be forgotten.[11]

My musings elicit the opening gesture of Sean Ferguson's *In the Flesh/Dans la chair* (2003). Articulated by celesta, harp, and glockenspiel, it creates a splash of colour across an empty palette from which emerges the sound of resonating crystals, defined not by their tone but by the feel of their sharp edges as they are slowly rotated. It is an effect created by sustained string harmonics scored at what science tells us is the threshold of human hearing. But the longer it persists, the more I feel it as a function of my own balance, as if it were my extended hand that was keeping the crystals in motion. And, eventually, having leaned too far forward, I hear the edge thicken to become the surface of a murky depth that pulls me down into its sounding space. It is not the first time I have heard this music. Unlike the first time, though, I find myself wanting to linger over the title of the work, a reference to Maurice Merleau-Ponty's phenomenological account of the role played by the body in perception and human understanding.[12] Ferguson's compositional process is based on psychoacoustic models of sensory dissonance, musical contour, and spectral envelopes,[13] all of which have been framed through research that has treated hearing as an isolated mode of sensory perception. Yet, as I struggle to find the words to describe Ferguson's music, I am acutely aware of the way in which my hearing seems to be sometimes a function of seeing, other times, of touch, and still other times, of balance. Many would dismiss my observations as a consequence of the limitations of language. But against the backdrop of the technology housed in this building and an ever-growing understanding of metaphor as the basic process through which we make sense of the world, I can hear them only as an affirmation of what Merleau-Ponty and others have described as the "inter-semiotic network" of senses that, while each having their own "individual rationality," work one through the other as a constantly evolving and ever developing system.[14] I am also reminded that at root hearing is a form of touch.

As I contemplate what the science of touch might have to contribute to our understanding of music listening, music to the science of touch, my thoughts assume the character of a free fantasy. Against the play of the changing light within the lobby as the sun rises, I am reminded of Jean Lesage's *Dischordia* (1990). It is a music that attempts "to usher different fragments of our nocturnal world of dreams into the domain of the sonorous."[15] Lesage describes his work "as a metaphorical music," a music in which he composes not only with sounds but with meanings. What I hear is a strange amalgam of the irrational and the coherent, with seemingly familiar themes and stylistic gestures appearing at disconcerting junctures, abrupt variations of atmosphere and movement, and an unrelenting sense of continuity born not from the development of a musical idea but seemingly from my own desire to wander. The effect is that of an ever-deepening present in which the play of symbolic, cultural, aesthetic, and formal or structural meanings creates a sense of endless possibility, a sense that here in this place, with this music sounding, my imagination has no bounds. Yet I am aware too that it is my imagination and that the future is not mine alone to chart. Others will bring to this music their own bodies, their own musical and scientific histories, their own sense of place. And it is in this that the beauty of art lies.

Ma fin est mon commencement.[16]

NOTES

1 Don McLean, "Introductory Remarks," Making a Space for Art Conference, Montreal, 14 October 2005.

2 Gilles Saucier, "The Schulich School of Music," Making a Space for Art Conference, Montreal, 15 October 2005.

3 Nicole Brossard is a Montreal postmodern poet and author. See *Intimate Journal* (Toronto: Mercury Press, 2004).

4 See, for example, Arthur Danto, *The Philosophical Disenfranchisement of Art* (New York: Columbia University Press, 2005).

5 Saucier, "The Schulich School of Music."

6 Edward Casey, "How to Get from Space to Place in a Fairly Short Stretch of Time: Phenomenological Prolegomena," in *Senses of Place*, ed. Steven Feld and Keith Basso, (New York: School of American Research Press, 1996).

7 Eleanor Stubley is the director of Graduate Studies at the Schulich School of Music. She teaches seminars in aesthetics and Canadian music. As a conductor, she has an international reputation for *The Pines of Emily Carr*, her recent film on a work of the same title by Canadian composer Jean Coulthard, and for the program book *Louis Riel: The Story, 2005*, written for Opera McGill's restaging of the opera *Louis Riel* by Harry Somers and Mavor Moore. She is also a celebrated musicologist, music educator, and freelance writer.

8 For further detail, see Marin Mersenne, *Harmonie Universelle* (Paris: Editions de centre national de la recherche scientifique, 1965), 210–20.

9 See Stephen Hawking, *The Future of Space-Time* (New York: Norton, 2002).

10 Christoph Neidhöfer, email communication, 14 October 2005. Niedhöfer uses similar words to describe other works in the program notes for the recording *Christoph Neidhöfer*, Musikszene, Grammont Portrait, CTS-M59.

11 This could also be usefully read against a theme of "forgetting" prominent in Montreal postmodern fiction writing; see, for example, Robert Majzels, *City of Forgetting* (Toronto: Mercury Press, 1997).

12 See, for example, Maurice Merleau-Ponty, *The Phenomenology of Perception* (London: Routledge and Kegan Paul, 1962); *The Visible and the Invisible* (Evanston, IL: Northwestern University Press, 1968).

13 For a detailed elaboration of these processes in Ferguson's *In the Flesh*, see Sean Ferguson and Richard Parncutt, "Composing in the Flesh: Perceptually-Informed Harmonic Syntax," unpublished paper provided by Sean Ferguson.

14 See, for example, the two publications by Maurice Merleau-Ponty cited in note 12 above, and Horst Ruthrof, *The Body in Language* (London: Cassell, 2000).

15 Lesage, introduction to *Dischordia* in the program notes for Montreal, Nouvelles Musiques, March 2005.

16 My end is my beginning. Heard first in Bruce Mather's *La Princesse blanche*; see chapter 10 of this volume. The long history of the phrase "ma fin est ma commencement" (my end is my beginning) includes the fourtheenth-century mass by Guillaume de Machaut, and resonates with various themes heard in the pages of this book: Bengt Hambraeus's interest in the past, John Rea's preoccupation with thirty years, the form of Bruce Mather's *La Princesse blanche*, and the importance of the "crossroads" epigram as the defining attribute of place for a book that begins in 1904 and ends in 2004.

Chronology

The information in this chronology focuses on the evolution of "new" music at McGill University, and was compiled by Prof. Eleanor Stubley, Heather White, and Associate Dean Bruce Minorgan, with the assistance of the Marvin Duchow Library and the McGill University Archives. This chronology is not intended as a comprehensive list of all of the "new" music or all the works by McGill composers that have been performed by McGill ensembles, including the Contemporary Music Ensemble. Rather, it documents works that were the result of a specific commission by an ensemble or that represent a milestone in the performance of "new" music by internationally recognized composers in Montreal. For a complete list of McGill Records featuring "new" music see Appendix 1.

THE MCGILL CONSERVATORIUM, 1894–1919

1894 Guillaume Couture suggests the creation of a chair of music theory at McGill.

1899 Lord Strathcona invites Clara Lichtenstein to establish a department of music in Royal Victoria College, offering vocal and piano instruction to women students pursuing bachelor of arts degrees.

1903 McGill University is appointed a representative of the Associated Board of the Royal Academy of Music, London, England, to conduct individual and school examinations across Canada.

1904 Conservatorium of Music is opened, with Charles Harriss as director and Clara Lichtenstein, as vice-director.

1908 H.C. Perrin replaces Charles Harriss as director of the Conservatorium.
The McGill Corporation approves appointment of H.C. Perris as the first full-time professor of music.

1909 The first orchestral concert is presented.

1910 Dr Howard Barnes gives a series of lectures in the Physics Building on acoustics, and he endeavours to seek an ongoing relationship between the Conservatorium and the department of science for research purposes.

Dr Wesley Mills is appointed to attend the International Music Concert in Europe.

The first choral concert is presented

Beatrice Donnelly becomes the first BMus graduate.

The McGill Conservatorium establishes its own examination system.

1911 Charles Henry Mills becomes the first DMus graduate; later he is appointed dean of Music at the University of Wisconsin.

1914 The McGill Conservatorium trains forty amateur singers to perform in a production of Wagner's *The Flying Dutchman* presented by the visiting Quinlan Opera Company.

THE EMERGENCE OF THE FACULTY OF MUSIC, 1920–30: H.C. PERRIN, DEAN

1920 The Faculty of Music is constituted, and H.C. Perrin is appointed as dean; the McGill Conservatorium continues as a preparatory school, providing instruction in theory and performance.

Sergei Prokofiev performs in Montreal.

1921 Redpath Hall, originally built in 1893, is refurbished as an auditorium and reading room.

Two music scholarships are established as a memorial to Sir William Peterson.

1922 Two music scholarships are established as a memorial to Sir William MacDonald.

Music is made an optional subject in the BA program.

1927 Three Beethoven centenary orchestral concerts are presented in Moyse Hall.

1928 A Schubert centenary orchestral concert is presented in Moyse Hall.

Maurice Ravel performs in Montreal.

THE FACULTY OF MUSIC, 1930–55: DOUGLAS CLARKE, DEAN

1930 Douglas Clarke is appointed dean of the Faculty of Music and director of the McGill Conservatorium.

The BMus requirements are changed to require seven years of study after the completion of a BMus degree.

1931 Douglas Clarke founds the Montreal Orchestra (later the Montréal Symphony Orchestra).

1932 The Montreal Orchestra first performs compositions by McGill students: Alexander Brott, Frank Hanson, Violet Archer.

1937 The Conservatorium of Music Opera Fund is established.

Igor Stravinsky performs in Montreal.

1939 The Carnegie Foundation donates a collection of gramophone recordings and library books to the Conservatorium.

Alexander Brott founds the McGill String Quartet (which became the McGill Chamber Orchestra in 1951).

1944 A BMus program in music education is introduced

1948 The McGill Conservatorium and the Faculty of Music move to Drummond Street.

A radio school involving collaboration with the Canadian Broadcasting Corporation (CBC) is proposed.

1949 A six-month program to acquaint music students and future radio music producers with microphone technique and radio music production, including plans for a microphone studio, is proposed but never implemented.

The first honorary degree is awarded to conductor Sir Thomas Beecham.

1950 Distinguished visitors to the Faculty include Yehudi Menuhin, Maurice Eisenberg, Emil Cooper, Ernest Ansermet, Ellen Ballon (graduate of McGill), and Thomas Young.

István Anhalt prepares and performs a groundbreaking concert presenting his own works and the Montreal premieres of Bela Bartók's *Sonata for Two Pianos and Percussion* and Igor Stravinsky's *Sonata for Two Pianos*.

Elizabeth Goldblatt, a piano instructor, presents a recital of works by Canadian composers.

1951 The Ellen Ballon Lecture Series is inaugurated.

1954 Pianist Ellen Ballon and soprano Pauline Donalda receive honorary degrees.

FACULTY OF MUSIC, 1955–64: MARVIN DUCHOW, DEAN

1955 Marvin Duchow is appointed acting dean of the Faculty of Music.

A graduate degree in musicology is proposed but refused because of the lack of adequate library and research resources.

The BMus program is extended from three to four years, with three streams: composition, performance, and school music.

Music listening sessions are added to all advanced history and composition courses.

A required arts component is introduced into the BMus program.

The Ellen Ballon Lecture Series features William Schumann, Ian Hunger (former director of the Edinburgh Festival), Rudolph Bing (general manager of the Metropolitan Opera), and Sir Thomas Beecham.

A radio school is again proposed at Senate and equipment is ordered.

1956 A free Campus Concert Series is introduced; many of the concerts feature works by student and faculty composers.

Luciano and Edith Della Pergola establish the McGill Opera Studio / L'atelier d'opéra McGill as an opera workshop.

1957 Marvin Duchow is appointed dean of the Faculty of Music.

1958 The McGill Opera Studio performs Cimarosa's *Il Matrimonio Segreto.*

Composer Norman Della Joio, critic Abram Chasms, and composer Deems Taylor give guest lectures on the role of the composer in a changing modern society.

Karlheinz Stockhausen gives a guest lecture, "New Electronic and Instrumental Music."

1959 Student compositions are presented in a New York radio program entitled "Hands Across the Sea."

István Anhalt produces the first concert of electronic music in Canada.

1960 The Netherlands Chamber Choir performs Samuel Barber's *Reincarnations* as part of the CBC Celebrity Series.

The Faculty of Music and the Conservatorium move to three terraced houses on McTavish Street.

1961 Ali Akbar Khan gives a series of lectures on Indian music through a grant from the Canada Council.

István Anhalt hosts John Cage and David Tudor.

Montreal hosts "La semaine internationale de la musique actuelle."

1962 Milton Babbit, professor at Princeton University, gives a series of guest lectures on music and science at the invitation of Anhalt.

1963 Hugh Le Caine loans a Multi-Track Tape Recorder to the Faculty of Music.

FACULTY OF MUSIC, 1964–76: HELMUT BLUME, DEAN

1964 Helmut Blume is appointed dean of the Faculty of Music.

RCA Victor and Decca Records contribute recordings for a listening library.

The Electronic Music Studio opens with István Anhalt as director.

Stockhausen returns to Montreal, sponsored jointly by McGill, l'Université de Montréal, le Conservatoire, Jeunesses musicales, and the CBC to give a lecture entitled "Invention and Discovery: Development of Musical Forms since 1951."

1966 An "Evening of Electronic Music" features the EMS and compositions by R. Murray Schafer and Pierre Mercure.

The Conservatorium becomes the McGill Preparatory School of Music.

Société de musique contemporaine à Québec (SMCQ) is established; McGill composers are among the founding members.

1967 R. Murray Schafer, guest composer from Simon Fraser University, completes two works for Expo '67.

István Anhalt, Alexander Brott, Kelsey Jones, Paul Pedersen, and Bruce Mather are among composers who receive centennial commissions supported by various organizations including the CBC, Expo '67, the University of British Columbia, Simon Fraser University, les Grands ballets canadiens, the Canadian Music Centre.

The Faculty is reorganized into three departments: Theoretical Music, Applied Music (Performance), and School Music.

1968 MMA programs in composition and musicology are introduced at the Faculty of Graduate Studies.

An International Young Composers Symposium is held in Montreal.

Conductor Wilfred Pelletier receives an honorary degree.

1969 Jazz composition and performance are introduced into the curriculum as workshops.

1970 An MMA program in music theory is introduced.

The Contemporary Music Ensemble is founded by Richard Lawton and Eugene Plawutsky.

Clément Morin (dean of music and conductor at Université de Montréal) receives an honorary degree.

SMCQ hosts Olivier Messiaen.

1971 The Faculty moves into two wings of the Royal Victoria College, remodeled and renamed after Lord Strathcona.

Paul Pedersen is appointed director of the EMS.

The SMCQ hosts Karlheinz Stockhausen.

The New Music Group, a student ensemble, is formed and performs in Toronto.

The 150th anniversary of McGill University is celebrated with a mixed media concert featuring works by Anhalt, Hurel, Pedersen, among others.

McGill graduate Violet Archer (composer) and scientist/composer Hugh Le Caine receive honorary degrees.

1972 The McGill Opera Workshop / L'Atelier d'opéra McGill becomes the McGill Opera Studio.

1973 Bengt Hambræus and alcides lanza are appointed co-directors of EMS.

1974 alcides lanza is appointed director of EMS.

A DMus degree in composition reappears after a dormant period of time with no graduates.

Mauricio Kagel, Earle Brown, and Philip Glass give guest lectures.

1975 Pollack Concert Hall (designed by John Bland of the firm Bland, Loyne/Shine/Lacroix) is inaugurated.

The tenth anniversary concert of the EMS involves collaboration with Métamusic Québec and the McGill Symphony Orchestra.

Visiting composer Mario Bertoncini introduces a course in musical design.

An MMus program in performance is introduced.

The McGill Opera Studio presents Benjamin Britten's *The Rape of Lucretia.*

Pianist John Newmark receives an honorary degree.

1975 Group MUD (MUsic Design), later renamed SONDE, emerges from the EMS.

Sergio Cervetti is visiting performer and composer at the EMS.

FACULTY OF MUSIC, 1976–86: PAUL PEDERSEN, DEAN

1976 Paul Pedersen is appointed dean of the Faculty of Music.

Edgar Valcárcel, from Peru, is visiting composer and pianist.

A BMus program in Early Music is introduced.

Masters degrees are renamed: MMus in Composition, MMus in Performance, MA in Theory, MA in Musicology.

The SMCQ performs at World Music Day in Montreal.

McGill Records is founded, with Paul Pedersen as director.

The McGill Wind Ensemble presents commission of Barbara Kolb's *Cross Winds* (USA).

The McGill Symphony Orchestra presents John Rea's *Pieces for Orchestra.*

1977 Mariano Etkin (visiting composer), Luciano Berio, Wlodzimierz Kotonski, Poul Rousing Olsen (Islamic Studies), and John Rothgeb give guest lectures.

Violinist Jean Carignan and composer Kelsey Jones receive honorary degrees.

1978 Makoto Shinohara is visiting professor.

French composer Claude Ballif replaces Bruce Mather, who is on sabbatical in France.

PhD programs in musicology, theory, and school music are proposed.

The McGill Preparatory School becomes the McGill Conservatory of Music.

The McGill Wind Ensemble presents the world premiere of alcides lanza's *eidesis IV.*

Pianist and composer Burt Bacharach and composer John Beckwith receive honorary degrees.

1979 An MMus program in Sound Recording is introduced.

The McGill Opera Studio commissions and premieres Byron Herman's *The Path of Light.*

A four-piano recital with pianists Bruce Mather, Pierrette LePage, Louis-Philipe Pelletier, Eugene Plawutsky, and Paul Helmer features works of Ivan Wyshnegradsky.

The McGill Concert Choir and the McGill Wind Ensemble premiere Bengt Hambræus's *Inductio* (composed for the installation of Principal David Johnston) and Donald Patriquin's *Sortilège.*

The McGill Opera Studio presents Menotti's *The Consul.*

The McGill Symphony Orchestra performs Donald Patriquin's *Karenna.*

The Faculty presents L'Atelier de musique contemporain de l'Université Laval, including a performance of Denys Bouliane's *Climat.*

1980 A modern sound recording studio is opened.

Researchers in the sound recording area and McGill Records develop surround sound.

Bruce Mather's *Musique pour Champigny* receives the Jules Léger prize for chamber music.

The McGill Symphony Orchestra commissions and premieres Donald Steven's *For Madmen Only* with cellist Tsuyoshi Tsutsumi.

The McGill Jazz Workshop premieres Kelsey Jones's *Jazzum Opus Novum.*

The McGill Symphony Orchestra premieres John Rea's *Hommage à Vasarely.*

The McGill Wind Ensemble performs Bengt Hambræus's *Invocation* (1971) and *Parade* (1977).

The McGill Women's Chorale performs Donald Patriquin's *Six Songs of Early Canada.*

Alexander Brott, founder and conductor of the McGill Chamber Orchestra, receives an honorary degree.

1981 Redpath Hall is outfitted with a French organ designed by Helmut Wolf.

A BMus program in Jazz Performance is introduced.

The McGill Symphony Orchestra premieres Brian Cherney's *Adieux.*

The McGill Symphony Orchestra performs Kelsey Jones's *Miramichi Ballad* (1954).

L'Orgue à notre époque is held; this symposium became the model for l'Académie festival d'orgue, with specifically commissioned works.

The Contemporary Music Ensemble presents the Canadian premiere of Berio's *Agnus*.

Organist and harpsichordist Kenneth Gilbert receives an honorary degree.

John Rea's *Com-possession* receives the Jules Léger prize for chamber music.

1982 The first McGill Contemporary Music Festival (a joint project of the composition area and the EMS) is held, with a focus on keyboard works and Carlos Santos as invited guest; Alexina Louie is commissioned to write, *Glenn Gould: In Memoriam*.

alcides lanza conducts the SMCQ in a concert titled, "Musiques nouvelles d'Amérique latine."

The Gerald Danovitch Saxophone Quartet wins the CBC's search for stars.

Composer István Anhalt, and contralto Maureen Forrester receive honorary degrees.

Pianist Tom Plaunt performs music of Brian Cherney.

1983 GEMS (Group of the Electronic Music Studio), a student-directed ensemble, emerges from within the EMS.

The Contemporary Music Festival features works for strings, with double bassist Bertrand Turetzky and violinist Manuel Enriquez as invited guests.

1984 Toronto and Montréal host World Music Day.

The first Graduate Student Symposium is held.

The Contemporary Music Festival features works for reed and wind instruments and organ, with organist John Grew as invited guest.

GEMS commissions McGill graduates Michel-Georges Brégent and Kristi Allik.

Guest lecturers include Philip Glass and Al Bregman (McGill Psychology, audio streaming).

1985 The McGill Concert Choir, the McGill Percussion Ensemble, and the Contemporary Music Ensemble perform Kelsey Jones's *Prophecy of Micah*.

The Contemporary Music Festival celebrates the twentieth anniversary of the EMS, with oboist Lawrence Cherney and clarinetist Jésus Villa Rojo as invited guests.

SMCQ hosts Steve Reich.

Brian Cherney's *River of Fire* receives the Jules Léger prize for chamber music.

FACULTY OF MUSIC, 1986–91: JOHN REA, DEAN

1986 John Rea is appointed dean of the Faculty of Music.

The Contemporary Music Festival features percussionist/musicologist Jean-Charles François and a commissioned work by José Evangelista.

The McGill Concert Choir performs Kelsey Jones's *Songs of Time* (1955).

Bruce Mather becomes conductor of the Contemporary Music Ensemble.

Denys Bouliane's *A propos ... et le bazaar perché* receives the Jules Léger prize for chamber music.

1987 A BMus program in music technology is introduced.

The optical music recognition project is begun.

School Music, once a department, becomes an area within the theory department.

The third Graduate Student Symposium focuses on "new" music.

The McGill Symphony Orchestra and Maureen Forrester premiere Donald Steven's *Pages of Solitary Delights.*

The McGill Chamber Singers and Symphony Orchestra premiere Bengt Hambræus's *Symphonia Sacra in Tempre Passionis.*

The McGill Concert Band and Chamber Winds perform Bengt Hambræus's *Parade.*

MusMars (Music, March) days, featuring Claude Lefèbvre as visiting artist, are introduced.

The EMS becomes fully digitized. Equipment used in the opening years of the EMS is donated to the National Museum of Science and Technology, Ottawa.

1988 PhD programs in musicology, theory, and school music are introduced.

The McGill Chamber Winds and Wind Ensemble perform Bengt Hambræus's *In the Stillness Between* (1982).

John Rea completes *Time and Again* for the opening of Calgary Olympic Games.

The Contemporary Music Festival pays hommage to Bengt Hambræus and alcides lanza on their sixtieth birthdays, with concerts featuring organist Werner Jacob.

1989 Honours BMus programs in computer applications and music theory are introduced.

The McGill Symphony Orchestra performs Mahler at Carnegie Hall in New York.

The McGill Opera Studio becomes Opera McGill, with Bernard Turgeon and Timothy Vernon as directors.

The McGill Wind Symphony and Concert Choir present the world premiere of alcides lanza's *un mundo imaginario* (1987).

The CBC produces a retrospective concert of Brian Cherney's compositions.

The Montreal Symphony Orchestra performs John Rea's *Vanishing Points.*

Maria Jacabek receives an honorary degree.

Peter Paul Kowprowski's *Sonata* receives the Jules Léger prize for chamber music.

Bengt Hambræus is named Swedish composer of the year.

1990 The twenty-fifth anniversary of the EMS features five concerts.

The McGill Wind Symphony performs Bengt Hambræus's *Nazdeer* (1989).

The Montreal Symphony Orchestra performs John Rea's *Over Time*.

FACULTY OF MUSIC, 1991–96: JOHN GREW, DEAN

1991 John Grew is appointed dean of the Faculty of Music.

An MMus program in performance and an MA program in computer applications in music are introduced.

The Faculty hosts the International Computer Music Conference.

Joel Wapnick produces a CD sampler of sounds with Sony.

SMCQ hosts Pierre Boulez.

The McGill University Chorus performs Donald Patriquin's *Palindrome (ladies long in the tooth)*.

The Marvin Duchow Music Library moves to 550 Sherbrooke Street West.

Donald Steven's *In the Land of the Pure Delight* receives the Jules Léger prize for chamber music.

Opera McGill presents Kurt Weill's *Street Scene*.

1992 Bruce Pennycook invents the MIDI time clip.

A graduate student exchange program is established with Sweden.

The name of the school music program is changed to music education.

Dixie Ross-Neill and William Neill are named directors of Opera McGill.

Opera McGill presents Benjamin Britten's *A Midsummer Night's Dream*.

Teacher, pianist, and commentator Maryvonne Kendergi and Ray Minshull (head of classical music at Decca Records 1967–94) receive honorary degrees.

John Rea's *Objets perdus* receives the Jules Léger prize for chamber music.

The first PhD (music) is awarded to Christine Beckett (music education).

1993 Morton Feldman and Toyohiko Satoh (Japanese lute) are visiting artists.

Schenkarian theory is added to the music theory program as an optional course.

McGill hosts the joint American Musicological Society and Association for Music Theory conference.

Composer Witold Lutoslawski and musicologist Colin Slim receive honorary degrees.

Bruce Mather's *YQUEM* receives the Jules Léger prize for chamber music.

1994 A PhD program in music media and technology is introduced.

A BA program with a major in music is introduced.

The Contemporary Music Ensemble gives the premiere John Rea's *Kubla Kahn* (1989).

Soprano Pierrette Alarie, tenor Leopold Simoneau, and conductor Paul Sacher receive honorary degrees.

1995 Walter Boudreau conducts the Contemporary Music Ensemble.

The McGill Symphony Orchestra premieres Bengt Hambræus's *Concerto for Piano* (1993), with pianist Marc Couroux.

The McGill Chamber Singers premiere alcides lanza's *in.../visible* (1994) with soprano Eva Lund.

Jazz musician Oliver Jones and violinst Isaac Stern receive honorary degrees.

1996 Denys Bouliane joins the faculty in the composition area and becomes conductor of Contemporary Music Ensemble.

Opera McGill presents Britten's *Albert Herring* and Stravinsky's *Le Rossignol*.

The McGill Wind Ensemble performs Kelsey Jones's *Musica d'occasione* (1978) and the world premiere of Bengt Hambræus's *Concertino* (1995).

Charles Dutoit, conductor of the Montréal Symphony Orchestra, receives an honorary degree.

FACULTY OF MUSIC, 1996–2001: RICHARD LAWTON, DEAN

1997 Richard Lawton is appointed dean of the Faculty of Music.

Opera McGill presents Quentin Doolittle's *Charlie the Chicken*.

Need for research scholars in ethnomusicology, popular music, and history of jazz is noted in Faculty's Annual Report.

L'Académie festival d'orgue / Summer Organ Festival, a biennial event with commissioned works, is established.

1998 The Contemporary Music Ensemble sponsors MusiNovember, featuring composer Nicolaus Huber, pianist Catherine Vickers, and Moritz Eggert.

GEMS sponsors a mini-festival focused on works of James Tenney.

1999 The Contemporary Music Ensemble, in conjunction with SMCQ, sponsors MusiOctober, featuring composer Louis Andriessen, soprano Ingrid Schmithusen, and Ensemble KORE.

Opera McGill presents the premiere of John Beckwith's *Taptoo!*.

A ioint BSc and BMus, with a major in computer science and music technology, is introduced.

A joint BMus in music education and BEd is introduced.

Jonathan Wild joins the Faculty as a composer and theorist.

Jean Lesage joins the Faculty as a composer.

Présences '99 (Paris) features a series of concerts showcasing Montreal composers.

Claudio Ferrari visits EMS from Argentina and composes a work for solo tape.

Pianist Norio Ohga (former CEO of Sony Music) receives an honorary degree.

Denys Bouliane wins the Quebec Music Personality of the Year Award.

2000 GEMS sponsors a visit by David Rokeby.

The Centre of Musical Excellence for Interdisciplinary Research in Music Media and Technology (CIRMMT) is jointly established by McGill University, l'Université de Montréal, and l'Université de Sherbrooke, with Wieslaw Woszczyk as director.

Denys Bouliane produces *Millennium Symphony* with contributions from nineteen composers.

A symposium celebrating the twentieth anniversary of sound recording at McGill is held.

Henryk Gorecki, Jean Claude Risett (French scientist and EMS composer) and Jorg Sennheiser (Chairman of Sennheiser Electronic) give guest lectures.

2001 A DMus program in performance is introduced.

The Contemporary Music Ensemble under Walter Boudreau performs Darius Milhaud's *La Création du monde* and Olivier Messiaen's *Oiseaux exotiques*.

Opera McGill presents Benjamin Britten's *Turn of the Screw*.

The McGill Wind Symphony performs Brian Cherney's *In the Stillness Between*.

A memorial concert for Bengt Hambræus is held.

Max Matthews, distinguished inventor in computer music, gives guest lecture.

McGill presents an Internet master class with Pinchas Zukerman (conductor of the National Arts Centre Orchestra) in real time.

Organist Marie-Claire Alain receives an honorary degree.

Chris Harmon's *Amerika* receives the Jules Léger prize for chamber music.

FACULTY OF MUSIC, 2001– : DON MCLEAN, DEAN

2001 Don McLean is appointed dean of the Faculty of Music.

2002 The Contemporary Music Ensemble, in conjunction with SMCQ and the Montreal Symphony Orchestra, sponsors MusMars, with Tan Dun, Alexina Louie, Melissa Hui, Denis Gougeon, and John Rea as featured composers.

The Distributed Digital Music Library Laboratory (a part of CIRMMT) is opened.

The music technology area sponsors an international conference on new interfaces for musical expression.

Sean Ferguson completes a doctorate and joins the Faculty as a composer.

Opera McGill performs Benjamin Britten's *Turn of the Screw.*

Tenor Ben Heppner and conductor Franz-Paul Decker receive honorary degrees.

2003 Montréal, Nouvelles Musiques festival international, to be held in alternate years, is founded and wins the opus prize for event of the year.

GEMS sponsors the visit of Keith Hamel and offers its final concert.

Ichiro Fujinago serves as acting director of CIRMMT.

Orchestre philharmonique de Radio-France premieres Sean Ferguson's *In The Flesh / Dans la chair* (jointly commissioned by Radio-France, Radio-Canada, and SMCQ) at the Presences 2003 Festival in Paris.

Pere Lindsay receives an honorary degree.

alcides lanza receives the Victor Martyn Lynch-Staunton Award from the Canada Council.

2004 MusiMars features Philippe Hurel as the Langlois Foundation (Centre for Innovation in Technology in the Arts) Visiting Professor; Howard Bradshaw pays tribute to Gèrard Grisey, a leader in spectral music.

The EMS is renamed the Digital Composition Studio; Sean Ferguson is appointed as director.

Dr Fernando Izaaetta, from Sao Paulo, Brazil, visits to explore composition and performance in real time.

The McGill Conservatory and the CBC commission Sean Ferguson to write *Les Bregmans* for chamber ensemble and narrator.

Stephen McAdams is appointed director of CIRMMT.

An interdisciplinary conference on the work of Joni Mitchell is held.

Pianist Anton Kuerti and singer-songwriter Joni Mitchell receive honorary degrees.

2005 Montréal, Nouvelles Musiques festival international premieres Brian Cherney's *Die klingende Zeit* (1994) and features works by Linda Bouchard, Pierre Boulez, Alexina Louie, Michael Colgrass, Olivier Messiaen, Denys Bouliane, Chan Ka Nin, Alain Dauphinais, Geof Holbrook, Jean Lesage,

Bruce Mather, John Rea, Gilles Tremblay, Philippe Leroux, Benjamin de la Fuente, among others.

Opera McGill presents a re-staging of Harry Somer's and Mavor Moore's *Louis Riel* (1967).

Martin Matalon, Yan Maresz, and Mauro Lanza are Langlois Foundation Visiting Professors.

l'Université de Montréal sponsors a conference on the theme, "Timbre in Composition, Performance, Perception, and Reception."

Philippe Leroux from IRCAM is a visiting professor.

The Optoelectronic Plethysmography and Respiratory Laboratory (part of CIRMMT) opens with Isabella Cossette as director.

Laurie Radford, Bruce Pennycook, and Andrew Culver return to the Faculty as guest lecturers and visiting professors.

Ethnomusicologist Simha Arom from IRCAM gives lecture on time organization in African music, using an approach developed through technological analysis.

Chris Harmon joins the Faculty as a composer.

The Andrew Svoboda Award for Music Composition and the John Bradley Memorial Prize in Sound Recording are established; these are the first scholarships to specifically focus on "new" music.

The Faculty of Music is renamed the Schulich School of Music, and a new building, supporting CIRMMT and the Marvin Duchow Music Library opens.

The Schulich School of Music and Concordia Fine Arts host the conference "Creating Space for Art."

Opera McGill commissions *Evangeline Revisited*, from librettist Alexis Nouss and conductor and composer Julian Wachner.

Soprano Jane Eaglen receives an honorary degree.

2006 MusiMars sponsors the premiere of R. Murray Schafer's String Quartet no. 10, played by the Molinari String Quartet.

APPENDIX ONE

Recordings

COMMERCIAL RECORDINGS OF WORKS CITED IN THE TEXT IN ALPHABETICAL ORDER BY COMPOSER

Note: Recordings of other works by Canadian composers may be obtained by contacting the composers through the Canadian Music Centre, 20 St. Joseph St., Toronto, Ontario, M4Y 1J9 or info@musiccentre.ca.

Anhalt, István. *Fantasia for Piano,* on "Glenn Gould Plays Contemporary Music." Sony Classical, SMK 52677.

Anhalt, István. *Foci,* with Phyllis Manning and Ensemble instrumental de Montréal. Radio Canada International LP, RCI 357; also included on "Anthology of Canadian Music: István Anhalt," Centrediscs, CMCCD 10204.

Anhalt, István. *Cento,* with Tudor Singers, Radio Canada International LP, RCI 357.

Anhalt, István. *Electronic Composition no. 3,* on "Electronic Essays," Marathon Music LP MS2111; also included on "Anthology of Canadian Music: Istvan Anhalt," LP ACM 22.

Bertoncini, Mario. *Cifre,* on "Mario Bertoncini," Edition RZ, LP 1002.

Bertoncini, Mario. *Tune,* on "Black Earth Percussion Group," Opus One, LP 22-2800.

Bouliane, Denys. *Douze tiroirs de demi-vérités pour alléger votre descente* on "La musique du réalisme magique," vol. 2, with Calamus Quintet and National Arts Centre Orchestra, Société nouvelle d'enregistrement, SNE-CD 567.

Bouliane, Denys. ... *Comme un silène entr'ouvert* ..., on "La musique du réalisme magique," vol. 1, with Ensemble Koln, Société nouvelle d'enregistrement, SNE-CD 543.

Cage, John. *Sonatas and Interludes,* on "Zeitenwechsel-John Cage," with Mario Bertoncini (piano), DAAD and Edition RZ, Parallele CD-20001.

Cherney, Brian. *In Stillness Ascending,* with Rivka Golani and Louis-Philippe Pelletier, McGill Records, 500036.

Davidovsky, Mario. *The Music of Mario Davidovsky,* vol. 3, Bridge 9171.

Etkin, Mariano. *Abgesang Mambo,* on "Octandre," Ars Musici, CD-AM 1147-2.

Etkin, Mariano. *Aquello,* on "New Music from the Americas, 1," Shelan, eSp 9301; on "Línea Adicional, Música Contemporánea Argentina," Melopea Discos, CCM 003.

Etkin, Mariano. *Locus solus* on *Hacen así,* Ensemble Perceum, CD-EUM 2318-2.

Etkin, Mariano. *Música ritual,* on "Serie Nueva Música Latinoamericana," vol. 3, T/E-7. Discos Tacuabé, LP 14319.

Etkin, Mariano. *Otros soles, Arenas, Caminos de cornisa, Frente a frente,* on "Otros Soles," Melopea Discos, CCM 002.

Etkin, Mariano. *Otros soles,* La revue Dérives (no. 47/48), LP insert.

Etkin, Mariano. *Perpetual Tango,* on "New Piano Works from Europe and the Americas," Mode Records, CD-31.

Etkin, Mariano. *Taltal,* on "Panorama de la Música Argentina," Fondo Nacional de las Artes, CD-IRCO 313.

Hambræus, Bengt. *Carillon for Two Pianos,* with Pierrette LePage and Bruce Mather, McGill Records, 77002.

Hambræus, Bengt. *Carillon for Two Pianos,* with Mats Persson and Christina Schomz, Caprice, CD 21331.

Harley, James. *Bien serré,* with KAPPA Ensemble (Philippe Keyser), Kappa, CD 002,2000.

Harley, James. *flung loose into the stars,* with Marc Couroux, ATMA Records, ACD22180; also on Music Works, CD 69.

Harley, James. *Per Foramen Acus Transire,* with Nancy Ruffer (flute), Metier Records.

Harley, James. *Windprints,* on "Canadian Music Centre Orchestral Repertoire," vol. 3, promotional CD, Centrediscs.

Harvey, Jonathan. *Bhakti,* with Nouvel Ensemble Moderne, Disques Montaigne, MO782128.

lanza, alcides. *arghanum Vpet,* with Joseph Petric (accordion), on "Orbiting Garden," Centrediscs, CMCCD 7802.

lanza, alcides. *arghanum Vð,* with alcides lanza, on "Music of the Americas, 1," Shelan, eSp 9301.

lanza, alcides. *trilogy,* with alcides lanza and Meg Sheppard, Shelan, eSp 9201.

lanza, alcides. *the extended piano,* with alcides lanza, Shelan, eSp, 9401.

Mahler, Gustav. *Ruckert Lieder,* with New York Philharmonic (Leonard Bernstein, conductor) and Dietrich Fisher-Dieskau, Sony, B00004SCUE.

Neidhöfer, Christoph, *Schichtung, Interplay, String Quartet, IXION, Zeitbogen*, with Ensemble Klangforum Wien (Johannes Kalitzke, conductor), Grammont, CTS-M59.

Oliver, John. *Icicle Blue Avalanche*, Earsay, 98004.

The Private Sea of Dreams, Il Gruppo. RCA Victor LP, LSP-3846.

Ravel, Maurice. *Miroirs* with Walter Gieseking. Pearl, B000000WVG.

Rea, John. *Une fleur du mal,* with Marie-Danielle Parent, soprano, G. Plante, clarinet, C. Best, cello, and J. Grégoire, percussion; on "Histoires extraordinaires," Riche Lieu/Radio-Canada, RIC 2-9958.

Schoenberg, Arnold. *Pierrot Lunaire*, with Ensemble Intercontemporain (Pierre Boulez, conductor) and Christine Schäfer, Deutsche Grammophone, B00000DBV6.

Schryer, Claude. *Autour*, with Simon Fraser University Sonic Research Studio, empreintes DIGITALes, IMED 9736.

Shinohara, Makoto. *Alternances*, on "Prospective 21e siècle," Philips, CD-836.991 DSY.

Shinohara, Makoto. *Fragmente*, on "Lucente Stella," Opus One, CD-30-122; on "The Japanese Recorder," BIS, CD-655; on "Clas Pehrsson," BIS, CD-202.

Shinohara, Makoto. *Mémoires*, on "Prospective 21e siècle," Philips, CD-836.991 DSY.

Shinohara, Makoto. *Nagare, Kyudo B, Tabiyuki, Birth of the Bass Koto,* and *Cooperation*, on "Portrait of Makoto Shinohara," Camerata, CD-375.

Shinohara, Makoto. *Obsession*, on "Oboe Obsession," Delos, CD-DE 3235.

Smalley, Denis. *Impacts intérieurs*, with Philip Mead and Roger Heaton, empreintes DIGITALes, IMED 9209.

Stockhausen, Karlheinz. *Elektronishe Musik*, Stockhausen Verlag, CD3.

Valcarcel, Edgar. *Flor de Sancayo [IV, solo cello]*, on "Luís Leguia," Luis and Clark Instrument Corp., unnumbered CD.

Valcarcel, Edgar. *Invencion, Checan IV*, on "New Music from the Americas, 1," Shelan, eSp 9301.

Xenakis, Iannis, and DJ Spooky. *Kraanerg* with ST-X Ensemble Xenakis, Asphodel, B000001PB2.

Zimmerman, B.A. *Photoptosis*, with Bernhard Kontrasky and Deutsches Symphonie-Orchester Berlin, Col Legno, B000004C13.

RECORDINGS OF COMPOSITIONS CREATED AT THE ELECTRONIC MUSIC STUDIO

eidesis IV (1977-II) by alcides lanza. McGill Records, MR 79008 (stereo LP).

"Electronic Music by Caron, Perron and Dawson." McGill Records, MR 80011 (stereo LP).

"Electronic Music by Hambræus: Tides – Tornado – Intrada: Calls." McGill Records, MR 76001 (stereo LP).

"SONDE," works by Culver, De Mestral, Pavelka, Dostie, and SONDE. Music Gallery Editions, MGE 14 (stereo LP).

"Tornado," EMS 35th anniversary with GEMS, works by Bruce Pennycook, alcides lanza, Hugh Le Caine, István Anhalt, Paul Pedersen, Bengt Hambæus, Pérez Miró, Osvaldo Budón, Laurie Radford, Brent Lee, Michael Picton, Alain Thibault, Frederico Richter, and Gilles Gobeil. McGill Records, MR 2001-01-2.

"Transmutations," works by Pennycook *(Praescio VII)* and lanza *(vôo),* with alcides lanza, piano and Meg Sheppard, voice. Shelan, eSp 9601.

RECORDINGS PRODUCED BY GEMS (GROUP OF THE ELECTRONIC MUSIC STUDIO)

"Vox Machina," works by Michael Picton, Raymond Luk, James Harley, Osvaldo Budón, and Sean Ferguson. McGill Records, 170 537-9 CD.

"Before the Freeze," works by John Oliver, Morton Feldman, Bruce Pennycook, Laurie Radford, Brian McCue, and Brent Lee. McGill Records, 750 038-2-CD.

"GEMS," works by Donald Steven, alcides lanza, Claude Schryer, and Richard Lloyd. McGill Records, MR 85027 (stereo LP).

CANADIAN COMPOSITIONS ON RECORDINGS PRODUCED BY MCGILL RECORDS (EXCLUDING JAZZ REPERTOIRE)

Anhalt, István, *Cento, Cantata Urbana,* MR 2001-01-2

Baculis, Alphonse, *Six Pieces for Saxophone Quartet,* 750042-2

Beckwith, John, *Arctic Dances,* 85026

Bélusc, Pierre, *Complicité,* 750052-2

Behrens, Jack, *Aspects,* 83017

Budón, Osvaldo, *Amorçage,* 750052-2

Budón, Osvaldo, *...para el trato con el desierto,* MR 2001-01-2

Budón, Osvaldo, *Territorios,* ISBN 7717-0537-9

Calvert, Morley, *Suite from the Monteregian Hills,* 80012 and 750051-2

Caron, Claude, *Japa,* 80011

Cherney, Brian, *Adieux,* 81013

Cherney, Brian, *Dans le crépuscule du souvenir...,* 750036-2

Cherney, Brian, *In the Stillness of the Seventh Autumn,* 750036-2

Cherney, Brian, *In Stillness Ascending,* 750036-2

Cherney, Brian, *River of Fire,* 85026

Cherney, Brian, *Shekhinah*, 750036-2

Culver, Andrew, *Signature*, 77003

Dawson, Ted, *Concerto Grosso*, 80011

Ferguson, Sean, *Vox Machina*, ISBN 7717-0537-9

Forsyth, Malcolm, *Three Métis Songs from Saskatchewan*, 85025 and 750028-2

Garant, Serge, *Circuit I*, 77003

Gobeil, Gilles, *Rivage*, MR 2001-01-2

Hambræus, Bengt, *Carillon*, 77002

Hambræus, Bengt, *Intrada: Calls*, 76001

Hambræus, Bengt, *Livre d'orgue*, vol 3, 85024

Hambræus, Bengt, *Sheng*, 85026

Hambræus, Bengt, *Tides*, 76001

Hambræus, Bengt, *Tornado*, 76001 and MR 2001-01-2

Harley, James, *Night Flowering … not even sand (II)*, ISBN 7717-0537-9

Hétu, Jacques, *Incantation*, 85026

Jones, Kelsey, *Jazzum Opus Unum*, 78006

Jones, Kelsey, *Passacaglia and Fugue for Brass Quintet*, 77004

lanza, alcides, *interferences III*, 85027

lanza, alcides, *eidesis IV* (1977–11, 79008

lanza, alcides, *sensors I* (1976 – 1), 77003

lanza, alcides, *interferences III* (1983-IV), MR 2001-01-2

lanza, alcides, *sensors V* (1985-II), 750052-2

LeCaine, Hugh, *Paulution*, MR 2001-01-2

Lee, Brent, *Clocks of the World*, 750038-2

Lee, Brent, *Deliberate Disguises*, MR 2001-01-2

Lloyd, Richard, *Breath Baby*, 85027

Luk, Raymond, *Semiotic Rifle*, ISBN 7717-0537-9

Mather, Bruce, *Musique pour Champigny*, 83019

Mather, Bruce, *Poème du Délire*, 83017

Mather, Bruce, *Sonata for Two Pianos*, 77002

McCue, Brian, *Premonitions I*, 750038-2

Morel, François, *Rythmologue*, 77003

Oliver, John, *Before the Freeze*, 750038-2

Patriquin, Donald, *Fête Carignan*, 80010 and 750045-2

Patriquin, Donald, *Hangman's Reel*, 80010 and 750045-2

Patriquin, Donald, *Overture to Christmas*, 750047-2

Patriquin, Donald, *Three Carols for Treble Voices, Harp and Flutes*, 750047-2

Patriquin, Donald (arr.), Carols Old and New, 750047-2

Patriquin, Donald (arr.), Noëls populaires pour choeur, 82014

Patriquin, Donald (arr.), Six noëls anciens, 750047-2

Pedersen, Paul, *Fantasie*, MR 2001-01-2
Pennycook, Bruce, *Amnesia*, MR 2001-01-2
Pennycook, Bruce *PRAESCIO-1*, 750038-2
Perrault, Michel, *Esquisses québécoises*, 85022 and 750050-2
Perron, Serge, *Fusion*, 80011
Picton, Michael, *Bagatelles*, MR 2001-01-2
Picton, Michael, *Ouvertures II*, ISBN 7717-0537-9
Radford, Laurie, *Enclave*, MR 2001-01-2
Radford, Laurie, *Minuit caché*, 750038-2
Rea, John, *Hommage à Vasarely*, 81013
Rea, John, *Com-possession*, 83019
Schryer, Claude, *A Kindred Spirit*, 85027
Steven, Donald, *For Madmen Only*, 81013
Steven, Donald, *Images – Refractions of Time and Space*, 85027
Steven, Donald, *Pages of Solitary Delights*, 85025 and 750028-2
Steven, Donald, *Rainy Day Afternoon*, 80012
Thibault, Alain, *Déca-danse*, MR 2001-01-2

CHRONOLOGICAL LIST OF RECORDINGS PRODUCED BY MCGILL RECORDS, 1976–2005

Recordings are generally listed under the year the music was recorded; release dates were sometimes a year or so later.

1976

76001: "Concrete and Synthesizer Music" – works by Bengt Hambræus

1977

77002: "Mather–LePage Piano Duo," – quarter tone music by Ivan Wyschnegradsky; works by Bruce Mather and Bengt Hambræus

77003: "Percussion" – McGill Percussion Ensemble

77004: "Mount Royal Brass Quintet" – transcriptions and contemporary brass quintet works

77005: "Romantic Flute Music" – Jeanne Baxtresser plays Schubert and Franck (reissued on CD MR 2002-01-1, under the title "Jeanne Baxtresser: Debut Solo Recording, Montreal 1977" with additional works by Saint-Saëns and Godard)

1978

78006: "McGill Jazz Band" – Jazz band standards plus 2 piano rags and a new work by Kelsey Jones

78007: "J.S. Bach Sonatas for Viola da Gamba and Harpsichord" – performed by Mary Cyr and John Grew (reissued on cassette 750034-2)

1979

79008: "McGill Wind Ensemble" – contemporary music for band

1980

80009: "Polychoral Brass Music" – the Mount Royal Brass Quintet

80010: "Jean Carignan and l'Orchestre des Grands ballets canadiens" – fiddle music played by Jean Carignan (reissued on CD 750045-2)

80011: "Japa – Fusion – Concerto Grosso" – Music from the McGill Electronic Music Studio

80012: "Brass Nova" – the Mount Royal Brass Quintet

1981

81013: Uri Mayer Conducts the McGill Symphony Orchestra" – works by Donald Steven, Brian Cherney, and John Rea, with cellist Tsuyoshi Tsutsumi

1982

82014: "Noëls" – Noëls populaires pour choeur et pour l'orgue

82015: "Love's Pashion"– ayres for lyra violl, played by Mary Cyr

1983

83016: "Buxtehude Cantatas for Advent, Christmas, and Epiphany" – McGill Chamber Singers and Collegium Musicum (reissued on CD 750029-2, under the title "Buxtehude Christmas Concert" with additional Buxtehude organ works in 1989)

83017: "Music for Three Pianos in Sixths of Tones" – works by Ivan Wyschnegradsky, Bruce Mather, and Jack Behrens

83018: "Tom Plaunt Plays Charles Ives" – the "Concord" Sonata

83019: "Winners of the Jules Léger Prize" – Works by John Rea and Bruce Mather

1984

84020: "Audio System Test Record" – technical tests and demonstration musical excerpts

84021: "Dietrich Buxtehude: Cantatas for Lent and Easter" – McGill Chamber Singers and Collegium Musicum

1985

85022: "Sketches / Esquisses" – Gerald Danovitch Saxophone Quartet (reissued on cassette 750032-4; reissued on CD 750050-2)

85023: "Louis-Philippe Pelletier, Pianist" – works by Robert Schumann and Alban Berg

85024: "Hambræus: Livre d'orgue, vol. 3" – performed by John Grew on the Redpath Hall organ

85025: "Forrester / Sea Pictures" – Maureen Forester and the McGill Symphony Orchestra (reissued on CD 750028-2 in 1988)

85026: "River of Fire" – Oboe works played by Lawrence Cherney

85027" "g.e.m.s." – Group of the Electronic Music Studio

1988

750031-2: "Buxtehude Alto Cantatas and Sonatas" – performed by Allan Fast with the McGill Collegium Musicum, directed by Mary Cyr

750033-2: "Day and Night" – McGill Jazz Band with David Liebman, solo saxophone

1989

750035-2: "Tangos" – performed by Arminda Canteros, piano

1990

750040-2: "Late Late Show" – McGill Swing Band directed by Gordon Foote

1991

750036-2: "In Stillness Ascending" – works by Brian Cherney with Rivka Golani, viola, and Louis-Philippe Pelletier, piano

750038-2: "G.E.M.S. – Before the Freeze" – Group of the Electronic Music Studio

750041-2" "Kevin Dean – Minor indiscretions" – Kevin Dean, trumpet

750042-2: "Celebration" – Gerald Danovitch Saxophone Quartet with Eugene Rousseau

750043-2: "Korngold Symphony in F Sharp" – McGill Symphony Orchestra directed by Timothy Vernon.

1992

750037-2: "missa sanci iacobi" – twelfth-century mass reconstructed by Paul Helmer

750039-2: "Jean-Philippe Rameau – Cantatas" – four cantatas, performed by Dominique Labelle, soprano, and Erik Oland, baritone

750044-2: "Cookin the Books" – McGill Jazz Ensemble directed by Gordon Foote

750048-2: "Poppin the Cork" – McGill Jazz Ensemble directed by Gordon Foote

1993

750047-2: "Noel" – Christmas music for choir, brass, strings and percussion.

750049-2: "Kevin Dean since 1954" – Kevin Dean, trumpet solo

1995

750051-2: "Mount Royal Brass Quintet" – CD reissue of works from LPs 77004, 80009 and 80012

1996

750052-2: "Percussion Music of the Americas" – McGill Percussion Ensemble, conducted by Pierre Béluse

1999

ISBN 7717-0537-9: "G.E.M.S. Vox Machina" – Group of the Electronic Music Studio, enhanced CD

2001

MR 2001-01-2: "Tornado – Electroacoustic Compositions" – McGill Electronic Music Studio 35th Anniversary, fourteen works on two CDs

2002

MR 2002-02-1: "Mahler: Symphony no. 5" – McGill Symphony Orchestra, conducted by Timothy Vernon

2003

MR 2003-03-1: "Conundrum" – McGill Jazz Orchestra, directed by Gordon Foote

2005

MR 2005-01-2: "Two Last Symphonies: Tchaikovsky and Mahler" – McGill Symphony Orchestra, conducted by Alexis Hauser, two CDs

APPENDIX TWO

The Aims and Philosophy of McGill University Records (1988)

For the past ten years, McGill University Records has operated principally as a promotional organ for the Faculty of Music. To date, all productions have featured McGill staff soloists, McGill staff composers, or McGill student ensembles. While high standards of performance and technical production have been maintained, the label is viewed, in the Canadian musical community, as serving primarily the McGill Faculty of Music. As we are now at the point of having to shift our production from analogue LPs to digital compact discs, it would be wise to examine the aims and philosophy of McGill University Records for the future.

While it might be possible to continue the same mode of operation as the past ten years, there is a danger of stagnation. If the same small group of soloists, composers and ensembles is continually featured, the interest of the buying public will wane and the enthusiasm of our staff in donating their time will vanish. However, the expansion of activities to include a larger scope than at present will have to be done creatively since McGill is obviously in no position to compete with the major commercial record companies.

It is proposed that McGill University Records adopt a philosophy analogous to that of a university press. As a university press publishes works of scholarly and social importance that may not be viable for the commercial press, so a university record company would produce music that is deemed to be important for the musical community and the country but which may not be popular enough to attract the commercial record companies.

The prime focus in selecting productions would be the repertoire. The following criteria are proposed:

1 A substantial proportion of the works on a disc should not be available on other commercial recordings.

2 Works by Canadian composers should be given special consideration.
3 The repertoire should be judged as being musically important.

Occasionally, productions may be selected to present a soloist or group without following the above repertoire guidelines. In these cases, the following criteria would be observed:

1 The soloist or group should be of outstanding quality.
2 The soloist or group should have a substantial professional performance record and a demonstrated commitment to developing a long term professional performing career.

Proposals for discs involving soloists, groups and composers from the staff of the McGill Faculty of Music must be judged by the same high standards as will be expected of soloists, groups and composers outside the Faculty of Music. If student ensembles are involved in a production, it is necessary that the final product be seen as being at a professional level. For all productions, the highest performance and technical standards must be maintained.

In summary, the aims and philosophy of McGill University Records should be broadened to include recording projects from outside the McGill Faculty of Music and should seek to ensure that all projects are of a high professional standard, both technically and musically.

Index